Rethinking Greenland and the Arctic in the Era of Climate Change

This groundbreaking book investigates how Arctic indigenous communities deal with the challenges of climate change and how they strive to develop self-determination. Adopting an anthropological focus on Greenland's vision to boost extractive industries and transform society, the book examines how indigenous communities engage with climate change and development discourses. It applies a critical and comparative approach, integrating both local perspectives and adaptation research from Canada and Greenland to make the case for recasting the way the Arctic and Inuit are approached conceptually and politically. The emphasis on indigenous peoples as future-makers and rights-holders paves the way for a new understanding of the concept of indigenous knowledge and a more sensitive appreciation of predicaments and dynamics in the Arctic.

This book will be of interest to postgraduate students and researchers in environmental studies, development studies and area studies.

Frank Sejersen is Associate Professor in the Department of Cross-Cultural and Regional Studies at the University of Copenhagen, Denmark.

Science in Society Series
Series Editor: Steve Rayner
Institute for Science, Innovation and Society, University of Oxford

Editorial Board: Jason Blackstock, Bjorn Ola Linner, Susan Owens, Timothy O'Riordan, Arthur Peterson, Nick Pidgeon, Dan Sarewitz, Andy Sterling, Chris Tyler, Andrew Webster, Steve Yearley

The Earthscan Science in Society Series aims to publish new high-quality research, teaching, practical and policy-related books on topics that address the complex and vitally important interface between science and society.

Vaccine Anxieties
Global Science, child health and society
Melissa Leach and James Fairhead

Democratizing Technology
Risk, responsibility and the Regulation of Chemicals
Anne Chapman

Genomics and Society
Legal, ethical and social dimensions
Edited by George Gaskell and
Martin W. Bauer

A Web of Prevention
Biological weapons, life sciences and the governance of research
Edited by Brian Rappert and
Caitrìona McLeish

Nanotechnology
Risk, ethics and law
Edited by Geoffrey Hunt and
Michael Mehta

Unnatural Selection
The challenges of engineering tomorrow's people
Edited by Peter Healey and
Steve Rayner

Debating Climate Change
Pathways through argument to agreement
Elizabeth L. Malone

Business Planning for Turbulent Times
New methods for applying scenarios
Edited by Rafael Ramírez,
John W. Selsky and
Kees van der Heijden

Influenza and Public Health
Learning from past pandemics
Tamara Giles-Vernick,
Susan Craddock and Jennifer Gunn

Rethinking Greenland and the Arctic in the Era of Climate Change

New northern horizons

Frank Sejersen

Routledge
Taylor & Francis Group

LONDON AND NEW YORK

from Routledge

First published 2015 by Routledge

2 Park Square, Milton Park, Abingdon, Oxon OX14 4RN
711 Third Avenue, New York, NY 10017, USA

Routledge is an imprint of the Taylor & Francis Group, an informa business

First issued in paperback 2016

Copyright © 2015 Frank Sejersen

The right of Frank Sejersen to be identified as author of this work has been asserted by him/her in accordance with sections 77 and 78 of the Copyright, Designs and Patents Act 1988.

All rights reserved. No part of this book may be reprinted or reproduced or utilised in any form or by any electronic, mechanical, or other means, now known or hereafter invented, including photocopying and recording, or in any information storage or retrieval system, without permission in writing from the publishers.

Notice:
Product or corporate names may be trademarks or registered trademarks, and are used only for identification and explanation without intent to infringe.

British Library Cataloguing-in-Publication Data
A catalogue record for this book is available from the British Library

Library of Congress Cataloging-in-Publication Data
Sejersen, Frank.
    Rethinking Greenland and the arctic in the era of climate change : new northern
    horizons / Frank Sejersen.
        pages cm
    1. Indigenous peoples—Ecology—Arctic regions. 2. Indigenous peoples—Ecology—Greenland.
    3. Inuit—Greenland. 4. Greenland—Environmental conditions. 5. Arctic regions—
    Environmental conditions. 6. Climatic changes—Social aspects—Greenland. 7. Climatic
    changes—Environmental aspects—Greenland. 8. Climatic changes—Social aspects—
    Arctic regions. 9. Climatic changes—Environmental aspects—Arctic regions. I. Title.
    E99.E7S423 2015
    305.897'0982—dc23
                                        2014038110

ISBN: 978-1-138-84515-2 (hbk)
ISBN: 978-1-138-28359-6 (pbk)

Typeset in Goudy
by diacriTech, Chennai

To Pernille, Emma Line & Rosa

Table of contents

Acknowledgements

Although this book draws on the fieldworks and anthropological research I have pursued in Greenland since 1995, the main two drivers for writing the book are the increasing and immense amount of research publications on climate change adaptation in the Arctic and the announcement of the Greenlandic authorities to start up hyper-industrialization. I am intrigued by the adaptation literature because it is difficult for me to recognize the people and living communities in the models and discourses to which these scholars subscribe. As the media also bases much of its coverage of Arctic climate change on the idea of Inuit as victims and vulnerable, the political agency, creative future-making and dynamic livelihoods of indigenous peoples tend to be put in the shadow or even forgotten. In 2006, when the Greenlandic authorities initiated a comprehensive political strategy to transform their society by opening large-scale and extractive industries, they set in motion a comprehensive rethinking of the Greenlandic society, what it means to be a Greenlander and what position the nation were to have in the world. So, two different tendencies were present: one that stresses victimization, and one that stresses creative future-making. It is between these two tendencies that this book emerged. Research into these issues became possible in 2009, when the European Research Council made a generous research grant (Project No: 229459) to the large cross-disciplinary project *Waterworlds: Natural Environmental Disasters and Social Resilience in Anthropological Perspective* with Professor Kirsten Hastrup as principal investigator. The ambition of the research project was to study local, social responses to environmental disasters related to water, as spurred by the melting of ice in the Arctic and in mountainous glacier areas, the rising of seas that flood islands and coastal communities across the globe and the drying of lands accelerating desertification in large parts of Africa and elsewhere. Furthermore, the aim was to contribute to a renewed theory of social resilience that builds on the actualities of social life in distinct localities, thus focusing on human agency as the basis for people's quest for certainty in exposed environments. I was part of this five-year project and my sub-project 'Ice, climate and development in Greenland' focused on how the changing icescape in the Arctic was creatively approached, understood and made part of people's futures.

During those five years of intensive research, I was so privileged to benefit from the inspiration and academic input from other team members as well as all the guest researchers we were able to invite to our sessions, meetings and conferences. I owe much to their input, critique and encouragement. The Department of Cross-Cultural and Regional Studies at the faculty of Humanities also supported my research financially as well as administratively, which made the pieces fall in place. The proofreading of the manuscript was done by Dan Marmorstein, whose suggestions for changes indeed improved the final result and the flow of my argument. The anonymous reviewers of the book proposal made some excellent comments and suggestions, which made me reorganize parts of the book. Finally, I want to thank the Royal Danish Academy of Sciences and Letters for giving me the permission to rewrite my chapter 'Resilience, Human Agency and Climate Change', which was first published in the anthology *The Question of Resilience*, edited by Kirsten Hastrup (Historisk-filosofiske Meddelelser 106, Copenhagen 2009 [ISBN: 978-87-7304-350-9]).

My biggest appreciation and thanks go to the persons in Greenland who took time off from their busy schedules during 2011 and met me with patience and openness. One-on-one conversations referenced in this book are from informal personal interviews with me that took place in Maniitsoq and Nuuk between February 22, 2011, and March 24, 2011. Through interviews and conversations, they invited me into their ideas, concerns and experiences related to the changing political and natural environment. Their positive attitude, creativity and encouragement are a constant reminder of the potential that lies in rethinking how we approach Arctic communities, agency and change. Thank you.

1 Introduction

Climate change and the emergence of a new Arctic region

The very landscape in which northern people have established societies is being shaken by the melting Arctic. Due to a changing icescape, hunters are experiencing greater difficulty gaining access to their prey. Due to changes in the temperature of the sea, fishermen are dealing with the fluctuating presence of fish. In certain places in the Arctic, communities are threatened by erosion when waves arise during storms, when rivers flood over and when the permafrost thaws. These natural phenomena carve out and undermine the very ground on which the dwellers have constructed their communities. It follows that communities in these locations are going to need to rethink their very existence, the way they perceive themselves and the way they organize their societies; indeed, they are going to have to anticipate new futures.

One of the stories circulating in the media that fosters a sense of hope is the story of Inuit people taking up and improving the harvesting of potatoes in Southern Greenland: Man may be in the midst of a crisis but he is nonetheless able to cope and adapt through change. Here, the constructed image of an Inuit turning into a farmer is used as a fantastic indicator of the possibilities of humankind to adapt and to pursue cultural change. Even though the Greenlandic potatoes are suggestive of a success story, in many ways it bespeaks only a minor portion of the sweeping social, cultural, economic and political changes that are taking place in the Arctic today, changes and developments that are being driven, to a certain extent, by climate change. Faced with a veritable procession of challenges, it is becoming increasingly more difficult to maintain the stance that people (just) have to adapt, because the process is neither simple nor linear.

Issues of climate change have put the Arctic on the map in new ways, and have incited the world to reconsider how the region and its population are being approached. The melting sea ice and the shrinking Greenlandic ice cap challenge the Arctic's special role in the imagination of the West. Now, the dominant understanding is that the Arctic is opening up. Its evident emergence has become, almost overnight, a powerful symbol of a new age. It is no longer distant but has become the focus, the concern and the interest of the world. Even within the Arctic itself, people's experiences with the changing icescape and their new role on the world stage have given rise to new self-perceptions and to new kinds of discourses that are related to social and environmental change.

According to the Danish novelist, Jens Christian Grøndahl (2009), various reports about the melting Arctic, and particularly the news stories about the two German freight ships that in 2009 managed to sail the Northeast Passage without any help from icebreakers on their way to South Korea, have caused existential unrest and a feeling of disorder. For Grøndahl, the Arctic has always occupied a dual and dynamic place in our imagination, somewhere between 'nature as the great other' and the civilizing project of man. In this sense, he claims, the Arctic has borne a familiarity with the rainforest and the desert, but those regions, according to him, have come to be crosscut by highways and pipelines and have thus become accessible. Only the frozen North, on the edge of the world, has maintained its relative impenetrability and inhospitality – primarily due to its cover of ice. In this imaginative perspective, the Inuit have only been able to survive because of their strenuous efforts and ingenuity. Grøndahl argues that it is this strong image of the North as the negation of human existence that has made the polar explorers, who were often struggling in vain against the forces of ice and snow, stand out as heroes in the context of a mythology about the nineteenth century's trials of strength that were played out between science and the wilderness (see also Bravo & Sörlin, 2002). This fascination or spell of the hostile and unconquerable Arctic was ruptured by the two German freight ships. He finds the consequences of this 'deflowering' of the Arctic myth, as he calls it, to be enormous and he compares it to a wall breaking down, allowing light to enter in and requiring us to re-orientate ourselves in space. He perceives it to be a state imbuing us with an alienated and homeless feeling that leaves us with a new and unsettling sense of the Earth as round. In many ways, he is addressing the concerns of a character and magnitude often expressed in the media. News from the Arctic about melting ice and news concerning the Inuit indeed create a sense of uneasiness about the stability of the planetary system. The research community has built a stronger and stronger case about how the Arctic ice and permafrost are disappearing, opening up the North while simultaneously challenging the existence of northern peoples' livelihoods and the future of the globe as we know it. The risks and dangers of the far North are linked not only to exploration and exploitation but have also taken on new meaning because changes in the Arctic have been linked to images of 'global tipping points' and irretrievable global processes which threaten everybody on this planet. It is within this concept of an inhospitable cold wilderness and an unstable global system that a new Arctic emerges. New positions and roles of Inuit and other Arctic peoples are emerging as well. Although indigenous peoples compose only some 10 per cent of the Arctic population of 4 million, they have been the focus of the public's interest and imagination. Considering the fact that indigenous peoples have gained land claims and self-governmental institutions in many regions, this places them in a highly influential position when it comes to influencing the direction of development in the Arctic.

This book is about how climate change in Greenland and the Arctic can be approached and about how strategies for dealing with these changes are entangled in complex webs of meaning, anticipations and politics of collective social goals to such an extent that it is hard to apprehend the challenges looming ahead. Moreover, the Arctic is facing an impending transformation. According to a scientific overview report produced by the Arctic Council, the diminished sea ice will very likely be concomitant with an increase in marine transportation, in the offshore extraction of oil and gas, and in the availability of access to other resources (ACIA, 2004, p. 11). This opening of the Arctic may have an impact on the economic, social, cultural and environmental spheres and may require that questions of sovereignty, security and safety will need to be revisited. A new landscape of risk and possibilities is emerging, indeed. This book's central argument is that we are going to have to rethink how we approach and understand the Arctic, not only because the ice is melting but also because the political and societal scenes are changing – and they are changing rapidly. The Arctic peoples are taking up a new and prominent political position, both as stakeholders and as collective rights-holders, and the international political cooperation in region-building institutions like the Arctic Council lays out a completely new political agenda. Arctic peoples are actively changing, creating and anticipating the very world they perceive to be their homeland. This creative process cannot be understood purely as adaptation or simply in terms of coping with climate change. The Arctic peoples are reorganizing and transforming their societies, and are entering into new political and economic partnerships in order to further their societal visions. The talk about climate change and ways of adapting do not take place in a vacuum and Arctic peoples are now in a position where they have to relate climate issues to contemporary political, social, economic and cultural barriers and drivers as well as to different visions of the future. Because Arctic people's societal visions are an important mover of anticipation and action, I consider them to be future-makers.

Climate change is certainly generating a new landscape of risk, which, in some areas, affects the life-nerve of communities and erodes the foundations of their way of life. In other areas, where climate-related changes are felt but understood to be transpiring as part and parcel of the world's natural cycles, concern is also prevalent because the changes are increasingly regarded as becoming entrenched. Although the Arctic is generally presented in the media and in scholarly culture as one single climate region, the diversity of the challenges related to climate change phenomena cannot be underestimated. The same is true of Greenland. Despite the fact that the country has a population of only 57,000 inhabitants, this huge island encompasses a natural and human diversity. For some hunters, the changing ice conditions open up new hunting opportunities while other hunters are experiencing curtailed mobility and waning accessibility to animal wildlife. In some cases, even small changes in the extent and quality of the sea ice have a massive impact on human activities and safety. The landscape of risk is, of course, not solely related to environmental matters, but is also constituted by the interplay of multiple factors including social organization, technology, skills and economic opportunities. As a consequence, many hunters and fishermen typically relate climate change concerns to other societal issues like questions about quotas, market possibilities, public investments and governmental priorities, just to name a few of the areas that are integrated in their total understanding of their landscape of risk. In some cases, climate change may not be the most pressing problem for people inasmuch as they are able to diversify their activities and innovate. In fact it may be the prices they are getting for their fish and the wildlife management regulations that might be straitjacketing their resource flexibility. In Chapter 7, which focuses on indigenous practices and knowledge, these issues, in correlation with an aggregate social field, are examined with an eye toward challenging our understanding of what we habitually perceive as 'local knowledge' and 'climate change problems'.

In this book, I aim to add a dimension to the climate change debate, a dimension that I find to be missing in much of the academic and public understanding of Arctic processes. Based on my studies in Greenland, I propose that the emphasis put on Arctic peoples as *victims* of climate change and on *adaptation* might be diverting our attention away from how people navigate a changed Arctic in multiple ways and from how climate change related issues may actually be emerging in unforeseen places and ways. It is not only a matter of commissioning more ethnographic studies but also a question of addressing the conceptual approaches with which we can try to understand life and change in the Arctic. The book redirects the focus away from the question of *how to adapt to climate change* in favour of the examining question of *who to become when adapting to climate change*. The point of departure is that who to become when adapting to climate change is tantamount to thinking of communities on another scale and to creating new images of social life. This perspective that I adopt here serves to redirect the focus away from the more environmentally based studies and away from vulnerability assessments.

By rethinking our approaches, we may catch sight not only of new problem-relations but possibly also of new human resources and how new routes and passages are anticipated and created. While some of the discussions and themes of the book are related to scientific and scholarly studies of community vulnerability, adaptation and resilience – primarily in Canada, where these studies are prevalent – the primary focus of the discussions relates to the *hyperindustrialization* of Greenland.

The political ambitions for a stronger and economically more self-reliant and self-governing Greenland fuel priorities and the societal changes that are taking place. In this perspective, some natural phenomena emerge as significant resources while other natural phenomena garner less attention. In Greenland, the increasing priority on the rapid development of oil and mining activities is immanent in societal discussions. However, one particular project stands out – and I have chosen this to be the focus of my discussions about societal change: it is the proposed construction of an aluminium smelter near the town of Maniitsoq on the west coast of Greenland. Even though its construction has not yet even been decided upon, this particular smelter has had an enormous impact on society and on the way the people living there understand the landscape of risk. It does so to such an extent that it stands out as a textbook case that clearly demonstrates how Arctic peoples, in their capacity as future-makers, are by the mere act of anticipation changing society as well as relating to – and making responses to – climate change. The emerging new Arctic may be understood as being driven by continuous constructions and negotiations of horizons of possibilities and expectations. In this perspective, the anticipation of futures stands out as the major driver and mobilizer of action. Moreover, emerging from this perspective is the fundamental question, 'How do we want the future society to be?' rather than 'How do we adapt to these changes?' By addressing the former question, the issue of climate change takes on another character and takes on a more socio-political and non-technical connotation.

The smelter can be understood as being entangled in climate change issues in many ways. First, the smelter is going to be powered by hydroelectricity that will be derived partly from the melting Greenland ice cap. Second, it will contribute significantly to Greenland's increased emission of CO_2, and thus position Greenland in a political predicament with respect to global climate. Third, it will add problems to the pallet of climate-related issues experienced in communities, even those that are far away from the smelter itself, and will thus come to influence their life worlds, choices and opportunities. By focusing on how Arctic peoples creatively mobilize and perform new societal ideas, as well as how they perceive and address the problems at hand, the Arctic emerges as more than the 'ground zero' of climate change, as is so often presented in the media. Furthermore, this approach stresses that environmental and climate change related problems are not to be regarded as detached from political strategies, economic priorities, social dynamics and cultural aspirations.

Zoning a region, assembling a problem and anticipating solutions

The Arctic is often envisioned as the cold zone north of the polar circle or the zone around the North Pole where the most salient characteristic is the ice. The delineations or zonings of the region have therefore followed biophysical criteria, such as the extent of the tree line, the boundary of continuous permafrost, the areas measured according to the winter and summer solstices, or the areas where the mean temperature for all months of the year is less than 10° Celsius. When the Arctic is primarily understood as an *environment*, it sets a particular stage that may not only conflict with how the North is approached by different parties but also impacts negotiations of perspectives and the dynamics of region-building that are taking place.

Today, there is a widespread perception that the Arctic is to be approached and understood as *one region*. The Arctic as one region is a product of political and scientific representation as well as of other human practices like network construction, political cooperation and the dissemination of news, etc.

The region evoked is the product of an effort and a systematic selection of features that are advocated as being genuine for the region (Keskitalo, 2004, p. 2) and are made relevant in institution building. The region is framed and practiced in ways that guide our attention in particular directions and influence how we formulate questions and answers. Thus, the framing influences what is considered to be relevant and valuable research and facts as well as what is to be seen as appropriate cooperation and networking. When the region is perceived in environmental terms, the environment becomes the framing device for the discourse posing both potentials and problems relevant to the way we understand agents and human relations. This further influences the role we assign to climate change in the interpretation of community dynamics.

The Arctic understood as one region is, according to Keskitalo (2004), a relatively new development. Historically, the North (as seen from the South) was – and particularly in North America – perceived not so much as a region but more as a *place* for explorers where fame and fortune were potential rewards (Delgado, 1999; Potter, 2007; Riffenburgh, 1993). The icy and barren North was a place to endure, overcome and fight against, with the ultimate purpose of returning home to the South. It was perceived as a sublime but fundamentally different and inhospitable environment that was not suitable for civilized human life. As pointed out by Brody, '[m]any [whites] believe that each degree northwards is a degree closer to the margins – or beyond them' (Brody, 1975, p. 80).

Numerous diaries and representations from polar explorations describe the immense hardships faced by the various expedition teams' members and depict the North as a region that is difficult to overcome and enter. Pictures of ships wrecked in – and taken down – by the ice, leaving the men exposed within an icy hell, are plentiful. Records kept by merchants and explorers also bear witness to catastrophic episodes, like the disaster in 1777 in East Greenland, when some 50 whaling ships were icebound and abandoned by their crews and the incident in 1835, where only 20 out of 70 whaling ships returned from the Davis Strait. These records and numbers similarly bespeak a history of intense European, Russian and American activity and resource extraction in the North with devastating consequences for the ecosystem and the indigenous peoples. The North was perceived and demarcated on the basis of its dangerous but promising environment. It was a resource-rich marginal zone, not a region to be appropriated as a whole.

In Canada, where the idea of the North as demarcated by the 60° north latitude increasingly took hold, the distinction was primarily administrative and political, as this formed the borderlines for separate political entities (provinces and territories). The boundary between the North and the South accordingly became one that was demarcated by political history and interests (Grace, 2001). In the Arctic Human Development Report (AHDR) (2004, pp. 17–18), the authors have also decided to demarcate the region in ways that take jurisdictional and administrative boundaries into consideration, and thus point our attention to the primacy of the practice of control as a pivotal aspect of region construction. For Armstrong et al. (1978: 1 cited in Keskitalo, 2004, p. 38), the integration of the region was defined quite flexibly in terms of both environmental and social characteristics, and the authors thought of the Arctic 'as a group of concepts and attributes, concerned with climate, vegetation, fauna, presence of ice and snow, sparseness of human habitation, remoteness from industrial centres, and many other factors, and not having precise boundaries'.

Applying a social constructivist perspective entails that the region cannot be regarded as a given and unproblematic entity. Rather, it has to be seen as being contested, practiced and evoked. The development of the Arctic as one region has its own specific history of practices, representations and political connotations that can be unfolded, as is so elaborately done by Keskitalo (2004), where region-building can be seen as following many of the same dynamics as nation-building and the construction of imagined communities (Anderson, 1983).

Region-building is an act of zoning. The social act of demarcating a zone is, according to Larsen (1992), also an act of evoking some sort of repetition, similarity or smoothness within a zone. Thus, mobility or cooperation may be understood and performed as being more possible within a zone than between zones that are blocked by a border. Furthermore, the symbolic status of zoning emphasizes recognition and value-adding as inherited aspects of the activity. This value-adding imparts identity to the zone. A region can, according to this perspective, be evoked by a social act of zoning that actively highlights differences on each side of the perceived zone border. These differences are arbitrary, no matter how physically apparent they may be. Following Simmel (1958, p. 467), the border is not a spatial fact with social effects but a social fact with spatial form. As Young also points out in the introduction to the AHDR (2004, pp. 17–18), there is 'nothing intuitively obvious about the idea of treating the Arctic as a distinct region'. He goes on to say that this uneasiness about how to zone the region and how to apprehend any kind of continuity and integration within such a large and diverse region may be understandable in some respects, but that 'this critique is falling increasingly on deaf ears among both those who live in the Arctic and others who think about Arctic issues today. More and more, the Arctic has emerged as a *distinct* region in public policy discussions'. In fact, Tennberg's analysis indicates that most states in the Arctic did not discover their 'Arcticness' until after the elaborate work of the Arctic Climate Impact Assessment (ACIA) published in 2005 (Tennberg, 2009a). It is this emerged distinctiveness as a special *integrated* region that is important to grasp. Also crucial to our further understanding are the questions of how its particular region-ness sets a new arena for the manner in which the Arctic is to be perceived and approached and how this can appear relevant and present to people who live far away from the North. People's sense of proximity to the Arctic is driven by, among other factors, the idea of global tipping points and global disasters caused by a melting polar region. Media messages about melting ice and rising sea levels are also drivers behind this perceptual development of what I would call a *region of flow*, intimately entangled in the rest of the world. In this sense, the Arctic epitomizes the marginal and the potent, as well as the isolated and entangled. Climate change and the position taken up by the Arctic in this process have made the North emerge more and more as one region – a perspective that for long has been promoted by the pan-Arctic nongovernmental organization (NGO) Inuit Circumpolar Council.

The age of the Arctic

The cartographical representations of the North have often pictured it as an area at the top of the world, closest to the upper edge of the map. Consequently, a clear sense about the space and time of the Circumpolar North is difficult to apprehend because, in these representations, the Arctic Ocean is reduced to a thin strip, if it even appears on the map at all. In these representations, the region becomes the North of particular nation-states which, historically speaking, have related to the regions in very different ways (Keskitalo, 2004) and have included the North in different national regimes. It was also these national regimes, which clashed during the Cold War period, that bifurcated the Arctic, and it can be said that the national *frontiers* were increasingly replaced by national and strategic *borders* as clearer claims and demarcations of sovereignty were made (Giddens, 1990, p. 73).

Recently, the Circumpolar North has been exchanged with another cartographical representation where the North is turned into an Arctic region of a spatially different character. This representation and zoning stresses and encourages new perspectives, even if it can still be seen as a spatial distortion. It can be understood more as a region of neighbours around the Arctic Ocean, neighbours that share an interrelated and unique environment that is undergoing rapid transformation and impact. It can be seen as a re-territorialization (Tennberg, 2009b). Around the time of the establishment of the Arctic Council, political scientist Oran Young commented on the remarkable changes that had taken place since the mid-1980s in the following way: 'Anyone who had the audacity to forecast in 1986 the emergence of this agenda of international cooperation in the Arctic within ten years would surely have been dismissed as a starry-eyed visionary' (Young, 1998, p. 49). Young finds the importance of the region to be underestimated within the political sciences and advocates establishing Arctic politics as a field of study in its own right, but he also argues that this be done for an even more encompassing research community (Young, 1992). The booming possibilities for industrial development in the Arctic that have been emerging since the 1970s, along with the military potentials, have indeed served to turn people's attention toward the Arctic. Accordingly, Young coined this altered view 'The Age of the Arctic' (Young, 1985–1986). Back in the mid-1980s, in continuation of this line of thinking, he urged the United States' policy makers to intensify their focus on – and their prioritizing of – the Arctic by stating: '[i]nterest in the Arctic is rapidly heating up worldwide' (Young, 1985–1986, p. 179). The rapid changes in the Circumpolar North that made the Arctic stand out as a new and important international region were also discussed in Young's collaboration with Gail Osherenko (1989).

Political cooperation has also actively evoked a regional identity. Not only has the work pursued by the working groups of the Arctic Council (e.g. Arctic Monitoring and Assessment Programme [AMAP]), an intergovernmental forum established in 1996, encouraged this new identity but it has also underpinned the ideological construction of the Council itself, which consists of members from the nation-states having an Arctic shoreline: Russia, United States, Canada, Denmark (including Greenland and the Faroe Islands), Iceland, Norway, Sweden and Finland.

The Council has also gradually expanded its field of concern, from being focused on environmental cooperation to achieving a broader political focus. This complex political landscape, however, is often over-simplified in cartographical representations of the Circumpolar North, where future claims on, for example, the North Pole are mapped out in a way that makes the nation-states stand out as the primary political agents. Such representations reinforce a traditional geopolitical understanding of state confrontation and sovereignty struggles over land and sea, a scenario with potential losers and winners. This view has especially been expressed by the media as the 'scramble' for the seabed or the 'great game' of international power politics, which is played out as the various nation's 'race' and 'rush' to extract an abundance of newly available resources. However, such a perspective deforms an understanding of contemporary political processes and potentials in the Arctic as well as ignores the long history of indigenous peoples' political mobilization across Arctic borders, which was already initiated at the Arctic Peoples' Conference in Copenhagen in 1973, where they began to think of the Arctic as one region.

While the five Arctic Ocean's littoral states – Russia, Canada, Denmark, Norway and the United States – are clearly endowed with enormous power and responsibilities, as stipulated in the international legislation, we can observe a political hybrid and complex scene that is characterized by cooperation, dialogue, devolution and transnational integration. Despite conflicts and problems, this constantly evolving political landscape in the Arctic may be the key to dealing decisively and successfully with the challenges of climate change and environmental change. In fact, political initiatives and changes may be as important as technological, cultural and social ones.

My argument is that the Arctic could increasingly be approached as *one* 'region of flow' in an era of climate change and that this new region can be perceived quite differently from the regionalizations of the North that have heretofore been predominant, historically speaking. The contemporary regional understanding has something to offer in cultural, social and economic terms and the area has increasingly been able to emerge as a distinct region in policy discussions (Arctic Human Development Report, 2004, p. 18). Martello (2004, 2008) contends that the Arctic itself has been constructed as a meaningful region largely through scientific institutions and research as well as through graphics, pictures, maps, quotes and tables that have been so elegantly applied in, for example, the ACIA (2005) and in the AMAP's assessment on Snow, Water, Ice and Permafrost in the Arctic (SWIPA) (AMAP, 2011a, 2011b). By localizing climate change in a particular way and among peoples that are being victimized, scientists and indigenous representatives are evoking and performing a certain region of flow – a relevant place for apprehending what is difficult for the public in general to see and experience.

Region of flow

Increasingly, the Arctic has come to be understood and performed as one region under rapid change. The environmental changes going on here are perceived as having severe consequences for northern populations as well as for the world in general. The changes are driven both by natural processes and human activities. Of concern in the Arctic and, accordingly, also points of focus for the Arctic Council, are the human-induced impacts stemming from hunting and fishing and industrial activities that persistently generate organic contaminants, greenhouse gas pollution, oil pollution, black carbon, heavy metals, noise, radioactivity and acidification. These industries are located both inside and outside the geographical Arctic region. Furthermore, the human-induced impacts that are being made on the Arctic are perceived to be locally and regionally non-containable due to the wind, the sea currents and the movement of ice, which quite easily transmit pollution to other geographical regions. Progressively, the region is understood as connected and entangled. From this analytical perspective or gaze, the Arctic comes to take on a double position: it becomes a 'region of attention' and also becomes a 'station' or a 'sink' in a region of flows of energy, species, particles and substances. Environmental concern and awareness have thus given rise to what I choose to call a *region of flow*, which assembles people from different geographical, social and political spaces around flow as a central theme into *one* field of entangled concern and responsibility. In this perspective, a *region* is thought of in terms of a *theme*. The demarcation and zoning of the North are broadening. Consequently, groups as well as nations far away from the Arctic are now expressing their wishes to partake in the Arctic Council because they have started to relate more directly to the North on the basis of ideas of flows and pathways. A new sense of totality has been developed and political action has been mobilized on the basis of a shared concern about these flows. A region of flow assembles problems and agents in new ways. When understood as such, the North's importance and entanglement in global relations certainly challenge our perception of the relevant objects of study as well as of well-established notions of sustainability, adaptation and vulnerability because the demarcation of the system itself is being challenged. In the 1970s, when Arctic indigenous peoples mobilized a new understanding of the Arctic as a neighbourhood in an indigenous homeland it was indeed a way to raise concern, to push governments, to fight anti-hunting organizations and to demand responsibility. The new Arctic was thus also a new way of understanding shame and blame, power and potentiality as well as an invocation of new system-understandings.

In this book, one of the arguments essentially holds that it is this transcendence of received notions of cultures, nations or even regions that may turn our attention towards societal dynamics, concerns and resources in new ways. The regionalization instilled by new environmental disasters implies that the mutual impact of phenomena belonging to different scales results in their inseparability and non-locality.

A region of flow criss-crosses national borders, climatic borders and biotopes, and thus encourages new ways of mobilizing and framing agency. A simple example of how a region of flow is constituted and used as a vehicle for policy-making is the formulation of conventions for the protection of migrating birds. The region of flow is demarcated by the routes of migrating birds and points toward potential agents that can take action in response to matters of concern. A region of flow is demarcated analytically on the basis of specific concerns and may aggregate geographical regions and people who would otherwise consider themselves to be separate. Another example is that the future and the welfare of Pacific islanders are increasingly being regarded in terms of their interconnections with the polar regions, since the melting ice is causing the ocean to rise and threatening the island life in the Pacific. In this region of flow, the Pacific islanders and a number of low-lying developing countries become extraordinarily dependent upon the polar ice, albeit in very different ways than the Inuit people, of course. However, they have caught sight of a commonality, and NGOs and institutions from these places have joined forces in the organization named Many Strong Voices. As its stated goal, the organization has – according to its homepage – an intention 'to promote the well-being, security, and sustainability of coastal communities in the Arctic and Small Island Developing States (SIDS) by bringing these regions together to take action on climate change mitigation and adaptation, and to tell their stories to the world' (Many Strong Voices, n.d.). The United Nations Economic Commission for Europe Convention on Long-Range Transboundary Air Pollution, which was signed by 34 governments and the European Community, is another example of how flows of particles are being dealt with on a broad cross-regional basis – or, more precisely, how flows of particles are being used to constitute interconnect-edness and consequently a region of flow. This reflects an understanding of how international political and scientific cooperation organized around a region of flow can reduce the damage to the environment and to human health brought about by transboundary pollutants. The concept of *region of flow* differs from the perception of a region as static and clearly demarcated.

Regions of flow have to be constructed and promoted since they are not necessarily directly perceivable; the spread of PCBs (poylchlorinated biphenyls), of DDT (dichlorodiphenyltrichloroethane) and of CFCs (chlorofluorocarbons) in the biosphere can only be detected through the aid of scientific equipment and the use of scientific research. Sometimes, even more visible flows of natural objects need to be apprehended through the mediation of science. This applies, for example, to migrating birds. For example, neither Iñupiat hunters in Northern Alaska nor sports hunters in California were necessarily aware of the extensive migrating routes of the birds they were shooting until scientists mapped the routes. Compared to bioregions and ecoregions, regions of flow have to be medi-ated to a much greater extent by science and have to be made visible and real in collages of cartographic and flow representations. The construction of a region of flow is often represented in the form of arrows, pathways, corridors or 'high-ways' on a map, thus indicating movement and flow rather than a clear bound-ary, which would generally be associated with the concept of a region (for a very good example please consult AMAP, 2003). By stressing cross-national and cross-regional pathways and entanglements while maintaining a centred Arctic focus, the Arctic Environmental Protection Strategy (AEPS), the AMAP and later on the ACIA have all made the Arctic one of the global 'environmental panopticons' (Tennberg, 2009b, p. 190) – a point from where extra-regional surveillance and observation is possible, necessary and appropriate.

During the social process of creating a region of flow and rendering it socially productive, certain notions of commonality (e.g. real or imagined problems, issues, concerns, disasters and risks) are demarcated. In this process, certain agents (e.g. Iñupiat hunters, Californian sports hunters and several governments [Huntington, 1992]) emerge as significant and certain solutions, rights and obligations are put into play and deemed to be relevant. The development of cross-scale and cross-geographical linkages is a social phenomenon and a work in constant progress, because it cannot be taken for granted. The permanence of these regions of flow has different temporalities and spatialities. The Chernobyl radioactive cloud, which moved over certain parts of Europe, had an extent in time and space that differs significantly from the airborne and seaborne pollution, which is being discharged continuously into the North. Regions of flow are thus essentially different from bioregionalism and from ecoregions, which are demarcated by particular attributes of natural characteristics like flora, fauna, water, soil, landform and climate (Sale, 1985). Regions of flow are demarcated not so much by boundaries as they are by movement, interrelations and connections which particular groups within society point out as being significant.

It is this sensibility about a *region of flow* that provides the rationale for pan-Arctic and international cooperation. Following this construction of a region, we have witnessed an increased awareness of scaling as well as a budding sense of uneasiness about the demarcation of problems and the complexity of inter-relationships. If the Arctic is approached as a *region of flow*, the development of political institutions and of cooperation emerges more clearly. The political cooperation was mobilized on the basis of environmental concern springing from a focus on flows, and the gradually developing programs for the scientific monitoring of the environment expanded the geographical national and Arctic areas and brought a sense of integration and continuity to the region, despite marked differences in the natural, social, economic and political environments. The process started in the mid-1980s (Keskitalo, 2004) and cannot be seen as separated from the intensified industrial activities taking place at that time (Osherenko & Young, 1989) as well as from the political ideas developing in the USSR. One could argue that the ground for more cross-boundary cooperation was explicitly being evoked by the former President of the USSR, Mikhail Gorbachev, in his 1987 Murmansk speech (Gorbachev, 1987). Here he attached special importance to the cooperation of the northern countries in environmental protection and demilitarization, in order to create 'a pole of peace', as he termed it, based on multilateral and bilateral agreements and cooperation. He also suggested that

> [we] attach special importance to the cooperation of the northern countries in environmental protection. The urgency of this is obvious. It would be well to extend joint measures for protecting the marine environment of the Baltic … to the entire oceanic and sea surface of the globe's North.

Gorbachev ended his speech by stressing his concern and encouraged 'The North European countries … [to] set an example to others by reaching an agreement on establishing a system to monitor the state of the natural environment and radiation safety in the region. We must *hurry* to protect the nature of the tundra, forest tundra, and the northern forest areas' (italics by the author).

A few years later, in 1991, an ambitious, albeit non-legally binding environmental protection strategy for the Arctic was established among the Arctic states. Although various states entered into this sphere of cooperation on the basis of different concerns, a common sense of urgency was developing (Keskitalo, 2004). At the first Ministerial Meeting in Rovaniemi in 1991, the Governor of Lapland made the following statement in his welcoming address: 'Our most *urgent* task is to find out true causes and set forth action together with *our neighbours* to eliminate the causes of damage' (cited in Keskitalo, 2004, p. 57, italics by the author). If we understand the processes of Arctic region-building as being based on an increasingly shared understanding of concern, risk, and urgency in the environment, shared among neighbours linked together by *flow*, the configuration of the problems becomes influenced by this focus on environmental issues. This has had an effect on indigenous peoples. Arctic indigenous peoples, who increasingly became players in this emerging environmental cooperation, were integrated on these environmental premises and rationales as set forth in the Rovaniemi Declaration on the Protection of the Arctic Environment, charted out in 1991 and outlining a framework for the AEPS. In the text of this declaration, the states emphasize 'our responsibility to protect and preserve the Arctic environment and [the importance of] recognizing the special relationship of the indigenous peoples and local populations to the Arctic and their unique contribution to the protection of the Arctic Environment' (Rovaniemi Declaration, 1991).

In Rovaniemi, four working groups were set up to deal with environmental issues of concern. Two years later, in 1993, the AEPS principles and issues were linked more directly to Arctic policies, health, economies and social initiatives designed to uphold the principles of sustainable development – a step that was, politically speaking, very difficult to navigate, as discussed by Keskitalo (2004). The indigenous peoples' representation opened up new political avenues for them (Koivurova, 2010; Koivurova & Heinämäki, 2006; Tennberg, 1998, 2010), but according to Keskitalo, they were caught in a dilemma: 'Indigenous groups… largely found themselves captured in an argumentative corner: while they argue for their rights to use not to be limited to the traditional, they gain their place in cooperation on the basis of relating their claims to a traditional connection to the environment' (2004, p. 99). The Arctic Council retained the Arctic as a region of flow defined primarily on environmental matters and concerns, accordingly limiting the breadth of discussions in the council and lacking for a broader consideration of the economic situation and ongoing development activities (Keskitalo, 2004, p. 99).

AEPS paved the road that eventually led, five years later, to the creation of the formalized political cooperation in the Arctic Council in 1996. It was first in the mid-1990s that AEPS took up climate change as an issue (Nilsson, 2009, pp. 81–82). The driving metaphors behind the perception of the North were thus being challenged in the period from the late 1980s to the 1990s. The North was no longer (only) to be perceived as a *frontier* for exploitation and resource extraction, a *theatre* for military operations, a *wilderness* of untouched and relatively undisturbed 'natural' surroundings or a *stage* for explorers striving to reach untouched, geographically and mentally, new territory. These metaphors have continued to be extremely powerful in the media's representation and in people's imagination. However, the idea of a North as a region of states and other parties (indigenous peoples and NGOs) that have joined forces in order to address their concerns about the future environment – as this is related to the level of pollution stemming from, flowing into and circulating in the Arctic – is emerging. This awareness, based on a new understanding of the scale of problems, also sets a new stage, assembles problems in novel ways and points at agents to bear the responsibility. In fact, some of the sources causing environmental problems and concerns in the Arctic are difficult to localize within the boundaries of what is perceived to be the Arctic and thus within the jurisdiction of the Arctic states to solve on their own. Problems related to the ozone hole, the greenhouse effect and transboundary pollutants like persistent organic pollutants and black carbon position the Arctic within global flows of pollutants. Taking the matter of black carbon into consideration, by way of example, Koch and Hansen (2005, p. 1) present the following research results:

> Black carbon (BC) particles, derived from incomplete combustion of fossil fuels and biomass, may have a severe impact on the sensitive Arctic climate, possibly altering the temperature profile, cloud temperature and amount, the seasonal cycle, and the tropopause level and accelerating polar ice melting. We use the Goddard Institute for Space Studies general circulation model to investigate the origins of Arctic BC by isolating various source regions and types. The model suggests that the predominant sources of Arctic soot today are from south Asia (industrial and biofuel emissions) and from biomass burning.

The region-building process can be understood as intimately entangled in the knowledge production that has taken place in, for example, the Arctic Council. Following the line of thinking expressed by VanDeveer (2004), it is the interaction of knowledge about nature and the visual representations of it in conjunction with associated forms of politics that result in the identity and autonomy of the Arctic as a region. Polar science accordingly plays an important role in supporting the governmental powers with knowledge that maintains and strengthens their positions and their practices of governing (Tennberg, 2009b) as well as their region-engineering. The scientific projects formerly pursued in the Arctic and encouraged by national policies have now changed into a more transborder, pan-Arctic monitoring system, with a greater focus on the region in its capacity of being entangled in global dynamics.

The Arctic Council (see the analysis by Tennberg [2000]) manifests a fine example of a high-level institution that is addressing pan-national issues. As one of its main tasks, it has been occupied with environmental data collection, monitoring, and eco-system interpretations that are of common benefit to the Council's members. The ACIA is one of the most salient climate-related initiatives of the Council; it conjoins climate change research and socio-cultural issues. Although one cannot speak of a coherent and comprehensive Arctic political regime, the Council has, through its soft-law framework, managed to come up with an agenda that emphasizes the importance of the Arctic, considered as a whole and globally entangled. For this reason, it is understandable that non-Arctic states like China are applying for membership in the Council. The interests of non-Arctic states in becoming engaged in the work of the Arctic Council reflect the fact that the region is being perceived as one that is opening up for commercial activities and also reflect the fact that more states that are non-Arctic are starting to consider changes and developments in the Arctic as being of relevance to them (Breum, 2011; Zellen, 2009). This new global position of the Arctic was also mirrored by the International Conference on Arctic Research Planning, which was held in Copenhagen in 2005. Here, the Arctic was stressed as being an important and unique part of the Earth system: environmentally, socially, economically, and politically. The conference's publication revealed, in its very title, the heart of the message: 'Arctic Research. A Global Responsibility'. The Arctic is indeed emerging as a unique region that is playing a special role in the global system, and non-Arctic institutions are producing this region as well. By constructing an Arctic that is entangled within a global system, certain concerns, interests and responsibilities emerge as evident. In his opening speech for the Arctic Frontiers Conference that was held in Tromsø in January 2009, Josephe Borg, Member of the European Commission Responsible for Fisheries and Maritime Affairs, emphasized that the Arctic is a place with a common heritage and a common responsibility (Borg, 2010):

> I sincerely hope that the discussions over the next few days will generate new ideas and help us take a step further towards securing a healthy Arctic region for future generations to come. Let me finish by quoting Henrik Ibsen: "A Community is like a ship, everyone ought to be prepared to take the helm." If the Arctic is our ship then we must all take the helm to preserve its future. Europe wants to contribute towards the sustainable development of the Arctic region while protecting it from environmental changes that result from increasing human activity. With that in mind, our message to you is clear. All of us in a position to make and influence policy must recognise the need to contribute to the decisive international action we need for the Arctic in order to preserve our common heritage. Let us be bold and protect this precious region in the interest of our planet as a whole.

Later the same year, the European Council did, in its conclusions on Arctic issues (Council of the European Union, 2009), provide formulations for an over-arching approach to EU policy on Arctic issues by recognizing 'the particular vulnerability of the Arctic region and its crucial importance to the world climate system' (p. 2) including 'the role of the Arctic region as an important part of the Earth ecosystem' (p. 3). When the Arctic, as a region, is increasingly becoming understood as being entangled in one or several systems and flows of global extent – and is gaining in importance precisely due to this perception of entanglement – the interests and concerns of non-Arctic states are mobilized as well. In the very first sentence of its 'Communication from the Commission to the European Parliament and the Council' concerning 'The European Union and the Arctic Region', The European Commission accordingly stressed that 'The European Union is inextricably linked to the Arctic region … by a unique combination of history, geography, economy and scientific achievements' (European Commission, 2008, p. 1). At an Arctic Dialogue meeting in Brussels between indigenous representatives and the European Commission in 2010, however, the Russian Ambassador at Large, Anton Vasiliev, voiced his objections to an 'entanglement' of this character. He stated that the EU is not at all inextricably linked to the Arctic and he regarded the declaration as being the European Commission's way of circumventing the interests of central Arctic governments. In a short article about the meeting, the representative from the Indigenous Peoples' Secretariat wrote the following statement, articulating the Russian stand on this matter (Gant, 2010):

> Objecting to the ideology of world heritage ideology that pervades the Northern Dimension policy, the Russian Ambassador at Large said that the Arctic is not some sort of virgin land or a state in itself. It is not the common home of everybody, he said, and no one should try and infringe on the responsibility of the Arctic States to administer the rights and obligations of their citizens.

This is a striking example of how the evocation of a system (e.g. global), of regions (e.g. the Arctic) and of different systemic entanglements involves the production of subject positions, and in this case, it was considered an attack on the sovereignty of the (Russian) state. Later on, the EU Commission elaborated their statement on entanglement by initiating a study, 'EU Arctic Footprint and Policy Assessment', which assesses the impact that the EU has on the Arctic environment and evaluates how this could change over time (Cavalieri et al., 2010). The EU's polluting activities, with specific consequences on the Arctic, are made transparent in the report. In doing this, the EU actively inscribes itself as being part of the *region of flow*.

In the Arctic, *cooperation* is emerging in many places (Young, 2009). A number of new agents and interrelationships are appearing on the political scene and taking responsibility on different levels of scale. Indigenous peoples have increasingly been successful in having their political rights and collective land rights strengthened. In 2009, for example, Greenland achieved self-governance and rights to the non-renewable resources. Cooperation between states can also be observed. According to the International Law of the Sea, claims made by Arctic states in the Arctic Ocean have to be scientifically based. This work is actually being pursued in a context of cooperation where Canada and Denmark, for example, are coordinating the data collection. The Danish scientific expedition that has taken on the task of investigating the Lomonosov Ridge, off the coast of Greenland, has also been reliant on the help of a Russian icebreaker. More and more, the coordination of search and rescue operations is being developed between countries (in Nuuk, in 2011, an agreement was signed by the Arctic ministers); in this light, the increased presence of military personnel cannot be regarded as an act of traditional re-armament echoing the Cold War militarization in the Arctic. On the Arctic Council's homepage, the Search and Rescue Agreement was commented on in the following manner (Pedersen, 2011):

> The Agreement is the first legally binding instrument negotiated under the auspices of the Arctic Council. It also represents the first legally binding agreement on any topic ever negotiated among all the eight Arctic states. The signature of the Agreement in Nuuk demonstrates the commitment of those states to enhance their cooperation in addressing emerging issues in the Arctic region.

Approached as a *region of flow*, cooperation among 'neighbours' along the flow emerges as one of the ways to handle future environmental challenges and opportunities. The active development of cooperation, which is supposed to constitute the framework within which ideas, priorities and visions for future societal transformations are to be negotiated and put into action, increasingly positions the *societal* on the centre of the stage, although the environment is still singled out as the primary concern. In the Arctic Council, which could rightly be termed the pivot point of Arctic cooperation, NGOs and non-Arctic states are granted the possibility of participating as observers. This inclusive political strategy allows other stakeholders to play a role in the development of activities in – and visions for – the Arctic. Apart from the states, the most important players in the Council are indigenous peoples, who have the status of permanent participants. The political rights they have gained since the 1970s have put them in the forefront of many political discussions and decisions, and they are indeed playing important roles in defining the new Arctic and the Arctic as *a region of flow*.

Indigenous peoples in the new Arctic

The Arctic Council estimates that about 500,000 people in the Arctic can be categorized as indigenous; this amounts to around 10 per cent of the total population in the Circumpolar North. The Arctic indigenous peoples have different histories and different cultural backgrounds, and often speak different languages. The designation 'Eskimos' or 'Inuit', as used in Alaska, for example, is essentially an 'umbrella' term encompassing the Iñupiat of the North Slope and Northwest Arctic boroughs and the Bering Strait region, the St. Lawrence Island (Siberian) Yupik and the Central Yup'ik and Cup'ik of the Yukon-Kuskokwim Delta in Southwest

Alaska (for further elaboration, see Dahl, 1993). These indigenous groups are often singled out as living under a great deal of climate change stress and both the scientific community and the media devote a lot of attention to them and their conditions. Indigenous peoples' role and position in climate change discussions have their own history and their own explanations. In what follows, I intend to cast light on this because doing so may serve to indicate some of the potentials and pitfalls in the roles and positions given to *and* taken by indigenous peoples in the contemporary debate on adaptation to climate change in the Arctic.

The cultures, histories, lifeworlds and conditions of these various groups are very dissimilar, and much like other population groups in the world, they cannot be approached as having only one voice, only one concern or only one vision. Within one and the same indigenous group, different attitudes with respect to, for example, land use can be a widespread occurrence (Nuttall, 2010). Notwithstanding the obvious diversity within and between groups, what I propose here is that they share *one* important thing: *the colonial experience* – no matter how different the respective colonial histories may be. This colonial experience has had a *marked* impact on the personal and collective lives of Arctic peoples (Minority Rights Group, 1994), and is still directly or indirectly playing a role in the issues that indigenous peoples are dealing with today – including climate change. The concept of indigenous is being used here not to point toward particular social and cultural characteristics, as is so frequently the errand, but rather to point at the problems, the relationships and the possibilities that have evolved out of the colonial experience.

The political struggles of indigenous peoples during the 1960s and 1970s targeted at raising a greater awareness about their situation and their visions of taking possession of their collective rights to self-determination, as well as land rights being acknowledged by the nation-states, have eventually proven to lead to a number of political developments and setups designed to deal with these collective wishes. Today, many Arctic indigenous peoples are engaged in institutions that are, to varying degrees, politically self-governing. Some of these institutions are demarcated by ethnicity (e.g. the Sámi parliament in Norway and the tribal councils in Alaska), by region (e.g. the self-government of Greenland and the regional government of Nunavut in Canada) or by land-claim agreements (e.g. Tungavik Federation of Nunavut [Dahl, 1993]). Furthermore, their ambitions of self-determination and concomitantly the rights to continue practicing a specific way of life, as well as the collective rights to determine their own future development, are also being pursued in political institutions, on different scales.

The position of indigenous peoples as permanent participants in the Arctic Council is one example of a non-indigenous political institution in which indigenous peoples are trying to further their agendas and raise their concerns. The North Slope Borough in Northern Alaska is another example where indigenous peoples are making a huge impact on the governing of the borough. Each of these political institutions gives indigenous peoples opportunities as well as problems. The Alaska Native Claims Settlement Act from 1971 offered relatively few political instruments as compared to what the Greenland Home Rule Agreement from 1979 offered and all indigenous peoples can be said to be standing inside an ongoing process of gaining more and more political control over their own futures. These political developments have been under continuous negotiations and improvements. In 2009, Greenland 'upgraded' the country's *home rule* to a *self-government*, giving Greenlanders additional and considerably expanded potentials as well as achieving recognition as a people with a right to independence from Denmark, should the people of Greenland wish to secede. These political developments put indigenous peoples in a position as collective *rights-holders* and their influence in political processes can no longer simply be reduced to stakeholder input (see Chapter 2). Furthermore, their political position and their claims to land render them pivotal partners in resource development or land use plans. Among other things, these various partnerships, governments and multi-level processes of cooperation make up the 'New Arctic', as proposed by Nordregio (2011). The political role and position of indigenous peoples in the 'New Arctic' are thus pivotal to constructive discussions about 'climate change adaptation in the Arctic'. However, indigenous peoples are often represented and assigned a position and role in these discussions that have a resonance in markedly different understandings of indigenous peoples' perspectives and agendas. The dominant framing is fuelled by a basic understanding of Arctic indigenous peoples as 'marginal'.

Indigenous peoples as the marginal other

The images and representations of indigenous peoples and the North have been widely studied and discussed (see, for example, Coates, 1994; Heininen, 2007). In an elegant manner, Ann Fienup-Riordan calls our attention to the image construction that has dominated the representation of Arctic peoples by coining the term, *Arctic Orientalism* (Fienup-Riordan, 1990, 1995). By making this explicit reference to Said's study of orientalism (Said, 1995), she is pointing at the role false assumptions and misrepresentations play in the discourse on Inuit culture and the Arctic, and how this production of difference lies at the heart of colonialism. It is this perception of indigenous peoples as well as its impact on political relations that Lill Rastad Bjørst terms *Arcticism* (2008). Our attitude to Arctic indigenous peoples plays a role in our relation to them and the way we understand the climate change problems they are facing. Very often, the idea of 'the marginal' is a dominant aspect in the discourse, and it has historically been a potent mover of imagination and ethnography. In 1932, for example, the famous Danish ethnographer, Kaj Birket-Smith, had this to say about the Eskimos, as the Inuit were termed at that time (Birket-Smith, 1932, p. 163, translated by the author):

> The Eskimos live at the world's back door, at the threshold to the empty polar wasteland and face to face with a nature that demands more of them than perhaps any other people of the inhabited world. The raw fight for food during both winter and summer makes such great demands on all human energies that it does not leave much time for anything else than to think of how to satisfy the most essential needs.

Here, Birket-Smith touched upon at least two notions related to marginality that are still prevalent in the discourse on indigenous peoples. First, the notion that Arctic indigenous peoples depend on natural resources; second, the notion that they occupy marginal territory. The widespread perception of Arctic indigenous peoples as simple hunter-gatherers can be related to the history and conception of the Arctic as a space for exploration and exploitation from the South. The Arctic emerges as a space that has predominantly positioned indigenous peoples as *marginal*, living their lives in a barren wilderness at the constant mercy of the environment. This discourse, which is based on the idea of marginality, produces several interrelated subject positions for indigenous peoples. They become geographically marginal, not only in terms of distance but also in terms of resources. Despite the history of an Arctic region that has come to be a 'hot spot' for international politics and attention as well as an extremely rich resource zone, which has fuelled Russian and Western economies for centuries, this discourse of marginality is maintained. The idea of marginality gives rise to a subject position where indigenous peoples have to adapt themselves to something more powerful. Adaptability becomes a central tool for dealing with this marginality. Arctic indigenous peoples (especially the Inuit) have been admired on account of their extraordinary knowledge of the environment and their skills when it comes to 'adapting' and 'surviving' in the North. Adaptation to a dominating nature and, later on, to a dominating culture (modernity) seems to be the fate of indigenous peoples and it is this concept of adaptation that has dominated the Western understanding of peoples and processes in the North. Even though post–World War II colonization was centred on bringing modernity to the North (see, for example, [Paine,1977]) the discourse never really disappeared. Indigenous peoples are still positioned as marginal, and adaptation is still the predominant analytical concept for apprehending their strategies. In fact, indigenous peoples have increasingly been positioned – within this discourse of adaptation and marginality – within a new triple marginal position. Now deeply entangled in colonial and postcolonial projects, and thus understood to be on their way into modernity, they have become marginal with respect to their own culture and, along with this, also marginal with respect to their skills and knowledge understood to be so decisive when it comes to making use of the environment. The triple marginality springs from being marginal with respect to one's own culture, to the environment and to modern culture. The marginality discourse proceeds with the following logic in mind: the more modern Inuit become, the less control they have, because they are thought of as becoming more and more alienated to themselves. In this way, they are understood as being situated *outside* the modern project of individual and collective emancipation. The discourse of marginality is highly explosive, as it can manifest itself in multiple ways: for example, when indigenous peoples are expected to be *incompetent* when it comes to dealing with new political systems and resource extractive activities. In Greenland, just to mention one example, the government's visions and oil-producing aspirations are sometimes met with a condescending attitude from Danish voices: Are Greenlanders competent enough to rule their own affairs and can they administer the economic bonanza from the oil industry? (see, for example, Mogensen, 2010). Stories about Greenlandic nepotism, socio-cultural decay and conditions bearing resemblance to a banana republic are often proliferating in Denmark. These stories not only address questions that would be important to any country faced with similar political and economic challenges; they also fundamentally question the competence of Greenlanders to deal with the problems and the new partners (e.g. multinational companies).

I maintain that indigenous peoples are centre-staged in their own lives. It is from such a position that they continuously and actively establish new strategies, navigate in a complex but negotiable setting, establish and negotiate new horizons of potentials and expectations and also create new futures. In some cases, marginality is used by indigenous peoples to apprehend a position or a situation and it is then used as a political tool (Paine, 1985) to further political agendas. In fact, the struggle of indigenous peoples worldwide does not essentially have to do with *receiving* or being *granted* rights to land, culture and self-determination; on the contrary, it is about having their collective rights to land, culture and self-determination *recognized* and *respected*. Basically, it is about being recognized as competent future-makers in possession of the necessary collective political, economic and intellectual resources. However, maintaining a discourse that posits marginality and adaptation as the organizing devices can work counter to this aspiration (see Chapters 6 and 7). As far as discussions of climate change and environmental change in the Arctic are concerned, the discourse of marginality is still dominating – currently, as an issue having to do with being at risk. The dominant storyline is accentuating a North that is melting at a speed that puts indigenous peoples in a new environment of risk. The speed of environmental change that challenges indigenous peoples' capacity for adaptability is linked with the discourse of the speed of cultural and social changes in the wake of modernization, with the upshot that the indigenous peoples are also seen as 'at risk' of not being able to adapt quickly enough. Climate change discussions combine these two understandings of being 'at risk' in an interesting and cogent manner. The risk of the Arctic indigenous peoples not being able to adapt to climate change is understood to be a function of their 'adaptation to modernization'. In Chapter 7, I will critically elaborate on this point and show how some climate change researchers link what they consider to be modern aspects of Arctic lifestyles with an increased risk of not being able to adapt to climate change.

The media brings forth stories of how, especially, Inuit are 'at risk', being faced with speedy changes in climate. In the *Daily Telegraph*, for example, the story of 'Why the Inuit people are walking on thin ice' was run in 2005 (Clover, 2005). The article's intention was evidently to show how global warming threatens Arctic culture and, as was made clear at the conclusion of the article, its objective was moreover to put a human face on climate change. The question is, however, what kind of human face is being evoked in the article. Here, stories related to dependence on the environment, marginality, rapid environmental changes challenging the status quo, inadequate skills and knowledge (or, more correctly, a deficiency in knowledge), and the dramatic risks of not being able to adapt were all unfolded quite vividly. Basically, Inuit were presented here as a deviant 'other'.

The story in the *Daily Telegraph* is based on a crisis narrative that is indeed dominant but may not necessarily reflect the multiple experiences and responses of northern people navigating a highly political landscape. 'The human face' is constructed with reference to an environmental framework and a human-environment disequilibrium. As a consequence, hunters, communities, stories and political stances emerge and obtain legitimacy from a discourse that gives rise to problems and solutions related directly to environmental issue. This discourse is not a pan-Arctic phenomenon. In Greenland, the news reflects a more complex situation where hunters, generally speaking, are well equipped to change strategies when faced with environmental change (see for example KNR, 2009; Olsen, 2011). However, what we are faced with here is a question of understanding Inuit responses adequately and thus a need to open up for other storylines. Moreover, what we are also being faced with is an urgent need to re-examine the relevance and the very foundation of the narrative that is based on adaptation, risk and marginality.

According to Michael Bravo (2008), this kind of marginality narrative masks the voices of Arctic peoples and ultimately impedes the development of different aspects of the northern citizens' civic participation with respect to climate change policy opportunities. He therefore suggests that indigenous peoples' responses to climate change problems are better understood in relation to emerging notions of citizenship than they are in relation to climate change crisis narratives that, by fiat, position these peoples as being intrinsically 'at risk'. Bravo finds the public and very potent crisis narrative to be too limited and critical inasmuch as it does not address issues of public participation, policymaking, or issues related to the growing inequalities of power and wealth. This incites him to ask the following question: 'Whom do climate change crisis narratives serve?' (Bravo, 2008, p. 2). In a similar vein, I argue that the quantitative rise in news from the Arctic, as seen in the wake of global warming, has not been followed commensurately by an increase in the general public's qualitative understanding of the Arctic, its inhabitants and the complex political scenario developing there. Accordingly, through the crisis narratives based on the vocabulary of risk, adaptability and resilience, indigenous peoples are being maintained in a marginal position. It becomes marginal since the Inuit, in this narrative, are used as the ultimate example of how people become vulnerable when the basis of their way of life (the basis here being understood to be *ice*) is eroded and disappearing. Bravo argues for alternative narratives and frameworks that are more sensitive to the highly social, political, economic and physical conditions in which Arctic communities will formulate their policy responses. Greenland's political self-government and its present political strategy to have extractive industries initiate activities is indeed an alternative narrative (see Chapters 3, 4 and 5). Within the scientific community focusing on Arctic vulnerability, adaptation and resilience some changes can also be observed. The Arctic Resilience Interim Report (Arctic Council, 2013) is an example of how human agency and indigenous political rights are starting to be integrated more in the system analyses.

The climate change crisis narrative is also scrutinized by Marybeth Long Martello (2008), where special emphasis is placed on how Arctic indigenous peoples are used as representations and representatives of climate change. She argues that the synthesis report (ACIA, 2004) of the comprehensive ACIA (2005) portrays, through its images and accompanying texts, Arctic indigenous peoples as exotic, expert, and endangered. This representation construes and constructs them as spokespersons for at-risk cultures and livelihoods. The scientific construction of the environment and environmental change itself thus impacts on the identity, representation, and intervention of particular groups (Martello, 2008, p. 354). Thus, even highly scientific studies, like the ACIA and its more than 500-page follow-up assessment in the so-called SWIPA report (AMAP, 2011b), subscribe to the marginality discourse. When human beings are framed as vulnerable as a direct consequence of their connection to a particular environment and a particular place, it generates the notion of a particular citizen whose lifeworld, problems, choices and strategies are already confined to being apprehended within such a frame (see also Martello, 2004). Martello finds that this perspective is rarely taken into account by vulnerability studies and argues, moreover, that the focus on what local people deem worthy and on what they are in need of gives them a new voice in the too environmentally focused assessment processes. It is the potentiality of this new voice which, among other things, has produced a new Arctic citizen, according to Martello (2004, 2008).

The agency of Arctic indigenous peoples is evolving and being shaped by the climate change narratives. However, the very focus on vulnerability and impact as the organizing device generates certain assumptions about indigenous agency and about the resources that can enable them to deal with the consequences (Martello, 2004, 2008). Indigenous peoples themselves have, according to Martello (2008), also been shaping the discourse on vulnerability and at-risk communities. A fine example is the prominent Inuit leader, Sheila Watt-Cloutier, who has argued that '[g]lobal warming has become the ultimate threat to Inuit culture and our survival as an indigenous people' (cited in Griffiths, 2007, p. 8). Another prominent Inuit spokesperson, Mary Simon, has argued that '[w]hen we [the Inuit] can no longer hunt on the sea ice and eat what we hunt we will no longer exist as a people' (cited in Griffiths, 2007, p. 9). Inuit are thus being represented as victims of climate change of a particular kind. It is one of cultural decay and destruction as a distinct people. A very strong co-relationship between the quantity and quality of ice and the existence of Inuit is being posited here.

These representations, however, employ very narrow ideas about human agency and about peoples' relationships to place and do not necessarily address the concerns of indigenous peoples and how they approach and enact a world undergoing rapid change. When indigenous peoples are integrated into scientific practices as contributors of knowledge – as was done in compiling the ACIA and suggested in the SWIPA report, for example – they move beyond a role as witnesses and take up a new position. Addressing these questions, Martello concludes that 'these methods of weaving together knowledge generation and societal agenda-setting allow Arctic indigenous peoples to imagine themselves as citizens of an emerging regional political community' (Martello, 2004, p. 114). Global climate change constitutes a new platform from which indigenous peoples can form, mobilize and articulate different concerns, but they run the risk of becoming ensnared in the discourse of marginality.

Indigenous peoples beyond the visible

Arctic indigenous peoples have a strong and powerful position in the climate change discourse. It is – among other things – the upshot of intense lobbying, of their presence at meetings and of their active involvement in drafting resolutions and in research projects that this position has become manifest. They have indeed become *visible* to the public; this is a position that indigenous peoples worldwide are struggling to gain as the first stepping-stone to recognition. Sheila Watt-Cloutier, an Inuit activist and the former president of the Inuit Circumpolar Council, gained worldwide recognition when she, was nominated in 2007 for the Nobel Peace Prize as a response to her struggle to make the world aware of the impacts of global warming on Arctic indigenous peoples. Furthermore, in 2005, she and 62 Inuit hunters filed a petition before the Inter-American Commission on Human Rights alleging that the emissions of greenhouse gases from the United States undermine and violate Inuit rights to culture and livelihood because of the devastating environmental effects of a warming Arctic. In doing so, she made global warming a human rights problem and directly linked Arctic environmental problems with industrial practices and governmental policies in the United States. The intensive lobbying work of, especially, indigenous peoples from the rainforest during the fifteenth session of the Conference of the Parties (COP 15) in Copenhagen targeted at their being included in the plans related to Reducing Emissions from Deforestation and Forest Degradation similarly underscores that the integration of indigenous peoples in climate change narratives and the explicit mention of them in official documents has not come about by itself. According to one of the chief indigenous lobbyists, Victoria Tauli-Corpuz: 'This is the first time in any legally-binding environmental convention that there is reference to human rights. And this has been our main concern from the very beginning' (cited in Indigenous Climate Portal, 2009). She continues by saying that '[t]he presence of a substantial number of indigenous peoples has considerably increased their visibility and highlighted their issues in the climate talks'. With respect to the Arctic, indigenous peoples are indeed visible, to such an extent, even, that Martello (2008) argues that non-indigenous peoples in the Arctic have become silenced. But this is a certain kind of visibility that is closely linked to an image of these indigenous peoples as closely linked to the environment and as potential victims of climate change. Therefore, they may emerge in the climate discussions as strong *stakeholders*. This might be one of the reasons that the European Commission invited (in March 2010) indigenous representatives from all over the Arctic to an Arctic Dialogue meeting in Brussels. After an introduction by Fernando Garces, the Directorate-General for

External Relations, welcoming the delegations to the centre of European politics and demarcating the meeting as one of several regular meetings between the EU and indigenous peoples, pursuant to a stipulation in the European Comission's communiqué to the European Parliament and the European Council (European Commission, 2008), a Gwich'in native leader from Alaska asked to have the word. He was pleased about having received the invitation to join in the dialogue meeting and had travelled several days to get here. The meeting – he suggested – was an opportunity to 'get things right' from the beginning and to make sure that the Arctic (and the indigenous peoples) was not going to be treated in the same way as other frontiers. He resolutely pointed out the long history of Alaskan native peoples and their struggle to have their collective rights to self-determination recognized. These rights are not negotiable, he stressed. The next indigenous representative who asked for the word was from the Inuit Circumpolar Council, and he elaborated on the various self-governance structures present in the Arctic and the long history of diplomacy, cooperation and partnership that has existed. Both of these statements demarcated the dialogue as being much more than a stakeholders' meeting.

The ambivalent relation between the position of collective rights-holders vs. the position of stakeholders is exactly what I will be elaborating further on in Chapter 2. Being recognized as collective rights-holders is certainly more gratifying and empowering than becoming visible as stakeholders, and the Inuit Circumpolar Council, in its Inuit Arctic Policy, clearly emphasizes that it is 'critical that Inuit be recognized and referred to … as a distinct "people". Inuit are not mere "populations" or "minorities". These latter terms serve to unfairly deny or undermine the true dignity, status, rights, and identity of Inuit as indigenous peoples' (Lynge & Steenbaek, 2011, p. 13) and this position encompasses the right to self-determination, which implies the right to self-government within states and meaningful participation in international cooperation. Since the end of the 1960s, the political developments in the Arctic have evolved in various ways in the different regions. But overall, the respect for and the recognition of indigenous peoples' rights have been developing, concomitantly resulting in a number of political institutions working to further indigenous self-determination. This is a development that has effectuated a political resonance in the United Nation's efforts to draft the Declaration on the Rights of Indigenous Peoples, which was finally adopted in 2007 after decades of discussions (Dahl, 2013). In this declaration, what is clearly stipulated, among other things, is that indigenous peoples have collective rights to self-determination, to freely determine their political status, and to freely pursue their economic, social, and cultural development. Such rights include the collective right to own, use, develop and control their lands, territories and resources and their right to ensure that no project affecting the land will proceed without their free, prior and informed consent. The political work in the United Nations has been progressing very slowly, ostensibly because the issues that are pertinent to indigenous peoples basically challenge the conventional understanding of state sovereignty as totally independent and absolute, internally as well as externally. However, the understanding of state sovereignty is continuously changing, due to processes of globalization, transboundary issues, transnational economic practices, international political cooperation and the development of new cross-border governmental institutions. The implementation of different regimes based on the recognition of indigenous peoples' rights to self-determination in the Arctic indicates that state sovereignty and indigenous rights cannot easily be understood as simply conflicting despite the obvious tensions of reciprocal interests. The issue of sovereignty is, however, recurrent, as illustrated by the following example.

Global warming causes the ice to melt. This process opens up the Arctic Ocean at a rapid pace. It has made the five coastal Arctic states confirm their claims, responsibilities and jurisdiction over territories as sovereign states. In 2008, their representatives met in Ilulissat, in Greenland, to address the challenges and possibilities. This meeting resulted in the Ilulissat Declaration, in which the Arctic states basically expressed their sovereignty in large areas of the Arctic Ocean, their commitment to the International Law of the Sea as a legal framework and their intention to bring about the orderly settlement of any possible overlapping claims. Less than a year later, the Inuit Circumpolar Council also adopted a comprehensive declaration on the sovereignty of the Inuit that was titled 'A Circumpolar Inuit Declaration on Sovereignty in the Arctic'. Here, they noted that the Ilulissat Declaration did not go far enough in affirming the rights that the Inuit peoples have managed to have recognized through international law, land claims and self-government structures. The Inuit Circumpolar Council's declaration stipulates the Inuit peoples' role and responsibilities as collective rights-holders and partners in both politics and development projects. With respect to industrial development, the declaration emphasizes that industrial development through partnership has to enhance the economic and social well-being of Inuit and safeguard environmental security. Indirectly, the declaration points our attention to the position of the Inuit peoples and the increased and renewed industrial activities made possible by an opening Arctic. By emphasizing their partnership, their rights and their possibilities as integral parts of any development of resource extractions or industries operating on their land – or affecting their land, they cannot simply be said to be positioned as *against* industrial development, as is often the perception that persists in the public's view of the situation. What they want is that their rights, their concerns and their interests to be respected and they want also to play an active role in shaping the future as well as to derive some measure of benefit from any development transpiring on their land. The long story of the political conflict over the pipeline in Canada (Nuttall, 2010) is a telling example of how both political involvement and the recognition of collective rights are pivotal to the indigenous people's acceptance of industrial activities (Robbins, 2006).

Thus the right to self-determination is considered by Inuit the right to choose and influence their own development and future; also if this entails their involvement in large-scale industrial projects. This stance is quite clear in the Arctic, although it is being practiced in different ways. Faced with global warming and international political initiatives to reduce emissions and the use of fossil fuels, the Inuit are confronted with a predicament. On the one hand, the Inuit are extremely aware of industry's impacts on climate change. On the other hand, their involvement in and support of industrial projects might serve to improve their economies and livelihoods in areas where cash-generating jobs are not so easily developed. This predicament became more and more apparent when the COP 15 meeting in Copenhagen in 2009 was approaching. Indigenous peoples from around the world met in Anchorage in April 2009 to prepare a common statement underlining the consequences and vulnerabilities of indigenous peoples due to the impacts of climate change. In the declaration (The Anchorage Declaration, 2009), they are 'deeply alarmed by the accelerating climate devastation brought about by unsustainable development ... Mother Earth is no longer in a period of climate change, but in climate crisis. We ... insist on an immediate end to the destruction and desecration of the elements of life'. Therefore, the declaration calls for binding emission reduction for developed countries, by at least 95 per cent below the 1990 levels, by the year 2050. For some Inuit groups, however, oil and gas development is important to their communities and their economy. The Iñupiat of Alaska, the Inuvialuit of Canada and the Inuit in Greenland are all – to different extents – engaged in the extraction of fossil fuels. This gave rise to certain controversies at the meeting and the declaration deals with this problem by presenting two options for action: one which calls for 'the phase out of fossil fuel development and a moratorium on new fossil fuel developments on or near indigenous lands and territories' and another that calls 'for a process that works towards the eventual phase out of fossil fuels, without infringing on the right to development of Indigenous nations'. The latter paragraph thus opens up for indigenous peoples' industrial use of their lands and resources, should they wish to do so in order to develop their societies.

As this chapter points out, indigenous peoples' collective rights, political self-government institutions and the devolution of power have become increasingly recognized and have been developed over the last decades and their claims of sovereignty, self-determination and right to development have been intensified since the beginning of the twenty-first century. Their strong political position in most of the Arctic (Shadian, 2014) is crucial to the shaping of relations between indigenous and non-indigenous peoples as well as between communities and enterprises. This is a position that indeed has little to do with marginality; it redefines the framework and the dynamics in what has been termed the new Arctic. It also affects how climate change policies and strategies are being approached, developed and implemented, and has an impact on what futures are to be envisioned.

Greenland and its climate challenges

The historical legacy of colonialism has served to link Greenland to Denmark since 1721. Over the years, the political climate in Denmark and Greenland has influenced the cultural, economic, educational, social and political developments in a variety of ways. The change that came about in 1953 – from having been a colony to being endowed with the status of being an integrated part of the Danish realm – signalled a major difference in the political relationship but it was with the introduction of Greenland 'home-rule' in 1979 that Greenlanders were enabled, to a much greater extent, to run their own affairs.

The Home Rule Act allowed Greenland to take the responsibility from Denmark for administering a number of important areas like education, health, fisheries, and environment. In order to finance the administration of these areas, Greenland received an annual block grant (subsidy) from Denmark. Today, the block grant amounts to DKK 3.6 billion (2013) and is one of the main pillars in the Greenlandic economy. Income from the fisheries and related activities is also important to the total income of Greenland, amounting to DKK 6.5 billion (2013). Between 1979 and 2009, the home rule was run by a Greenlandic government and a parliament elected by people living in Greenland. The Home Rule was thus not a political system based on ethnic criteria because Danes and other non-Greenlanders living in Greenland could vote and were eligible to run for election to Parliament. However, because the ethnic Greenlanders are in the majority, they have *de facto* been able to run a great many of their own affairs.

The growing wish of Greenlanders to take greater and greater responsibility of their own affairs and to elevate the home rule to a new level incited the Greenland government to establish a Greenlandic self-government commission, which was operating from 2000 to 2003. It put forward a comprehensive report on the possibilities for self-government (Selvstyrekommissionen, 2003). This work laid the cornerstone for a Greenlandic-Danish self-government commission in 2004, the members of which were appointed by the Danish Premier and the Greenlandic Premier. Its efforts resulted in the Act on Greenland Self-Government (hereafter referred to as the Act), which was adopted by the Danish Parliament in June 2009, officially empowering Greenland with self-governance from June 21, 2009. The Act boosts the political possibilities and responsibilities of Greenland and is important for some of the decisions, priorities and the political navigation that are all being carried out by the Greenland Government and the Parliament. It is within this political framework that environmental disasters and change (real, anticipated and feared), risk assessments, climate change impacts, adaptation and mitigation strategies, as well as societal choices are negotiated and made. The Act is neither to be considered the context nor to be considered the background upon which the choices are made. It constitutes the very lifeworld as well as the horizon of possibilities and is therefore to be considered integral in all choices. The Act cannot be situated strictly in its own domain but needs to be seen as being entangled in all the choices and strategies. Thus, when the Greenlandic government invites in extractive industries the Act not only frames the possibilities but drives the strategic thinking, ambitions and the process itself.

The new Greenland

In 2008, in connection with the referendum on self-governance in Greenland, 21,355 people voted 'yes' to the Act while 6,663 voters were opposed. The Act certainly changes the position and the agency of Greenland. The Act is complex

and its implications can be interpreted in a variety of ways. In what follows, I will
point out some of its elements and certain perspectives that ought to be kept in
mind when trying to understand the new position of Greenland and when trying
to understand its new potentials in an era of climate change.

The Act recognizes the people of Greenland as a people, pursuant to
international law, with the right of self-determination and the right to independence as a state, should the people wish to have this independence. Furthermore,
it recognizes Greenlandic as the official language in Greenland. This can be
regarded as a major step in the more than 290 years of historical relations between
Denmark and Greenland. Furthermore, revenues from mineral resource activities
in Greenland shall accrue to the Greenland Self-Government authorities; in stipulating this, the Act puts the resources, the development and the benefits thereof
in the hands of Greenland. With respect to Greenland's foreign policy, the Act
confirms the new partnership between Denmark and Greenland to be developed
over the years, wherein the two governments (Denmark and Greenland) will
be cooperating on international affairs with a view to safeguarding the interests
of Greenland as well as the general interests of the Realm of Denmark. This
partnership implies that Naalakkersuisut (the Greenlandic Government) may,
on behalf of the Realm, negotiate and conclude agreements, under the umbrella
of international law, with foreign states and international organizations, including administrative agreements that exclusively concern Greenland and relate
wholly to fields of responsibility that have been taken over from Danish control. Greenland's contemporary and future activities on the international scene
are thus recognized. However, the Act also stipulates expressly that the Danish
authorities' constitutional responsibilities and powers in international affairs
cannot be limited by the Act. Matters related to foreign policy and security
(i.e. military) policy are still considered affairs of the Realm (Denmark, Greenland
and the Faroe Islands) and thus matters that will continue to be handled by the
Danish authorities. As a result, the Greenland Self-Government authorities are
subject to those obligations arising out of agreements under international law and
other international rules that are binding, at any time, on the Realm. This entails
that the agreements signed by the Danish authorities during the global climate
negotiations at the COPs as well as the agreements forged in the International
Whaling Commission are binding for Greenland as well.

The political room for manoeuvring is accordingly quite complex and
Greenlanders' 'adaptation to climate change' has become highly entangled in a
political web spun partly by the Greenlanders themselves.

The partnership on foreign policy applies to negotiations and agreements where
Denmark and Greenland have been jointly involved in the negotiations. In such
cases, they must be signed by the Government *together* with Naalakkersuisut, as far
as it is possible to do so. In matters where the Danish authorities negotiate agreements under international law that are of particular importance to Greenland
they must, according to the Act, be submitted to Naalakkersuisut for comment
before they are concluded or terminated. The possibilities, responsibilities and
limitations with respect to Greenland's involvement in international politics

therefore amount to a delicate balancing between the different authorities – this is a fact that can eventually impact Greenland's possibilities for pursuing its own climate policy.

Running the administrative functions of Greenland requires considerable annual subsidies from Denmark. The Act secures a continuation of these subsidies. One consequence of this is that the fields of responsibility that have been taken over by the Greenland authorities since 1979 can be secured and maintained. The new Act includes a list of about 30 new fields of responsibility over which Greenland can exercise legislative and executive power, should they wish to do so. Among these fields are police and prosecution services, and the administration of justice, including the establishment of courts of law and provisions for processing cases related to criminal matters. Furthermore, the Act presented Greenland with the possibility of taking over the area of administrating mineral resources, which is, in fact, one of the first areas for which they assumed responsibility back in 2010. The legislative power lies with the Greenlandic Parliament (now to be called Inatsisartut); the executive power lies with the Greenlandic government (Naalakkersuisut); and the judicial power is to lie with the courts of law to be established by the Self-Government authorities (presently the Greenlandic courts are part of the Danish court system).

There is no doubt about the fact that the new Act on Greenland Self-Government constitutes a giant step forward and that it falls neatly in line with the sovereignty and partnership discourse that is so prevalent in the Arctic. It opens up for new constellations of partnership and cooperation that were seen, for example, in 2011, when Greenland, the Faroe Islands and Denmark jointly announced a common strategy for the Arctic (Denmark, Greenland, & the Faroe Islands, 2011).

The Act constitutes a framework in which certain logics have been carved out. These, in turn, influence political strategies and ambitions in addition to creating certain problems. The possibility of taking over new fields of responsibility is met with the requirement that Greenland itself has to finance the selected fields. Increased juridical responsibility, which is considered to be expensive, is therefore dependent upon a substantial increase in public finances. This requirement presents an additional challenge to the Greenlandic authorities, which are also trying to navigate their way through the financial crisis and the increasing discrepancy between public expenses and income. On top of this fiscal challenge, the subsidy (block grant) from Denmark has been 'frozen' at DKK 3.4 billion and the subsidy is re-adjusted annually in accordance with increases in the general wage and price index, as indicated in the Finance and Appropriation Act for the year concerned. Due to the fact that the rate of inflation is higher in Greenland than it is in Denmark, the subsidy is slowly being hollowed out, and in the years 2010 and 2012, Greenland received a block grant that was reduced by DKK 50 million.

For these reasons, it is understandable that Greenland is willing and interested in engaging in activities that may serve to increase the public income. Without the introduction of new sources of income, it is neither possible to maintain the current level of public services nor to widen the spectrum of fields of responsibility that could improve the country's possibilities for practicing self-determination in a more extensive manner. According to the Economic Council that was established by Naalakkersuisut in 2009, the contemporary standards existing in the welfare society, in conjunction with the current availability of finances from various sources, are going to precipitate larger and larger deficits in the public finances, and the welfare society is perceived as being under severe pressure (Økonomisk Råd, 2011). Fisheries and tourism do not constitute viable areas of expansion that can generate sufficient capital for meeting these challenges. As the Commission on Welfare and Taxes concluded in 2010, 'Status quo is not a possibility…[and] there are no easy solutions' (Skatte- og velfærdskommissionen, 2010, p. 6). Greenland is therefore looking into mineral resources, oil and gas, and large-scale industries as new sources of income, and as expressed by the Minister for Industry and Mineral Resources, '[O]ur minerals deposit resources can create the future welfare society' (Berthelsen, 2011, translated by the author). From 2008 to 2009, the total area of oil licenses expanded from 6,882 km² to approximately 130,000 km² (Bureau of Minerals and Petroleum, 2009). In 2010, companies were given licenses for oil exploration in an area that is larger than 200,000 km², and mines near Nuuk (iron) and Narsaq (uranium/rare earth elements) and in Citronen Fjord (zinc/lead) are all under development. Additionally, the rich hydropower resources are attractive to energy-demanding industries, and the potential establishment of an aluminium smelter in West Greenland near the town of Maniitsoq has, since 2006, stood as a political priority.

The dimensions and number of industrial projects on the drawing board being sketched out with an eye toward boosting the Greenlandic economy, projects that are envisioned for being implemented as soon as possible, indeed make it appropriate to refer to these ongoing processes as *hyper-industrialization*. Even though one may be able to comprehend each project in an isolated fashion, it is hard to apprehend the cumulative effects on society. Naaja Nathanielsen, from Inuit Ataqatigiit, airs concern in the Greenland Parliament about the speed with which these projects are being planned and encourages people to consider how many large-scale projects Greenland will be able to initiate without there being severe consequences on human beings and on the country's economy (Nathanielsen, 2011). Faced with the expert judgment that 'status quo is not a possibility', Greenland has chosen to pursue a large-scale societal process of transformation that has partly been influenced by the Act itself. The Greenlandic newspaper Sermitsiaq concluded that 'the times when we were spoiled are over. No one is going to stand ready with a bag of money to help us … In modern Greenland, it is all about creating our own economy and our own society' (Sermitsiaq, 2011, translated by the author); taking hold of the economy and creating a viable income is considered, by this newspaper's writer, to be the essence of self-government. The political aims are to improve the economy by increasing the number of job opportunities, to empower people to provide for themselves without receiving public support and to enhance the revenues from non-renewable resource activities. A major restructuring and reformation of the society is currently taking place in order to support these goals. The enhancement of the level of the educational programs that are available to the population and the reformation of important sectors (e.g. the fisheries, where new quota systems aim to decrease the number of fishermen in order to make the business more economically sustainable for the remaining fishermen) are among the strategies currently on the table. People are not only going to benefit from the direct jobs in the new industries but also from the indirect ones that are concomitantly created in the service sector. These reforms are being driven by the notion that new jobs will create a better and more solid tax base and that persons who are currently dependent on public support can eventually become active on the labour market. Greenland also has high expectations of revenues that stem from the mineral resource industry since they will be channelled directly back to Greenland. However, the Act stipulates that when annual revenues exceed DKK 75 million, Denmark will reduce the extended subsidies by an amount that corresponds to half that portion of the annual revenue that exceeds DKK 75 million. That is to say, if Greenland should receive DKK 100 million in revenues in any one year, the Danish subsidies will be reduced the following year by DKK 12.5 million (i.e. one-half of 25 million).

In the long run, the perspective is to make Greenland economically independent from Denmark while care is taken that this be accomplished without jeopardizing the stability created by the subsidy system. In the event that Greenland should annually receive more than approximately DKK 7 billion in revenues, the Danish Government's subsidy to the Greenland Self-Government authorities would be reduced to zero. Following such a scenario, the two governments would have to renegotiate the future economic relations, including the distributions of revenues. In short, the new Act redefines the 'rules of the game', not only with respect to the relationship to Denmark and other nation-states, but also within the bounds of Greenland.

Environmental change and political ambitions

Inspired by political ecology as outlined by, for example, Biersack (2006), my anthropological approach addresses climate and environmental issues as being deeply entangled in the political life, in its ambitions, and in its strategies. I understand questions of risk and change to be an inherent aspect of how people – as actors with choices, expectations and ambitions – navigate their way through the world as a whole. Thus, environmental changes (e.g. melting ice) cannot be understood in isolation from the social and political spheres. Political ecology differs from cultural ecology by virtue of its emphasis on reflexivity on power and institutions, by virtue of its targeting of traversing linkages through which people are embedded in – and are producing – larger structures, and by virtue of its insistence that mankind co-produces nature. Cultural ecology pursues a more apolitical focus on issues of adaptation to an environment, with less attention paid to political structures and rights that mediate the human-nature articulation.

The foregoing outline of the political situation in Greenland is thus, from a political and ecological point of view, not to be read as simply a context: it is rather to be understood as an inherent aspect of the way various natures, climates, citizens and the world are being enacted and performed. Environmental change and disasters are not merely natural; they are also socially co-produced. A study on this basis ought to be occupied with social actors and their choices and how they continuously construct, navigate, and negotiate the world in order to render it meaningful. In a similar sense, the analytical approach of the research apprehends neither 'region' nor 'community' nor 'culture' as being closed and bounded entities. These are to be perceived as being embedded in and produced by larger powerful structures but also as being co-producers of particular structures.

The analysis of hyper-industrialization points toward how industrial companies and Greenlandic agents are continuously engaged in negotiating the extent, the content, the direction, the embeddedness and the results of industrial activities. Greenland has become what Biersack (2006, p. 16) has termed an intensive *site* for local-global articulation and interaction. Sites are understood as both locations and relations, and are under dynamic re-negotiation and re-interpretation in terms of scale, demarcation and content. The local and the global are seen as being intertwined and the global and globalization are being produced, enacted, and perceived by people in these places. People in Greenland are, according to this perspective, not considered to be 'victims' of either progress, climate change or globalization that is penetrating its way into the local, but are perceived, rather, as co-producing progress, climate change and globalisation, as will be discussed in Chapters 5 and 6. The 'outside' or 'extra-local' becomes a constituent part of a place and it is through the particular links and wider social relations that places are rendered distinct and dynamic. What imparts to a place its specificity and uniqueness is, according to Massey (1993, p. 67), emerging out of the constructions of

> particular interactions and mutual articulations of social relations, social processes, experiences and understandings, in a situation of co-presence, but where a large proportion of those relations, experiences and understandings are actually constructed on a far larger scale than what we happen to define for that moment as the place itself, whether that be a street, a region or even a continent.

What are considered global powers (e.g. capitalism) must then be understood as being flexible in relation to people's diverse and conflicting engagements, imaginations, anticipations and expectations in particular places (Featherstone, 1993). This approach makes it possible to study globalizing processes as they unfold on the ground, where people create, exploit and contest the transnational spaces and flows. In Chapters 5 and 6, I will pursue such an analysis.

Various analytical approaches, frameworks and terminologies have been proposed and applied for purposes of comprehending environmental and climate change processes in the Arctic, as well as being applied to the analyses of vulnerability, risk and adaptation. In this book, I discuss some of these, along with the analytical implications, including the position of people standing in these approaches. In doing so, the researchers involved are apprehended as being co-producers of nature, people, places, problems and solutions by virtue of their sheer acts of scaling, framing, and contextualizing. The discussions presented in this book are not being pursued with an eye toward making the representations of Arctic processes more 'correct' and 'accurate' but rather with the aim of developing and encouraging a critical awareness of the perceptions of research in the Arctic and its salient implications on the very dynamics it happens to be scrutinizing. Such discussions of analytical approaches are not merely 'academic' but may also be correlated with policy claims and objectives. On the one hand, one needs analytical closure to take action and the adaptation- and risk-frameworks offer such closure. On the other hand, if one chooses to maintain an open-ended appreciation of the empirical and its explosive and unpredictable dynamics (see also Hertzfeld, 2001, p. x), one is continuously confronted by a resistance to closure.

The social intensity of ice and the transformation of society

Conflicts and problems related to water (especially ice and the sea) are highly intensive in the Arctic as climate change and societal change alter fundamental ecological and political relations. Challenges of climate change, whether in the form of melting sea ice, the receding glaciers, the thawing of permafrost or changes in biodiversity and resource presence, put Arctic societies in an intense situation, where difficult societal choices have to be made and expectations have to be reconsidered. It is often the case that attempts are made to synthesize people's manner of dealing with these challenges under the umbrella concept of *adaptation*, and multiple studies examine the vulnerabilities of people and communities with respect to pursuing successful adaptation. Water and ice are, however, so deeply entangled in people's lives that the concept of adaptation does not adequately address the social intensiveness of a changing world of water and the transformative choices that people are making and negotiating in the Arctic.

Throughout this book, the concept of adaptation (and resilience) is not employed for purposes of analysing societal changes and practices but is used as a background for discussions about agency (Chapter 2), anticipation (Chapter 3), socialization of technology (Chapter 4), place-making (Chapter 5), scaling (Chapter 6), and contextualization of knowledge and future-making (Chapter 7). By avoiding adaptation as an organizing device for analysis, I hope to turn the analytical focus toward transformative processes that are driven by a multiplicity of factors. The value of transformation as a useful term for approaching water dynamics is also apparent when applied to the history of Greenland. Generations of Greenlanders have experienced fluctuating temperatures that are followed by changes in sea ice as well as shifts in the presence of renewable resources. The boom and bust cycles of Arctic economies are still within the memories of people living in the present generations, and even though these economic cycles may also be affected by economic demand, natural resource fluctuations, technological pressure and the overuse of resources, they are very often understood to be under the influence of changes in temperatures and ice-conditions. In the famous study conducted by the Danish biologist, Christian Vibe (Vibe, 1967), and in a later one conducted by the Greenlandic historian in local knowledge, Hans Christian Petersen (Petersen, 2007, 2010), what is rendered apparent is that the cycles of resource presence are related to changing temperatures. Formerly, these cycles between good and bad periods could have a crucial impact on the physical survival of the population while today, in an urbanized Greenland (Sejersen, 2007, 2010), the possibility of impending 'disaster' takes on an entirely different character. In some cases, towns have specialized in a particular resource such as Atlantic cod, Greenland halibut, northern shrimp, snow crab or a combination of these. When a resource happens to disappear due to a change in sea temperature, the economies of families and towns can be hit extremely hard. In Paamiut in South Greenland, for example, the disappearing Atlantic cod in the 1970s (Rasmussen & Hamilton, 2001), something in which the town had specialized, resulted in outmigration and a dearth of larger investments, leaving behind a depopulated town with very little resources. For Paamiut, it was a transformation. Even though a disaster can be coined as natural, it is always perceived and defined as such from a societal point of view. The predicaments of Paamiut brought about as a consequence of its resource specialization serve to draw our attention to the close relationship between resources, human settlements and practices, although this correlation should not be understood as environmental determinism or adaptation, but rather as human worlds evoked and made possible by political choices and societal strategies.

In the 1950s and 1960s, when the Danes made massive investments in localities with particular water and ice qualities as part of a modernization of Greenland, the social organization around and the valuation of water and ice changed – dramatically. This modernization process resulted in development paths (centralized fisheries), which boosted urbanization, the educational level, the economy, the welfare and the health of the Greenlandic population but also made towns sensitive to changes in resources and political goodwill. The new way of organizing society transformed it as well. Greenlandic towns share the problems of many other cities of the world that rely on a few central resources. In Greenland, however, the problem is amplified by the fact that there are no roads connecting the towns and regions, and it is only possible to move from one place to another by using expensive and unstable means of transportation – namely, by air and by ship. The commuting culture, which some of the world's regions rely on in order to maintain a flexible labour market and a more permanent settlement pattern, is consequently not realistically a viable option for Greenland. If there are no jobs, people quickly consider moving away; this results in an outmigration and a brain drain that can prove devastating to towns and communities. These urban dynamics can be observed many places in the world and may strike the life nerve of a town as hard elsewhere as they do in Greenland, but its small population of 57,000 people makes Greenland particularly vulnerable. The crash of the Atlantic cod population in the 1970s and the speedy emergence of northern shrimps due to falling sea temperature, just to mention one example, triggered a new specialized economy in Greenland but also new job opportunities, which led to a reshuffling of the settlement pattern. This was indeed a societal transformation.

Changes in sea temperature can therefore be of paramount importance, not only for a sector (e.g. the fishing sector) and a community (e.g. Paamiut) but also to the demographic and socioeconomic organization of the country as such. Closely linked to sea temperature in the Arctic are the presence, the quality and the extent of sea ice, which not only play a major role in the Arctic ecosystem but also in forming access to resources. The dynamics of sea ice are quite complex and in some cases, ice hinders people's access while in other cases, it is the decisive factor in making accessibility to resources possible. The yearly and cyclic movement of sea ice has an impact on the dynamics and seasonality of the Greenlandic societies and the diverse livelihoods that are being enacted in different parts of the country. The sea ice has always been the centre of focus for Greenlanders, but lately, the Greenlandic ice sheet has also become important for Greenlanders because its withdrawal is understood to be influencing the environment in different ways. For example, in the town of Qeqertarsuaq and in the small community of Kangerluk, some people expressed concern about how the disappearing glaciers bring about concomitant decreases in humidity and bring about the drying out of important trout rivers (personal interviews in 2009). In other regions of Greenland, the withdrawal of the ice sheet opens up new land for resource prospecting (AMAP, 2011a, p. 9; Råstofdirektoratet, 2007, p. 53). In Greenland, much of the focus on the rapidly melting ice sheet is, however, linked to the use of the melt water for hydroelectricity harnessed for purposes of boosting mega-industries. The water supply of the lakes has always been partly viewed in relation to the glaciers. Already in the mid-1970s, the potential for hydroelectricity was being explored by Danish engineers. Today, however, lake water is strategically and actively turned into – and pursued as – a resource, not only to meet the national energy demands, but also to attract mega-industries.

In essence, Greenlanders are organizing water and society in new ways in order to diversify their economy to support the welfare ambitions of the state. By doing so, they are renegotiating the significance of places and global relations. This book will, particularly in Chapters 3, 4 and 5, analyze the strategies, ideas and concerns related to the planned construction of the aluminium smelter and point out the radical transformations of society that are to take place. A significant issue that will be analyzed is the way that the new society is being anticipated and controlled as well as the emerging idea of a new Greenlandic citizen that can boost and embrace these transformations. This focus on societal transformation will serve to direct our attention toward how people perceive and navigate new resource opportunities, new potential dependencies, risk landscapes and new societal dynamics.

Today, the problems, choices and ambitions of people, even those who are living in what are considered far away, remote communities, cannot be fully grasped by positioning them in more or less closed systems. Since the beginning of the century, climate change has indeed become the dominant discourse, to such an extent that other societal issues related to gender, human rights, poverty, good governance, and Third World development have become 'overrun' and 'colonized' (personal comment by Petra Tschakert). Questions related to these issues had to be reinvented and reformulated in order to be adjusted to the climate change discourse. It even took some time before climate change was understood to include a human rights dimension and researchers in the social sciences and in the humanities were also reluctant, at the outset, to engage fully in the climate change discussions. Since the period that was ushered in by COP 15 in 2009, the social sciences and the humanities have entered the debate and the direction in which they may take the public debate and the influence that they may come to have on policy priorities are now being taken seriously by other disciplines (Hulme, 2011). Initially, the climate change discourse was weighed down by environmental concerns, economic perspectives and technical considerations. However, as more and more societal, political and cultural issues were able to enter the discourse, it became harder to maintain a simple understanding of climate change, human vulnerability and adaptation in the discussions as being solely related to environmental issues (Tschakert, 2012). It is often hard to boil down the problems of people and environmental concerns and reduce them to issues of climate change, solely, and people's climate change related choices and strategies are always inscribed in a larger societal vision and thus informed by other factors (Nuttall, 2008). In this sense, the demarcation and the encirclement of climate change disasters are as difficult as any other disaster, as has been discussed, for example, in Perry and Quarantelli (2005), Oliver-Smith & Hoffman (2002), Hastrup (2011) and Wisner, Blakie, Cannon, & Davis (1994). In Chapters 2, 6 and 7, I will discuss some of the climate change related vulnerability and adaptation studies pursued in the Arctic and will be analysing the implicit understandings of humans and societies in the study approaches as well as some of the cognate problems.

I want to address climate change and societal change in the Arctic from a different vantage point than adaptation. I perceive lifeworlds to be continuously unfolding and unfinished. People are experiencing certainty and uncertainty in their lives and any effort to flesh out and contain climate change challenges from ongoing social, political, environmental and economic experiences analytically freezes the composite and dynamic worlds of people. When everyday life is conceptualized through climate change and adaptation strategies, it may form analytical closures that have consequences on the way we understand community dynamics, human agency and environmental change. Such a view may set climate change responses apart from the many other relevant activities and choices that people pursue.

I have chosen to pursue fieldwork in Greenland, which is often considered the 'ground zero' of climate change. Here, climate is indeed on the agenda but not in the way one might have expected. The ambitions of the Greenlandic government to introduce industrial mega-projects in order to boost the economy propel the discussion in directions that depart from many of the studies of climate change in the Arctic. In the winter of 2011, I travelled to Maniitsoq and Nuuk on the West coast to interview persons who were involved, in one way or another, with the plans to construct an aluminium smelter: activists, entrepreneurs, politicians, citizen groups, consultants, scientific experts, lobbyists, etc. They all related the smelter to environmental and climate change issues but referred to the smelter in different ways in order to comment on or reflect upon societal development. The role and consequences of the smelter were framed in diverse ways and were the cause of much social reflection. However, all of the people I interviewed expected that the reorganization of water and melting ice for purposes of powering the smelter is going to provide grounds for a transformation of Greenland and the development of new horizons of potentiality in an era of climate change.

References

ACIA. (2004). *Impacts of a Warming Arctic: Arctic Climate Impact Assessment.* Cambridge: Cambridge University Press.

ACIA. (2005). *Arctic Climate Impact Assessment.* Cambridge: Cambridge University Press.

AMAP. (2003). *AMAP Assessment 2002: The Influence of Global Change on Contaminant Pathways to, within, and from the Arctic.* Oslo: Arctic Monitoring and Assessment Programme.

AMAP. (2011a). *Snow, Ice, Water and Permafrost in the Arctic (SWIPA) – Executive Summary.* Oslo: Arctic Monitoring and Assessment Programme, Arctic Council.

AMAP. (2011b). *Snow, Water, Ice and Permafrost in the Arctic (SWIPA): Climate Change and the Cryosphere.* Oslo: Arctic Monitoring and Assessment Programme (AMAP).

Anderson, Benedict. (1983). *Imagined Communities. Reflections of the Origin and Spread of Nationalism.* New York: Verso.

Arctic Council. (2013). *Arctic Resilience Interim Report 2013.* Stockholm: Stockholm Environment Institute and Stockholm Resilience Centre.

Arctic Human Development Report. (2004). Akureyri: Stefansson Arctic Institute.

Berthelsen, Ove Karl. (2011, October 21). Vores undergrund kan skabe fremtidens velfærdssamfund, *Sermitsiaq,* p. 35.

Biersack, Aletta. (2006). Reimagining Political Ecology: Culture/Power/History/Nature. In A. Biersack & J. B. Greenberg (Eds.), *Reimagining Political Ecology* (pp. 3–40). Durham & London: Duke University Press.

Birket-Smith, Kaj. (1932). Grønlandsk folkekunst. *Tilskueren, februar,* 163–176.

Bjørst, Lill Rastad. (2008). *En anden verden. Fordomme og stereotyper om Grønland og Arktis.* København: BIOS.

Borg, Joe. (2010). The European Union's Strategy of Sustainable Management for the Arctic. Opening Presentation at the Arctic Frontiers Conference. Retrieved January 3, 2012, from http://europa.eu/rapid/pressReleasesAction.do?reference=SPEECH/09/9&type=HTML.

Bravo, Michael. (2008). Voices from the Sea Ice: The Reception of Climate Impact Narratives. *Journal of Historical Geography, 35*(2), 256–278.

Bravo, Michael, & Sörlin, Sverker (Eds.). (2002). *Narrating the Arctic: A Cultural History of Nordic Scientific Practices.* Canton: Watson Publishing International.

Breum, Martin. (2011). *Når isen forsvinder. Danmark som stormagt i Arktis, olien i Grønland og kampen om Nordpolen*. København: Gyldendal.

Brody, Hugh. (1975). *The People's Land: Eskimos and Whites in the Eastern Arctic*. Harmondsworth: Penguin.

Bureau of Minerals and Petroleum. (2009). *Exploration and Exploitation of Hydrocarbons in Greenland: Strategy for Licence Policy 2009*. Nuuk: Nalaakkersuisut.

Cavalieri, Sandra, McGlynn, Emily, Stoessel, Susanah, Stuke, Franziska, Bruckner, Martin, Polzin, Christine, Koivurova, Timo, Sellheim, Nikolas, Stepien, Adam, Hossain, Kamrul, Duyck, Sébastien & Nilsson, Annika E. (2010). *EU Arctic Footprint and Policy Assessment* Berlin: Ecologic Institute.

Clover, Charles. (2005, October 17). Why the Inuit people walk on thin ice, *The Daily Telegraph*, p. 13.

Coates, Ken. (1994). The Discovery of the North: Towards a conceptual framework for the study of northern / remote regions. *The Northern Review* (12–13), 15–43.

Council of the European Union. (2009). *Council Conclusions on Arctic Issues. 2985th Foreign Affairs Council Meeting, Brussels, 8 December 2009*. Brussels.

Dahl, Jens. (1993). *Indigenous Peoples of the Arctic*. Reykjavik: The Nordic Council's Arctic Conference, The Nordic Council.

Dahl, Jens. (2013). *The Indigenous Space and Marginalized Peoples in the United Nations*. New York: Palgrave Macmillan.

Delgado, James. (1999). *Across the Top of the World*. London: British Museum Press.

Denmark, Greenland, & the Faroe Islands. (2011). *Kingdom of Denmark: Strategy for the Arctic 2011–2020*. Copenhagen: Ministry of Foreign Affairs (Denmark), Department of Foreign Affairs (Greenland) and Ministry of Foreign Affairs (the Faroe Islands).

European Commission. (2008). *Communication from the Commission to the European Parliament and the Council, November 20*. Brussels.

Featherstone, Mike. (1993). Global and local cultures. In J. Bird, B. Curtis, T. Putnam, G. Robertson & L. Tickner (Eds.), *Mapping the Futures: Local Cultures, Global Change* (pp. 169–187). London: Routledge.

Fienup-Riordan, Ann. (1990). *Eskimo Essays*. New Brunswick and London: Rutgers University Press.

Fienup-Riordan, Ann. (1995). *Freeze Frame: Alaska Eskimos in the Movies*. Seattle: Washington University Press.

Gant, Erik. (2010). Arctic Dialogue Workshop. Retrieved January 3, 2012, from http://icr.arcticportal.org/index.php?option=com_content&view=article&id=1276: arctic-dialogue-workshop&catid=108:news-latest&Itemid=4&lang=sa.

Giddens, Anthony. (1990). *The Consequences of Modernity*. Cambridge: Polity Press.

Gorbachev, Mikhail. (1987). Mikhail Gorbachev's speech in Murmansk at the ceremonial meeting on the occasion of the presentation of the Order of Lenin and the Gold Star to the City of Murmansk, 1 October. Retrieved December 12, 2011, from http://teacherweb.com/FL/CypressBayHS/JJolley/Gorbachev_speech.pdf.

Grace, Sherrill. (2001). *Canada and the Idea of North*. Montreal: McGill-Queen's University Press.

Griffiths, Franklyn. (2007). Camels in the Arctic? Climate change as the Inuit see it: 'From the inside out'. *The Walrus Magazine* (November), 1–15.

Grøndahl, Jens Christian. (2009, December 11). Tankens hvide pletter, Essay, *Weekendavisen*, p. 1.

Hastrup, Frida. (2011). *Weathering the World: Recovery in the Wake of the Tsunami in a Tamil Fishing Village*. New York: Berghahn Books.

Heininen, Lassi K. (2007). Different images of the Arctic, and the Circumpolar North in world politics. In P. Kankaanpää (Ed.), *Knowledge and Power in the Arctic: Proceedings at a Conference in Rovaniemi, April 16–18, 2007* (pp. 124–134). Rovaniemi: University of Lapland, Arctic Centre.

Hertzfeld, Michael. (2001). *Anthropology: Theoretical Practice in Culture and Society*. London: Blackwell.

Hulme, Mike. (2011). Meet the humanities. *Nature Climate Change 1* (July), 177–179.
Huntington, Henry P. (1992). *Wildlife Management and Subsistence Hunting in Alaska.* London: Belhaven Press in association with the Scott Polar Research Institute, University of Cambridge.
Indigenous Climate Portal. (2009). IPs Gain in COP 15. Indigenous Peoples Achieve Major Gains in Climate Change Negotiations. Retrieved December 30, 2011, from www.indigenousclimate.org/index.php?option=com_content&view=article& id=93%3Aips-gain-in-cop15&catid=3%3Anews&lang=en.
Keskitalo, E. Carina H. (2004). *Negotiating the Arctic: The Construction of an International Region.* New York and London: Routledge.
KNR. (2009, October 29). Fangere tilpasser sig klimaforandringer. Retrieved December 28, 2011, from http://knr.gl/da/news/fangere-tilpasser-sig-klimaforandringer.
Koch, Dorothy, & Hansen, James. (2005). Distant origins of Arctic black carbon: A Goddard Institute for Space Studies ModelE experiment. *Journal of Geophysical Research, 110*(D04204), 1–14.
Koivurova, Timo. (2010). Limits and possibilities of the Arctic Council in a rapidly chang-ing scene of Arctic governance. *Polar Record, 46*(2), 146–156.
Koivurova, Timo, & Heinämäki, Leena. (2006). The participation of indigenous peoples in international norm-making in the Arctic. *Polar Record, 42*(2), 101–109.
Larsen, Svend Erik. (1992). *Gadens rum – byens grænse.* Humanities Research Center/ Man & Nature: Working Paper 9.
Lynge, Aqqaluk, & Steenbaek, Marianne. (2011). *Inuit Arctic Policy.* Nuuk: Inuit Circumpolar Council.
Many Strong Voices. (n.d.). The goal of Many Strong Voices. Retrieved April 14, 2011, from www.manystrongvoices.org/.
Martello, Marybeth Long. (2004). Global change science and the Arctic citizen. *Science and Public Policy, 31*(2), 107–115.
Martello, Marybeth Long. (2008). Arctic indigenous peoples as representations and repre-sentatives of climate change. *Social Studies of Science, 38*(3), 351–376.
Massey, Doreen. (1993). Power-geometry and a progressive sense of place. In J. Bird, B. Curtis, T. Putnam, G. Robertson & L. Tickner (Eds.), *Mapping the Futures: Local Cultures, Global Change* (pp. 59–69). London: Routledge.
Minority Rights Group (Ed.). (1994). *Polar Peoples: Self-Determination and Development.* London: Minority Rights Publications.
Mogensen, Lars Trier. (2010, August 10). Fremtiden tegner sort for Grønland. Retrieved September 1, 2010, from http://politiken.dk/debat/signatur/ECE1044389/fremtiden -tegner-sort-for-groenland/.
Nathanielsen, Naaja. (2011, December 9). Kan ting blive for store, *Sermitsiaq*, p. 85.
Nilsson, Annika E. (2009). A changing Arctic climate: Science and policy in the Arctic Climate Impact Assessment. In T. Koivurova, E. C. H. Keskitalo & N. Bankes (Eds.), *Climate Governance in the Arctic.* New York: Springer, Environment & Policy 50.
Nordregio. (2011). *Megatrends.* Stockholm: Nordic Council of Ministers, TemaNord 527.
Nuttall, Mark. (2008). Climate change and the warming politics of autonomy in Greenland. *Indigenous Affairs* (1–2), 44–51.
Nuttall, Mark. (2010). *Pipeline Dreams: People, Environment, and the Arctic Energy Frontier.* Copenhagen: IWGIA.
Oliver-Smith, Anthony, & Hoffman, Susanna M. (Eds.). (2002). *Culture and Catastrophe: The Anthropology of Disaster.* Santa Fe, New Mexico: The School of American Research Press.
Olsen, Oline. (2011, December 8). Fiskerne drager fordel af varmere klima. Retrieved December 28, 2012, from www.knr.gl/da/nyheder/fiskerne-drager-fordel-af-varmere -klima.
Osherenko, Gail, & Young, Oran. (1989). *The Age of the Arctic: Hot Conflicts and Cold Realities.* Cambridge: Cambridge University Press.

Paine, Robert. (1977). *The White Arctic*. St. John's: Institute of Social and Economic Research, Memorial University of Newfoundland.

Paine, Robert. (1985). The claim of the Fourth World: The quest for autonomy and nationhood of indigenous peoples. In J. Brøsted, J. Dahl, A. Gray, H. C. Gulløv, G. Henriksen, J. B. Jørgensen & I. Kleivan (Eds.), *Native Power* (pp. 49–66). Bergen, Oslo: Universitetsforlaget.

Pedersen, Ivalu Søvndahl. (2011). Search and rescue in the Arctic. Retrieved December 13, 2011, from www.arctic-council.org/index.php/en/oceans/search-and-rescue.

Perry, Ronald W., & Quarantelli, E.L. (Eds.). (2005). *What is a Disaster? New Answers to Old Questions*. Bloomington: Xlibris.

Petersen, Hans Christian. (2007). Iagttagelser over klimaets svingninger. *Tidsskriftet Grønland*, 55(2–3), 94–104.

Petersen, Hans Christian. (2010). *Kalaallit Ilisimasaat. Pisuussutit Uumassusillit Nunatsinnilu Pinngortitap Pisuusutai. Local Knowledge: Living Resources and Natural Assets in Greenland*. Montreal: IPI International Polar Institute Press.

Potter, Russell A. (2007). *Arctic Spectacles: The Frozen North in Visual Culture, 1818–1875*. Seattle & London: University of Washington Press.

Rasmussen, Rasmus Ole, & Hamilton, Lawrence C. (2001). *The Development of Fisheries in Greenland*. Roskilde: NORS, Roskilde University.

Riffenburgh, Beau. (1993). *The Myth of the Explorer: The Press, Sensationalism, and Geographical Discovery*. London: Belhaven Press.

Robbins, Joel. (2006). Properties of nature, properties of culture: Ownership, recognition, and the politics of nature in a Papua New Guinea society. In A. Biersack & J. B. Greenberg (Eds.), *Reimagining Political Ecology* (pp. 171–194). Durham and London: Duke University Press.

Rovaniemi Declaration. (1991). Retrieved December 12, 2011, from http://arcticcircle.uconn.edu/NatResources/Policy/rovaniemi.html.

Råstofdirektoratet. (2007). Råstofdirektoratets bidrag til klimaworkshop. In G. H. Direktoratet for Miljø og Natur (Ed.), *Klimaworkshop* (pp. 52–55). Nuuk: Direktoratet for Miljø og Natur.

Said, Edward. (1995). *Orientalism*. New York: Pantheon Books.

Sale, K. (1985). *Dwellers in the Land: The Bioregional Vision*. San Francisco: Sierra Club Books.

Sejersen, Frank. (2007). Indigenous urbanism revisited – the case of Greenland. *Indigenous Affairs*(3), 26–31.

Sejersen, Frank. (2010). Urbanization, landscape appropriation and climate change in Greenland. *Acta Borealia*, 27(2), 167–188.

Selvstyrekommissionen. (2003). *Betænkning af Selvstyrekommissionen*. Nuuk: Grønlands Hjemmestyre.

Sermitsiaq. (2011, December 2). Vi skal selv - og vi kan selv, *Sermitsiaq*, p. 36.

Shadian, Jessica M. (2014). *The Politics of Arctic Sovereignty. Oil, Ice and Inuit Governance*. London & New York: Routledge.

Simmel, Georg. (1958). *Soziologie. Untersuchungen über die Formen der Vergesellschaftung*. Berlin: Duncker & Humblo.

Skatte- og velfærdskommissionen. (2010). *Hvordan sikres vækst og velfærd i Grønland?* Nuuk: Grønlands Selvstyre.

Tennberg, Monica. (1998). *The Arctic Council: A Study in Governmentality*. Rovaniemi: University of Lapland.

Tennberg, Monica. (2000). *Arctic Environmental Cooperation: A Study in Governmentalilty*. Hants and Burlington: Ashgate Publishing Company.

Tennberg, Monica. (2009a). Is adaptation governable in the Arctic? National and regional approaches to Arctic adaptation governance. In T. Koivurova, E. C. H. Keskitalo & N. Banks (Eds.), *Climate Governance in the Arctic* (pp. 289–302). New York: Springer, Environment & Policy 50.

Tennberg, Monica. (2009b). Three spirals of power/knowledge: Scientific laboratories, environmental panopticons and emerging biopolitics. In J. M. Shadian & M. Tennberg (Eds.), *Legacies and Change in Polar Science: Historical, Legal and Political Reflections on The International Polar Year* (pp. 189–200). Farnham: Ashgate.

Tennberg, Monica. (2010). Indigenous peoples as international political actors: a summary. *Polar Record*, 46(3), 164–170.

The Anchorage Declaration. (2009). Agreed by consensus of the participants in the Indigenous Peoples' Global Summit on Climate Change, Anchorage, Alaska, April 24, 2009. Retrieved August 13, 2012, from http://unfccc.int/resource/docs/2009/smsn /ngo/168.pdf.

Tschakert, Petra. (2012). From impacts to embodied experiences: Tracing political ecology in climate change research. *Geografisk Tidsskrift, Danish Journal of Geography, 112*(2), 144–158.

VanDeveer, Stacy C. (2004). Ordering environments: Regions in European international environmental cooperation. In S. Jasanoff & M. L. Martello (Eds.), *Earthly Politics. Local and Global in Environmental Governance* (pp. 309–334). Cambridge, Massachusetts: MIT Press.

Vibe, Christian. (1967). Arctic animals in relation to climatic fluctuations. *Meddelelser om Grønland, 170*(5), 1–227.

Wisner, Ben, Blakie, Peiers, Cannon, Terry, & Davis, Ian (Eds.). (1994). *At Risk*. London: Routledge.

Young, Oran. (1985–1986). The Age of the Arctic. *Foreign Policy* (61), 160–179.

Young, Oran. (1992). *Arctic Politics: Conflict and Cooperation in the Circumpolar North.* Hanover: University Press of New England.

Young, Oran. (1998). *Creating Regimes: Arctic Accords and International Governance.* New York: Cornell University Press.

Young, Oran. (2009). Whither the Arctic? Conflict or cooperation in the circumpolar north. *Polar Record*, 45(232), 73–82.

Zellen, Barry Scott. (2009). *Arctic Doom, Arctic Boom*. Santa Barbara, California: Praeger.

Økonomisk Råd. (2011). *Økonomisk råds rapport 2011*. Nuuk: Nalaakkersuisut.

2   Resilience, human agency and Arctic climate change adaptation strategies

People's possibilities for dealing successfully with climate change and establishing viable adaptation strategies, including coming up with solutions to contemporary and anticipated problems, depend, among other things, on the ability to cross a number of barriers. In its publications, the Intergovernmental Panel on Climate Change (IPCC) fleshes out these barriers and addresses the complexity of issues. One of these barriers is the institutional and legal setup. However, even though equity and the diversity of potentials for coping are both addressed by IPCC, the structures of critical institutions and the derived allocation of decision-making authority have been underplayed by IPCC in its work on resilience. This is striking, since political institutions often have a crucial impact on people's abilities to take action and to propel human resources and innovation. The Arctic presents interesting perspectives on the complexities and path dependencies of the institutional and legal setup as well as on potential solutions. The institutional change and reorganization, which are presently taking place in the Arctic at great haste, may constitute an important tool for Arctic societies to improve their horizon of possibilities and to pursue strategies that are aligned with their visions and capabilities. In the Arctic, indigenous rights, decentralization, participation, empowerment and self-determination figure very prominently in the rhetoric of Inuit organizations, due to the colonial history and the relations that indigenous peoples have with the nation-states. The focus of Inuit organizations is both on how to empower people and on how to identify and evaluate people's vulnerabilities. Seen from an indigenous point of view, the limitations of Inuit's political elbowroom and agency may actually make them vulnerable to climate change.

In this chapter, these political and institutional limitations are discussed in relation to Arctic climate change and the concept of resilience. Agency is to be understood in this chapter as the potential to seize, create, develop and pursue opportunities as well as to change, create, negotiate and develop policy. Improving peoples' agency may improve their possibility for adapting to climate change and for creating viable futures for their communities. However, one should not be so naïve as to assume that enhanced agency in the hands of indigenous peoples will, in itself, lead to greater equity and social justice or will automatically reinforce sustainability, resilience and workable climate change adaptation strategies. As is the case everywhere else in the world, conflicting knowledge, claims, visions, positions, ideas and needs within and between communities are indeed part of the indigenous world. In fact, any conceptualization of an unambiguous relation between indigenous empowerment and improved resilience and adaptation fails to acknowledge the ironical possibility that positive responses to and applications of such a conceptualization could actually result in social and political conflict as well as in a lack of adaptation.

However, the focus on agency might urge us to change our focus from *how to adapt to* change to *how to create* change when working with climate change adaptation strategies. A focus on agency favours a more complex representation of political processes in order to widen the scope of contexts in which climate change has to be dealt with. It is futile to attempt designing climate change adaption strategies without having a broader perspective that encompasses the legal and institutional setup. Furthermore, the focus on agency challenges one-sided solutions and simple systemic representations because it provides an analytical platform on which to approach the dynamic, open and conflicting nature of social, cultural and political life. As such, a focus on agency may challenge the definition of resilience. Resilience is commonly understood as being related to a system's ability to maintain stability in times of shock or under stress, either through reaction or by means of change (Folke et al., 2002). In the words of Holling, Gunderson and Ludwig (2002, p. 22), the pursuit of resilience supports a future 'that encourages innovative opportunity for people to learn and prosper, that incorporates responsibility to maintain and restore the diversity of nature, and that is based on a just and civil society'. The concept of resilience and its built-in normative content may, however, not be the best all-encompassing analytical tool with which to navigate humanity in a more sustainable direction when faced with the complexity, openness and dynamics in systems that are supposed to be made resilient. Especially when it comes to climate change, we are facing challenges, on all scales, that need to be addressed with more prevailing approaches than those that stem from the theories of resilience and adaptation. The focus on agency may prove to add a dimension to the resilience discussions since it questions the systems and their structures that are to be made resilient, and it opens up for creativity and alternative futures in constantly changing systems, which are difficult to demarcate. A focus on agency in climate change adaptation strategies serves, furthermore, to turn our attention toward the temporal aspect of agency employed in any adaptation strategy. This chapter will show how the temporal aspect may influence both contemporary and future strategies related to pursuing societal goals.

Vulnerability and victimization

The issue of agency has not been ignored by IPCC and policy makers who clearly acknowledge that people's proclivities for adapting to climate change are unevenly distributed throughout the world, where aspects like gender, ethnicity, education, economy, and dependence on particular ecosystems, among other parameters, are stipulated as factors affecting people's coping potentials (Bruce, Lee, & Haites, 1995; Garcia-Alix, 2008; Tauli-Corpuz & Lynge, 2008; United Nations High Commissioner for Human Rights, 2009). Research into people's vulnerability has been pursued in parallel with studies of vulnerable regions. The extreme vulnerability of very large segments of the world's population and the need to push for adaptation strategies incorporating and benefitting these marginal groups have become increasingly pressing because contemporary and future mitigation policies cannot, neither in the short nor in the long run, successfully obviate the challenges and problems of vulnerable groups facing the double exposure of problems related to both climate change and globalization processes (Leichenko & O'Brien, 2008; O'Brien & Leichenko, 2000). Globally, these groups are increasingly demanding that the international response to climate change should also focus on their adaptation problems and capacity building, due to the damaging climate events that are likely to occur (Pielke, Prins, Rayner, & Sarewitz, 2007).

Marginal and vulnerable people are already struggling with existing societal and economic problems. Their potentials to cope with climate change thus have to be viewed within a larger framework (Arctic Council, 2013; Nuttall et al., 2005). Therefore, the solutions for reducing their vulnerability are extremely complex and involve issues related to societal transformations that are related only distantly to what we normally consider relevant and necessary for climate change adaptation. In line with this, the Working Group II of IPCC points out that '[r]ecent studies on the implications for adaptation…indicate that such changes may imply larger policy shifts; for example, towards protection of the most vulnerable' (Klein et al., 2007, p. 759).

Indigenous peoples all over the world often perceive their position to be marginal, on both the national and international levels, and they are demanding greater influence in decision making when it comes to climate change and similarly pushing for greater respect for their self-determination and collective land rights as essential tools for adapting to climate change (C. Nilsson, 2008). Indigenous peoples experience different kinds and degrees of colonial and post-colonial asymmetrical power relations with state institutions. For these groups, any climate strategy is carried out within these relations – and thus carries political implications. With respect to the climate change discourse, indigenous peoples are often placed in a position of being victims (Bravo, 2009). However, the concurrent discourse on self-determination emphasizes agency and it is actually altering and challenging their position as victims.

Although the 400,000 indigenous people of the Arctic comprise less than 1 per cent of the world's indigenous peoples, their experiences with a rapidly changing and destabilized Arctic ecosystem due to climate change and the profound implications that this has on their societies may serve as a case not only for other indigenous peoples but also for marginalized and vulnerable groups worldwide. The Arctic as a region is unique with respect to the de-colonization processes that have taken place since the 1960s. In 1971, Alaska natives got the Alaska Native Claims Settlement Act; in 1975, the Cree and Inuit signed the James Bay and Northern Québec Agreement; in 1979, Greenland got Home Rule; in 1984, the Inuvialuit signed the Inuvialuit Settlement Agreement; Inuit in Northern Canada established Nunavut in 1999; in 2005, Nunatsiavut was settled in Labrador; and in 2007, steps to establish a Nunavik government in Northern Québec were taken. These are but a few examples of the many agreements in the Circumpolar North that have been signed since the 1960s. In 2008, Greenland and Denmark negotiated an act establishing a greater degree of self-governance to Greenland and opening up for total independence, should the people of Greenland wish to gain this. This act was launched in June 2009 on the national day of Greenland and marks a major step forward in the relationship between Denmark and Greenland. Despite a common point of departure (a widespread wish for a greater degree of self-determination among indigenous peoples), these pan-Arctic processes of political devolution are quite diverse and assign different potentials of agency to indigenous peoples.

In their essential character, the agreements vary from region to region. By using very broad categories, one could characterize the conditions as state capitalism in Greenland, state intervention in Canada and state subventionism in Alaska (Rasmussen, 1999, p. 222). Some agreements work with regional self-government, some with land claims and others with ethno-political governments (Dahl, 1993). Some indigenous peoples (e.g. Iñupiat of Northern Alaska) have pursued greater autonomy under existing political structures (boroughs). In some regions, the political solutions are combinations – for example, in Nunavut (Canada) where regional self-government is combined with land claim. The complexities and diversities of processes of de-colonization and path-dependencies make indigenous empowerment a very unclear path but what this points to is an ambition and a process of increased agency rather than a definite end.

The extraordinary movement of indigenous empowerment and regional political decentralization that we observe in the Arctic (Dahl, 1993) directs our attention to three points: *First*, these political and institutional setups are products of negotiation and reflect the possibilities, agendas and contexts that existed when they were adopted. *Second*, these agreements and laws are regularly revisited and changed in order to meet new challenges. *Third*, the institutional setup is an important tool to enable Arctic peoples to cope with societal challenges (e.g. climate change) themselves. It is therefore crucial to ask the following questions: Do these agreements act as institutional and legal barriers or do they really and truly provide Arctic peoples with agency to cope successfully with changes in their society? And if so, what kind of agency do they provide?

Vulnerability and institutional barriers

When evaluating vulnerability and the possibilities for improving the adaptation capacity of people, communities and societies, the institutional, legal and political setup is critical (Adger & Kelly, 1999; Arctic Council, 2013; Chapin III et al., 2006; Handmer, Dovers, & Downing, 1999; Keskitalo, 2008; C. Nilsson, 2008; Nuttall, 2008a, 2008b; Yohe et al., 2007). It has often been mentioned that the political realities at different scales influence vulnerability. Anisimov et al. (2007, p. 673), for example, state that

> [r]esilience and adaptability depend on ecosystem diversity as well as the institutional rules that govern social and economic systems. Innovative co-management of both renewable and non-renewable resources could support adaptive abilities via flexible management regimes while providing opportunities to enhance local economic benefits and ecological and societal resilience…Although Arctic communities in many regions show great resilience and ability to adapt, some responses have been compromised by socio-political change.

Increasingly, institutional structures are being singled out as constituting barriers. Adger et al. (2007, p. 728) for example, mention that: 'New studies carried out since the …[Third Assessment Report (TAR)] show that adaptive capacity is influenced not only by economic development and technology, but also by social factors such as human capital and governance structures'. In Smit et al. (2001, pp. 895–897), six features of communities or regions that determine their adaptive capacity are put forward: economic wealth, technology, information and skills, infrastructure, institutions and equity. However, in the Fourth Assessment Report (FAR) of IPCC, political and institutional barriers are neither treated in any detail nor dealt with separately in the section (17.4.2) entitled 'Limits and barriers to adaptation' (Adger et al., 2007, pp. 733–737). Future assessment reports from IPCC may include this aspect in somewhat more detailed fashion but currently, it is worthy of note that the scattered remarks on institutional barriers by IPCC offer very few hints as to what importance institutions exert on climate change adaptation strategies and resilience.

Framing the adaptation problem as an institutional one helps to address the political and legal contexts within which adaptation is implemented and discussed. Vulnerability then becomes a problem *of* society rather than a problem *for* society (Hewitt, 1995, 1997). FAR (Klein et al., 2007) deals to a limited degree with the policy and institutional contexts within which adaptation and mitigation can be implemented and discusses interrelationships in practice (Klein et al., 2007, p. 766). The institutional perspective is relevant inasmuch as it directs our attention to different arenas and levels where solutions to climate change adaptation can be found. Governance and the distribution of rights and benefits are crucial factors when it comes to how adaptation capacity is distributed and activated. The lack of sufficient local political institutions and hindrances to accessing political frameworks may constitute barriers to institutional changes that can support local people's adaptation strategies and ways of doing, being and knowing (see also Arctic Council, 2013; Keskitalo, 2008). Despite the fact that institutions shape, enforce, constrain and reduce adaptive capacity and prefigure adaptive action accordingly, (Pelling, High, Dearing, & Smith, 2008), vulnerability and adaptation discussions have, for quite some time now, according to Keskitalo (2008, p. 23), 'exhibited a rather instrumental and management-oriented view of adaptation in social systems and excluded explicit discussions of power and politics from the process of adaptation, despite acknowledging their importance.' Smit and Wandel (2006, p. 289) suggest that where political constraints are particularly binding, adaptation may be considered by attempting to change those structures themselves. This is an endeavour that, in some cases, moves *beyond* rectifying institutional inefficiencies, instabilities and weaknesses.

I suggest that political and legal institutional structures should be addressed directly when evaluating adaptation capacity (see also C. Nilsson, 2008, p. 15). This is particularly important when working with indigenous peoples because their relationship to the authorities carries a particularly political dimension, where the question of *collective rights* to self-determination is of paramount importance. For many indigenous peoples, the question of collective land rights (and the right to manage and develop the use of those lands) is a core issue, albeit a political can of worms when addressed directly to the state. The Arctic Resilience Interim Report (Arctic Council, 2013, pp. 59, 86) mentions state-imposed constraints on indigenous peoples' cultural practices and political-economic activities as a hindrance for indigenous peoples to deal with climate change problems. However, the report does not address the question of indigenous rights to a full extent, even though it emphasizes that '[the] power of self-determination through active and meaningful participation in decision-making processes is central to the environmental justice issues involved in any normative approach (such as a resilience analysis) to decision-making' (Arctic Council, 2013, p. 24).

All the problems that indigenous peoples will face due to climate change are, in some ways, already taking place, and a part of recent history: the deterioration of the environment that threatens subsistence activities; forced or strongly encouraged relocation to new areas and central communities; changes in social organization and cultural values giving rise to potential inter-generational problems, the introduction of new industries and businesses run by rationales not necessarily beneficial to local communities; and the experience that government strategies are inadequate for dealing with the magnitude and diversity of problems. Without a doubt, climate change will have a huge impact on the political, social, cultural and economic dynamics in the Arctic (ACIA, 2005; Anisimov et al., 2007) and it will indeed amplify some of the current and anticipated problems with which people already struggle. The public sector's focus on climate change related problems as the primary driver for change in the Arctic has prompted human geographer Rasmus Ole Rasmussen to put forth an appeal to apply a more nuanced perspective (see Arctic Council, 2013; Nuttall, 2009, p. 307 for a similar argument):

> most discussions tend to forget that there are other ongoing social processes which – independent of the processes of changing climate – may become much more decisive for the future of many of these settlements (Rasmussen, 2010, p. 219).

The danger of segregating climate change issues from other political and societal issues is also accentuated by the Arctic Climate Impact Assessment (ACIA, 2005).

This assessment points out that the contemporary institutional setting and the colonial history constitute a framework that can act as a barrier to adaptation. It therefore states that

> [e]mpowering northern residents, particularly indigenous peoples, through self-government and self-determination arrangements, including ownership and management of land and natural resources, is a *key* ingredient that would enable them to adapt to climate change…National governments, often slow moving and ill equipped to think and act in the long term, must also understand the connections between empowerment and adaptability in the north if their policies and programs are to succeed in helping people respond to the long-term challenge posed by climate change (ACIA, 2005, p. 91, italic by author).

By placing an emphasis on the political context as the key factor in adaptation, ACIA contributed a seldom-mentioned and controversial input to the climate debate in the Arctic. ACIA's emphasis on political and institutional reforms as an important strategy to be deployed when relating to the challenges of climate change is, of course, to be found elsewhere in the Arctic Council's publications and also – but to a much lesser degree – in the Snow, Water, Ice and Permafrost in the Arctic assessment (AMAP, 2011) and the Arctic Resilience Interim Report (Arctic Council, 2013), which were follow-ups of ACIA.

This chapter will show how climate change research pursued in Arctic Canada in cooperation with indigenous peoples often places the emphasis on their past experiences and patterns of action. As a consequence, research into ways of strengthening adaptation capacity often reinforces habitual approaches rather than focusing on adaption to alternative future societal scenarios and activating human agency in relation to those. In Greenland, the climate change debate is tightly tangled up in questions related to future self-determination, economic reforms and new occupations. This focus stimulates an agency potential that is somehow detached from past and present experiences. In both regions, the fundamental understanding of what constitutes adequate human agency has an impact on the selection of participants in policy and strategy design, on the implementation of strategies and on the manner in which future engagement and agency are framed.

Double agency

Indigenous peoples are often labelled as being vulnerable with respect to climate change and they are indeed experiencing what Robin Leichenko and Karen O'Brien term 'the double exposure of processes' related to both globalization and climate change (Leichenko & O'Brien, 2008; O'Brien & Leichenko, 2000). Their vulnerability is, among other things, closely linked to their political and legal status, which limits their agency. Indigenous peoples in the Arctic are aspiring to activate what I term *double agency*. Both aspects of this double agency are important and the question before us is how to mobilize human resources in order to activate the human potential of creativity that is so necessary for dealing with climate change.

The first aspect of double agency is people's possibilities of influencing and of supplying knowledge, experiences, perceptions, anticipations and perspectives to political processes and decisions; in short, their possibilities of making a difference in climate change adaptation strategies and policies. This aspect emphasizes *stakeholder participation* and *integration* and often involves connecting people who happen to be standing on different levels of decision-making. Co-management regimes in Canada (Berkes, 2001) stand as textbook examples of an institutionally integrative system where indigenous peoples participate in most aspects of decision-making concerning resource management in what they consider to be their homeland. This aspect of agency is primarily being pursued within existing structures.

The second aspect – and, for indigenous peoples, often a crucial one – is people's possibilities of actively pursuing creative, flexible and innovative strategies that create change and transform society in directions that lie within a horizon of expectation and possibilities related to the group in question. This aspect emphasizes *rights-holder possibilities* and *self-determination* and involves expanding the framework of choices and decisions. This entails considering mechanisms that can improve peoples' political and legal entitlements and collective rights to negotiate, create, plan for, seize and pursue opportunities and change, whether this change be societal, political, economic, technical, cultural or institutional. This aspect of agency thus supports the creation of new institutions and structures, among other things. Consequently, it necessitates that the political context and institutional setup be revisited and evaluated in relation to indigenous peoples' rights to land and self-determination. In the Arctic, a clearer understanding of both the contemporary political context and indigenous peoples' political and legal struggles can be gained by applying both aspects of agency.

By stressing the two aspects of agency, our attention is directed to the fact that coping with climate change is not only about improving the *integration* of stakeholders and their knowledge. For indigenous peoples, it is also a matter, in a number of cases, of *removing* legal barriers and a matter of *creating* enhanced governance opportunities. In doing this, indigenous peoples have the potential to more effectively carve out their own collective spaces of hope and vision rather than – as is so often the case – be reduced to knowledgeable stakeholders or clients to be integrated into existing programs and institutional setups. Having agency as an analytical focus, it is possible to accentuate potentials, directions and limitations in political processes, strategies and actions.

We often see that human agency in relation to a changing environment due to climate change is afforded priority in comparison with human agency in relation to society (Bertelsen, 1996, p. 67). For Arctic indigenous peoples, as for most of the world's population, adapting to climate change may imply making radical societal changes and reforms. Even though group solidarity and coherence cannot and should not be taken for granted, indigenous peoples' communities often want to act as a collective, to improve their possibilities as a collective and to deal with their disagreements about strategies, priorities and even the demarcation of the collective in question. What I am suggesting is that when indigenous peoples strive to gain a political platform, furnishing what I term double agency, they are able to pursue strategies that build on the basis of their dual status as *stakeholders* (participation and integration) and as *rights-holders* (self-determination). Both aspects of human agency for indigenous peoples spring from a collective categorization and representation that often combines indigenous cultural identity with expansionist colonial histories. Group legitimization and justification thus assume vital importance and climate change adaptation strategies are, in some way, tangled up in the politics of identity. In fact, the politics of identity may inhibit strategies that reflect the diversity within indigenous communities. This will be shown later on in this chapter, where the politics of identity situate local people in a position as hunters because this jibes with the general discourse.

When formulating climate change adaptation strategies, the participation and integration of indigenous peoples within existing and improved institutional structures constitute an important platform for agency. The second aspect of double agency has to do with people's possibilities to actively pursue new, flexible and innovative strategies and to activate the human resources that are needed in order to navigate towards a horizon of expectation and possibilities. There has been a lot of focus on the first aspect in IPCC but very little on the second one.

Human agency is, according to Emirbayer and Mische (1998), a temporally embedded process of social engagement that may orientate in different ways towards the past, the future and the present. The temporal dimensions of agency exert implications on how societal problems are approached and how solutions are designed. According to the authors, some actors approach projects and realize them on the basis of the habitual and selective reactivation of past patterns of thought and action as routinely incorporated in practical activity, where stability and order are emphasized (the iterational element). Other actors apply a more projective approach, where the possible future trajectories of action may be creatively reconfigured in relation to the actor's hopes, fears and desires for the future (the projective element). Finally, actors may apply a more practical and normative approach based on emerging demands, dilemmas and ambiguities of presently evolving situations (the practical-evaluative element). When analyzing how human agency is advanced in the Arctic, it quickly becomes apparent that people shift between these temporal orientations while, in certain contexts, some of them become more dominant. In the Arctic, several adaptation strategies are in the process of being formulated (see Furgal & Prowse, 2008; Indian and Northern Affairs Canada, 2006, n.d.; Kleman, 2008; Northwest Territories – Environment and Natural Resources, 2008) and each process emphasizes different aspects and temporal dimensions of agency that may influence coping strategies in fundamental ways. In the following, the focus will be on Greenland and Canada, and their separate issues and strategies related to the field.

Climate change adaptation strategies in Canada and Greenland

The politics of scale and the temporal dimensions of climate change adaptations strategies set the stage for Arctic peoples' participation and also serve to map out the framework for – and the eventual success of – strategies. These aspects have to be closely revisited, especially now when the thawing ice is making the Arctic accessible to resource extractive industries and the shipping sector to a degree never seen before. The future global attention and activity in the Arctic will transform the possibilities and have impact on the socio-economic, cultural, political and security setting of the Circumpolar North. The expansion of economic activities in a rapidly transforming Arctic poses management challenges to the entire Arctic region that are related to security, governance and international cooperation.

A major challenge in adaptation strategies is to raise awareness of the long-term view (Folke et al., 2002) and to provide the foundation for human agency to deal innovatively with developments in the region. Otherwise, the people living here might not be in a position to seize new opportunities. Inuit Tapiriit Kanatami, representing the Inuit in Canada, also wants to break away from the history of dependence and has expressed a desire to bring about a reduction in outside support and to reduce the heavy reliance on public sector activities and subsidies (Inuit Tapiriit Kanatami, 2008) with the upshot that Inuit are pushing for change (see also Inuit Tapiriit Kanatami, 2007). This political agenda, coupled with the challenges of climate change, poses legal questions, as pointed out by Beach (2000): '[w]ere the climate to change so as to demand or make possible new forms of livelihood for northern indigenous peoples, the new livelihoods would not entail the legal or moral justifications for Native monopoly of resource access enjoyed by many Natives today'. Beach is thus directing our attention to the fact that indigenous peoples' present status as rights-holders is not sufficient for securing any legal basis for alternative futures.

With respect to the Arctic, climate change presents yet one more challenge to many communities that are struggling already with a number of cultural, legal, social, economic and political problems. Climate change may magnify existing local problems and serves to amplify the international stakes in the Arctic. The number of cross-cutting issues and scale-crossing relations, even in the most remote communities, present the researchers and policy makers with a setting of great complexity that does not lend itself to simple reductions. In spite of this, many researchers have a particular interest in how climate change will affect the indigenous way of life based on hunting and fishing (see Chapters 6 and 7). This is a convenient focus in relation to climate change discussions because indigenous peoples are easily pointed out as vulnerable. Indeed, this focus may also spring from the very fact that indigenous peoples themselves place emphasis on these activities as an important element in their own culture, their political identity and their group justification vis-à-vis the state. In the contribution made by the Working Group II to the TAR of the Intergovernmental Panel on Climate

Change, Anisimov et al. (2001, p. 827) predict, for example, that climate change in the Arctic 'will entail adjustments in harvest strategies as well as in allocations of labor and resources'. Other authors (Nuttall, 2008a) emphasize that the hunting way of life is affected and constrained by many factors, of which climate change is but one and they accordingly add more complexity to the contemporary Arctic reality. Still, the hunting way of life is the centre of focus.

In the Canadian north, the institutional and political setting emphasizes the inclusion of communities and indigenous peoples. A good many workshops have been held there for purposes of integrating local perspectives, indigenous knowledge and local perceptions of vulnerability and risk (Ford et al., 2007; Ford & Smit, 2004; Ford et al., 2008; Ford, Smit, Wandel, & MacDonald, 2006; Government of Nunavut, 2005a, 2005b, 2005c, 2005d). By this means, the strategies specifically respect and become more related to local needs, local conditions and local ideas, and the strategies and capacity-building strategies thus elicit a strong local resonance. This local integration and partnership is one aspect of human agency: it opens up for alternative ways of doing, being and knowing and thus challenges the privileged voices of authorities and scientists. This approach is a direct result of the empowerment of Arctic indigenous peoples since the 1970s and of Canada's special commitment to honour indigenous peoples' interests and concerns (Inuit Tapiriit Kanatami & Inuit Circumpolar Council [Canada], 2007). Several studies on indigenous peoples' observations and vulnerability have been pursued in the Circumpolar North. Canada, in particular, has used these kinds of down-scaled studies to strengthen research into how climate change is experienced and how it is going to influence local communities, as seen from the local point of view. According to Ford et al. (2008, p. 55), these 'down-scaled projections provide detailed regional and site scenarios of climate change for community-based vulnerability analyses' and the approach can identify what capacity exists for coping with change and concomitantly inform the development of adaptation policies. This local focus circumvents the problems linked to national adaptation programs of action, which are often lacking in micro-level socio-economic information, and are often riddled with gaps in stakeholder participation in the planning, design, implementation and monitoring of projects (Adger et al., 2007, p. 733). In Chapters 6 and 7, these down-scaled studies will be critically examined.

Viewed from an indigenous perspective, this involvement and respect for indigenous knowledge are quite different from the relations of being subdued and subjugated that indigenous peoples have previously experienced with scientists and state authorities alike. In this perspective, their observations, their experiences, their worries and their ideas suddenly *matter*. Social vulnerability is defined at the local level, and Ford et al. (2007, p. 155) find that local knowledge and the land-based skills allow 'response with experience'. People-participatory processes are important because cultural traditions and livelihoods are at stake.

Community-based studies integrating community stakeholders, studies that aim to contribute to adaptation practices, are indeed important for indigenous capacity building, for policy recommendation and for suggesting the direction of action to be taken. Part of the methodology (Smit & Wandel, 2006) is to identify *relevant* conditions within the community and then apply risk and vulnerability assessments that aim to provide suggestions regarding new initiatives, policy modifications, economic and technological support programs and capacity-building plans that will enhance the adaptation capacity of the community in question.

Institutional aspects are integrated, but what is often addressed, rather than the creation of new systems, are questions of how to make the existing systems better. In Canada, the focus on the hunting system results, among other things, in proposals to provide financial support to the purchase of new equipment that can cope with the changing environment (Ford et al., 2008, p. 54). Adaptation policy identifies what policy measures are required 'to moderate or reduce the negative effects of climate change, as well as how best to develop, apply, and fund such policies' (Ford et al., 2007, pp. 151–152). The focus is primarily on ways to change behaviour (such as a change in hunting strategy or the sharing of meat) as the main adaptive strategy (Ford et al., 2007, p. 154), although Ford and Smit (2004, p. 395) in one (and only one) sentence mention that 'increased political autonomy and comprehensive land-claim agreements may further strengthen the adaptability of communities'.

These local studies of potential coping strategies are certainly informative. However, by virtue of its extreme down-scaling and sector-focusing, the research approach detaches itself from the complex social, economic, cultural and political setting which certainly influences changing behaviour and perspectives, even within the chosen sector of analysis. Societal and economic changes related to tourism, militarization, the commercialization of harvests, industrial development (e.g. mining), and wage-based activities, are treated as factors from the *outside* that influence the coping strategies *within* the hunting sector, rather than as factors that have to be apprehended as integral parts of the system and the community's adaptation capacity. Inuit are, therefore, in these approaches maintained in their position as hunters – an image that fits into the discourse of indigenous peoples as traditional and as being closely linked to the land solely through their hunting activities. These studies do not consider urbanization or industrialization as part of Inuit adaptation strategies even though most communities have experiences with and orientate themselves towards these two modes of life (Arctic Human Development Report, 2004). Therefore, some of the conclusions that are drawn in the local studies appear to be somewhat disconnected from the complex contemporary Arctic context. For example, it is stated that the 'adaptability of younger generations to future climate change will depend upon how well they acquire Inuit traditional knowledge and land-based skills' (Ford et al., 2008, p. 58; Ford et al., 2006). Seeing that climate change is certainly going to transform the ecosystem and can also reasonably be expected to boost many non-indigenous activities in the North, the younger generation is probably going to need more than this acquisition. Conducting sector-oriented analyses in a manner that remains detached and uninformed about the political institutions is a way of 'deconstruct[ing] actors to a point where adaptation to change is no longer possible' (Keskitalo, 2008, p. 2). When *mainstreaming* adaptation strategies, this takes place within existing structures of power and discourses. Indigenous peoples struggling to break away from their asymmetrical power relation to the state and struggling to establish platforms of agency may not benefit much from mainstreaming, which can be perceived as a continuation of their marginal position. Rather, indigenous peoples need to have existing institutional and political structures revisited and changed in order to facilitate adaptation strategies that place agency more firmly in the hands of indigenous peoples, accordingly empowering them with the right to pursue alternative societal strategies that may or may not prove to be viable in their dealings with climate change. It is on account of these institutional and political restrictions, which straitjacket Inuit agency, that George Wenzel (2009, p. 97) suggests that Inuit 'must make negotiation part of their adaptive toolkit'. The potential strategies of the hunter to maintain the relationship in the life-giving world by shifting to new resources are, paradoxically, to be fought in the political arena. Whereas the hunters formerly followed the animals, they now have to follow the national and international policies, which diminish the hunters' mobility, agency and choice.

The focus on local and traditional knowledge linked to the hunting sector is so strong in the Canadian Arctic that, among other things, it raises the question of the 'politics of scale' (see e.g. Lebel, Garden, & Imamura, 2005; A. E. Nilsson, 2007), both with respect to spatial and temporal dimensions. First, the clear demarcation of locality and community as the point of departure and main frame of reference underplays local people's entanglement in the extra-local structures of economy and urbanization. The research projects that inform policy makers down-scale human relations and human agency and, in doing so, they wind up fixating Arctic communities in an arena of limited resources which is going to affect the understanding of them as vulnerable. The urban entanglement is, for example, taken out of the strategies by down-scaling the focus, and the potentials in the urban structure for local people are left out, even though urbanization is an extremely predominating factor in the Arctic, both with respect to migration-patterns and the positive and negative impacts on peoples' lives – even for people living far away from urban centres (Nielsen, 2005; Sejersen, 2007).

Inuit knowledge is a major resource in the adaptation strategies, as it is intimately bound up with the understanding of Arctic peoples as being closely linked to the natural surroundings of their communities (see Chapter 7). In this case, the temporality of agency is characterised by an intense and extreme cramming of the past into the present. This perspective, which may in fact be supported by a majority of Inuit community members, also demarcates relevant knowledge and thus carves out only a fraction of the experiences and perspectives that local actors have and may use to mobilise new ideas, strategies and scenarios. In these adaptation processes, the history and political experiences of Arctic indigenous peoples as well as their visions of establishing and maintaining self-governing and economic viable regions are all omitted. The down-scaling of perspective is linked closely to a discourse of *societal maintenance*.

In Greenland, on the contrary, climate change adaptation strategies are being *upscaled* to such an extent that Greenland is being turned into a single community. This national point of departure silences local concerns and the Greenlandic authorities, in the few discussions they have held on climate change, have not fostered any major processes that integrate the local people to any significant extent. The knowledge regime and the research that have been pursued place an emphasis on scientific understandings of economy and technology, and the government has been encouraging the younger generation to pursue education in technical and academic disciplines. The discourse is one of *societal transformation*, where extra-local structures (e.g. the global financial market) are important in defining adaptation strategies. Urbanization is not only accepted as a major force in society but is being used actively by the Inuit-run government to strengthen self-determination (Sejersen, 2007). The eagerness to work towards more self-governance and economic development is supported by the population (75 per cent voted 'yes' to the referendum on self-government in 2008). In Greenland, the strategy is to diversify the economy through hyper-industrialization, which involves a major transformation of society. The society is hoping, by doing so, to be able to break away from its economic dependence on the fishing industry, which is currently facing severe changes due to climate change and other factors. The integration of elaborate local knowledge and community studies in policy making is not afforded the same priority as macro-studies of the national economy and the labour market. Greenland may thus be limited in the adaptation strategies, due to lack of adequate research and local involvement. The extreme push for societal transformations and the political drive to gain more self-determination affect the temporality of agency in Greenland in ways that cram the future into the present (K. Hastrup, 2007).

Double agency in the Arctic

Ecological changes effected by climate change are, along with socio-economic changes, increasingly pushing for the need to diversify the economies of Arctic communities. Many communities are now orientating their concerns, attention and activities towards non-renewable resource industries operating in the Arctic, in one way or another. If the Arctic communities are to adapt to climate change and diversify their economies, indigenous peoples will therefore have to benefit from these industrial activities, and any adaptation strategy has to integrate this. The main question is, then, the extent to which the legal and institutional setup will stimulate them to activate agency in this direction when it comes to climate change adaptation strategies.

The first aspect of agency (*participation*) is already quite elaborate in Nunavut and Greenland. In Nunavut, for example, land claim agreements clearly stipulate that Inuit are to benefit from these industrial activities when it comes to job opportunities, etc. through the settlement of Inuit Impact and Benefit Agreements. This is an integral aspect of the first aspect of agency, which is based on respect, integration and benefit. However, if one looks at the second aspect of human agency (*rights-holder possibilities* and *self-determination*; the capacity to act and work for change) it is possible to identify political and institutional barriers for change not only within the existing co-management regimes, but also within the land claim agreements. Stated differently, although the Nunavut Land Claims Agreement is the most far-reaching agreement ever signed in Canada between an indigenous group and the federal government (Légaré, 2008, p. 346), it may be appropriate to revisit and evaluate the existing land claims agreement in Nunavut in order to find out whether it is geared to meet the challenges of climate change. The Agreement gives Inuit ownership rights to 18 per cent of the 1.9 million km^2 of land in Nunavut, of which 10 per cent includes subsurface rights where Inuit can benefit from any mineral or energy extraction. Benefits stemming from company taxes and royalties from the remaining 82 per cent go to Canada primarily. Therefore, it may strengthen Inuit communities when they get a larger share of the revenues as rights-holders and enable them to broaden up their horizon of possibilities and to seize new opportunities by acquiring more control, management and benefits over Crown lands and resources in Nunavut (O'Reilly & Eacott, 1998). This is going to require major political renegotiations like those that we have seen being forged between Denmark and Greenland, which have acknowledged Greenland's subsurface property rights. Considering the fact that mining is, by far, the most dynamic private sector in Nunavut, it is therefore interesting to note that this sector has not yet been integrated to any great extent in climate change adaptation strategies at the community level, neither by the researchers nor by the indigenous peoples.

However, Nunavut, specifically, and Canada, more generally, have recently taken steps to address questions of community development that might prove to have an influence on climate change adaptation strategies. By doing so, they are deviating from the predominant trend in the United States, where the main focus is to pursue research into risks and uncertainties related to climate change (Trainor, III, Henry P. Huntington, & Kofinas, 2007, p. 633). The Inuit Action Plan (Inuit Tapiriit Kanatami & Inuit Circumpolar Council [Canada], 2007) is designed to give sustenance to a long-term vision and comprehensive planning, where solutions designed in full partnership with Inuit are implemented. The new partnership established between Canada and Inuit (as established in 2005 in the Partnership Accord between the Inuit of Canada and Her Majesty the Queen in Right of Canada [Inuit Tapiriit Kanatami & Inuit Circumpolar Council (Canada), 2007, pp. 91–95]) calls for a new and more positive relationship between Inuit and the government. The action plan states that even though its success is linked to the ability to use existing structures, the plan will 'research the creation of new or reformed institutions and processes to address Inuit issues be they national or international in nature' (p. 22). It contains a full section (pp. 53–74) on the inclusion of Inuit into foreign policy related to the management of the oceans and coastline. These institutional changes are also reflected in the Aboriginal and Northern Community Action Plan (ANCAP) (Indian and Northern Affairs Canada, 2006), which encourages Inuit organizations, businesses and authorities to apply for funding in order to '[r]eview existing policy and legislation, including land claims and implementation plans, as well as Aboriginal dimensions of international initiatives to identify major policy gaps and options for addressing climate change adaptation' (Indian and Northern Affairs Canada, 2006, p. 3). These initiatives are revisiting the political structures and the cross-scale relations, partnerships and cooperation that are available for communities and important to further development (Folke et al., 2002, p. 21; Keskitalo, 2008, p. 22). Thus, the dominant perspective emphasizing habitual and past patterns of thought and action as well as stakeholder participation and integration is slowly beginning to be replaced by a focus on collective rights-holder possibilities and perspectives, which emphasize projective approaches that address alternative futures. The Arctic Resilience Interim Report (Arctic Council, 2013) is also a step in this direction.

One may approach the new self-government agreed upon by Denmark and Greenland with a similar focus on agency. Self-government provides Greenland with the possibility of taking control over its own affairs, to a considerable extent, and thus supports the unfolding of the second aspect of double agency. However, the premise of the new act is that Greenland should initiate an industrial revolution of a magnitude, the consequences of which are difficult to anticipate. The act – the legal framework for future agency – may in fact limit Greenland and may not provide the tools and means for this industrial revolution and for the societal transformation that the changing climate opens up for. In a more globalized Arctic, the ability to act on the international arena and to attract foreign investments is a necessity for a successful adaptation. Greenland already has competences and political possibilities with respect to foreign policy and these are now formally being integrated into the self-government act. But are they sufficiently far-reaching? For example, the act does not give Greenland much latitude to pursue its own foreign policy on matters related to climate mitigation strategies.

Inuit in Nunavut do not share these international political openings to the same extent and this may in fact limit their adaptations strategies since the international arena and the Arctic as a global geo-political and economic hot spot is going to call for more and more involvement in international negotiations and relations. However, the Inuit Action Plan paves the road for greater involvement in foreign policy affairs and Inuit in Nunavut may thus be standing in a position where they can influence issues of sovereignty and international engagement in the Canadian North. The Arctic Council, where indigenous peoples are permanent participants, also offers a regional circumpolar arena for Inuit to put forward these international concerns, but the policy mandate of the Council is rather limited and, moreover, it is difficult for the Council to fully address and act on the complexities of climate change. A focus on institutional barriers standing in the way of adaptation to climate change could thus also include a revision of the Council.

The two Arctic examples presented in the chapter each evince the difficulties in demarcating the system that agents have to navigate in and adapt to. In Nunavut, the dominant discourse demarcates a system that *shrinks* reality beyond recognition whereas in Greenland, the discourse demarcates a system that *slings* reality in all directions. This is also reflected in the research studies that are being pursued. In Canada, they focus on processes at the community level while in Greenland, they focus on processes on a national level. There is such a wide-spread uneasiness about system demarcation that agency becomes limited in both cases. In both regions, people are facing rapidly emergent futures where 'learning to manage by change' may be a too vague a strategy for creating any latitude for manoeuvring where agents have the ability to navigate, take responsibility and anticipate the future trajectories of life (F. Hastrup, 2011). This chapter's focus on agency also directs our attention to institutions and political structures as potential barriers when pursuing climate change adaptation strategies. What we are going to need, in all likelihood, are total transformations and the rethinking of institutions and systems. When it comes to taking on these challenges, adaptation may prove to be a concept that is too instrumental (Thompson, Robbins, Sohngen, Arvai, & Thompson, 2006, p. 2), a concept that does not adequately accentuate the role of humans as social and cultural engineers.

It appears that the concept of adaptation reduces the full potentials of human agency and creativity and downplays the fact that what is perceived as climate adaptation has to do with making societal choices that are informed by a great variety of concerns and challenges other than climate. The questions in the Arctic revolve around who it is that influences these choices and whether there is sufficient institutional capacity for dealing with entangled and perforated socio-ecological systems that are complex, dynamic and prone to non-linear, uncertain and often abrupt changes. Faced with major contemporary and future changes, it is crucial in climate adaptation strategies to address Arctic peoples' capacity to play a key role in the regional and global dialogues about the kind of development that ought to be taking place in the Circumpolar North (Nuttall, 2001, p. 28). Adaptation strategies being developed now are going to set the framework for future agency. Paying attention to the legal and institutional setup in climate change adaptation strategies and studies is therefore of paramount importance. This attention may also serve to assign priority to a broader perspective and other factors that are presently being downplayed in IPCC.

References

ACIA. (2005). *Arctic Climate Impact Assessment*. Cambridge: Cambridge University Press.

Adger, W. Neil, & Kelly, P. Mick. (1999). Social vulnerability to climate change and the architecture of entitlements. *Mitigation and Adaptation Strategies for Global Change* (4), 253–266.

Adger, W. Neil, Agrawala, Shardul, Mirza, M. Monirul Qader, Conde, Cecilia, O'Brien, Karen, Pulhin, Juan, Pulwarty, Roger, Smit, Barry & Takahashi, Kiyoshi. (2007). Assessment of adaptation practices, options, constraints and capacity. In M. L. Parry, O. F. Canziani, J. P. Palutikof, P. J. v. d. Linden & C. E. Hanson (Eds.), *Climate Change 2007: Impacts, Adaptation and Vulnerability. Contribution of Working Group II to the Fourth Assessment Report of the Intergovernmental Panel on Climate Change* (pp. 717–743). Cambridge: Cambridge University Press.

Anisimov, Oleg, Fitzharris, Blair, Hagen, Jon Ove, Jefferies, Robert, Marchant, Harvey, Nelson, Frederick, Prowse, Terry & Vaughan, David. (2001). Polar regions (Arctic and

Antarctic). In J. J. McCarthy, O. F. Canziani, N. A. Leary, D. J. Dokken & K. S. White (Eds.), *Climate Change 2001: Impacts, Adaptation, and Vulnerability. Working Group II (WGII) Contribution to the Third Assessment Report (TAR) of the Intergovernmental Panel on Climate Change (IPCC)* (pp. 803–841). Cambridge: Cambridge University Press.

Anisimov, Oleg, Vaughan, David, Callaghan, Terry, Furgal, Christopher, Marchant, Harvey, Prowse, Terry, Vilhjálmsson, Hjalmar & Walsh, John. (2007). Polar regions (Arctic and Antarctic). In M. L. Parry, O. F. Canziani, J. P. Palutikof, P. J. v. d. Linden & C. E. Hanson (Eds.), *Climate Change 2007: Impacts, Adaptation and Vulnerability. Contribution of Working Group II to the Fourth Assessment Report of the Intergovernmental Panel on Climate Change* (pp. 653–685). Cambridge: Cambridge University Press.

Arctic Council. (2013). *Arctic Resilience Interim Report 2013*. Stockholm: Stockholm Environment Institute and Stockholm Resilience Centre.

Arctic Human Development Report. (2004). Akureyri: Stefansson Arctic Institute.

Beach, Hugh. (2000). Social and economic aspects of climate change in Arctic regions Retrieved April 16, 2013, from www.thearctic.is/articles/topics/socialecon/enska /index.htm.

Berkes, Fikret. (2001). Cross-scale institutional linkages: Perspectives from the bottom up. In E. Ostrom, T. Dietz, N. Dolsak, P. C. Stern, S. Stonich & E. U. Weber (Eds.), *The Drama of the Commons* (pp. 293–321). Washington D.C.: National Academy Press.

Bertelsen, Kristoffer. (1996). *Our Communalised Future*. Aarhus: Aarhus University (Ph.D. handed in at Dept. of Ethnography and Social Anthropology).

Bravo, Michael. (2009). Voices from the sea ice: The reception of climate impact narratives. *Journal of Historical Geography, 35*(2), 256–278.

Bruce, James P., Lee, Hoesung, & Haites, Erik F. (Eds.). (1995). *Climate Change 1995: Economic and Social Dimensions of Climate Change. Contribution of Working Group III to the Second Assessment of the Intergovernmental Panel on Climate Change.* Cambridge: Cambridge University Press.

Chapin III, F. Stuart, Hoel, Michael, Carpenter, Steven, Lubchenco, Jane, Walker, Brian, Callaghan, Terry, Folke, Carl, Levin, S. A., Mäler, Karl-Goran, Nilsson, Christer, Barrett, Scott, Berkes, Fikret, Crépin, Anne-Sophie, Danell, Kjell, Rosswall, Thomas, Starrett, David, Xepapadeas, Anastasios & Zimov, Sergey A. (2006). Building resilience and adaptation to manage Arctic Change. *Ambio, 33*(4), 198–202.

Dahl, Jens. (1993). *Indigenous Peoples of the Arctic*. Reykjavik: The Nordic Council's Arctic Conference, The Nordic Council.

Emirbayer, Mustafa, & Mische, Ann. (1998). What is agency? *The American Journal of Sociology, 103*(4), 962–1023.

Folke, Carl, Carpenter, Steve, Elmqvist, Thomas, Gunderson, Lance, Holling, C. S., & Walker, Brian. (2002). Resilience and sustainable development: Building adaptive capacity in a world of transformations. *Ambio, 31*(5), 437–440.

Ford, James, & Smit, Barry. (2004). A framework for assessing the vulnerability of communities in the Canadian Arctic to risks associated with climate change. *Arctic, 57*(4), 389–400.

Ford, James, Smit, Barry, Wandel, Johanna, & MacDonald, John. (2006). Vulnerability to climate change in Igloolik, Nunavut: What can we learn from the past and present. *Polar Record, 42*(221), 127–138.

Ford, James, Pearce, Tristian, Smit, Barry, Wandel, Jahanna, Allurut, Mishak, Shappa, Kik, Ittusujurat, Harry & Qrunnut, Kevin. (2007). Reducing vulnerability to climate change in the Arctic: The case of Nunavut, Canada. *Arctic, 60*(2), 150–166.

Ford, James, Smit, Barry, Wandel, Johanna, Allurut, Mishak, Shappa, Kik, Ittusarjuats, Harry, & Qrunnut, Kevin. (2008). Climate change in the Arctic: Current and future vulnerability in two Inuit communities in Canada. *The Geographical Journal, 174*(1), 45–62.

Furgal, Christopher, & Prowse, Terry. (2008). Northern Canada. In D. S. Lemmen, F. J. Warren, J. Lacroix & E. Bush (Eds.), *From Impacts to Adaptation: Canada in a Changing Climate 2007*. Ottawa: Government of Canada.

Garcia-Alix, Lola. (2008). The United Nations Permanent Forum on Indigenous Issues discuss climate change. *Indigenous Affairs* (1–2), 16–23.

Government of Nunavut. (2005a). *Inuit Qaujimajatuqangit of Climate Change in Nunavut 2005. A Sample of Inuit Experiences of Recent Climate and Environmental Changes in Baker Lake and Arviat, Nunavut*. Iqaluit: Government of Nunavut.

Government of Nunavut. (2005b). *Inuit Qaujimajatuqangit of Climate Change in Nunavut 2005. A Sample of Inuit Experiences of Recent Climate and Environmental Changes in Clyde River, Pond Inlet, Resolute Bay, Grise Fiord, Nunavut*. Iqaluit: Government of Nunavut.

Government of Nunavut. (2005c). *Inuit Qaujimajatuqangit of Climate Change in Nunavut 2005. A Sample of Inuit Experiences of Recent Climate and Environmental Changes in Kitikmeot, Nunavut*. Iqaluit: Government of Nunavut.

Government of Nunavut. (2005d). *Inuit Qaujimajatuqangit of Climate Change in Nunavut 2005. A Sample of Inuit Experiences of Recent Climate and Environmental Changes in Pangnirtung and Iqaluit, Nunavut*. Iqaluit: Government of Nunavut.

Handmer, John, Dovers, Stephen, & Downing, Thomas E. (1999). Societal vulnerability to climate change and variability. *Mitigation and Adaptation Strategies for Global Change*, 4(3–4), 267–281.

Hastrup, Frida. (2011). *Weathering the World: Recovery in the Wake of the Tsunami in a Tamil Fishing Village*. New York: Berghahn Books.

Hastrup, Kirsten. (2007). Performing the world: Agency, anticipation and creativity. In E. Hallam & T. Ingold (Eds.), *Creativity and Cultural Improvisation* (pp. 193–206). Oxford: Berg.

Hewitt, Kenneth. (1995). Excluded perspectives in the social construction of disaster. *International Journal of Mass Emergencies and Disasters*, 13(3), 317–319.

Hewitt, Kenneth. (1997). *Regions at Risk: A Geographical Introduction to Disasters*. Essex: Longman.

Holling, C.S., Gunderson, Lance, & Ludwig, Donald. (2002). In quest of a theory of adaptive change. In C. S. Holling & L. H. Gunderson (Eds.), *Panarchy: Understanding Transformations in Human and Natural Systems* (pp. 3–22). Washington: Island Press.

Indian and Northern Affairs Canada. (2006). Aboriginal and Northern Community Action Program (ANCAP). Impacts and Adaptation Funding. Call for Projects 2006–2007. Retrieved April 14, 2013, from www.docstoc.com/docs/104795919/Aboriginal-and-Northern-Community-Action-Program.

Indian and Northern Affairs Canada. (n.d.). *Report on Adaptation to Climate Change Activities in Arctic Canada*. Ottawa: Indian and Northern Affairs Canada. Northern Affairs Program. Environment and Renewable Resources.

Inuit Tapiriit Kanatami. (2007). *ITK Strategic Plan 2007–2009* Ottawa: Inuit Tapiriit Kanatami.

Inuit Tapiriit Kanatami. (2008). *An integrated Arctic strategy*. Ottawa: Inuit Tapiriit Kanatami.

Inuit Tapiriit Kanatami, & Inuit Circumpolar Council (Canada). (2007). *Building Inuit Nunaat. The Inuit Action Plan* Ottawa: Inuit Tapiriit Kanatami.

Keskitalo, E. Carina H. (2008). *Climate Change and Globalization in the Arctic: An Integrated Approach to Vulnerability Assessment*. London and Sterling: Earthscan.

Klein, Richard J.T., Huq, Saleemul, Denton, Fatima, Downing, Thomas E., Richels, Richard G., Robinson, John B., & Toth, Ferenc L. (2007). Inter-relationships between adaptation and mitigation. In M. Perry, O. Canziani, J. Palutikof, P. v. d. Linden & C. Hanson (Eds.), *Climate Change 2007: Impacts, Adaptation and Vulnerability: Contributions of Working Group II to the Fourth Assessment Report of the*

Intergovernmental Panel on Climate Change (pp. 745–777). Cambridge: Cambridge University Press.

Kleman, Ilan. (2008). *Vulnerability and Adaptation to Climate Change in the Arctic (VACCA): An Analysis of the Scoping Study Data. A report prepared for the Sustainable Development Working Group of the Arctic Council.* Oslo: CISERO.

Lebel, Louis, Garden, Po, & Imamura, Masao. (2005). The politics of scale, position, and place in the governance of water resources in the Mekong region. *Ecology and Society, 10*(2), online article no. 18.

Légaré, André. (2008). Canada's experiment with aboriginal self-determination in Nunavut: From vision to illusion. *International Journal on Minority and Group Rights, 15*, 335–367.

Leichenko, Robin M., & O'Brien, Karen. (2008). *Environmental Change and Globalization: Double Exposure.* Oxford: Oxford University Press.

Nielsen, Jens Kaalhauge. (2005). Industrial development. In M. Nuttall (Ed.), *Encyclopedia of the Arctic* (Vol. 2, pp. 966–969). New York & London: Routledge.

Nilsson, Annika E. (2007). *A Changing Arctic Climate: Science and Policy in the Arctic Climate Impact Assessment.* Linköbing: Linköping University, Department of Water and Environmental Studies.

Nilsson, Christina. (2008). Climate change from an indigenous perspective. Key issues and challenges. *Indigenous Affairs* (1–2), 9–15.

Northwest Territories – Environment and Natural Resources. (2008). *NWT Climate Change Impacts and Adaptation Report.* Yellowknife, Northwest Territories: Northwest Territories. Department of Environment and Natural resource.

Nuttall, Mark. (2001). Indigenous peoples and climate change research in the Arctic. *Indigenous Affairs* (4), 27–33.

Nuttall, Mark. (2008a). Climate change and the warming politics of autonomy in Greenland. *Indigenous Affairs* (1–2), 44–51.

Nuttall, Mark. (2008b). Editorial. *Indigenous Affairs* (1–2), 4–7.

Nuttall, Mark. (2009). Living in a world of movement: Human resilience to environmental instability in Greenland. In S. A. Crate & M. Nuttall (Eds.), *Anthropology & Climate Change: From Encounters to Actions* (pp. 292–310). Walnut Creek: Left Coast Press.

Nuttall, Mark, Berkes, Fikret, Forbes, Bruce, Kofinas, Gary, Vlassova, Tatiana, & Wenzel, George. (2005). Hunting, herding, fishing and gathering: Indigenous peoples and renewable resource use in the Arctic. In C. Symon (Ed.), *Arctic Climate Impact Assessment Scientific Report* (pp. 650–690). Cambridge: Cambridge University Press.

O'Brien, Karen, & Leichenko, Robin. (2000). Double exposure: Assessing the impacts of climate change within the context of economic globalization. *Global Environmental Change*(10), 221–232.

O'Reilly, Kevin, & Eacott, Erin. (1998). *Aboriginal Peoples and Impact and Benefit Agreements: Report of a National Workshop.* CARC: Northern Minerals Programme Working Paper 7.

Pelling, Mark, High, Chris, Dearing, John, & Smith, Denis. (2008). Shadow spaces for social learning: A relatial understanding of adaptive capacity to climate change within organisations. *Environment and Planning A, 40*(4), 867–884.

Pielke, Roger, Prins, Gwyn, Rayner, Steve, & Sarewitz, Daniel. (2007). Climate change 2007: Lifting the taboo on adaptation. *Nature* (445), 597–598.

Rasmussen, Rasmus Ole. (1999). Conditions for sustainable development in the Arctic – a general perspective. In H. Petersen & B. Poppel (Eds.), *Dependency, Autonomy, Sustainability in the Arctic* (pp. 217–228). Aldershot: Ashgate.

Rasmussen, Rasmus Ole. (2010). Climate change, the informal economy and generation and gender response to changes. In G. Winther (Ed.), *The Political Economy of Northern Regional Development* (pp. 219–238). Copenhagen: Nordic Council of Ministers (TemaNord 2010:521).

Sejersen, Frank. (2007). Indigenous urbanism revisited – the case of Greenland. *Indigenous Affairs* (3), 26–31.

Smit, Barry, & Wandel, Johanna. (2006). Adaptation, adaptive capacity and vulnerability. *Global Environmental Change, 16*(3), 282–292.

Smit, Barry, Pilifosova, Olga, Burton, I., Challenger, B., Huq, S., Klein, R.J.T., & Yohe, G. (2001). Adaptation to climate change in the context of sustainable development and equity. In J. J. McCarthy, O. F. Canziani, N. A. Leary, D. J. Dokken & K. S. White (Eds.), *Climate Change 2001: Impacts, Adaptation, Vulnerability. Contribution of Working Group II to the Third Assessment Report of the Intergovernmental Panel on Climate Change* (pp. 876–912). Cambridge: Cambridge University Press.

Tauli-Corpuz, Victoria, & Lynge, Aqqaluk. (2008). *Impact of Climate Change Mitigation Measures on Indigenous Peoples and on Their Territories and Lands.* Report E/C.19/2008/10: submitted to the Permanent Forum on Indigenous Peoples, United Nations Economic and Social Council.

Thompson, Alexander, Robbins, Paul, Sohngen, Brent, Arvai, Joseph, & Thompson, Tomas Koontz. (2006). Economy, politics and institutions: From adaptation to adaptive management in climate change. *Climatic Change, 78*(1), 1–5.

Trainor, Sarah F., III, F. Stuart Chapin, Henry P. Huntington, David C. Natcher, & Kofinas, Gary. (2007). Arctic climate impacts: Environmental injustice in Canada and the United States. *Local Environment, 12*(6), 627–643.

United Nations High Commissioner for Human Rights. (2009). *Annual Report of the United Nations High Commissioner for Human Rights and Reports of the Office of the High Commissioner and the Secretary-General.* Report GE.09-10344 (E) 220109: Report of the Office of The United Nations High Commissioner for Human Rights on the relationship between climate change and human rights.

Wenzel, George. (2009). Canadian Inuit subsistence and ecological instability – if the climate changes, must the Inuit? *Polar Research, 28*, 89–99.

Yohe, Gary W., Lasco, Rodel D., Ahmad, Qazi K., Arnell, Nigel, Cohen, Stewart, Hope, Chris, Janetos, Anthony & Perez, Rosa. (2007). Perspectives on climatic change and sustainability. In M. L. Parry, O. F. Canziani, J. P. Palutikof, P. J. v. d. Linden & C. E. Hanson (Eds.), *Climate Change 2007: Impacts, Adaptation and Vulnerability. Contributions of Working Group II to the Fourth Assessment Report of the Intergovernmental Panel on Climate Change* (pp. 811–841). Cambridge: Cambridge University Press.

3 Mega-industrializing Greenland

On a global scale, Greenland has been singled out as the showcase for global climate change and designated as an indicator of the accelerating speed of global warming. What has made this image so strong and compelling is the combination of the presence of the colossal Greenlandic ice sheet, the ever-changing sea ice and the idea of environmentally dependent hunters and fishermen. However, Greenland is also undergoing processes of industrialization that position the country as a new global agent – not only as a producer of important and strategic non-renewable resources like oil, aluminium and rare earth elements, but also as a contributor to the emission of greenhouse gases. Although these industries still face major challenges with respect to extraction, due to the Arctic's environmental conditions, it is a fact that climate change has made the Arctic more accessible.

The presence of large-scale industries in Greenland is not a new phenomenon. Since the beginning of the twentieth century, the Greenlandic fishing industry has formed the commercial backbone of the country and has been *the* economic pillar. Furthermore, there have been several mining projects operating with and without the use of Greenlandic labour (Sejersen, 2014). The contemporary process of industrialization – this could be called the 'second wave of industrialization' – is, however, of a somewhat different nature, speed and extent. One primary difference is that the Greenlanders themselves are driving the processes of industrialization. Moreover, an integrated part of the post-colonial intention has been to become less dependent on economic support from Denmark. The 'second wave of industrialization' therefore has a strong national component and includes a reorganization of society.

This chapter will focus on one of the most significant industrial initiatives that has been on the drawing board: the construction of an aluminium smelting plant. This is but one of many projects currently on the table, but it has gained a lot of attention due to the anticipated consequences for Greenland and its labour market.

The chapter will, on the basis of reports and the public debate, unfold the strategies, the ideas and the concerns related to the construction of the smelter.

The chapter will focus especially on issues related to anticipation and control of knowledge, and lead up to a discussion of the socialization of technology in Chapter 4.

A mega-industry in Greenland – only the beginning

Only a handful of people in Greenland were aware of the fact that an aluminium company had approached the Greenlandic authorities and asked whether it would be possible to construct an aluminium plant. However, in December 2006, the mayors of each of the three West Greenlandic municipalities, Sisimiut, Maniitsoq and Nuuk, received an invitation from the Home Rule government in Nuuk, an invitation that involved their being briefed on a new and yet unknown development project that was on the drawing board. Each one of these three municipalities was struggling, at that time, with its own societal problems related to widespread unemployment, rapid changes in the composition of demography, and economic stagnation. Despite this, these three municipalities are considered some of the more progressive and productive towns in Greenland. In fact, the towns of Nuuk and Sisimiut have, together with the towns of Ilulissat and Qaqortoq, been singled out as being the 'centres of growth' in Greenland, which means to say that these four townships receive the lion's share of the national investments. Being designated 'centres of growth' also entails that the towns are supposed to be 'growth engines' for the benefit of the rest of Greenland. The authorities perceive the town of Maniitsoq as lacking in any development potentials and it is thus a town that has been left outside the cluster of the 'centres of growth'. In Maniitsoq, people have often mentioned to me in the course of our conversations that they feel disregarded and deserted by the authorities. The three towns, whose mayors turned up at the aforementioned meeting, are indeed facing very different kinds of conditions. Nuuk, with its population of 16,000 and its status as the capital city, enjoys certain advantages when compared to the much smaller town of Sisimiut (with 5,000 inhabitants), which is located 320 km north of Nuuk. Sisimiut is, however, an industrious town in the domains of fishing, tourism and education. In between these two towns, and located on an island, we find Maniitsoq, with a population of only 2,600. The city has experienced the cycles of boom and bust within its fisheries and has been seeing a period of steady decline since 2001, when Royal Greenland decided to close down the fish factory that was located in the town.

The mayor of Maniitsoq at that time, Søren Lyberth, told me that the new project that was being introduced to the three mayors at the Nuuk meeting came as a total surprise to him: a welcome, albeit challenging surprise, as he put it. He recalled how one of the participants at that first meeting noticed and subsequently commented, happily, on the expression on the mayor's face at the moment he was informed about the plans to locate a huge aluminium smelter in one of the three towns. The sheer magnitude of the project (in terms of space, time and investment) certainly surpassed anything that Greenland has experienced since the time it was empowered with Home Rule in 1979. For good reasons, it can be termed a mega-project – not only will it influence the specific town close to the location of the smelter – it will also affect the whole of Greenland, inasmuch as it will generate economic development and potentials for people and regions elsewhere in Greenland and will, furthermore, serve to supply a much-needed economic injection to the national economy.

The authorities requested that each of the three towns come up with potential locations for the smelter within less than two months' time, in order for the aluminium company, Alcoa, to consider Greenland as a potential place for their activities.

The aluminium industry

The size and the potentials of the project quickly became apparent to those who were taking part in the Nuuk meeting. The American firm, Alcoa, had approached Greenland in order to investigate whether it would be possible and whether it would be desirable to locate an aluminium smelter on the west coast of Greenland. Alcoa - an acronym for Aluminum Company of America – has, since the time of its establishment in 1888, become one of the world's leading producers of alumina and aluminium, and one of the world's leading miners of bauxite (the raw material needed for aluminium production). It is involved in major aspects of the industry, ranging from mining through fabrication to recycling and has roughly 59,000 employees working in 31 countries (Alcoa, 2010). The company thus has more employees than the number of inhabitants in Greenland, and it is the third largest aluminium industry in the world, surpassed only by Rio Tinto Alcan and Rusal. Alcoa expects the global demand for aluminium to increase by 6,5 per cent annually and expects it to double within 10 years, as a response to increased urbanization, to population growth and to widespread energy and environmental concerns (Alcoa, 2010, p. 3). The market potentials are thus very promising and the aluminium companies are constantly on the lookout for new sites where they can establish production facilities. The aluminium industry is a huge and profitable industry that provides the world with a lightweight and easily malleable metal with a low density and an ability to resist corrosion. These remarkable qualities make aluminium useful in many industries and products, and this type of metal is especially vital within the construction and transportation industries. It is used widely and enters the everyday lives of people all over the world in the form of cans, cars and foils for cooking and storing foods. Additionally, aluminium has another attractive quality: it is easy to recycle.

Aluminium is abundant in the world even though it does not exist, in its pure form, in the environment. It is, in fact, produced from bauxite ore, which is found in high concentrations in Australia, Brazil, Guinea, Jamaica, Ghana, Indonesia, Russia and Surinam. Bauxite ore is deposited in the earth quite close to the surface, and mining is pursued from open pits where soil from large tracts of land is removed by bulldozers and transported to a processing plant where the bauxite is turned into a fine white powder known as alumina, which is the aluminium oxide separated from the iron oxide in bauxite. Although aluminium is the world's most abundant metal on the Earth's crust, in was not until 1825 that the Dane H.C. Ørsted produced an impure sample of aluminium (Emsley, 2001, p. 23); the major challenge is to get the aluminium oxide separated from the iron oxide. Since the moment of Ørsted's breakthrough, the processing carried out through electrolysis has continuously been refined. In 1854, the world's aluminium production was enhanced by the opening of a mine in the southern part of Greenland (Ivigtut and Arksukfiord), where the very rare mineral, cryolite, can be found. Cryolite contains aluminium, but, more importantly, it was used as the major ingredient in the electrolytic processing of bauxite, since it facilitates the process. This mine was closed down in 1987 and stands as a milestone in the history of Greenland, due to its alleged profitability for the Danish mining company. Today, another product has replaced cryolite in the electrolysis. Energy to drive the electrolysis is one of the primary resources needed for the production of aluminium. Therefore, alumina is shipped from the processing plants to smelting plants located at sites where inexpensive energy is available in enormous and reliable quantities. These three requirements of the energy resource (that it be inexpensive, that it be large-scale and that it be reliable) are used for assessing the quality of the site of the smelter. Currently, Iceland, Norway, New Zealand, China, Russia, Ghana, Canada and the Middle East are among the countries that host smelters. Iceland has actually turned aluminium production into one of its major economic activities, and in 2007 its aluminium exports accounted for more than a quarter of its total goods exports in terms of value. In 2008, the value of the nation's aluminium exports exceeded that of its fisheries' products for the first time (Institute of Economic Studies, 2009, p. 13). A profitable aluminium production is accordingly dependent on multiple factors where long-distance transport makes it possible to combine the deposit (mine) with inexpensive energy (smelter). The position of Greenland along the aluminium production chain is the stage before the metal enters the market.

Alcoa approached Greenland as a possible site for a smelter because of its potential and on account of previously unused hydroelectric energy resources that appear to be available in connection with some of the large lakes in West Greenland. The energy supply is of paramount importance because 26 per cent of the total expenditure related to the production of aluminium is energy, which thus becomes a competitive parameter if a country wishes to attract and maintain this kind of industry (Grønlands Hjemmestyre Erhvervsdirektoratet, 2007). In some countries, the aluminium industry has difficulties upholding favourable energy agreements because other industries and private users are willing to pay higher prices (Grønlands Hjemmestyre Erhvervsdirektoratet, 2007, p. 9). Greenland already has some experiences with hydroelectric power plants. Since 1993, Greenland has been trying to comply with the national energy requirements by constructing small-scale hydroelectric facilities close to the larger towns. In 1993, a power plant was constructed in Nuuk; in 2004, one in Tasiilaq (2004); in 2007, one close to Qaqortoq and Narsaq; and in 2010, the town of Sisimiut also got their own plant. In 2013, a hydroelectric power plant was opened in Ilulissat. Now, Greenland will be getting 70 per cent of its energy from hydroelectric power. One more power plant is on the drawing board and is slated to provide energy to Aasiaat and Qasigiannguit (Nukissiorfiit, n.d.). The priority being placed on hydroelectricity is also part of Greenland's strategy to reduce its CO_2 emissions as well as to become more self-sufficient when it comes to energy. Hydroelectric power is thus being used in a variety of ways: to reduce emissions, to strengthen energy independence, and to attract industries. Hydroelectricity indeed offers a potential that Greenland has not fully been able to use until now. However, the resource itself and the way it is being used to further mega-industrialization possess transformative societal consequences insofar as the organization of technology and the people linked to mega-industrialization are both driving the society in new directions.

The socialization of the factory

Seen from the industry's point of view, Greenland stands out as a most suitable prospective site for a smelter. From a Greenlandic point of view, a smelter offers job and tax revenue potentials for a township and for the country as a whole. However, the size of the project will have a potential impact on many aspects of the social and cultural dynamics as well as on the environment. In the following, I will analyze and discuss how the factory has been appropriated, assembled and redefined by different groups within the Greenlandic society. I have chosen to term the dynamics by which technology (in this instance, a smelter) is anticipated as being integrated into society a 'process of socialization'. This 'socialization' of technology is a process of socio-technological becoming, where members of society pursue critical reflection on social dynamics and societal vision triggered by the introduction of technology (this process will be discussed in Chapter 4). From Alcoa's point of view, Greenland could potentially offer stability and a suitable site for a profitable smelter. From a local point of view, the factory could be inscribed in, support and expand the existing social and economic life. The factory thus acts as an interface between two different social systems (and two different systems of practices). For Nuuk, Sisimiut and Maniitsoq, the process presupposed that they would have to re-examine their self-perception and their cultural, social, educational and environmental support for a given industrial project. The towns set out to appropriate the logics of the industrial corporation and reorganized their resources and ambitions in relation to the proposed factory. As I will elaborate later on, in the section in Chapter 5 on place-making, the process of reorganization also set in motion a process of local re-evaluation of place.

The localization of a national factory

Each of the three Greenlandic mayors welcomed the invitation to pursue further research on finding the best site for a smelter in their municipalities. Alcoa set up a number of criteria that a site was supposed to meet: proximity to a town (this was not a mandatory requirement), ice-free harbour facilities (so as to ship in alumina and ship out aluminium), access to fresh water and the possibility of establishing a working camp that could host 2,000 workers in the vicinity of the factory (Grønlands Hjemmestyre Erhvervsdirektoratet, 2007, p. 10). Quickly, all three mayors set up working groups to evaluate whether or not their own municipality could satisfy the criteria. Such a situation of competition was not new to the municipalities. For some time, the three towns had been competing for limited goods in the form of national investments in public facilities and administration – a competition that is very political inasmuch as it relates to the national distribution of benefits. As with many other large-scale projects in Greenland, the central authority positioned itself not only as a facilitator or mediator but also as an organizer of the factory project. In order to take on this role, the government set up a special section named Greenland Development, which it organized as a limited company (Greenland Development A/S). In this way, the project was still in the hands of the government and the government was accordingly able to oversee its progression as well as to regulate policies and economic benefit-sharing on a national scale. From the outset, the project was thus practiced, understood and scaled as being *national* by the Greenlandic authorities.

At the meeting in Nuuk, the authorities informed the mayors about the economic potentials of the project for the respective towns as well as for Greenland on the whole. The task presented at the meeting was for the three towns to go about locating, within circa one and a half months' time, appropriate sites for a smelter and a harbour. It was indeed a mega-project that was as of yet unknown to Greenland and the assignment that had been put before the three mayors required that they approach their social and natural environment with new eyes. Locally, in Maniitsoq, the working group that was assigned to come up with potential sites chose to approach the project by stipulating seven factors that were constructed on the basis of the initial requirements (Maniitsoq kommune, 2007, p. 2). First and foremost (factors 1 and 7), they suggested that the site of the factory be situated close to the hydroelectric power plant and that developing the site ought to be inexpensive; these factors can, of course, appear to be lucrative for the company but they also gave Maniitsoq an edge over the two other towns. Second in importance (factors 4, 5 and 6), the site should be easily accessible the whole year round (requirements related to the harbour and the airport, etc.) and finally (factors 2 and 3), the site should be in the vicinity of the town of Maniitsoq in order to create road infrastructure so as to facilitate the convenient and easy mobility of the workers. These seven factors defined by the municipality added a particular social dimension to the project. It is especially the insistence on locating the factory close to the town of Maniitsoq that can be regarded as a means of giving the project a social dynamic that is very different from mine camps and industrial enclaves, where the sites are often located far away from the communities. Maniitsoq municipality wanted to set up a dynamic interaction between the factory and the town; this is something that people in Maniitsoq stressed continuously to me during interviews. The interaction is elaborated in the municipality's report, where it is expected to result in the following: (1) a more socially and culturally well-functioning family life for the labour force (as compared to the more artificial and seasonal 'camp' lives lived at some other project sites); (2) an interface that will provide work and educational potentials for other family members; (3) a possibility of attracting and maintaining the necessary labour force whose members often have requirements and expectations that cannot be met in working camps; (4) the reduction of the costs of construction, if the existing infrastructure could be put to use; and (5) mobility of the labour force, facilitated by a road, would result in stability, as compared to a site located far away from the town (Maniitsoq kommune, 2007, p. 4). From the very outset, Maniitsoq thus seized hold of the project and socialized it into a project of its own – as much as it was possible to do so.

Part of the towns' reorganization of resources and ambitions was relational in nature. In order to appear attractive and progressive, each municipality did much to promote itself, to portray their town as an urban centre and as a dynamic place of the future – as a proper site for investment. They all tried creatively to establish a vision, to anticipate a story or a line of future development. By doing so, they brought 'the unprecedented into effect by way of imaginative power and thus expand[ed] the community's awareness of itself' (Hastrup, 2007, p. 200). Special emphasis was placed on how to link local possibilities – physical as well as cultural – to global requirements and national benefits. The socialization of the factory was linked closely to self-awareness building, to the anticipation of national dynamics and to the positioning of the nation in a global economy. In this new and budding perspective, an uninhabited stretch of coastline emerged as a harbour front for large-scale shipping operations and a far-away plateau turned into an area for the location of a factory. In three leading newspaper articles, the mayor of each municipality presented his or her own case, and each of them inscribed the envisioned factory into spaces of rationality and anticipation. The mayor from Maniitsoq (Lyberth, 2007) actually stressed the reasonability of giving his own particular community this chance for development. This argument thus framed the Alcoa project within what was primarily a nation-wide political management and resource distribution discourse, emphasizing that it was now his own municipality's turn to get some political attention, in order to climb out from economic dead waters. The mayor of Sisimiut (Berthelsen, 2007), on the other hand, pointed toward the self-perceived dynamic, innovative, self-confident 'can-do' culture that is thriving in his town as well as to his town's potential to attract and to hold workers and their families, as a consequence of the number of recreational attractions. This mayor insisted on making a conjunction of the existing successes of his town with the potential success of the project. Nuuk's mayor (Davidsen, 2007) adopted a meta-perspective, which combined the local, national and global perspective in such a way that Nuuk's position and potentials appeared very clearly. While arguing on behalf of Nuuk, she simultaneously pointed out that the project should benefit the whole of Greenland, as it is engaged in a global economy. She would be content if Greenland could host the smelter no matter where it might be located. That was indeed the privileged perspective of the capital.

Alcoa evaluated the multiple sites proposed by the municipalities (Maniitsoq kommune, 2007; Nuup Kommunea, 2007; Sisimiut kommune, 2007) and one year later, in the spring of 2008, the decision that the smelter would be located in Maniitsoq was handed down. Immediately, the announcement resulted in a public outbreak of joy in the town, where people drove around in cars, tooting their horns. In my interviews with Maniitsormiut (the people from Maniitsoq), they recall this day as a new beginning for the town which has been burdened for so very long with decreasing job opportunities and difficulties in attracting and maintaining qualified workers.

All three mayors linked development in general terms with town-development and increased centralization. They thus anticipated that the urban processes would be playing a significant role in the transformation and demographic reorganization of society. This reorganization may result in an uneven geographical distribution of economic benefits in Greenland, inasmuch as people living in areas considered marginal are going to be receiving less economic and political attention. The Alcoa process is interesting because it reflects a split position of urban governance in Greenland: between the managerial approach pursued since the 1950s (see e.g. Adolphsen & Greiffenberg, 1998) and a more recent entrepreneurial one. The latter is based on each of the towns' promotion of itself, in competition with the other towns, in order to attract externally financed projects. Under the managerial approach (Harvey, 1989), the competition was taking place within a national financial arena where the Greenland authorities would make a choice that could be inscribed within a broader national political management strategy. For decades (at least, since 1950), urban development plans in Greenland have been positioned in relation to national development and have had to be evaluated on the basis of local and regional benefits but also with respect to their contributions to more comprehensive national strategies. The aluminium project was indeed an example of bureaucratic managerialism combined with an entrepreneurial approach. The Alcoa request also shows how capitalist interests of this magnitude stimulate a redefinition, a re-configuration and a re-scaling of both the towns and the landscapes (see also Chapter 5).

The assemblage of a project

From the beginning, the socialization of the factory was a process driven by factory deconstruction and reconstruction, mediated by anticipated directions of national development. Reports, hearings and public discussions can be understood as links in a process of project-assemblage, where recurrent activities of project deconstruction and reconstruction were being pursued for purposes of establishing creative relations between the existing conditions and the anticipated consequences.

The physical, economic and social magnitude of the project quickly became apparent. An aluminium smelter is approximately 1.5 km long and needs close access to a harbour at least 16 m deep, to the steady supply of energy, and to the labour force (Maniitsoq kommune, 2007). Initially, three large lake systems were designated as the potential sites for hydroelectric power plants which could provide the necessary 600–750 MW: Tasersiaq, Sondre Isortup Isua and

Imarsuup Isua. Long-distance electric transmission cables from the lakes to the factory needed to be set up, since these lake systems are situated far away from Maniitsoq. Already during the initial period of investigation, it quickly came to light that the costs of construction at Sondre Isortup Isua would be too high and no more consideration was given to this lake system as a potential site for the project (Departementet for Erhverv, 2008, p. 18). Furthermore, in order to house the approximately 600 factory workers, the infrastructure in Maniitsoq would have to be expanded and renovated on a large-scale. What they decided to do in Maniitsoq was plan for the construction of a new section of town and for an 11-km-long road leading to the factory. According to a Danish newspaper, this was going to be one of the biggest private-sector investment projects in the history of Denmark (Andersen, 2011).

During my fieldwork in Maniitsoq, it quickly became apparent that people were concentrating their focus on certain elements and aspects of the project and making these relevant to their vision of the town and of Greenland as such. Thus, in order to demarcate and apprehend the project, people singled out local-izable project aspects and creatively constructed a factory narrative from these. Analytically, I understand such project aspects as *sites of activity*, which were joined together in order to function as a totality and as an integrated system of flow. Through an act of *compartmentalization*, these sites were tailored – and carved out. From these pieces, a total project could be imagined and assembled. The primary sites of activities being carved out were: the factory, the working camp, the harbour, the electric cable transmission system, the hydroelectric power plants, the new road and the new town. Some *sites of activity* were put in the foreground while others were left in the shadows, so to speak. In this way, people in Maniitsoq were able to navigate a highly complex project and creatively construct desirable narratives based on a variety of different project-assemblages.

When the authorities launched several studies related to demarcated areas, the focus was aimed on what could be termed *sites of concern*: environment, health, culture, economy, society, educational system and the labour market. The act of compartmentalization continued. A complex and living project was thus decon-structed into formalized, controllable and manageable components that could be synthesized and cumulated in different ways in order to apprehend the project in new totalities. The primary driver of this assemblage-process was the initiation of a large-scale Strategic Environmental Assessment (SEA), which was set in motion in 2007, having been initiated by the government. The SEA included the scientific investigation of prescribed sites of concern as well as a number of public hearings (Hansen, 2010). An SEA is not only to be seen as a tool for policy makers to understand projects but also as a creative way of assembling projects and socializing them.

As will be seen in this chapter, my interviews, the reports and public discus-sions reflect that people made use of certain common concepts in order to relate to the project. These concepts were not only directly related to what I term *sites of activities* and *sites of concern* but also added a temporal dimension to the pro-ject by constructing it in distinctive phases. These temporal distinctions, which can be termed as acts of compartmentalization, not only highlight temporality but also mark socio-economic challenges and possibilities. I term these temporal compartmentalizations *sites of phases*. The mega-project was deconstructed, during conversations and in reports, into demarcated phases (hearing/assessment, negotiation, construction and operation), where each phase fashioned a temporal conjunction of issues related to sites of activities and sites of concerns. Of special interest was especially the number of foreign workers required for the *construction* phase and the direct and indirect employment possibilities for Greenlanders during the *operational* phase. Compartmentalization, in the form of demarcating sites of activities, concerns and phases, has become a crucial aspect in controlling the process and the factory's stories. These devices are politically saturated and are employed strategically. One issue in particular was central and emerged from a discussion that was centred on sites of phases: for each phase of the project, Alcoa wanted to introduce different conditions for workers. This request came as a surprise – this is clear to see when we look back at a report made to the Parliament in 2007 (Grønlands Hjemmestyre Erhvervsdirektoratet, 2007), where the following framework was presented (on p. 26): the salaries and working rights of foreign workers engaged in the construction phase were to be regulated by agreements applicable to the Greenlandic labour market rather than by 'international salaries', as it was termed. Seeing as the foreign workers were expected to be Chinese, primarily, 'international salary', in this context, could be taken to be synonymous with wages that are substantially lower than the minimum wage offered in Greenland. Later on, however, this issue of wages nearly became a deal-breaker because Alcoa insisted on reducing the costs of construction substantially by paying 'international salaries'. In order to appear internationally competitive for mega-industries, it was, later on, in 2011, eventually accepted by the Greenlandic authorities that Alcoa – during the *construction* phase – should have the possibility of employing workers on contracts that had not yet been seen in the Greenlandic labour market, while the wages during the *operational* phase were supposed to follow Greenlandic standards. The demarcation of these sites of attention (concerns, activities and phases) thus also opens up for the construction of different subjects being given different rights and obligations. Furthermore, each site of attention positions the factory in different networks and landscapes.

In fact, more than 50 reports have been used to assemble the factory project, since 2007. People had to relate to a large and continuously expanding paper world. The SEA, as well as other assessments and reports, are major and official devices that have been set in motion in order to *model* and *engineer* not only projects but also the anticipated futures. The creative process of modelling and engineering a project – and thus the basic political aspects of the endeavour, became an issue during the SEA, where questions of representation and positioning were raised. As soon as these questions were raised, the whole project as an engineering process was put into focus. The question of representation was raised in several ways. Implementing an SEA posed a new challenge for the Greenlandic authorities, and they lacked the experience and the juridical background needed to undertake it. However, due to both the scale of the project and the precedent to which it may give rise, Alcoa and the Environmental Department of the Home Rule paid for a Ph.D. project (Hansen, 2010) that would follow and analyze the SEA process. This study points at several positive results of the SEA process and particularly emphasizes the increased awareness related to, for example, the stakeholders' understanding of the matter, the quality of existing environmental knowledge and the procedural and institutional limitations and possibilities. However, the study stops short of concluding that the actual Social and Environmental Assessment was taken into consideration during the political decision-making process, and notes that the decisions about the project and the location appear to have been made beforehand. The problems raised in the SEA were also critically addressed by anthropologist Mark Nuttall (2008, p. 50):

> In Greenland, the SEA for the aluminum smelter has identified areas of considerable concern with respect to the Alcoa proposal. In doing so, it has revealed that Greenland's regulatory review process, environmental impact assessment procedures, mechanisms for considering cumulative impacts and public hearings process lag far behind some of its circumpolar neighbors, and that Greenland is ignorant of processes that have shaped historical patterns of resource use and socioeconomic development elsewhere in the indigenous world.

The SEA, which should have served, in itself, to render the project process transparent, whirled up a number of other issues that threw light on some broader issues related to societal development, the inclusion of civil society and governmental structures. In a provocative manner, the Greenlandic intellectual and former politician, Finn Lynge (2010, pp. 8–9), put forward the following comments based on the experiences gleaned from the SEA and other processes related to large-scale industrial projects in Greenland:

> The public cannot help being confused. Even if the environmental department is given more personnel and an increased range of responsibilities, an important part of the public will still be at a loss about what to make of it all. At the same time, the situation is bedevilled by a further conundrum, a burden of oddly adverse tradition. The fact of the matter is that large segments of the Greenland population do not see the need for any kind of increased rule-setting in environmental matters at all. They have always been users of nature, and many resent what they experience as uncalled-for meddling on the part of outside specialists in matters of hunting and fishing. The pre-cautionary principle is not a part of Inuit tradition, and restrictive measures are not the most popular part of modern-day rule-setting.

Hansen, Nuttall and Lynge all point to concrete problems related to the specific process but, moreover, they expose some wider public concerns that may emerge when Greenland enters into large-scale industrial projects. What their comments may reflect is that Greenland is entering into a very new landscape of risk and decisions, which require a new public awareness, new governmental procedures and structures and also a particular global view. Presently, it is 'much learning by doing' – and is often 'two steps behind', as one involved bureaucrat expressed to me – because a project the size of the aluminium smelter has never been experienced in Greenland before. An SEA or an Environmental Impact Assessment (EIA) requires much more than merely assessing projects, as if such a report were nothing more than an act of knowledge gathering and coordination. These assessments can be understood as political devices for assembling projects and for mobilising anticipation. Two major questions, then, are: 'How do people and institutions anticipate the future?' and 'How do they organise socially in relation to these anticipated futures in a new landscape that is well suited to mega-projects?'

Anticipating a future project world

While it was still on the drawing board, people were busy trying to envision the aluminium project in different ways. It is one thing to comprehend the impacts of a given 'site of activity' (e.g. the costs, the impacts and the potentials of a road leading from the town to the factory); it is another to envision the totality of the project. In order to furnish a wider understanding and to aid in decision-making, different devices for advancing imagination were mobilized: assessments, reports, hearings, radio discussions, trips to other aluminium smelters (in Iceland), homepages, lectures, pamphlets, maps and graphics, photos, posters, workshops, meetings, etc. To put it simply, these activities can be understood as ways of 'getting around' the project as much as possible, and of engaging with – as well as informing – the public. It is within these activities that the project is assembled, envisioned and represented. It is through these channels of communication, scenarios and sources of ideas and information that the project is evoked, shaped and understood; in short, this is where it comes into being. In order to strengthen imagination and anticipation, the project was rendered as concretely as possible. The potential future of Greenland was creatively given a life in distinctive locations, for example. Certain Icelandic factory sites, especially, became places from which Greenlanders mirrored their ambitions of development. Several delegations of local representatives, politicians and project leaders travelled to Iceland in order to visit existing smelters, to witness what was there and to 'see it with our own eyes', as it was often explained to me. Icelandic communities with aluminium smelters were used to evoke representations of potential Greenlandic futures and the visiting delegations were creating, so to speak, *proxy-futures.* The Icelandic factory – the proxy – is not, in itself, of any great interest (you would not want to work there or to invest in the factory and you would not exactly campaign against it) but it happens to be a place from where you can obtain and test out variables. The proxy variable becomes powerful when it is understood as having a close correlation with the inferred value – the Greenland condition. Throughout the course of repeated visits to Iceland, the smelters were used as proxies for an analogous Greenlandic factory and thus employed to indicate a potential future.

I have chosen to use the term 'proxy-future' in order to differentiate it from the more common approach of conceptualising 'scenario-making' which was used intensively. The latter is primarily a way of establishing a dialogue among agents concerning a given situation based on a platform in which new strategies are tested in order to inform decision-makers about potentialities in situations of uncertainty and complexity. 'Scenarios' signify attempts at grasping the risks, the challenges and the potentialities of various imagined futures with the intention of informing strategic decision-making. Therefore, scenarios are different from visions and projections, where visions signify formulations of wished/feared futures and projections signify some anticipated future that is based on existing conditions. The creation of a proxy-future is a more powerful construction, which combines scenario, vision and projection. This construction can be linked directly to life lived and used for social and political mobilization lying along a particular line of an anticipated future. The future is proxy because it is presented and understood as real and as being lived out by a proxy. Proxy-futures are powerful movers of opinion and social energy, and thus can be regarded as politically interesting trading zones that can be entered and as political important implements that can be controlled. The *potentialities* of a factory are turned into *real* futures by the means of proxy-futures. The productive strength of a constructed proxy-future is that it appears to be grounded. It ties the temporal moments of knowledge-making, decision-making and implementation very tightly together, in such a way that the future becomes a temporal location that 'speaks to' the present. This causes it to be different from scenarios, visions and projections. A wish or a concern can, through the mobilization of proxy-futures, appear to be grounded and its imagined and figurative character can be bypassed.

A proxy-future, in this case, is a juxtaposition of the wanted and the expected, framed in the form of something that is realizable: a transfiguration of the wanted into the world where it becomes a significant part of the reality to which one relates, and towards which one navigates. Proxy-futures can, in a different way, also be evoked in reports, where futures are designed and given their own life by means of repetition and probability assessments. More than 50 reports about the aluminium smelter have been made available to the public and political decision-makers. It is within this matrix of reports that an image of the future appears and stands out clearly and controllable. Where the life around the Icelandic aluminium smelters is used in connection with proxy-futures, the proxy-futures emerging from such reports are more subtle and indirectly rendered, inasmuch as they take on the character of laboratory simulations.

The project has been analyzed, criticized, evaluated and adjusted to such an extent in the numerous reports that, in many people's minds (and this is very often presented as such by Greenland Development A/S), what we have here is a matter of fine-tuning, improvements and corrections. The project appears as not only a scenario, a projection, a vision or a prophecy but as a reality that is right at hand. The project has been given, so to speak, a test-run in the reports (which can be understood as a controlled laboratory setting) and by means of this simulation, the reports cumulatively come to constitute a proxy-future. The evocation of a proxy-future makes the future project appear real and it simply becomes a matter of a few pieces that have to be looked into a bit more closely and have to be fixed before the project can be launched. On June 10, 2011, Greenland Development A/S announced, at a public meeting held in Maniitsoq, that while it normally takes 5 to 15 years to develop such a comprehensive project, the process, in this case, has unfolded very quickly. Greenland Development A/S has continuously been able to provide status reports and to point at factors that facilitated progression. Due to the rapid process, to the many reports and to the control exerted by Greenland Development A/S, the project details have been highly compressed and the factory has been configured as being in a state of continuous progress – its existence-to-be is thus taken as a given and the reports have naturalized the 'taken for granted'. By visiting Iceland (the proxy), one can see what the future may look like. But also, this proxy-future emerges sheerly by reading the reports, because the projected smelter is nearly up and running in the report – the laboratory and all the potential hindrances have already been examined. At the meeting on June 10, 2011, Greenland Development A/S, for example, assured the public that 'the consequences on society have been well looked into' (Greenland Development A/S, 2011, translation by the author), as if everything were ready and under control. The reports are used as 'rationality badges', in the words of Clarke (1999), which signifies a practice where documents are used as statements to the public, telling the people that things are under control. The reports construct proxy-futures that are difficult to argue against because it is impossible to argue against the presence of smelters in Iceland (because they are already there!). The cautious use of terminology related to uncertainty, likelihood and probability and thus the acceptance of open future storylines come, in proxy-futures, to be exchanged with terminology related to certainty and assurance. Acts of imagining the future or investigating representations of it are thus resulting, in some cases, in a process of bypassing the fact that the projections and anticipations are figurations and nothing more. However, anticipatory knowledge represented as a proxy-future turns our imagination in controlled and limited directions.

Coordinating anticipated futures

In the case of Greenland, the evocation of a proxy-future is now in the hands of few people who can set the discourse. To facilitate the difficult process of project appropriation, the Home Rule set up a company in 2006 that was named Greenland Development A/S. It concentrates fully on the aluminium smelter and is dedicated to coordinating activities related to getting the plant to Greenland. This includes requesting and producing feasibility studies, conducting analyses of requirements and supervising project preparations. Members of Greenland Development A/S have played a significant role – through its homepage, lectures, meetings, interviews, articles, reports and briefings as well as by coordinating visits to Iceland – in informing the public and the politicians about the smelter and its expected impacts. The company is thus a major producer and coordinator of the anticipated future that people are supposed to use as a reference point for how 'the good life' can evolve and what this requires. Given such a task, the company is standing in the eye of the storm, since it has to facilitate negotiations with the aluminium company, disseminate information and hold hearing campaigns for the public, while providing background materials to the policy makers. To strengthen this work, its main office in Nuuk has been expanded to include an office in Maniitsoq, which has been set up for purposes of facilitating local discussions and responding to questions that are put forth locally.

The pivotal position of Greenland Development A/S has continuously been an issue. My own conversations with ardent advocates of the smelter reveal that they are pleased with the information that is being made available to them by Greenland Development A/S as well as with the support they get when asking for it. However, some of these advocates also air concerns about the dominant role that Greenland Development A/S plays, because they feel that the company does not fully represent alternative voices. It is not the intention here to analyze whether this is true or not, and even a cursory perusal of the material that is being made available by Greenland Development A/S indicates openings of alternative and even critical storylines. However, what might be relevant here is that some people (even some who advocate for the establishment of the smelter) feel that the centralized facilitation of the project through only one organization (company) reduces the *sense* of diversity of concerns and potentials. In their eyes, Greenland Development A/S produces *one* storyline – one proxy-future – and this makes these critics feel uncomfortable even though they might otherwise be supportive of the project. Other more critical views concerning Greenland Development A/S are being voiced and they are centred primarily on the direct control and dominance of the company in setting the discourse. In one newspaper article published in Sermitsiaq, political activist Sara Olsvig raised her concerns about Greenland Development A/S in the following way: 'My best personal judgement is that there is a clear conflict of interest when Greenland Development A/S, on the one hand, has to inform the public without being biased and, on the other hand, has to sell the country to the big multinational companies' (Olsvig, 2010, translated by the author). There is a delicate balance that has to be mastered here and Greenland Development A/S is compelled to navigate in a political minefield and has to run the risk of being accused of controlling the process as well as the flow of information. Another risk is that the company formulates *one* proxy-future, and by doing so, diminishes the voices, the concerns and the desires that are being raised by the public.

The questions here are not whether or not Greenland Development A/S controls the process, or whether or not it bends the reports in order to furnish and maintain a special discourse in order to get the project accepted and up and running; that would require another study. The issue here is that people are trying to imagine a future not only for Maniitsoq and the communities in Greenland; their concern also has to be understood as a concern with a future for Greenland as a more self-sustaining nation. In Maniitsoq, people are trying to imagine how it would be to have a smelter as a neighbour or as a working place, while in other communities other people are trying to imagine what it is going to mean to have Maniitsoq as the new national centre of economic activity. Meanwhile, everyone is trying to understand the significance of this change for the Greenlandic economy as such. Very diverse anticipations are being put into play and they all have to be appreciated and communicated by the one and same company, which is dedicated to the project and eagerly promoting it. The power and potential of constructing a proxy-future are closely linked to the producer and its communication. Trust-making becomes an essential requirement for the viability of a proxy-future and a lot of the criticism aimed at Greenland Development A/S has actually concentrated on the issue of trust rather than on the data and projections presented in reports presented by the company. Similarly, supporters of the aluminium project often make references to trust by stressing how one can rely on the reports, thereby underlining that the reports' anticipated future is at hand.

Greenland Development A/S has formulated, financed and obtained reports concerning the aluminium project's requirements and impacts (e.g. environmental, financial, economical and educational). The sheer number of reports is overwhelming, both in their detail, their complexity and their extent, which reflects an unprecedented analytical prioritization in Greenland. The reports have cumulatively given rise to a strong sense of *project direction* and *control*. As will be seen later in the chapter, the smelter was evoked in reports in such a way that the smelter and its positive effects on Maniitsoq and Greenland can increasingly be perceived as already having been investigated and already having been brought under control; the question becomes one of simply getting things right, of closing gaps of uncertainty and of getting things rolling in the right sequence. This is not the result of the individual reports, but rather of the way Greenland Development A/S has positioned itself and has been positioned by the government in the discourse as the primary and predominant storyteller of an anticipated future based on the enormous corpus of reports, which can be difficult for the public to approach, comprehend and question. During a coffee break at one conference, a centrally placed Greenland negotiator directed my attention to the power of these reports by stating that decisions in Greenland are no longer taken on the basis of hearsay or on feelings: 'Today, society thinks itself through reports', he assured me. This being the case, the life and trails of reports become of paramount importance when it comes to public anticipation, imagination and planning. This paper world can be seen both as paradigmatic of modern knowledge practices but also as an ethnographic world where agents creatively form, negotiate and manipulate anticipations through the construction of the particular project (Riles, 2006).

In the following, the project will be described in detail. The description will be based on the reports that are sequenced here, more or less, in chronological order. This approach allows the emergence of the project itself to appear, through the presentation of the documents and reports as ethnographic artefacts. It is thus never a complete project but a project in the making and a project that is constantly undergoing change albeit not without a sense of direction. By following the trails of the reports, it ought to be possible, also, to see the social life of the project and to see how the project is scaled and assembled in various ways. The analysis of the documents makes use of the focus on sites of activities, sites of concern and sites of phases as organizing devices.

The life and trails of reports

From the very beginning, reports have been a part of the process – perhaps one of the most important parts when it comes to reflecting activity, progress and momentum. Throughout the year 2006, negotiations with Alcoa proceeded and as the Home Rule gained more awareness of the potentials as well as the potential impacts, the government initiated an environmental investigation. In February 2007, Nuuk, Sisimiut and Maniitsoq each handed in their respective reports suggesting sites for smelters that would comply with the requirements of Alcoa. In order to trigger, encircle and support the project development, a flow of documents and reports was set in motion. It is the development and the contents of these publications that will be used here as the backbone for a presentation of the project itself and of the changes in focus and concerns that have appeared over time. These changes in focus not only illustrate the social life of a project but also its perforated nature and the inherent difficulties associated with apprehending a project of this size. Furthermore, the flow of reports also shows how the project is being evoked and how contours increasingly come to be accepted. In the following presentation and analysis, I will make use of publically available documents, because they are also decisive in forming the public opinion and political discourse.

The documents can roughly be divided into three categories: documents linked to the SEA; reports and documents produced by the authorities and by consultant firms; and, finally, white papers and parliamentary papers. My work with these documents has been expanded by exploratory interviews with the producers and the users of the reports. As an upshot of the centralized process, nearly all of these documents have been available on the homepage of Greenland Development A/S. This strong emphasis on data gathering and on the production of projections marks a paradigm shift in Greenland politics. This is reflected, among other places, in the perception that concerns are best dealt with either by making references to reports or by arguing for more investigation – i.e. 'we need more comprehensive investigations before we take the final decision' – see e.g. the press release by Juliane Henningsen (2011). Some of the reports were produced in dialogue with communities and organizations; this was primarily the case with the SEA reports, where public hearings were an inherent requirement. During interviews made in Maniitsoq, people singled out these kinds of meetings as some of the primary places where coherent information about the project was made available to them. However, the involvement of the civil society as co-producers of reports was truly rare.

Before the environmental assessments were initiated, the Home Rule requested an overview report from the National Environmental Research Institute DMU (Johansen, Asmund, & Aastrup, 2007) that was supposed to outline and pinpoint some of the critical environmental issues that ought to be taken into account when pursuing an SEA and when discussing the smelter and the hydroelectric project.

The overview report was then used as a point of reference for a working group that was set up by the government (Arbejdsgruppen vedrørende Infrastruktur-, Miljø- og Naturforhold). The task of the working group was to identify and unfold the different areas of concern and uncertainties that needed to be investigated and the legislative requirements needed in order for the government, the parliament and the public to understand and discuss the effects and implementation of the project in relation to issues of environment, health and cultural heritage. The working group prepared a report (Arbejdsgruppen for Infrastruktur Miljø og Natur, 2007) that recommended – among other things – making an SEA and also pointed out that the project would – independently of location – make a large impact on regional dynamics as well as on the overall balance in Greenland, both in the short and the long term (p. 20). Furthermore, the report stressed that the authorities should approach the project from a holistic societal perspective and that they would need to look into the global issue of CO_2 emission, because the smelter would nearly double the emissions of Greenland (p. 31). The working group also called attention to the legislative requirements that would be necessary in connection with handling such a large-scale industrial project. The report was one of three reports that were handed in by parliamentary working groups in order to approach the project in all its complexity. Another working group looked into the labour market and occupational development (Arbejdsgruppen for Arbejdsmarkeds- og Erhvervsudvikling, 2007), and finally, a report was produced to pinpoint economic investments, benefits and ownership models (Arbejdsgruppen for Samfundsøkonomi, 2007).

These three reports eventually came to fashion the background for another overview document, which was presented to the Parliament in the spring 2007 (Grønlands Hjemmestyre Erhvervsdirektoratet, 2007), in which it was stated, among other things, that the project may require a change in lifestyle and a readjustment of the educational system (p. 29). At the bi-annual gathering in the Parliament, it was resolved that an SEA be pursued, an assessment that was finalized and sent into public hearing in December 2007. This was a comprehensive report (Grønlands Hjemmestyres SMV arbejdsgruppe, 2007) that focused primarily on environmental and health issues; the production of the report involved public meetings in Sisimiut, Maniitsoq and Nuuk (for an elaborate discussion of the SEA please consult Hansen, 2010). In November of that same year, NIRAS, a consultancy firm, had tabulated some initial estimates of the needed labour force capacity and put forward suggestions for how to meet those requirements (NIRAS, 2007). The latter included several ways to increase the available labour force: by reforming the fisheries (e.g. reducing the number of fishermen); by reducing the subsidies offered to different occupations (thus forcing people to find new jobs); by granting fewer people early retirement benefits (p. 11); and by withholding public investments – for example, in the construction sector situated outside the site of the smelter (p. 13). The report was also quite explicit about the difficult and unpopular decisions that had to be taken (p. 14) and about the centralization of the population that might eventually be one of the consequences of the project (p. 16).

Among the figures presented were also the expected investments, which were computed as amounting to more than 1.5 times the size of Greenland's GDP, as well as the positive secondary employment possibilities, estimated as being 1.7 (which means for every 100 persons employed at the factory, there are 70 persons who will find employment elsewhere). The 115-page report was the first attempt to make qualified estimations of the societal consequences and the requirements of the project. In these initial reports, the extent of the project, its requirements and it impacts are thus elaborated quite clearly, and the factory was scaled in a way to make it emerge as a national project.

The ability to attract the needed Greenlandic labour force to serve the factory was understood as being dependent upon the willingness, the understanding and the perception of Greenlanders. For this very reason, the firm, HS Analyse, conducted a public analysis of the knowledge and attitudes in Greenland with respect to the aluminium smelter in 2007 (HS Analyse, 2008) and this firm has continued to do so every year in order to monitor the progressive trends in the public's attitudes. Later on, in December, the Danish embassy (Danmarks Ambassade Danmarks Eksportråd) handed in a comparative analysis of the rules, requirements and benefits from similar industries in Iceland, Canada and Norway (Danmarks Ambassade Danmarks Eksportråd, 2007). This empowered the parliament with a better understanding of the aluminium industry – an insight that, earlier on, had already been analyzed with respect to Iceland in the NIRAS report (2007). Furthermore, a report on four different ownership models and associated economic risks was prepared (CRU Strategies, 2007).

Hence, within the time-span of only one year, several institutions, companies and the public were set in motion to comprehend the extent and complexities of the project and also to initiate public and political discussions. Reports from working groups, consultancy firms (NIRAS, HS-Analyse, CRU Strategies), institutions (Eksportrådet), scientific institutions, stakeholders (municipalities) and public hearing processes (SEA) constitute an impressive collection of background material, recommendations, questions that could be investigated further and tough decisions that had to be made. In the years to follow, this bulk of reports came to lay the foundation for the discourse. Due, perhaps, to the initial and exploratory status of the reports, in which many questions were raised, many of the complexities and risks were unfolded at an early phase. Cumulatively, the initial reports point toward sites of concern and toward the new risk landscape that Greenland was about to enter. An aluminium smelter would inscribe Greenland as a new production site in a globalized metal industry and the reports point at the transformative societal consequences this may have on the mobility and settlement patterns, the educational requirements, the public investments and subsidy policies, the landscape use and the economic benefits throughout the whole of Greenland. Without a doubt, the reports draw the contours of a project that will transform the Greenlandic society and that will require continuous attention and adjustment of policies. The reports make it apparent that the project was understood as a national project, which would underpin the development of Greenland, and that the project was going to require large-scale reforms in the whole of Greenland.

In the wake of the SEA, there was a need that emerged to look more thoroughly into regional development and the social and economic impacts of the project. In January 2008, the Department of Environment hosted a conference where international researchers addressed the issues that were based on case studies from elsewhere in the North. The SEA process itself generated a parallel and integrated track within the flow of the projects, where issues related to environment, health, heritage and regional development were positioned in the forefront. It was a much more localized discourse than the national discourse that had emerged from the initial reports. After no more than approximately one year of research, hearings and meetings, the factory project emerged as a whole, where potentials, risks and challenges were increasingly brought together. This is apparent in the 'Decision paper for the establishment of aluminium smelter in Greenland' presented to the Parliament by the Department of Industry, Labour Market and Vocational Training in February 2008 (Department of Industry, Labour Market and Vocational Training, 2008). This paper introduced the project in detail, compared it to other similar industries in the North, inscribed it into the global CO_2 and climate question, presented pros and cons with respect to different smelter sites, addressed financial and ownership questions, summarized the conclusions of the SEA and pointed toward certain overall social impacts and requirements. A special report (Bennetzen & Lonka, 2008), focusing on the more close relationships between the smelter, the nearby town (whether it be Sisimiut, Maniitsoq or Nuuk) and ideas for a sustainable relationship, was used as a background to judge the financial aspects and town-enlargement requirements. The 'Decision paper' was a key document in the sense that it constituted the very basis on which the Parliament approached and understood the project in its totality. The Parliament's own working group on the aluminium project had meetings and discussions with principal Greenlandic stakeholders in the labour market (SIK, GA and NUSUKA) about the project and eventually prepared and handed in an elaborate paper (Landstingets ad hoc udvalg vedrørende eventuel etablering af en aluminiumssmelter i Grønland, 2008) to the Parliament in May 2008. Here, major issues and questions raised by the political parties were addressed. This paper, moreover, made a number of recommendations for further investigation and monitoring, especially with respect to economy and its impacts on the Greenlandic society.

The direction of and work with the factory project was influenced by two major political changes that took place in Greenland, changes that totally influenced the project's dynamics. On January 1, 2009, the 18 municipalities in Greenland were merged into only four – a manoeuvre in which the two competing towns of Sisimiut and Maniitsoq were united. It was a long process and was part of a major administrative reorganization of Greenland. However, the merging of municipalities also brought political issues to the forefront in new ways, since former towns that were used to competing for a limited supply of goods now had to cooperate, and the reduction of centres was raised as an issue of concern among many of the smaller communities, because they felt more marginalized in the new structure. Actually, a similar process of municipality-merging transpired in Denmark in 2007. Later the same year, the Danish Parliament adopted an act giving Greenland self-government. This was a major step towards greater independence and the act stipulates that Greenland's aspirations toward self-government should be met by creating more economic self-reliance. Therefore, the act stipulates that all income from resources is to go to Greenland, with the one requirement that some part of this income is supposed to reduce the block grant from Denmark. These two changes in 2009 altered the relations between different regions in Greenland and altered the relationship between Greenland and Denmark (see Chapter 1 for an elaboration of this). It similarly made it only more apparent that economic development in Greenland should be organized in new directions – a setting within which the smelter became an even more important driver and instrument for what was considered 'positive change'.

Removing deal-breakers

The aluminium factory project involves a range of problems and concerns related to, for example, environmental consequences, income potentials and investment and ownership models. As the project took on more and more shape in 2009, certain concerns started to dominate the debate. In one case, it was even suggested that the project be abandoned altogether. In the following, three issues will be set in the foreground because they call attention to different arrangements of *sites of activities*, *sites of concern* and *sites of phases*, and they appeared as potential deal-breakers.

Flooding the past – a site of activity

One issue in particular was a potential deal-breaker: the question related to the flooding of the landscape surrounding the lake of Tasersiaq for the purpose of establishing hydroelectric facilities. The entire project is dependent upon this flooding and damming activity carried out at this particular site. The reason why an obstacle to moving forward appeared was not due to the location itself, as this site had been demarcated very early on in the process; rather, it was because archaeological investigations carried out in the area of Tasersiaq revealed extraordinary findings related to several groups of Eskimos and a unique settlement pattern that was evidently in use more than 4,000 years ago. The cultural landscape was so very unique that the National Museum in Greenland (Nunatta Katersugaasivia Allagaateqarfialu [Greenland National Museum and Archives], 2009, p. 13) recommended that the area be listed as a UNESCO World Heritage Site on the basis of the following argument:

> The coherent complexes of settlements and hunting areas by Tasersiaq make up unparalleled opportunities for the study of prehistoric Inuit's activities in the cultural landscapes as traditional knowledge from historical use of the landscapes are available [...] For these reasons the contiguous landscapes are of great value for the study of prehistoric hunting activity and the interplay between human and nature in general.

This was indeed a deal-breaker. However, in a white paper (Ministry of Industry and Mineral Resources, 2009) published October 2009, the Greenlandic government suggested changing the law on cultural heritage so that the government would then be able to overrule the museum and thus allow the project plans to continue. The issue indeed gave rise to new ways of understanding culture, place and temporality, as will be analyzed in Chapter 5.

Polluting the world – a site of concern

The second phase of the SEA was running throughout the year 2009 and included a life-cycle assessment of a smelter in Greenland as compared to another one located in another country (Schmidt & Thrane, 2009). Essentially, the report analyzed the pollution made by the factory, examined its CO_2 footprint and inscribed all of this in a global context – a scaling that opens up a new site of concern. Emissions of CO_2 indeed became a hot international topic during 2009, when the fifteenth session of the Conference of Parties (COP 15) that convened in Copenhagen gave rise to renewed focus on the Kyoto Protocol, in relation to which Greenland had promised Denmark that it would actively pursue a reduction of 8 per cent in its CO_2 emissions. In a report on the costs of different CO_2 quota systems (PriceWaterhouseCoopers, 2009), it was stressed that Greenland could potentially find itself in a situation where it would have to purchase quotas for a substantial amount of money, thusly reducing the financial benefits of industrial development (mining, oil and heavy industry). This could potentially serve to position Greenland as a place where initiating industrial growth was simply too expensive. The newly appointed premier, Kuupik Kleist (appointed premier in 2009), spent considerable time negotiating with Denmark to find a solution to this predicament, which could have been a potential deal-breaker, since the smelter would presumably increase the CO_2 emission of Greenland by 75 per cent. Greenland, like many other non-industrial countries, was eager to pursue a path of industrial development in order to improve its economy and to buttress its ambitions of promoting the general welfare but now found itself standing as the 'odd man out' in Denmark because the Danish political environment was so focused on reducing emissions. This presented a precarious situation for Denmark because on the one hand, it was struggling to forge an ambitious global settlement on emissions and, on the other hand, it was busy negotiating with Greenland to open up for a substantial increase in emissions. The distribution of uneven development potentials for the world's populations, which became the crux of the matter during the COP 15 negotiations, was accordingly taking place *internally* in Denmark. In the end, the controversy was handled politically in such a way that it did not stand out as being controversial (Bjørst, 2011). In a footnote (Kleist & Friis, 2009) to the Copenhagen Accord that was formulated at COP 15, there is a brief formulation that stipulates that Greenland is not to be considered a party to any agreement being made here. After COP 15, the United Nations was informed that Greenland is not to be bound by the targets and obligations taken on by Denmark as a member of the European Union and will be setting up its own reduction targets. Just as in the case of the archaeological controversy surrounding the territory in Tasersiaq, political ingenuity and diligence on the part of the Greenlandic government played a decisive role in solving the problem. The issue of CO_2 emission not only indicates that a mega-industrializing Greenland has entered a new political landscape of expectations and requirements, but also that navigating a new Greenland in a world concerned with climate change requires new political strategies and new ways of scaling the activities of Greenland. These requirements also call attention to the essential problem of understanding climate change related issues in Greenland, in particular, and in the Arctic, in general, as solely being matters of adaption.

Reorganizing the workers – a site of phase

A significant issue that had been raised several times, but that was never really addressed in Greenland was the question of how mobile people were in Greenland. Without a willingness to move from other regions in Greenland to Maniitsoq, the domestic labour force would not be able to satisfy the projected expectations. Consequently, the potential tax revenues stemming from the project and the concomitant benefits to the population would be diminished. Furthermore, lack of mobility would result in an influx of foreign workers. If a Greenlandic labour force is not available to work during the operational phase of the project, at the right site, the project will not come to make the expected positive benefits on the economy of Greenland. This is not a new issue. In a report put forth in 2003 by the Greenlandic Self-Government Commission, which was set up by the Home Rule of Greenland, this mobility requirement was formulated in the following way: 'A decisive political problem that is related to the labour market is the fact that the population has not moved in synch with changes in the nation's employment opportunities' (Selvstyrekommissionen, 2003, p. 363, translated by the author).

In May 2008, a large study of the mobility dynamics in Greenland was therefore initiated. Some of the preliminary results of this study were presented already in the 2009 white paper (Ministry of Industry and Mineral Resources, 2009, pp. 24–25), while the study's final results were published in 2010 (Nordregio, 2010) and called attention, variously, to the unique mobility patterns in Greenland and to some of the drivers and barriers for mobility. The report's national focus also supported the government's wish to mobilize as many workers as possible from all over Greenland and the need to design plans and programs in order to 'achieve the highest possible positive effects, and the least possible negative consequences' (p. 24). With this new report in hand, the government could substantiate its aspirations to mobilize the Greenlandic labour force. The report's conclusions with respect to the willingness of the population to move and to engage in new industrial activities (Nordregio, 2010, p. 149) could be interpreted as a support of the project as such (Ministry of Industry and Mineral Resources, 2009, p. 25). The report has given the authorities an understanding of some of the drivers of mobility and has singled out groups within the society based on their mobility-related 'readiness'. The new juxtaposition between the conception of Greenland as an industrial frontier, made possible in part by climate change, and the Greenlanders' aspiration to acquire more economic independence from Denmark has made *individual* mobility a central component of the country's political discussions and strategies to enforce a *national* community. The focus on and understanding of the need to have a mobile working force configures a new citizen in Greenland (this will be analyzed later on in Chapter 4) and evokes the factory as a national project. The expectation of the authorities is that during a particular site of phase (the operational phase) the factory will be run by Greenlandic workers primarily. As will be discussed later on in Chapter 4, the factory thus turns into a particular national socio-technical configuration, which can be expected to give rise to new economic opportunities and challenges. This new socio-technical configuration, in turn, draws the focus to some of the potential negative social issues related to the project. In the following, the issue of uneven development, which could potentially be generated in the wake of the project, will be investigated, taking its mark in the reports' ways of dealing with the matter and in how this was integrated into a more social and economic holistic perspective.

Uneven development

Throughout 2009, the project's consequences were investigated in further detail while its temporal, spatial and financial consequences and impacts continued to emerge, increasingly. The three potential deal-breakers – the preservation of Tasersiaq, the need to finance the acquisition of CO_2 quotas and the potential lack of a mobile labour force – were addressed and dealt with, head on. The initial results of the mobility study cast light on the contours of the possibilities of using the domestic labour force and also on the contours of some regional consequences of the changed settlement and mobility patterns. The potential for this uneven development had been raised several times before – in white papers, reports, etc. – but now, the differentiated impact on regions in Greenland had become more apparent and was addressed quite directly in the reports. This awareness indicates a more conscious up-scaling of the project in the discussions and simultaneously signals a challenge being posed to the previous demarcation and downscaling of the project to the site of activity, primarily. Thus, the factory could not be seen in isolation (i.e. as being separated) from development issues happening in the rest of Greenland. In 2010, the government initiated a process to formulate a regional development strategy where municipalities and the government should consider ways of coordinating and implementing a strategy with the aim of living up to the requirements for national economic development (Naalakkersuisut, 2011b) – in a report published in 2011. The report identified regions and growth sectors to be invested in to boost the national economy, and concomitantly singled out regions and sectors that will get less attention because they are considered economically unviable. The process was driven not only by the new aspiration to become economically self-reliant but moreover by economic projections that pointed out how expenses for what is primarily public welfare were presumably not going to be met by the national income (pp. 9–12). Greenland was thus experiencing some of the same dynamics and predicaments as other social-welfare societies in the Western world. A national deficit in the near future due to a decreasing labour force appeared to be the primary driver in the regional development strategy. The factory project was accordingly whirling up issues related to future development, priorities and consequences on a much larger scale than the particular piece of technology. Two issues stood out as central: a new and emerging socio-economic differentiation of society and new processes of centralization.

A new socio-economically differentiated society

Of special interest in 2010, as reflected in the reports published that year, were the socio-economic consequences of the project. Increasingly, Greenland Development A/S and the government were trying to comprehend the local, regional and national impacts of the project and thus trying to identify the areas that called urgently for special attention. Apart from the SEA, which was published in its final version in 2010 (and covered the topics of environment, health, culture and regional development), the majority of reports delved more deeply into examining educational requirements, economic impacts on other regions and Maniitsoq, and the local consequences of a changed mobility pattern in the labour force, just to mention a few examples. Overall, the emphasis was placed on understanding the project in a more socially and economically holistic manner. These issues had been raised from the very outset of the process, but it was not until now that the reports focused explicitly on these issues to a degree not previously seen. The reports were used as background materials for the 2010 white paper on the aluminium project, which concentrated specifically on these matters. New concerns were thus brought into focus. If the projections and calculations were correct, an up-and-running project with Greenlandic workers would change the make-up of many communities, change their future development possibilities, alter their social stability and potentially lead to uneven development in Greenland. For example, in the report on the economic impact upon municipalities (Jervelund & Winther, 2010) the municipalities of Kujalleq and Qaasuitsup are expected to lose DKK 11 and 19 million annually due, respectively, to out-migration and brain drain. If Greenland is to gain financially from the project it is important – according to NIRAS (2010) – to make sure that Greenlandic workers from outside Maniitsoq move to Maniitsoq and that the reduced population in other regions of Greenland be followed up by a reduction in public services offered in those regions. What this entails is that a financially lucrative project for Greenland will subsequently lead to deep cuts in the financial and human capital of communities throughout all of Greenland! This is going to require a reforming of what is considered reasonable, proper, important and necessary with respect to community dynamics. The premier, Kuupik Kleist, appealed to the population by saying that 'If these projects are to be realized, it is of the utmost importance that the population as such – the fellow citizens of

Greenland – exhibit, to a significant extent, active citizenship in the sense that everyone will be contributing by shouldering the burden' (cited in M. Lynge, 2011 translated by the author).

Centralization and decentralization

The 2010 reports do serve, very clearly, to identify the pervasive nature of the project and to suggest that it is going to mark the beginning of a new society – in Maniitsoq as well as elsewhere in Greenland. In Greenland, the settlement structure has always been a political 'hot potato', since the balance between decentralized and centralized settlement patterns is culturally and economically sensitive. In the public and political debates, there have been two very dominant ideas. One emphasizes *centralization* fuelled by a particular economic understanding (i.e. centralization will reduce public expenses and will boost economic development), while the other emphasizes *decentralization* as it is understood to underpin Greenlandic culture, lifestyle and respect for diversity (i.e. small is beautiful, economically sustainable and more in line with Greenlandic mentality) (see Forchhammer [1997] for a historical study of this polemic). One upshot of this discourse conflict can be spotted in the frequent avoidance of explicit political statements promoting centralization, urbanization and the encouraged depopulation of small communities. However, there is no doubt that the tendencies in settlement patterns, in political focus and in investment planning are setting their sights on centralization (Sejersen, 2007). These are tendencies that promote centralization while avoiding any detailed considerations of the long-term effects on people who are living in smaller and more out-of-the-way places.

The establishment of a smelter in Maniitsoq – and its resulting effects – is, at one and same time, trying to bypass this question and trying to address the issue directly. The concentration of a large part of Greenland's labour force in Maniitsoq as well as the need to channel large investments into the town and the project will – according to the reports – be felt everywhere in Greenland. What, on a *national scale*, can be seen as a diversification of the economy and as the potential consolidation of a more self-reliant national economy can result in a specialization that enforces concentration and thus the economic and human drying out of other regions. With the smelter, the centralization–decentralization polemic has taken on a new form; however, the question has been coined in such a way that it is not a discussion about whether or not centralization is a good – or a bad – idea, but whether Greenland wants to seize hold of this industrial opportunity, which could potentially accelerate Greenland's development. In the 2010 SEA (Grønlands Selvstyres SMV arbejdsgruppe, 2010, p. 9), the following, concerning the pervasive nature of the project, was stated: 'Such a large-scale operation, with so many jobs, has never been seen in the history of Greenland and in a Greenlandic context, it can be regarded as a mega-project, which is likely to influence the economic, social, political and cultural conditions in Maniitsoq and in other parts of Greenland' (translation by the author). The NIRAS report (NIRAS, 2010, p. 15) was more open and direct about the project's effects in other areas of society. It related the potential economic benefits directly to changes in other spheres: 'a greater supply of labour [which will have a positive effect on the Greenlandic economy] can be realized by undertaking changes in structural conditions such as education, mobility, rules and incentive structures, behaviour, family patterns, traditions and so forth' (translated by the author). The report suggested several tools that could potentially furnish a greater supply of labour and suggested ways to make sure that public expenses will continuously balance changes in the settlement patterns – both parameters (an increase in recruitment and decreases in public expenses) are decisive and will need to be pursued continuously if Greenland is going to benefit economically from the project. This will, according to the report, force the politicians to make some potentially unpopular decisions (pp. 17–18). In the white paper submitted to the Parliament in September 2010 (Naalakkersuisut, 2010), these issues were clearly fleshed out. The government warns that it ought to 'be taken into account that those moving to Maniitsoq from other parts of the country will, to a large extent, be socio-economically advantaged people. This means that some towns and settlements should expect to do without those people who they rely on in the local community and who may have been particularly enterprising or supportive in society' (Naalakkersuisut, 2010, p. 21). This indeed signalled a change in socio-economic focus – from the more national (importance for the national economy) to the potential uneven regional development and also toward a focus on how the project might accelerate already existing regional problems.

Factory figuration

The national vision of a more self-sustaining economy was centred on a single mega-industry driven by hydroelectricity. It was envisioned as helping Greenland to be better equipped at responding to the increasing public welfare expenses but would presumably also have negative social impacts in regions situated far away from the site of the smelter. The new and focused organization around water use (in this case, hydroelectricity) for special purposes (in this case, aluminium) gives rise to consequences that are external to the particular sites of activities, and the contours of this new world became increasingly apparent in the reports. The water-project conjoins the regions of Greenland and gathers them in a particular movement of society. In fact, hunters in Northern Greenland – living hundreds of kilometres away from Maniitsoq – who are already busy trying to comprehend and deal with the disappearing sea ice (Hastrup, 2009), are now also expected to engage in and relate to a water-related world, which will increasingly come to dominate their livelihood. By means of the hydroelectric-dependent smelter, a new Greenland emerges and mobilizes. Even though the factory and the hydroelectric electric power plants are the central manifestations of the project (and the centre of attention (with respect to pollution, infrastructure, etc.), the new Greenland is also about the cultural, social and economic realities prompted by the factory and the hydroelectric electric power plants. The project thus transcends itself and there is more at stake here than 'just' a factory, dams and many kilometres of transmission cables. It is apparent that the factory world is a social world and that the new factory world that will materialize with the appearance of the smelter is about something more than mere hydroelectricity and a potentially polluting factory – it is also about values, about consciousness of place and about ways of understanding community sustainability and subject responsibility.

The long trail of reports and the paper construction of a factory are thus interesting in several ways. The smelter in the reports is constructed and treated as an entity with certain characteristics. For example: it is huge, it requires large investments, a reorganization of the labour force, the flooding of the landscape, and the pollution of the atmosphere, etc. In this way, it is as much performed as it is reflected upon. In order to handle the complexity of the matter, the reports compartmentalise the project in what I term *sites of activities*, *sites of concern* and *sites of phases*. The reports lay out the matrix of the project and create the texture through which we are to understand its implications and requirements. All reports maintain a strong focus on the particular project and all of them refrain from integrating the requirements and consequences of other large-scale industrial projects, which are currently on the drafting tables in Greenland. This focus can be interpreted as an act of project compartmentalization and isolation.

The reports thus evoke the project and make it more tangible, albeit in a particular figuration. This is not meant to be taken as a critique of the reports and the way that they have been orchestrated but more as a reminder of the relations between the analysis and the object matter – or more precisely as a reminder of how the analytical process and the object under study co constitute each other. The figuration of the project in reports causes certain places, phases and concerns to emerge as a generalized system from which data has to be obtained, assessed, evaluated and communicated. The task that lies before us, then, is to be more and more precise with respect, for example, to the numbers of workers required, to the impact on migrating geese or to the investment that is going to be needed. The constant striving for more and more precise data and the pursuit of proper public hearing procedures underpins the idea of pre-existing elements and problems that have to be systematically investigated, put in their place and (hopefully) solved in order for an informed decision to be made.

However, the structuring of reports, the questions asked and the applied perspective generate a particular project figuration. In the SEA, this becomes quite clear. To meet the requirements of a SEA, the researchers are supposed to use a SEA template, so to speak. They have to research the following areas (defined as 'environment'): nature (animal and plant species, etc.), environment (health, pollution, etc.), culture (cultural heritage, etc.) and regional development (increased migration, etc.). This chosen analytical take on a mega-industrial project and on the creation of a new world is valuable and has indeed led to the production of numerous informative reports and posters. The latter are particularly interesting, seeing as they were made available to the public in easy-to-read language at the public hearings and thus constituted an important constituent ingredient in raising public awareness. At the hearings, there were specialists that represented each of the respective areas of the 'environment'; these special experts made presentations, answered questions and took notice of good ideas and new perspectives from the audience. The structuring of the individual SEA sections is supposed to follow a more or less strict pattern – with baseline studies, and consequence and risk assessments – thus working with clear temporal and spatial demarcations and scales. In the report on Regional Development and Migration (Grønlands Selvstyres SMV arbejdsgruppe, 2010, p. 16), the chosen demarcation was briefly discussed and the inclusion of another temporal scale suggested (an 'exit phase') in addition to the ones officially decided upon (construction phase and operational phase) as well as to inscribe the smelter in a more general vision of regional and national development. In a lengthier interview, one of the researchers pointed out to me that the applied phases were somehow supporting a politically convenient discourse, where the smelter would *first* be constructed by foreign workers and *then* Greenlanders would take over the operation, accordingly landing most of the jobs. These two phases are socially opportune and easy to understand. Indeed, this way of understanding the two phases jibes nicely with the general understanding of the project locally: outside workers will help build the factory and then Greenlanders will take over the operation.

The compartmentalization and the 'freezing of phases' have made generalizations and comparisons possible, not only between phases but also between reports. Each phase represents social, economic, cultural and political dynamics; the first phase is understood as a necessity (Greenland does not have the skills or the labour force needed to construct the project), and the several thousand workers who will enter Greenland during this phase will be located in camps with little or no access to the Greenlandic society. The idea of *containment* is dominant in this phase, not only with respect to the restricted physical movement of the workers and a demarcation of their ethnic background but also with respect to their rights. However, in the operational phase, many Greenlanders are going to be expected to orientate towards the factory and associated activities. They are going to be involved in a dynamic factory environment, where rights and wages match the general requirements associated with the Greenlandic labour force. The idea of *inclusion* is dominant in this phase. Thus, two different kinds of subjects are being produced and two different social settings are being engineered by this particular factory figuration. The separation of practices of containment and inclusion, respectively, is maintained by the existence of two radically different phases. One of the questions emerging from this understanding is the process of transfer from one phase to another, while a second question has to do with the transfer's temporal, economic and social implications. The analytical demarcation of the project in phases can, in and of itself, be seen as a disciplining act, which is highly political. One concern raised by a bureaucrat during a conversation with me was the reports' lack of appreciation of the transition processes between the phases. He was worried about the socio-cultural and political challenges emerging *in between* the construction phase and the operational phase. Here, he expected an as-of-yet unnamed (and thus untamed) phase of perhaps 15 years, where the factory would be in operation, but with only a few Greenlandic workers. Hence, a difficult cross-cultural situation would potentially emerge, with political and legislative challenges that have not been addressed within the existing phase demarcations and factory figuration.

The empire of expertise

Largely, the factory figuration and the different sites of attention have been maintained throughout the project period. This has been possible because much of the knowledge-building, interpretation and communication related to the project have been organized by a single company, Greenland Development A/S. We may understand this as an *empire of expertise*, where an institution sets the dominant discourse and organizes the flow of information.

More than 50 reports related to the project reflect not only its mega-ness but also a special commitment on the part of the Greenland self-government to grasp the project in all its complexity. Comprehending the corpus of reports can be overwhelming and it indeed requires a certain kind of expertise to be able to find, to read, to interpret and to compare the reports. Most of the reports are available on the homepage of Greenland Development A/S (www.aluminium.gl) where they are organized in different ways to help users to navigate. On the homepage, one has to enter the 'Library' and choose among three entrances, which categorize the reports in chronological, alphabetical and thematic order. On the homepage, each report is accompanied by a brief summary. In the thematic section, the reports are ordered chronologically, with the more recent ones at the top. This is a valuable entrance point for knowledge-building. Elsewhere on the homepage, one finds links to other reports that might be relevant to the theme in question. For example, under 'Environment and climate', there is a link to the reports produced under the SEA and to the archaeological reports. These reports, however, are *not* found in the 'Library' even though they have been produced as part of the development of the project.

Navigating in this corpus of reports requires expertise simply because the different reports have to be found at different places and because their relational and absolute importance is not explicated. The most recent report, for example, may not necessarily be the most important inasmuch as it may be highly specialized and might be a constituent part of a larger and more comprehensive investigation. The status of reports is thus difficult to appreciate fully. If users are to make a qualified access into this corpus of reports, they are going to need a mediation of expertise. This expertise lies in the hands of Greenland Development A/S, and they make oral presentations on a regular basis at a variety of institutions and organizations, at all different kinds of levels. For example, the company gave a presentation to the local business community in Maniitsoq in February 2011 titled, 'Up and down in the reports of the aluminium project'. Because this presentation was directed to the business community, the chosen focus was primarily on salary, taxes, income, origin of labour force, employment, economic consequences and potentials. To understand what is really 'up and down' in the reports is also a way of appreciating what is up and down in the project as such. It requires expertise in judgement, in outlook and in communication. Greenland Development A/S has to make choices of relevance and choices of relations. This applies to everybody who might venture so much as to claim to offer an 'up and down' presentation. The self-government of Greenland has granted Greenland Development A/S the expertise to request, produce, present and make available reports to the public and the politicians. Such a task requires a lot of interpretation and choice, which renders the task a politically saturated enterprise. One of the choices they have made is not to include the SEA reports and the archaeological reports in their 'Library'. The point here is not whether this changes the level and quality of information on the homepage but that the position of Greenland Development A/S is central in the communication and interpretation of the entire process. We may understand this as an *empire of expertise*, which narrows the perspective and ultimately leads to a silencing of alternative or critical voices, storylines, and narratives. This is not meant here as a criticism of the work that is being done by Greenland Development A/S but more as a reflection upon the relationship between the state and the public that is being mediated by a single company.

An *empire of expertise* can be understood as a knowledge regime that dominates through the construction by certain experts of certain selected narratives. By creating relations between reports and formulating the 'up and down', the project as a whole, the project's subjects and elements are simultaneously evoked and activated in one and the same manoeuvre. The project becomes ordered, disciplined, and rendered more and more real, manageable, easy to grasp and, in the words of Hargadon and Sutton (1997), change becomes routinized. It is grounded, placed and turned into a given, not only by the individual reports, the totality of reports or their public availability, but also by virtue of the processes and procedures under which they were produced (e.g. by following the proper hearing procedures). Following the proper procedures (e.g. by refraining from either sidestepping or questioning the report's set-up) and maintaining the defined demarcations (culture in one report and environment in another, or analyzing the overall dynamics by using only two project phases) are ways of understanding, ordering and staging the world. In a sense, the company creates a new kind of literacy by means of controlling the flow of reports; this serves to maintain and authorize a recurrent order of sites of attention and serves to secure a consistent factory figuration.

The work of Greenland Development A/S consists, so to speak, in grounding the project by scrutinizing different aspects of the project for the Greenland government, so as to systematize a chaos of potential risks, and potential needs. The company coordinates negotiations and cooperation with Alcoa in order to develop the project and – at the same time – communicates the project to the public, while helping to involve the public in the discussions. The construction of reports, narratives and factory stories are not solely the privilege of Greenland Development A/S, seeing as there are, in fact, other institutions, organizations and agents engaged in the construction of factory stories, whether they be unfolded in newspaper comments, research reports, hearing letters or the like. However, the special position of Greenland Development A/S as an empire of expertise emerges as a result of the authority, position, status and funding entrusted to this company by the Greenlandic government and the expectations that the government invests in doing this. The chairman of the board of Greenland Development A/S pointed out, in a newspaper article (Holmsgaard, 2006), that the work related to the aluminium project is of such a comprehensive extent and nature that the government wants to encapsulate the preparatory work in a special company. The company was established on the basis of a wish to create a 'one door' principle and to create total transparency with respect to the work. This 'one door' decision only serves to bolster the position of Greenland Development A/S as an empire of expertise and also calls attention to the *active* delegation of expertise to one particular group in society – in this case, a particular company. The neo-liberal construction of the empire of expertise is interesting insofar as the company's structure hinders the public's rights of access to internal documents. The presence of members of the company's staff at most hearings and meetings about the project, as well as their willingness to provide professional advice on what is up and down for all interested groups in society, underpin its dominance and the widespread acceptance of their right to define the extension of the project in the world.

The concept of an 'empire of expertise' directs our attention to the *institutionalization* of a certain group of experts, which ascribes to them a certain *centred* and *dominant* role and position in public discourse. The role and position of, for example, the IPCC, the universities or the national museums in society can be understood in a similar way, but they may be more open to public scrutiny and internal critical reflection than a company with the mandate that has been delegated to Greenland Development A/S. In a written comment made in response to a report on the economic consequences of the smelter, the Employers' Association of Greenland – Grønlands Arbejdsgiverforening – did take the opportunity to criticize the position of Greenland Development A/S. The Employers' Association termed the construction of Greenland Development A/S harmful to the climate of openness about the project, seeing as the efforts of Greenland Development A/S had resulted in document confidentiality, which undermined critical and public reflection (Grønlands Arbejdsgiverforening, 2010). In an open letter to the government, Sara Olsvig (2010) also raised concerns about the credibility of Greenland Development A/S because of its construction and its dual role of public service and of attracting large-scale industries to Greenland. In a radio debate broadcast on KNR, on November 11, 2010, many listeners who called in to the station questioned the role of Greenland Development A/S and aired their sense of trepidation about the company's priority evidently being assigned to give service to Alcoa rather than to the public (Olsvig & Merrild, 2011). This uncertainty about the role being performed by – and the dominant position granted to – Greenland Development A/S has often overshadowed discussions about the actual work pursued by the company.

Domination by project figuration

Looking at Greenland Development A/S as an *empire of expertise* evokes a focus on ways of dominating and securing control over the ordering of elements. It may be useful to make use of an analogy (a national museum and a laboratory) to illuminate the underpinnings and consequences of control by means of ordering. In a national museum, things are put on display and are made to represent, for example, cultures. Things, in and of themselves, do not represent 'a culture', 'a region', 'a people' or 'a period', but are made to do so by creative force and choice. Things are turned into objects for a particular purpose (e.g. for purposes of an analysis or for an exhibition), from a particular point of (theoretical) view. According to Bruno Latour (2007), this process can be seen as a 'figuring of the world' where things are turned into figures via the conscious connection to and embeddedness in other figures (see also Williams & Edge, 1996). Things do not speak for themselves, but are actively made to speak. In this process, the thing emerges as an object to be displayed or analyzed. The distances between system and observation, between theory and data, between background and foreground, and between whole and part can be questioned (as is done, for example, by Latour (2007)) and the contraries can be seen, instead, as co-producing one another. Inside the museum, things become objects for display, by virtue of the questions we (and the curators) ask and by virtue of the narratives that are expected to emerge from the thing and its relation to other objects in the exhibition. Relations between objects in an exhibition can, for example, be induced on the basis of ideas related to chronology and region. Certain temporal and spatial understandings are systematizing and figuring objects by means of the organization and the sequences of rooms, the showcases, and the displays. Nathalia Brichet and Frida Hastrup's critique (2011) argues that this system and the configuring of things are often perceived as being natural and external to the things, and in ethnographic exhibitions, the system predominantly reproduces an idea of a direct natural matching of thing, place and people. Such an understanding leads to a tragic predicament, where collectors can never obtain enough things or the right things to map the world, a people, a place or a period because these categories are considered external to the objects that are supposed to represent exactly this externality.

This focus on figuring points to yet another conception of whole and part, where the whole figures the part and the part figures the whole. In a dynamic relation of co-production, the figures emerge *through* each other. This idea of co-production is also dominant within Science and Technology Studies (STS), where a renewed understanding of the relationship between the social and the technological, cultural and natural is explored. Here, a scientific experiment in a laboratory, for example, is considered a social process where a thing, a patient, a particular substance, an animal, or whatever, is figured to be a certain kind of *object* that is supposed to be put through an experiment in a controlled and external environment, where factors can be neatly isolated in sequences, causes and consequences. The experiment is then pursued in this way, in order to appear stable and reproducible. STS – among other things – critically studies how the culture and sociality of laboratories reproduce the idea that knowledge of a given object (phrased as 'facts') is possible to acquire in isolation from the laboratory that configured the object in the first place.

According to STS, the laboratory is precisely a place where a thing is taken out of its ordinary network of relations and creatively configured, by placing it in a new spatial and temporal regime, which *reduces* it and *amplifies* it, at one and the same time (Roepstorff, 2003, p. 378). According to Karin Knorr-Cetina (cited in Roepstorff, 2003, p. 367), the lab can be seen as making a particular order possible, an order where elements are reconfigured and controlled in order to make it possible to construct knowledge. She understands the lab as a *hyper-version* of reality. The cultural logic of the lab makes it possible to reconfigure temporal and spatial parameters and to evoke a narrative (about, for example, blood cells or about HIV) that can travel and make sense outside the lab, where it then becomes re-figurated and set into new relations (e.g. the human body of the patient). As Roepstorff (2003, p. 367) points out, the analytical approach to studying the logic of labs and experiments is not confined to laboratories alone but can also be applied to practices where controlled figurations take place – e.g. in museums or anthropological research. The focus on controlled reduction, amplification, figuration, as well as on the co-production of parts and wholes can be analytically inspiring when looking at the Greenland Development A/S-generated reports which are linked to the aluminium project.

The project is mega not only in its spatial extent (the factory's size, the landscape, the flooding due to dams, etc.) but also in the extent of its impact on society. This has incited the politician, Juliane Henningsen (2011), to claim that the project is so large-scale that it will have 'an immense social, economic, cultural and political influence on the whole of Greenland and not only on Maniitsoq'. Therefore, she and other politicians maintain the perception that further, better and more accurate and thorough investigations need to be pursued in order to obtain more 'complete' information. Or, to put it differently, that it is going to be necessary to get more facts about the project. It is the task of Greenland Development A/S to make sure that a setting is constructed in which these investigations are initiated and made available in order for the politicians to make what can be considered 'informed' decisions. There are indeed a number of futures, consequences and complexities to appreciate and take into account. Reports are one means of trying to grasp the potentialities and consequences, and specialized research within demarcated fields like the environment, health, culture, economy and mobility have also been carried out. Each field represents, so to speak, a laboratory, where elements (e.g. birds, bodies, history, the labour force and families) are pointed out and configured in new and simpler, more controllable and more identifiable relations.

Part of this process involves constructing baselines that have to be established as the grounding texture of the experiment. From the establishment of a number of causal relationships, it is possible to make a number of projections, where different parameters can be altered in a controlled manner (see e.g. NIRAS, 2010). For example, it becomes clear from this 'experiment' that public finances are going to be affected positively if the workers at the factory are recruited from that segment of the population that has previously received public subsidies (pp. 4–18). Subsequently, this can be compared to how the economy will presumably appear if workers are recruited from other societal groups. The experimental character of the projection is explicitly mentioned (e.g. pp. 13ff), since there are many uncertainties – not only in the relation between the chosen parameters (e.g. how many workers are required) but also with respect to other developments in society (e.g. what the developments are in the policies, settlement patterns and the labour force in general). On the one hand, the complexities of the project need to be *boiled down* to a couple of parameters in order to make projections and, on the other hand – and conversely – there is a need to *amplify* the potentials and consequences in detail. Several other projections are being made (for example, about the need for foreign workers, and about housing, export/import, level of consumption, etc.) and it is through the combination of such projections that the aluminium project re-figures or re-emerges in a new totality: a new project narrative, which is expected to guide the decision-makers.

As in any laboratory, the object has to be creatively configured as such. In this case, it is a project in two phases with which different socialities, different incomes and different investment needs are associated. The project could have been configured quite differently – a configuration that may not necessarily amount to an improvement – and consequently, the object under study and the whole experiment, as such, would be changed. Because Greenland Development A/S has produced or ordered most of the reports, the company can maintain the figuration. By stabilizing and maintaining the same figuration, a comparative perspective becomes possible, to some extent, while it simultaneously promotes the idea of project-grounding. The latter implies that the project is an external system that has to be explored and filled out with data, so to speak, just as the rooms of the museum have to be filled with things from 'cultures'. Furthermore, a totality (the ultimate amplification) becomes achievable by forming a bond of union between the different reports that investigate each of their spheres (e.g. environment, health, culture, etc.) separately. On the basis of this mode of understanding, a full overview of the project can be obtained by entering the 'Library' on the homepage and by reading the most recent reports, in much the manner that one can get a sense of viewing the whole world by walking through all the rooms of the ethnographic exhibitions at the national museum. Such a sense of total outlook amounts to a figuration that takes for granted that a totality can indeed be inferred from the produced parts.

The figuration of citizens

Reports with projections may constitute one very important and indispensable way of appropriating and evaluating a mega-project like the aluminium smelter in Greenland. The processes of evaluation, estimation and projection are, in themselves, constructing and evoking the factory itself; they are demarcating the totality of the project, as well as the citizens, within a new project reality. Unlike many of the industrial oil- and mining-related projects going on in Greenland, there is a particular citizen that appears to be emerging in the reports that deal with the aluminium project.

One of the primary goals of attracting the smelter to Greenland is to better the public finances through an improved tax base. In a report on the economic importance of the aluminium project (NIRAS, 2010), different scenarios are set up, indicating a variety of possible dimensions (and thus income), but also a variety of subjects within the project reality. The centre of attention in the report is the labour force and the spatial and social mobility of people, which are fleshed out as key areas of concern if Greenland is going to benefit from the project. The report states that a precondition for the anticipated goal (an improvement in the nation's economy) is the willingness of people to move to and work in Maniitsoq. Growth is linked to the supply of labour, in addition to being linked to the reduction of public expenses in those regions from where the labour force is being recruited. The report thus recommends that people should be activated and mobile and it specifies that the financial prospects of the nation will increase if the labour is recruited from that particular group of people who have been the recipients of public subsidies. As part of a 'new' labour market policy, young people ought to be encouraged to work and to get an education (p. 13) – this is a strategy that could allegedly result in a financial improvement of DKR 300 million annually. An improved supply of labour that would underpin the employability of Greenlanders at the smelter must –according to the report (p. 15) – involve nothing less than structural changes within the educational system, and within mobility patterns, family patterns, and traditions.

Furthermore, behaviour and inducement culture need to be changed. According to the report, this reorganization of society could be stimulated by reducing or removing subsidies extended to sectors of labour that are considered uneconomic (e.g. hunting and small-scale fishing) (p. 16), by reducing public spending on construction work, and by encouraging large-scale mobility away from certain communities in order to reduce the public-sector expenditures in these places (p. 16). The report explicitly points out that a number of difficult and unpopular political decisions need to be taken but suggests that these decisions are to be seen in a totality, and states that one way of bringing about a totality is the creation of 'aluminium packages', where popular and unpopular decisions would be bundled together and voted through parliament, as a totality (pp. 17, 58–59). Such a suggestion – which may be neither politically nor bureaucratically feasible – amplifies the extent of the project and casts light on how it depends upon and influences many other sectors of society. But it also promotes the smelter as a *national* project. A changed settlement pattern in which people are centred in productive areas, according to the report, also results in a better use of the (human) resources and of the 'labour force reserve' – as people are referred to in the report – that is presently placed in the smaller communities (p. 58). The term 'labour force reserve' is used by Heidegger in his critique of technology, which he perceives to be overtaking us in our modern society and in the way that we are engaged in the gradual transformation of the entire world and ourselves into 'standing reserves', i.e. into raw materials that are supposed to be mobilized in technical processes (see Feenberg, 1991, p. 7). The citizens of Greenland are, in the reports, being turned, in a variety of ways (either by force or by inducement), into individuals who are supposed to pursue an education, as well as to move and to work, in order to underpin an economically self-sustaining society. In Greenland, the drive to establish a national economic base for self-governance is a strong force in forming the developments of the country and meanwhile, an emergent utilitarian perspective prevails over the former ways of understanding the rights and obligations of the individual. The workings of society and culture have to support and have to be coordinated with the overall national ambitions toward economic self-reliance. When a labour market policy that stimulates qualified and mobile workers becomes essential as part and parcel of this national ambition, new subjects are constructed in the process and called upon. A new Greenlander is constructed and described as an individual who is ready to move into the hands of planners for the common good. In the words of Anna Tsing (2003, p. 129), such an individual becomes the allegorical source of the nation's Everyman, where he or she, in Greenland, appears as movable, as re-trainable and as being ready to embrace changes in a country fused with productivism, and nationalism. This is a new Greenlander, in the sense that this individual deviates from former translations and transformations of Greenlandicness, as has been described by Gimpel and Thisted (2007, p. 195). It may be difficult to visualize this new self-government citizen but the contours are apparent in many political statements. For example, in his foreword to the 2010 white paper on the aluminium project, Ove Karl Berthelsen, Minister for Industry and Mineral Resources, concludes his presentation in the following way (Naalakkersuisut, 2010, p. 3):

> By continuing the thorough development work, the project will be an important contribution to our joint goal of creating a self-sustaining society on sustainable foundations. The positive effects should not just permeate those areas where new growth businesses are emerging, but also the populations of other towns and settlements. We need as many work-capable forces as possible for the continued development of our society.

The statement can be interpreted as uplifting in the sense that it promotes a vision of a society where uneven development will be avoided. However, the minister's statement also stresses that everyone is needed and that everyone has to 'serve their country', so to speak, as part of the striving to gain a self-sustaining society. Former premier Hans Enoksen stressed this obligation clearly in his New Year's speech 2006/2007, when he stated that '[p]roductivity, efficiency enhancement and persistent supplementary training must be our goals. We all have a duty to be informed about the right way to independence' (Enoksen, 2007, p. 28). This means that new perceptions of the good life (for example, where to live, what to be educated to do, and what to pursue as an occupation) and the premises for judging personal and collective productivity and welfare need to be revisited and adjusted. This is an evocation of a new social contract and a new Greenlander; this can also be seen in the political vision report prepared by the government that was headed by Kuupik Kleist during the Alcoa negotiations (Naalakkersuisut, 2012).

Economic self-reliance and a new national subject

The production of aluminium in Greenland is by no means to be considered in isolation from the aspirations of the national community of Greenland – this becomes apparent in the above sections. The focus on a reformed Greenland also reforms the way Greenlanders are construed as subjects. Reforming Greenland thus implies reforming Greenlanders. This process of transformation is evident in many political reports. In its Political and Economic Report 2011, the Greenlandic government clearly points out that if Greenland is going to continue to finance the welfare state, then structural reforms are required. The aim is to 'ensure that a greater proportion of the population is given the basis to provide for itself' (Naalakkersuisut, 2011a, p. 31, translated by the author) – meaning that they should no longer be receiving public support. In order to emphasize the importance of a focused strategy and national co-operation, the report makes it clear that '[t]he narrow pursuit of special interests should therefore give way to the desire for a more sustainable development and for what best serves Greenlandic society as a whole' (p. 31, translated by the author). In its document discussing the possibility of a governmental coalition, the vision for a reformed Greenland is fleshed out in the following formulation: 'A strong self-government with a self-sustaining economy is a task that can only be realized if all participate actively. […] Development is to be anchored in the existing and future growth centres, because a genuine and cost-effective development can be secured there' (cited in Naalakkersuisut, 2011b, pp. 3–4, translated by the author). This line of thinking is also found in some of the other reports and documents that have become infused into the debate. Together with the municipalities, the government has, for example, formulated a regional development strategy (Naalakkersuisut, 2011b) in order to initiate and coordinate the required reforms necessary for attaining the following strategic goal: 'to develop a self-sustaining society where everyone has an opportunity to develop and maintain life by active self-support' (Naalakkersuisut, 2011b, p. 7, translated by the author).

The particularities of the national reforms, as reflected in the above citations, became very explicit in 2009, when Greenland experienced a major political change from a Siumut-dominated government (social democratic/conservative) to a government with a majority of politicians from Inuit Ataqatigiit (socialist/social democratic). This change signalled a turning point and the spectrum of reforms that was being sought changed, radically. Whereas the latter government saw renewable and non-renewable resources as the primary basis for economic development (Siumut & Atassut, 2007, p. 3), the new government added the labour market and the resources embedded in the population. This can be described as a change from an understanding of resources as external (e.g. minerals and fish) to an understanding of resources as internal (mobile and educated individuals, and the reorganization of society [e.g. in growth centres]). This is a policy devoted to the creation and construction of a new neo-liberal context within which to think about society, individuals and the state. In fact, by stressing the importance of the individual, the government re-appropriates the physical bodies of citizens, and Greenland as space (e.g. in regional growth centres) and mediates relationships in the national self-sustaining project. Citizenship is now – in this new Greenland – revolving, to a significant degree, around active participation. The government proposed a new plan called (in my translation of the banner-slogan) 'From passive to active support' (Inuit Ataqatigiit, Demokraterne, & Kattusseqatigiit Partiiat, 2009, p. 17) and this indeed signalled a new take on social issues and expectations, even though it compared its own plan with the livelihood strategies of the historical Inuit hunters as though there were some significant similarities: 'Just as Inuit has always followed the animals in order to support oneself and one's family, we have, today, an opportunity to follow jobs through mobility-promoting arrangements' (Inuit Ataqatigiit et al., 2009, p. 17, translated by the author).

Thus, the new government's strategy is to unite the population in a common project that is supposed to be directed towards an economic self-reliant Greenland and towards activating and developing human resources for the common good by encouraging education, mobility and growth in a few well-chosen and cost-effective centres. Expectations, negotiations and transformations of cultural norms and social worlds have been initiated. A societal reform of this magnitude will affect the livelihood strategies of people for many years to come. The ideas put forward by the new government actually reflect the ideological basis of the vast and comprehensive preliminary political study of the potentials to obtain self-government in Greenland – a study carried out by the Greenlandic Self-Government Commission in 2003. Here, the new productive and self-supporting citizen that has to be activated is referred to, in the following manner, by way of reference to people who are in need of public support: 'they do not contribute enough to our common basis for living. Their tax payment is small or even absent. On the basis of this, it can be maintained that they do not contribute sufficiently to the societal economy' (Selvstyrekommissionen, 2007). The need to reform the economy is a primary driver and what is underlined in several government documents (Naalakkersuisut, 2011a, 2011b) is that a reform is needed in order to maintain services and pursue the ambition of becoming more economic self-reliant.

The social, cultural and economic world of Greenland is indeed undergoing a rapid process of transformation. This is going to challenge people's perceptions of rights, obligations, personhood and the good life, and is also going to have an impact on laws and regulations. The special combination of growing aspirations toward self-governance and toward realizing a self-sustaining economy, the requirements of a mobile labour force, the new technology and the consolidation of growth in what is perceived as cost-effective centres furnishes the basis for a new Greenland, where people and space are being appropriated in new ways. It is in this light that the smelter stands out as a piece of technology that is envisioned as playing a decisive role in the reform – a role to be discussed in the next chapter.

References

Adolphsen, Jes, & Greiffenberg, Tom. (1998). When planning in Greenland began: The role of the construction commission. In T. Greiffenberg (Ed.), *Development in the Arctic* (pp. 83–87). Copenhagen: Danish Polar Center.

Alcoa. (2010). *Seizing Opportunity, Accelerating Value – 2010 Annual Report and form 10-K*. Pittsburgh: Alcoa.

Andersen, Marianne Krogh. (2011, November 11–17). Chinatown i Maniitsoq, *Weekendavisen*, pp. 1–2.

Arbejdsgruppen for Arbejdsmarkeds- og Erhvervsudvikling. (2007). *Arbejdsmarkeds- og erhvervsudviklingsmæssige betragtninger i forbindelse med etablering af tung energikrævende industri i Grønland*. Nuuk: Grønlands Hjemmestyre.

Arbejdsgruppen for Infrastruktur Miljø og Natur. (2007). *Den endelig rapport med en indledende vurdering af konsekvenserne for infrastruktur, sundhed, miljø, natur og kulturhistorie ved anlæggelsen af en aluminiumssmelter mellem Sisimiut og Nuuk*. Nuuk: Grønlands Hjemmestyre.

Arbejdsgruppen for Samfundsøkonomi. (2007). *Samfundsøkonomiske betragtninger i forbindelse med etablering af et aluminiumssmelteværk og tilhørende vandkraftværker i Grønland*. Nuuk: Grønlands Hjemmestyre.

Bennetzen, Niels, & Lonka, Anders. (2008). *De byudviklingsmæssige konsekvenser ved etablering af en aluminiumssmelter i Grønland*. Nuuk: Greenland Development A/S.

Berthelsen, Allattoq Herman. (2007, September 7). Aluminiumsindustri ved Sisimiut, *Inuussutit* p. 8.

Bjørst, Lill Rastad. (2011). *Arktiske diskurser og klimaforandringer i Grønland. Fire (post)humanistiske klimastudier*. København: Institut for Tværkulturelle og Regionale Studier (PhD indleveret til det Humanistiske fakultetet).

Brichet, Nathalia, & Hastrup, Frida. (2011). Figurer uden grund. *Tidsskriftet antropologi* (64), 119–136.

Clarke, Lee. (1999). *Mission Improvable: Using Fantasy Documents to Tame Disaster*. Chigago: University of Chicago Press.

CRU Strategies. (2007). *Greenland Aluminium (Ownership Models)*. London: CRU.

Danmarks Ambassade Danmarks Eksportråd. (2007). *Rammevilkårsanalyse for Greenland Development Inc*. Oslo: Danmarks Eksportråd.

Davidsen, Agnethe. (2007, September 21). Aluminiumssmelteværk i Nuuk, *Inuussutit*, p. 4.

Departementet for Erhverv, Arbejdsmarked og Erhvervsuddannelser. (2008). *Beslutningsgrundlag for etablering af aluminiumssmelter i Grønland*. Nuuk: Grønlands Hjemmestyre.

Department of Industry Labour Market and Vocational Training. (2008). *Decision Paper for Establishment of Aluminum Smelter in Greenland*. Nuuk: Greenland Home Rule.

Emsley, Roy. (2001). *Nature's Building Blocks: An A-Z Guide to the Elements*. Oxford: Oxford University Press.

Enoksen, Hans. (2007, January 5). Kære alle borgere i vort land, *Sermitsiaq*, pp. 28–29.

Feenberg, Andrew. (1991). *Critical Theory of Technology*. New York, Oxford: Oxford University Press.

Forchhammer, Søren. (1997). *Gathered or Dispersed?: Four Decades of Development Policy Debate in Greenland*. Copenhagen: University of Copenhagen (Ph.D. handed in at the faculty of Humanities).

Gimpel, Denise, & Thisted, Kirsten. (2007). Lost – and gained – in translation. Kulturel oversættelse som transformativt rum. *Tidsskriftet Antropologi* (56), 179–204.

Greenland Development A/S. (2011). Status for projektet. Retrieved July 12, 2011, from www.aluminium.gl/media(851,1030)/GD_8._juni2011_pr%C3%A6senteret_af_Juaaka.pdf.

Grønlands Arbejdsgiverforening. (2010). Kommentar fra Grønlands Arbejdsgiverforening. In NIRAS (Ed.), *Aluminumsprojektets økonomiske betydning* (pp. 74–75). Nuuk: NIRAS.

Grønlands Hjemmestyre Erhvervsdirektoratet. (2007). Redegørelse om energiintensiv industri i Grønland. Nuuk: Grønlands Hjemmestyre.

Grønlands Hjemmestyres SMV arbejdsgruppe. (2007). Sammenfatning af strategisk miljøvurderings rapport (SMV 2007 rapport - DK). Udsendt i offentlig høring fra December 10, 2007 til January 15, 2008. Version 11. December 2011. Nuuk.

Grønlands Selvstyres SMV arbejdsgruppe. (2010). *Regionaludvikling og migration – Strategisk miljøvurdering.* Nuuk: Grønlands Selvstyre.

Hansen, Anne Merrild. (2010). *SEA Effectiveness and Power in Decision-Making: A Case Study of Aluminium Production in Greenland.* Aalborg: University of Aalborg (Ph.D. handed in at The Danish Centre for Environmental Assessment).

Hargadon, Andrew, & Sutton, Robert I. (1997). Technology brokering and innovation in a product development firm. *Administrative Science Quarterly, 42*(4), 716–749.

Harvey, David. (1989). From managerialism to entrepreneurialism: The transformation in urban governance in late capitalism. *Geografiska Annaler. Series B, Human Geography, 71*(1), 3–17.

Hastrup, Kirsten. (2007). Performing the world: Agency, anticipation and creativity. In E. Hallam & T. Ingold (Eds.), *Creativity and Cultural Improvisation* (pp. 193–206). Oxford: Berg.

Hastrup, Kirsten. (2009). The nomadic landscape: People in a changing Arctic environment. *Geografisk Tidsskrift-Danish Journal of Geography, 109*(2), 181–189.

Henningsen, Juliane. (2011). Alcoasagen skal ikke fremskyndes. Retrieved May 23, 2011, from www.ia.gl/index.php?id=1256.

Holmsgaard, Erik. (2006, December 1). Nyt selskab skal forberede aluminiumssmelteværk, *Sermitsiaq,* p. 48.

HS Analyse. (2008). *Kendskab og holdning i Grønland til aluminiumsprojektet – efterår 2007.* Nuuk: HS Analyse.

Institute of Economic Studies. (2009). *The Effect of Power-Intensive Industrial Developments on the Icelandic Economy* Reykjavik: Institute of Economic Studies, University of Iceland.

Inuit Ataqatigiit, Demokraterne & Kattusseqatigiit Partiiat. (2009). *Landsstyrekoalitionsaftale for 2009–2013.* Nuuk.

Jervelund, Christian, & Winther, Christian Dahl. (2010). *Effekt på kommunernes økonomi af aluminiumsprojektet.* København: Copenhagen Economics.

Johansen, Poul, Asmund, Gert, & Aastrup, Peter. (2007). *Miljømæssige problemstillinger og løsningsmuligheder i forbindelse med anlæg og drift af vandkraft og en aluminiumssmelter i Grønland. Redegørelsen til Grønlands Hjemmestyre, Direktoratet for Natur og Miljø.* Aarhus: Afdeling for Arktisk Miljø, Danmarks Miljøundersøgelser, Aarhus Universitet.

Kleist, Kuupik, & Friis, Lykke. (2009). *Forståelsesdokument vedrørende fodnote om Færøerne og Grønland til den/de nye politiske klimaaftale(r) indgået under COP 15-møder i December 2009 i København.* København: Naalakkersuisut & Klima- og Energiministeriet.

Landstingets ad hoc udvalg vedrørende eventuel etablering af en aluminiumssmelter i Grønland. (2008). Betænkning afgivet af Landstingets ad hoc udvalg vedrørende eventuel etablering af en aluminiumssmelter i Grønland vedrørende Forslag til Landstingsbeslutning om placering af aluminiumssmelteværk samt principbeslutning om ejerskabs- og finansieringsmodel, hvis det på et senere tidspunkt endeligt besluttes at etablere en vandkraftbaseret aluminiumsproduktion i Grønland. Nuuk: Home Rule of Greenland.

Latour, Bruno. (2007). *Reassembling the Social: An Introduction to Actor-Network-Theory.* Oxford: Oxford University Press.

Lyberth, Søren. (2007, September 14). Aluminiumssmelteværk i Maniitsoq. Naturligvis, *Inuussutit,* p. 8.

Lynge, Finn. (2010). Foreword. In A. M. Hansen (Ed.), *SEA Effectiveness and Power in Decision-Making: A Case Study of Aluminium Production in Greenland* (pp. 7–9). Aalborg: The Danish Centre for Environmental Assessment.

Lynge, Mads. (2011). Kuupik Kleist: Alle skal være med til at løfte opgaverne. Retrieved July 13, 2011, from www.knr.gl/da/nyheder/kuupik-kleist-alle-skal-v%C3%A6re-med-til-l%C3%B8fte-opgaverne.

Maniitsoq kommune. (2007). Aluminiumssmelteværk i Maniitsoq. Områdeforslag. Maniitsoq.

Ministry of Industry and Mineral Resources. (2009). *White Paper on the Status and Development of the Aluminum Project*. Nuuk: Greenland Self-Government.

NIRAS. (2007). *Økonomiske konsekvenser af etablering af aluminiumsindustri i Grønland.* Nuuk: NIRAS.

NIRAS. (2010). *Aluminiumsprojektets økonomiske betydning.* Nuuk: NIRAS.

Nordregio. (2010). *Mobilitet i Grønland: Sammenfattende analyse.* Stockholm: Nordregio.

Nukissiorfiit. (n.d.). Fremtidsvisioner. Retrieved April 26, 2011, from www.nukissiorfiit .gl/dk/om_nukissiorfiit/fremtidsvisioner/.

Nunatta Katersugaasivia Allagaateqarfialu (Greenland National Museum and Archives). (2009). *Culture Historical Significance on Areas Tasersiaq and Tarsartuup Tasersua in West Greenland & Suggestions for Salvage Archaeology and Documentation in Case of Damming Lakes.* Nuuk: NKA.

Nuttall, Mark. (2008). Climate change and the warming politics of autonomy in Greenland. *Indigenous Affairs* (1–2), 44–51.

Nuup Kommunea. (2007). Kortlægning af lokaliteter for aluminiumsværk ved Nuuk. Nuuk: Nuup Kommunea.

Naalakkersuisut. (2010). *White Paper on the Aluminium Project Based on Recent Completed Studies, Including the Strategic Environmental Assessment (SEA).* Nuuk: Greenland Self-Government.

Naalakkersuisut. (2011a). *Politisk-økonomisk beretning 2011.* Nuuk: Naalakkersuisut.

Naalakkersuisut. (2011b). *Redegørelse om regional udviklingsstrategi.* Nuuk: Grønlands selvstyre.

Naalakkersuisut. (2012). *Vores fremtid - dit og mit ansvar. På vej mod 2025.* Nuuk: Naalakkersuisut.

Olsvig, Sara. (2010, January 29). Hvorfor får vi ikke alt at vide?, *Sermitsiaq*, p. 30.

Olsvig, Sara, & Merrild, Anne. (2011, March 11). Vi har brug for professionelle beslutningsprocesser og det haster!, *Sermitsiaq*, p. 52.

PriceWaterhouseCoopers. (2009). *Grønland og CO₂ kvoter.* København: PwC.

Riles, Annelise. (2006). Introduction: In response. In A. Riles (Ed.), *Documents. Artifacts of Modern Knowledge* (pp. 1–38). Ann Arbor: University of Michigan Press.

Roepstorff, Andreas. (2003). Laboratoriet. Stedet for erkendelse. In K. Hastrup (Ed.), *Ind i verden. En grundbog i antropologisk metode* (pp. 365–382). København: Hans Reitzels Forlag.

Schmidt, Jannick H, & Thrane, Mikkel. (2009). *Life Cycle Assessment of Aluminium Production in New Alcoa Smelter in Greenland.* Nuuk: Government of Greenland.

Sejersen, Frank. (2007). Indigenous urbanism revisited – the case of Greenland. *Indigenous Affairs*(3), 26–31.

Sejersen, Frank. (2014). *Efterforskning og udnyttelse af råstoffer i Grønland i historisk perspektiv.* København: KU, Ilisimatusarfik & Udvalget for samfundsgavnlig udnyttelse af Grønlands naturressourcer.

Selvstyrekommissionen. (2003). *Betænkning af Selvstyrekommissionen.* Nuuk: Grønlands Hjemmestyre.

Selvstyrekommissionen. (2007). Betænkning afgivet af Selvstyrekommissionen, chapter 2.5 Alle skal bidrage til samfundsøkonomien. Retrieved July 12, 2011, from http:// dk.nanoq.gl/Emner/Landsstyre/Selvstyre/Selvstyrekommissionen/Betaenkning_afgivet_af_Selvstyrekommissionen/25_Alle_skal_bidrage_til_samfundsoekonomien .aspx.

Sisimiut kommune. (2007). Potentielle aluminium smeltersites i Sisimiut kommune. Sisimiut: Sisimiut Kommune.

Siumut, & Atassut. (2007). *Landsstyrekoalitionsaftale. Fælles ansvar og samarbejde*. Nuuk: Landsstyret.

Tsing, Anna Lowenhaupt. (2003). Agrarian allegory and global futures. In P. Greenough & A. L. Tsing (Eds.), *Nature in the Global South – Environmental Projects in South and Southeast Asia* (pp. 124–169). Durham and London: Duke University Press.

Williams, Robin, & Edge, David. (1996). The social shaping of technology. *Research Policy, 25*, 865–899.

4 Reforming a society by means of technology

Judging by the outlook of the situation in Greenland, the proposed aluminium smelter in Maniitsoq is, first and foremost, a factory in need of cheap energy and a reliable labour force in a stable political environment. Water of a certain quality and quantity is required to produce hydroelectric power and it has been possible to locate water resources that comply with these needs. Apart from the water needed in connection with energy production, Greenland can offer ice-free harbour facilities and freshwater in large quantities for production. Thus, by controlling and using water in a very specific and goal-oriented way, it becomes possible to evoke a *site* that is fit for the smelter. These different water potentials merge in Maniitsoq and the place becomes interesting and competitive for global industrial companies that are on the lookout for new cost-effective sites of production. Indeed, the melting local glaciers, the melting Greenlandic ice sheet and the melting sea ice improve the water potentials of Greenland for mega-industries. Greenland is now beginning to organize water in certain purposeful ways and also starting to reorganize the society itself in order to realize what is considered (by some people, in any event) the best outcome for the national economy. This involves a process of social engineering where people have to move to productive centres and have to rethink their understanding of the good life. Because the water-dependent aluminium smelter is the largest development project in Greenland, one that will make a significant impact – or even a 'dramatic' impact, in the words of one report (Bennetzen & Lonka, 2008, p. 46) – on many parts of Greenland, with irreversible consequences, it is safe to say that Greenland is undergoing a process of creative reformation. This is a reformation where new kinds of balances between regions and social groups as well as among new dynamics and dependencies will emerge.

It is indeed relevant to relate the mega-project to a general vision of Greenland and to all the complex decisions and investments that have to be made. The integration and use of new (mega-)technology in Greenland will be discussed in the following sections, the discussion being based primarily on the work of Andrew Feenberg (1991), which – on the basis of philosophy of technology – focuses on the complex interaction between technology and society and also deals with the role technology plays in the transformation of social values as well as with how society socializes technology. Feenberg, among other things, aims the analytical focus at questions of power, democracy and causality.

Although the aluminium case is linked to climate change, Greenland's potential engagement in the aluminium industry is not a question of *adaptation* or *coping* – it is rather an example of *transformation* made possible by a confluence of climate change (melting ice), water control (dams), political vision (self-government), global markets (aluminium prices), technological requirements (a smelter) and national management (centralized administration). I choose to refer to this engagement as *transformation* because it entails a re-appropriation of space and population and also stimulates acknowledgement of creative ways to reformulate the project related to the state and the individual, and also examines how they are entangled. It is a normative and political endeavour, mediated by technology. The basic requirements of the factory will transform the Greenlandic society; the government is using this as a naturalized leverage for a reforming of society. With this, I am implying that the smelter and its production requirements are going to become mediating factors for political decisions that would otherwise be difficult to agree upon (e.g., forced changes in settlement patterns and changes in subsidy policies). The smelter turns into a naturalizing mediator between political areas that are normally difficult to link because the relations are believed to be political sensitive. This is a view on technology that emphasizes the idea that certain social forces, groups, interests and powers within society use technology to push social, political and economic agendas. Technology is the means for human ends. In the case of Greenland, technology in the shape of the smelter is being used to push for a better national economy, among other things, and to organize society in new ways. People are expected to adjust to the technical requirements of the smelter (and several studies are annually testing the attitude and willingness of Greenlanders to actually do so) in ways that would have met more resistance if these changes were being suggested on the grounds of political reasoning alone. This opens up for a more general discussion on the role and position of technology in societal change and reform.

Simpson (1995, pp. 13–14) points our attention to a process that resembles this mediation but which accentuates the role and position of technology itself in this process. When society makes use of technology for the purpose of enhancing social values (e.g. using the smelter to create a more self-reliant Greenlandic society), the values, he claims, become the ends of the technology, and this posits technology as autonomous. The values migrate, so to speak, into – or are handed over to – the realm of technicians and bureaucrats, who render them divorced from the context of human lifeworld. The difficult but pressing public political debate on 'What do we want the future self-governing Greenland to look like?' is turned into a simple discussion of how to regulate the smelter, how to make it work for the benefit of self-government and how to avoid environmental problems. The mediation is thus carried out on technology's terms. According to philosopher Jacques Ellul (see Feenberg, 1991, p. 7), the technical phenomenon has become a defining characteristic of all modern societies, regardless of political ideology. A more complex understanding of the process is contributed by Feenberg (1991), who, on the one hand, focuses on the problems related to the restructuring implications of technology (taking care to remind us that technology is not neutral) while maintaining, on the other hand, that we can appreciate the potentials and use of technology for the benefit of society. He argues that societies can control how and what values technology mediates. By maintaining a balance, he claims, we avoid the discussions between instrumentalist and substantivist approaches. All too often, these two approaches understand technology and culture as 'reified and opposed to each other in arguments about 'trade-offs' between efficiency and substantive goals such as participation or environmental compatibility' (Feenberg, 1991, p. vi). By this, he means to say that the debate often boils down to simple negotiations, where instrumentalists and substantivists basically accept the technology in question and then negotiate the 'amount' of technology and culture, respectively. The more technology, the less culture – and vice versa. Feenberg, however, maintains the right to talk about a better society and he proposes a new awareness about – and a new approach to – technology because technology has become so pervasive that the consensus leaves little of practical import on which to disagree. He argues that 'the degradation of labor, education, and the environment is rooted not in technology *per se* but in the anti-democratic values that govern technological development' (Feenberg, 1991, p. 3). He conjoins this democratic discussion with existential choices about what it means to be human but notes that '[t]oday these choices are increasingly mediated by technical decisions. What human beings are and will become is decided in the shape of our tools no less than in the action of statesmen and political movements' (Feenberg, 1991, p. 3). How technology is being organized and used is thus fraught with political and moral consequences, and Feenberg finds that the 'exclusion of the vast majority from participation in this decision is the underlying cause of many of our problems' (Feenberg, 1991, p. 3). These discussions are hampered not (solely) by the political organization of society but moreover by the pervasive nature of technology, which leaves little room for discussions that do not transpire on its own terms.

Very often, the Greenlandic discussions on the proposed smelter have a lot to do with obtaining better information, better data and more thorough analyses. It has to do with gaining a deeper understanding of the project's positive and negative sides in order to be able to weigh the pros and cons. Voices that contest such an approach and that fundamentally question the industry or the speed of its implementation (even though they may not subscribe to either anti-development or anti-industrialization) do not have a prominent place in the debate. Critique and concern about the smelter must be phrased within the discourse of the project technology so that it can conveniently be approached – and answered – by the bureaucrats, academics and engineers that possess the expertise about the technology and the project. Feenberg argues that '[t]his approach places "trade-offs" at the centre of the discussion. [...] On this account, the technical sphere can be limited by non-technical values, but not transformed by them' (Feenberg, 1991, p. 6). Habermas proposes that the technologization of the public sphere, where its functions are transferred to technological experts, may destroy the very meaning of democracy, which he understands as the commitment on the part of the citizens to engage in rational arguments in public life (see Feenberg, 1991, p. 8). Whereas Feenberg advocates a more critical approach to technology, Habermas's critique is pivotal: '[r]edeeming power of reflection cannot be supplanted by the extension of technically exploitable knowledge' (cited in Feenberg, 1991, p. 9). By following this line of thinking, human agency gains a strong position in technological transformations.

The neutrality ascribed to technology, which makes it possible to apply technology in the service of particular social and political projects, is basically an instrumentalist understanding that stands in opposition to a substantive theory, where the neutrality of technology is denied. Feenberg looks over at Ellul and Heidegger and points at their strategies of arguing for a substantive theoretical understanding of technology as constituting a new type of expansive cultural system that restructures the entire social world as an object of control. Implicated in this suggestion is that '[t]echnology is not simply a means but has become an environment and a way of life' (Feenberg, 1991, p. 8). Thus, by choosing to employ a particular technology, whether it be a dog sledge, a water pump or an aluminium smelter, man concomitantly makes many unwitting cultural choices and is affected by the technology itself. That the technical apparatus requires and shapes society in certain ways was argued, already in 1872, by Engels, in his essay, 'On Authority'. Here, Engels claimed, on the basis of his analysis of three socio-technical systems (cotton-spinning mills, railways and ships at sea), that '[t]he automatic machinery of a big factory is much more despotic than the small capitalists who employ workers ever have been' (cited in Winner, 2009, p. 217) and continued with the even more sweeping formulation: 'If, man, by dint of his knowledge and inventive genius, has subdued the forces of nature, the latter avenge themselves upon him by subjecting him, insofar as he employs them, to a veritable despotism independent of all social organization' (cited in Winner, 2009, p. 218).

The construction of an aluminium smelter may, from this perspective, require the establishment, structuring and maintenance of a particular set of social conditions as the operating environment of that factory. Langdon Winner (2009, p. 223) terms this relationship 'the political qualities of artefacts'. He argues for a dialectic perspective on the political quality of technology: the use of artefacts may have intentional or unintentional consequences on society, authority and power but may also tend, due to the design, the use, the maintenance and the running of crucial technological systems, to eclipse other sorts of moral and political reasoning. Through the use of a theory of technological politics, he draws 'attention to the momentum of large-scale socio-technical systems, to the response of modern societies to certain technological imperatives, and to the ways human ends are powerfully transformed as they are adapted to technical means' (Winner, 2009, p. 211). In an earlier publication (1977, p. 227), Winner even argued for the following relationship between society and technology:

> The goals, purposes, needs, and decisions that are supposed to determine what technologies are in important instances no longer the true source of

their direction. Technical systems become severed from the ends originally set for them and, in effect, reprogram themselves and their environments to suit the special conditions of their own operation. The artificial slave gradually subverts the rule of its master.

The technology complex in question (a smelter, two dams, electric transmission cables, etc.) carries by virtue of its large-scale systematic socio-technical nature an enormous potential. The astronomical economic investments that are required, its spatial and temporal consequences, and also the political expectations invested in the project give it a certain momentum. This concept of 'technical momentum' is proposed by Hughes (2009), in an attempt to bridge technological determinism and social constructivism, and he suggests that the investment of money, effort and resources required to develop, maintain and use technological systems can make it difficult, if not impossible, to change those systems (p. 141). From his vantage point, the system thus both shapes and is shaped by society.

Technological artefacts function within particular social relations, practices and networks; they cannot work without them. Technological artefacts may thus more correctly be termed 'socio-technical systems' – the social is part of the technological and the technological part of the social. The smelter technology, for example, cannot operate without a labour force. Therefore, the smelter, regarded as a socio-technical system cannot be detached, no matter how autonomously it may seem to be operating, from human practices, values and aspirations, and thereby it enables certain social relations while constricting others. The technology may thus reinforce a particular system of values and relations.

A socio-technical system that is fit for Greenland

The smelter complex in Greenland is huge and expensive and certainly does constitute, in the terminology put forth by Thomas Hughes (2009), a 'technical momentum'. In addition to the factory itself and a harbour, the two hydroelectric power plants have to be constructed. This will indeed make an impact on Greenlandic society. However, if we understand the project complex as a socio-technical system, our attention to the social relations, the values and the political anticipations is intensified. The question is thus not only one of how to make the technology work, but also a question of what kind of society the system should stimulate. In fact, the smelter could run profitably, both for the Greenlandic society and for the aluminium company, by bringing foreign workers to Greenland (NIRAS, 2010, pp. 28–32) but the government has decided that the factory should benefit the Greenlandic population directly as a workplace. That the factory should underpin a certain socio-technical system has been a conscious political decision. Therefore, the government has entered into an agreement with Alcoa which specifies the aluminium company's obligation to employ, in the service of the project, as many qualified Greenlanders as possible. In the Arctic and in Canada, in particular, the development of Impact and Benefit Agreements (Caine & Krogman, 2010; Fidler & Hitch, 2007) has become common practice, by means of which industries address community needs and aspirations in the development areas. The Greenlandic aspiration to boost the economy and the productivity of its population has informed the government's requirements that have been put forth to Alcoa. The authorities want the factory to be embedded in the lifeworld of Greenlanders instead of designing it as an industrial activity that turns Greenlanders into bystanders, even if such a solution could also improve the island's economy – through royalties and company taxes.

In a certain way, circumpolar peoples' expectations to be engaged in and to benefit directly from industrial activities as well as their claim to economic development set a new framework around industrial expansion and activities in the North. It makes industrialization quite different from former industrial activities and from the former ways of approaching the North: as a frontier and as a resource-platform for southern-based centres. This decision and requirement for involvement are pivotal in understanding the socio-technical system that will emerge from the smelter complex. The smelter's strict requirements for a stable labour force now have to be filled out by Greenlanders rather than by foreign workers, who could just as well have been migrating workers settled in work camps for shorter or longer periods. The mobilization of a qualified and stable Greenlandic labour force, to be located in Maniitsoq with their families, and the appurtenant requirement that this mobilization could also help to improve the national economy – as a consequence of recruiting workers from special social groups – will both serve to change the socio-technical system. Thus, the particular choice of socio-technical system made by the authorities may have more impact on Greenland than the smelter itself. To put this in different way, the government has changed the social life of the smelter and socialized it, in a particular way, by means of its decisions.

The smelter should not be understood as a means that a community is supposed to control merely in order to reach certain ends. The point is rather that – following Bruno Latour (1999, p. 212) – it is impossible to have an artefact that does not incorporate social relations and it is similarly impossible to define social structures without accounting for the large role played in such structures by nonhumans (e.g. technology). The socio-technical is thus a hybrid, consisting of crossovers, thusly eliminating humans and technology as polar opposites. By applying this perspective, Greenland socializes the smelter (e.g. by giving it a particular life and a history of construction, operation and death) and the smelter itself socializes Greenland (by re-importing the workings of the factory into the social realm). Humans and nonhumans (in this case, a smelter) have exchanged properties at crossovers and each of those crossovers 'result[s] in a dramatic change in the scale of the collective, in its composition and in the degree to which humans and nonhumans are enmeshed' (Latour, 1999, p. 201). In the words of Latour (1999, pp. 197–198):

> techniques are not fetishes, they are unpredictable, not means but mediators, means and ends at the same time; and that is why they bear upon the social

fabric. Critical theory is unable to explain why artifacts enter the stream of our relations, why we so incessantly recruit and socialize nonhumans. It is not to mirror, congeal, crystallize, or hide social relations, but to remake these very relations through fresh and unexpected sources of action…[M]ost of the features of what we mean by social order – scale, asymmetry, durability, power hierarchy, the distribution of roles – are impossible even to define without recruiting socialized nonhumans.

Controlling a mega-project

The discussion of the factory technology in Greenland has not been seen either as totally external to or as being divorced from cultural values and organizations, a perception that Arnold Pacey (1983, p. 5) singles out as an overhanging danger. The smelter is not being considered 'only technology'. In most project reports, the aim is to construct baseline studies and background material in order to understand the requirements, impacts and potentialities of the aluminium smelter. Although the project is, in the reports, socialized and tamed in a particular way, the reports never try to bypass uncertainties or the project's tremendous and uncontrollable influence on society. However, even in the vocabulary of impacts, consequences, anticipations and projections, one particular image of the smelter-society relationship is maintained: it can be monitored and, assuming enough data can be gathered and weighed in relation to baseline studies and political ambitions, this relationship can be controlled through proper management, through the prudent use of expertise and through adept decision-making that is based on due diligence. In a white paper, the Greenlandic government, for example, stated: 'These studies have now been completed and the [study] project has documented the present situation against which future development can be assessed.' (Naalakkersuisut, 2010, p. 9). Later in the same report, it was underlined that '[o]ngoing updates of data in the mobility study are recommended as part of the follow-up monitoring. Such data updates will be a core element in the future planning of societal development throughout Greenland.' (Naalakkersuisut, 2010, p. 12). The reports were thus framed as ways of targeting the project through technical intervention, planning and expertise – a strategy that calls to mind James Ferguson's anti-politics machine (Ferguson, 1994), which points at ways that politics are removed from development.

Such studies of impacts and baselines become desirable and possible when the socio-technical system is figured and understood in a particular way. The dominant figuration of the project becomes apparent when comparing it to other figurations produced by opponents. The project opponents' arguments are based on discourses that socialize the project along different lines. One group of opponents focuses its concern and critique on the quality of the studies pursued and on the probability of impacts; their line of critique is 'Can the studies be trusted and have they told us everything?'. Their concern is not only related to the uncertainty and limits of science but also to the credibility of the institutions that are framing and communicating the studies. However, their critique can be seen as existing *within* the same socialization process as that which is being constructed in the reports – the factory can be controlled, its impacts can be monitored and decisions can be made; the problem is – according to these opponents – that the present assessment system cannot (yet) meet the requirements.

Other opponents socialize the project quite differently. Then, another kind of critique emerges. In their project-story, the smelter is configured in a global capitalist network, where it is linked to other companies, markets, peoples and environments elsewhere. The factory in Maniitsoq cannot function, in this system and according to *their* optics, without the global network of transportation, without the increasing and – as seen from their point of view – unnecessary consumption of aluminium, without the concentration of capital winding up in the pockets of a handful of companies, without the emission of large quantities of CO_2 leading to global warming and without the destruction of environments elsewhere in the world – due to mining (see e.g. Avataq, 2010a). The Greenlandic environmental organization, Avataq, condenses this view in the following way: 'Can we, as a society, have faith – and place our trust – in a company like Alcoa, at all, while we can simultaneously observe how the company behaves in the rest of the world?' (Avataq, 2010a, translated by the author). The organization links Alcoa to what they call 'rogue states' and claims that the company's involvement in, for example, Guinea in West Africa, helps a regime to maintain its violations of human rights and its oppression of the population. The opponents that are primarily organized in Avataq socialize the factory in a totally different way than what transpires in the reports made available by Greenland Development A/S, by virtue of their focus on the multitude of phases of aluminium production from the beginning to the end of the process.

Avataq's understanding of the social embeddedness of the factory within a global network of other factories, industrial activities, transport and economic competition is met with critical responses from Greenland Development A/S, where the Greenland Development A/S pursues what could be termed a factory re-socialization. This was, for example, the case in 2010, when the reservoir walls containing poisonous red mud stemming from the production of alumina (the product that is subsequently used in aluminium smelters) were broken by accident in Hungary. 3.2 million m³ of mud flooded three villages and the authorities struggled gallantly to avoid a major pollution of the Danube and Raba Rivers. Authorities placed three regions in a state of emergency and labelled the incident an 'ecological disaster' (Tran, 2010) and called it the worst chemical disaster in the history of the country (Kennedy, 2010). Due to the potential overflow into the Danube River, the EU feared that the spill could turn into an ecological disaster for several countries and urged Hungarian authorities to focus all their efforts on keeping the sludge away from the Danube (Pidd, 2010). In order to avoid any misunderstandings and any unnecessary fear in Greenland of an analogous risk of pollution, Greenland Development A/S appeared on the national television station and explained that there are no resemblances between the two factories – a smelter does not produce toxic red mud. Avataq responded with a press release in which they accused Greenland Development A/S of manipulation and of propagating a conscious misrepresentation of the aluminium industry. Avataq maintained that '[i]t is a fact that in order to produce aluminium, bauxite has to be produced somewhere in the world. The process of refining bauxite into alumina will result in red mud as a waste product, as was the case in Hungary. Irrespective of how you regard the catastrophe in Hungary, it is a fact that in order for the proposed smelter in Maniitsoq to produce aluminium, there will – somewhere in the world – be a lake of red toxic mud.' (Avataq, 2010b, translated by the author). This conflict serves to demonstrate how the factory is socialized in two quite different networks, where one focuses on containment within a closed system (Greenland) while another focuses on linking the factory into a global system of interdependence. These differing system understandings point at the importance of the relationship between system understanding and factory figuration. When different system understandings can evoke diverse factory figurations, the definition of 'baseline' and even the demarcation and dynamics of the socio-technical system itself emerge as politically driven and contentious.

Avataq sees the aluminium industry as being interlinked in a global business where certain values are exposed through its technologies, activities and investments. By up-scaling the socio-technical system, the risk landscape of aluminium production in Greenland is therefore tied into a global network of interdependent technologies, people, environments and production phases. This perspective is underpinned by the organization's referral to networks with organizations elsewhere in the world that stand in opposition to the aluminium industry (e.g. Saving Iceland and International Rivers Network) and by its diligent activity of correlating material on aluminium-related issues from all over the word (e.g., the book, 'Out of this Earth' (Padel & Das, 2010)). As I will show later, in the chapter on place-making (Chapter 5), Greenland Development A/S and the supporters of the factory in Maniitsoq also establish an understanding of the smelter and the technology that integrates Maniitsoq in a global network of technologies. Analytically speaking, they evoke a socio-technical system that is also global but nonetheless of a totally different nature, where the factory is understood as a global market supplier and as an alternative to the polluting smelters found in foreign countries. Thus, the conflict is not constructed as one that is based on different processes of socializations that can best be understood in terms of local/national versus global but rather on socio-technical systems that can best be understood as being embedded in different global networks of interdependence. The point here is that one and the same technology can be socialized in various ways, by means of demarcating its boundaries and networks differently. Thus, it is not a question of framing the issue as a global industry that happens to be intruding on a local setting but rather as a question of framing different ways of socializing industrial technology.

Technology and alternative rationalizations

The new Greenland is being pursued by a very conscious appropriation of technology, with a special purpose (a self-sustaining economy) in mind. The reports are quite elaborate about the fact that this entails a reorganization of society and a change in the competences as well as a change in the mobility of the labour force, among other things. Kwame Gyekye (1995, p. 139) defines appropriation as the method that features the 'active, adroit, and purposeful initiative and participation of the recipients in the pursuit and acquisition of a technology of foreign production'. It is, quite precisely, through the government's insistence upon the involvement of the Greenlandic labour force in the project that the project makes its anticipated extensive social and demographic impact. The authorities expect to enhance, rather than to undermine, the political and economic aspirations of Greenland. In fact, by demanding the involvement of the local population, Greenland re-designs the socio-technical system to make it fit to the needs of self-government. Critics of instrumentalism, like Heidegger, might presumably have pointed out that it is impossible to create a fundamentally different form of industrial society through a different instrumentalization of the existing technological base (see Feenberg, 1991, p. 11). Furthermore, Heidegger might very well have stressed that technology is relentlessly overtaking us to such an extent that the technical restructuring of modern societies is rooted in a nihilistic will to power and in a degradation of man and Being to the level of mere objects (see Feenberg, 1991, p. 7). The technology has – from this point of view – become autonomous and has transformed individuals into standing reserves and raw materials for the benefit of technological processes. In 1966, Lewis Mumford formulated this process of alienation in the following way: 'Instead of functioning actively as a tool-using animal, man will become a passive, machine-serving animal whose proper functions…will either be fed into a machine, or strictly limited and controlled for the benefit of depersonalized collective organizations' (1966, p. 303). If this is the case, we are doomed, according to Feenberg, unless we return to a more traditional and primitive way of life, as would be expected to be the consequence of this line of thinking.

Feenberg finds the discussions on technology and society to be stranded between instrumentalist and substantive theories and he offers a critical theory of technology in which *both* arguments are maintained. His theoretical formulation resembles the substantive theories by arguing that the technical order shapes – and perhaps even structures – the world, in a more or less autonomous fashion (p.12), but that humans make choices and take action in order to make use of technology for particular purposes: 'In choosing our technology we become what we are, which in turn shapes our future choices' (Feenberg, 1991, p. 12). Thus, by rejecting a strong substantive stand and concurrently following a more instrumentalist line of thinking, Feenberg argues that his critical theory does indeed integrate human choice and human action, where human beings make use of technology for particular purposes; it is for this reason that political struggles continue to be important. However, Feenberg argues that technical rationality becomes political rationality (p. 12). This is a point that was originally advanced by Herbert Marcuse. In his groundbreaking 'One-Dimensional Man' (1964, p. xlvii), it is expressed in this way:

> As the project [the transformation and organization of nature as the mere stuff of domination] unfolds, it shapes the entire universe of discourse and action, intellectual and material culture. In the medium of technology, culture and politics, and the economy merge into an omnipresent system which swallows up or repulses all alternatives. The productivity and growth potential of this system stabilize the society and contain technical progress within the framework of domination. Technological rationality has become political rationality.

Even though Feenberg finds a footing in such a deterministic stand, based on substantive theory, he does not write off human agency, choice or the will to transform the goal-horizon through technological means. He maintains that technology can be bent to serve cultural values and political ambitions. Therefore, he argues that '[f]rom an economic standpoint, the dependence of technology on culture means that *alternative rationalizations* are possible, each equally "efficient" in terms of achieving its own ends, but employing different configurations of means to do so' (Feenberg, 1991, p. 115, italics in original). The technological order is thus, for Feenberg, a potential starting point for divergent developments depending upon the cultural environments that shape it. What Feenberg does is to deny that one single technical phenomenon (such as a factory) can be demarcated, characterized and rejected as a whole. This is a non-deterministic approach, where technological development is influenced by both technical and social criteria of progress which, according to him, opens up for changes in society in a variety of directions depending on the prevailing hegemony (Feenberg, 1991, p. 130). At the same time, he finds the adaptive relationship between technology and society to be one of reciprocity, which entails that 'technology changes in response to the conditions in which it finds itself as much as it influences them' (Feenberg, 1991, p. 130). The foundation for this relationship is that technical objects are considered social objects, which is also reflected in the use of the term, 'socio-technical systems'. The technological changes and their relationship with society are thus to be considered particular cases of industrialism that need to be considered in relation to the particular society in question. 'The content and meaning of industrialism is not exhausted by our experience of it since technology still contains *potentialities* that might yet be actualized in a different cultural context' (Feenberg, 1991, p. 131).

If this analytical focus on *social potentialities* is to be applied in Greenland, it is going to be necessary to look at how society discusses and evaluates the smelter project, i.e. the technology in question, and at how its potentialities are constructed and understood on a broader scale rather than as being compartmentalized within the environmental and economic fields. One could thus ask the following question: What kind of society is envisioned and mobilized by this particular future socio-technical system?

Imagining social potentials

The social potentials are seldom touched upon in the reports, in discussions in the newspapers and in the Parliament. The different discussions centre on how to make the project possible, how to evaluate its consequences and how to make as many people as possible benefit from it. These questions are in line with the analyses published on the homepage of Greenland Development A/S, where the focus is on how to organize society so as to make it fit the requirements of the smelter. Here, the centre of focus is to produce and assess as much data as possible by experts. The potentialities that Feenberg is pointing at are framed by the project itself and concomitantly coupled with a powerful desire to boost the economy.

Few voices in the Greenlandic society have pointed at other aspects of the socio-technical system that have to be examined, discussed and managed. However, Karl Lyberth, who happens to be a strong advocate of the smelter, points at some of the broader questions that need to be addressed. In a newspaper article (K. Lyberth, 2011), he asked the following questions: How will Greenland deal with the large number of foreign workers who, in the long run, may turn the Greenlandic population into a minority? What will happen to the Greenlandic language if the English language becomes more dominant? Is Greenland ready to be a multicultural and multi-religious society? What will happen to sectors that will be reduced (like fishing and hunting)? Concern is also expressed by one strong opponent of the project who finds that the project will change the unique value system and Greenlanders' connection to the land because the future will be put into the hands of the rationality of large-scale industries (M. L. Lyberth, 2011). In the white paper presented to the Parliament in autumn 2010, the government, in addition, raises a serious social concern that is related to the communities from which the Greenlandic labour force is to be recruited (Naalakkersuisut, 2010, p. 21):

> It should also be taken into account that those moving to Maniitsoq from other parts of the country will, to a large extent, be socio-economically advantaged people. This means that some towns and settlements should expect to do without those people who they rely on in the local community and who may have been particularly enterprising or supportive in society.

Such questions raised by supporters, by opponents and by government itself, are not being pursued in detail. Indeed, discussing these matters on a 'thorough and fully informed foundation' – which is the phrase that is often used – does appear to be difficult. Doing so, in a proper way, will certainly require a broader and more democratic discussion in society, which could include more stakeholders throughout Greenland, as has been suggested by Jane Petersen, member of Parliament, in the discussions that were carried on in Parliament on November 10, 2010 (personal observation of the author from watching the discussion on on-line television). Petersen's proposal finds resonance in Fennberg's argument that 'democratic control of industry is a condition for generating an interest in a new direction of technological progress' (Feenberg, 1991, p. 143). The argument thus perceives democracy as a productive force that is shaping innovation. When Jane Petersen asks about how to integrate Greenlandic nongovernmental organizations and the public in discussions, it is not tantamount to asking whether Greenland is a democracy or not. Her point can be better understood as a question about how Greenland has organized its democracy and how it has integrated stakeholders in the debate about the future of Greenland. Similar worries about the public's democratic participation are also put forth in a report (K. G. Hansen, Sørensen, & Jeppson, 2009) that analyzes newspaper articles related to major decisions which have been made in relation to the smelter. It concludes that: '[o]ur analysis indicates that during the period in question (almost three years), levels of public debate relating to the aluminium furnace have gradually risen. A large number of stakeholders have been represented in this debate. In general, however, it would seem that public discussion has been displaced, as it were, which is what has occurred after administrative and internal political decision-making processes have taken place. Considered in relation to the process' democratic character, this is, of course, most unfortunate' (K. G. Hansen et al., 2009, p. 58).

Throughout the project period, Greenland has tried to control the factory set-up and to maintain as much oversight on the project as possible, in order to organize it (and the factory, for that matter) as a socio-technical system that will serve the interests of the self-government. The requirements and consequences have been analyzed and the impacts and benefits appear to be nationwide and related not only to the factory's immediate surroundings. The different effects have been formulated and advanced in reports but there has never been a real and coherent discussion of the vision of the Greenland that emerges from these effects. The factory project has not configured itself as an explicit *moral project,* where the state and the public enter into a new social contract of rights and obligations based on a novel perception of what citizenship means. Instead, it seems as if these moral concerns have been lived out by proxy, through a preoccupation with procedures, representation, data gathering, and economic technicalities. The scene of political democratic struggles (and accordingly, the ideas about different visions for society and about how technology can be used to promote such a society) has been dominated by the expert culture (the empire of expertise) guided by an overall societal vision: economic self-reliance supporting the self-government. When economic self-reliance becomes the main driver, the economic imperative stands out as predominant to such an extent that people who question the smelter project (even though they might not necessarily happen to oppose the project) are criticized as undermining self-governance and the nationwide development (see e.g. M. L. Lyberth, 2011).

The question thus becomes whether Greenland has managed to fully understand and discuss the societal transformation that the new socio-technical system sets in motion. Due to the dominance of a certain group of experts and the pervading political ambitions of a self-sustaining self-governing Greenland, the project has been socialized and figured in a coherent way. The result is that other ways of understanding the socio-technical system have been marginalized. The political and economic aspirations embedded in the project have twisted the social imperative in a certain direction, where landscape, communities, citizens and nationhood are assembled in a factory project within which dreams, standards and practices are wrapped together in finite moments of politically pervasive and materially effective configurations (see Greenough & Tsing [2003, p. x] and Tsing [2003, p. 11]). To put this in a different way, the factory is constructed as a particular spatial and temporal socio-technical system that is being used to figure a new national society and a new citizen.

Even though the discussions of the unfinished and not yet commenced project are largely being carried on along the lines determined by technical aspects, environmental impacts, ownership models, economic potentials, factory phases and the wages of foreign workers, the shadow issues are social and political. Instead of looking into the social aspects of a technical revolution (which seems the way things are proceeding in Greenland), it might be useful to refocus and concentrate, alternatively, on the technical aspects of a social revolution. In fact, the factory technology, in and of itself, does not require society to be reorganized or require that citizens to be moved, etc. Rather, it is a particular social vision that requires the figuration of a particular socio-technical system rendered possible by this particular smelter, in which the social world and its citizens are going to be reshuffled in order to meet new national political and economic goals. This factory technology gives rise to certain path dependencies, which differ from those that we see in mining and oil and gas extraction. It is most especially its need for a large and reliable labour force that will be working 24 hours a day, 365 days a year, for at least 60 years, that affects the temporality of the project and its potential impact on Greenland. Choosing an aluminium smelter as a national socio-economic leverage thus has certain potentials for maintaining the permanence and direction in the national project. The factory is not seasonal – neither is nationhood: this makes a perfect match. The factory is used to transform Greenland's goal horizon and this process of world-making is accompanied by a reinterpretation of citizenship, place and landscape as well. Even so, these aspects are not part of the debate, explicitly.

Project compartmentalization and the re-configuration of society

Greenland's ambition to create an economically self-reliant and politically self-governing country cannot be realized without effectuating some major re-configurations of the society. During the 1950s and 1960s, the Danes pursued what may be termed a total reorganization of Greenland. Greenlanders refer to this period as the time when the effects of Danish colonization were felt to be the harshest; this was largely due to an extensive modernization process that was centrally planned by the Danes, a strategy of modernization that followed the tenets of Danish design. This was the case even though Greenland was not officially a colony any longer. Often, this period is spoken about as being a traumatic period because it involved the more or less forced relocation of many Greenlanders to towns. The effects of this centralization process were, in fact, one of the underlying reasons for a growing Greenlandic political resistance to Danish 'remote control' (*fjernstyring* in Danish, as it is often referred to), which eventually led to a movement demanding Home Rule: a claim toward self-determination that Greenland finally succeeded in attaining in 1979 when it was granted Home Rule and which was, moreover, enhanced and expanded in 2009 when self-government was obtained.

The present aluminium project has – according to the reports – nationwide impacts and will be the largest project ever in the history of Greenland. Furthermore, the aluminium smelter is only one out of several large industrial projects that are on the drawing board and are in their first stages. If all these projects are taken into consideration, in the aggregate, the potentialities of technology are significant; this is something to which Feenberg (1991) draws our attention. In order to benefit from these projects, a particular socio-technical system has to be built where the educational level, the skills in general, the mobility patterns, the demographic set-up, the urbanization processes and the subsidy distribution system, just to mention a few examples, have to be organized and coordinated in order for the system to work. According to the managing director of the Employers' Association of Greenland, Henrik Leth, this process of social crafting and engineering is going to make the modernization period of the 1950s and 1960s look like a 'Sunday school project' (Leth, 2008). Leth does have, of course – as the managing director of the employers' association – a vested interest in boosting economic potentials, but he raises concerns: '[the projects] require a number of democratic reflections and a thorough public debate. And this requires a totally new and visionary political plan for the future of Greenland. After all, in what direction are we headed with Greenland?' (Leth, 2008 translated by the author). In a similar way, one of the working groups under the Strategic Environmental Assessment pointed out that it is not (only) a matter of better understanding the details, trends and projections but (also) a matter of relating this mega-project to a general vision of Greenland (Grønlands Selvstyres SMV arbejdsgruppe, 2010, p. 16). This wish to have a more coherent vision of the future of Greenland is worthy of note because it reveals that the future cannot (solely) be modelled or anticipated through technology; neither as individual projects nor as pooled. In essence, what this means is that even though all industrial projects are closely monitored, evaluated, impact-assessed, and infused by public opinion – a process that indeed increases control over the individual projects, their progression and their implementation – this is an endeavour that is separated from a coherent vision related to livelihood. This is the kind of vision that Henrik Leth is calling for.

Although one may take up a critical stance in response to the way these processes are taking place (e.g. A. M. Hansen, 2010) the point I would like to make here is that knowledge and control over the project has been pursued on the basis of a particular figuration of the project and on the basis of a narrowing of vision in order to make the project work and grow. According to James Scott (1998, p. 11), '[t]he great advantage of such tunnel vision is that it brings into sharp focus certain limited aspects of an otherwise far more complex and unwieldy reality'. One could say that this is the strength, as well as the predicament, of all analytical endeavours. However, as with all analytical work, one must ask the pressing questions: 'What is obtained and what is left out and what are the consequences of this?' Scott elaborates how, for example, cadastral maps and modern forest management are ways of ordering, controlling, measuring, standardizing and appropriating the world (as well as, respectively, the population and the trees) in the service of a state power, from where there issues an illusion about a synoptic view of the entire project. However, Scott emphasizes that this knowledge is gained by accepting a rather static and myopic view of the social practices and dynamics. In order to infuse this technical vision into processes of project evaluation and assessing, compartmentalization is necessary. By compartmentalization, I mean the disciplining of the project through the vehicle of deconstructing it into commensurable and demarcated elements and phases that are related to importance and unimportance as analyzed in Chapter 3. Furthermore, the project itself is also compartmentalized from other projects and thus shielded from the world. Scott points out that 'a whole world lying "outside the brackets" returned to haunt this technical vision' (p. 20).

In the projects related to the aluminium smelter, there are only a few thoughts expressed about how the smelter, in combination with other large-scale industrial projects, will influence Greenland (a result of *project compartmentalization*) and there is neither any analysis nor any discussion about how communities that are expected to experience smelter-related outmigration are going to wind up looking (a result of *site compartmentalization*). The livelihood and welfare-related problems in negatively affected communities are mentioned but not considered. Rather, these communities are referred to as merely being *impacted* by the smelter. The point here is not to question the analysis of impacts but rather to question the act of compartmentalization that leads to a loss of vision which has consequences for people and on their perception of the projects. Arguing for the evocation of a societal vision, as Feenberg urges us to do, is one way of addressing the potentialities of the technology. It can be claimed that the vision of an economically self-reliant and politically self-ruling Greenland is a compelling vision and that everything has to be judged in relation to that – and that alone. However, the other questions that also come into view are: What kind of life does the population want to live in an economically self-reliant and politically self-ruling Greenland? What potentials within this framework do they want to activate and pursue? Thus, it is a more ethical and socio-cultural discussion of a societal vision that emerges from Feenberg's work. He finds that this democratic discussion could be positioned in the centre of the public debate and could be used as a yardstick for judging project elements, potentialities and assemblages. When the projects and the technological requirements dominate the political discourse and accordingly infuse a utilitarian logic into the debate, it can cast a shadow over more immanent understandings of changes and transformations, as well as a shadow over the contours of state organization and citizenship. The social contract between state and citizen is being redefined in the reports although the reports are highly technical and economical. Processes of societal engineering, patterning, control and expertise are unfolded in the technical reports which, by virtue of their facts, their charts, their statistics, their representations and their projections are, on the one hand, transforming and constructing a society and, on the other hand, are not quite capturing (and are not really supposed to capture) the new society in its totality and lived diversity. Scott (1998, p. 88ff) terms these processes 'state simplifications', which are part and parcel of an ongoing state project of legibility. 'Simplification' is used here, however, as signifying anything else but simple or related to simple-mindedness (p. 81). Five characteristics of facts that state simplifications give rise to are listed in his analysis – and he points out that state simplifications are observations of only those aspects of social life that are of official interest (p. 80): a) utilitarian facts; b) written, documentary facts; c) static facts; d) aggregate facts; and e) standardized facts. The relationship and dependencies among the different kinds of facts are scrutinized by Scott (1998). He also examines how these 'state simplifications' are employed in structural reforms and grandiose plans. In his analysis, the state project of legibility is not only about how to produce, order and use these facts but also has to do with articulating a strategy about how to create a population that can live up to those standardized characteristics embedded in the facts, because only then will the inhabitants be easier to monitor, count, assess and manage (pp. 81–82). He is actually suggesting that 'many state activists aim at transforming the population, space and nature under their jurisdiction into the closed systems that offer no surprises and that can best be observed and controlled' (Scott, 1998, pp. 81–82).

If we transpose this into a Greenlandic context, then the aluminium reports and all the descriptions, observations, calculations, assessments, mappings and projections are, in fact, also part of a civilizing mission that is being carried out by the Greenlandic authorities. When politicians request more data and analysis they are, at the same time, supporting a state project that is supposed to produce a particular kind of citizen and supposed to evoke, in the end, special focus areas of politics. This is, of course, the job and the burden of all politicians, everywhere. In Greenland, however, the civilizing mission of the state is tailored in a special way, due to its unique post-colonial position and occupational history. The Self-Government Act of 2009 has the boosting of economic activity as its basic point of departure; this makes mega-industries attractive. Mega-industries may be challenging in themselves, but they are maybe even more challenging in a country like Greenland, where this kind of industrialization has not appeared before. Therefore, concerns about the consequences are raised in the Strategic Environmental Assessment. However, what has been suggested is that this concern can be counteracted if 'thorough base-line study is put in place, which may be used as the point of departure for an ongoing and long-term monitoring program of the regional developmental tendencies in areas of out- and in-migration. When implementing potential mitigating or facilitating measures, the effects of these should also be monitored...In this way, a baseline data can be obtained, which can then be used as a measure of warding off unwanted – as well as encouraging – socio-economic and regional economic consequences in the future' (Grønlands Selvstyres SMV arbejdsgruppe, 2010, p. 15, translated by the author). Amassing data and ongoing monitoring thus seem to be important tools in helping policy makers. The danger is that collections of statistical facts (which are generated with a certain vested interest in mind and configured accordingly) may be turned into social causalities that politicians have to react to or have to design their policies after.

The process of statistical facts being turned into social causalities is, for example, apparent in the migration studies. Migration patterns are a central and decisive trend that has to be understood if plans for concentration and labour force mobility are going to be set up. The mobility report (Nordregio, 2010), for example, finds statistical evidence for singling out hunters and fishermen as less mobile than other occupational groups, presumably due to their attachment to their hunting and fishing territories (p. 17). Of course, the social life and mobility of hunters, as well as their territorial attachment, are essentially more complex and dynamic (Sejersen, 2003, 2004) and there may be good reasons for hunters and fishermen to be resistant to the idea of moving (on account of, for example, the lack of affordable housing and the lack of adequate jobs elsewhere) and to say so when they are being interviewed for the mobility reports. Their answers may also be seen as constituting a critique of the large-scale attempt to re-design community life and production from above. However, their answers and the statistical analyses derived from such answers are then turned into social causality, which is further underpinned by stressing their territorial attachment. Occupational hunting (an activity of a social group), territorial attachment (cultural dimension) and lack of mobility (practices) become three interrelated elements in a positive feedback loop enmeshed in a dominant narrative that is considered to be causally related: the more successful the hunter is, the more attached he is to the hunting territory and the more immobile he becomes, the argument seems to go. Statistical data that is turned into laws of social causality gain a particularly strong status and such data may be used to mobilize political opinion, funding and intervention. In the new emerging system, hunters and fishermen have been re-valued and turned from a productive group that has been looked upon with a certain measure of respect into a place-bound group that is standing in the way and hindering the envisioned flourishing of a resourceful and mobile labour force that would be of benefit to the common good.

In the new political environment of mega-industrialization, this narrative makes a boomerang effect on the hunters and the fishermen, who now have to stand as targets of political intervention and reform. The rules of the game, so to speak, are changing with great haste in this nation-wide reconfiguration process. This leads to new requirements and logics: no longer is 'small' being equated with 'beautiful'. In 2011, MP Niels Thomsen suggested, in Parliament, that hunters earning less than DKK 150,000 per annum should be offered the possibility of being re-educated: 'If the hunters start to educate themselves to take on a new occupation, it will be of benefit to their families. There is no doubt that their economy will be improved. […] In the long run […] it will be to the benefit of the national economy [*landskassen,* in Danish] and the individual towns if this responsible initiative were to be supported' (cited in Andersen, 2011 translated by the author). This is a suggestion that falls right in line with the underlying logic of Naalekkersuisut's Regional Development Strategy (2011) which, making a reference to an earlier report that was written by the Home Rule (Hjemmestyre, 2008), states the following (Naalakkersuisut, 2011, pp. 25–26, translated by the author):

> The changes can continue to be severe in the coming years. Therefore, it is necessary to look at the problems in a holistic way and it is important to establish basic principles for the political efforts that are related to the development of the future labour market. Therefore, a renewed focus shall be put on the upgrading of the labour force for new job functions but there is also a need to focus on the readiness for change [*omstillingsparathed* in Danish] among each individual in the labour force. The premises for a societal strong economy are the labour force's continuous search for new jobs that offer the best possible salaries and responsibilities in order for the human resource, as an effort factor [*indsatsfaktor* in Danish], to be paid the highest possible wage.

In the Parliament, Thomsen's proposal was turned down. The political party, Siumut, argued, among other things, that hunters and fishermen should not be singled out as beneficiaries of a special program – it should be applied, instead, to everybody who stands in need of educational improvement. A number of other political parties were against the proposal, and actually on the basis of the special respect they harbour for hunters and their occupation, but they did acknowledge the need to reorganize the occupational field and the market in order to make it more cost-effective. The status of hunters has indeed changed over the last decades and many of the positive attributions are still maintained – partly, perhaps, because hunters are thought of as being emblematic of a saliently 'Greenlandic' way of life.

However, Thomsen's proposal indicates the emergence of an attitude in Parliament that has already become dominant in the reports. In the reports, the need to re-educate hunters and fishermen is often referred to, albeit in indirect fashion: in the Regional Development Strategy, one of the tactical goals with respect to fisheries is, for example, to increase the individual fisherman's income by modernizing the fishing fleet with the use of as few public subsidies as possible (Naalakkersuisut, 2011, p. 40). The structural reforms indicated here are functioning to concentrate the fleet and the quotas in as few hands as possible. In practice, this entails that a large group of active fishermen will have to reduce their fishing activities – or stop altogether. The fishery reform thus requires that many hunters and fishermen are going to have to re-evaluate their lifestyles and their competences. In a parliamentary report focusing on the labour market and on aluminium production, the possibility and the need to retrain hunters and fishermen – and other persons who are presently working within the fishing industry – is also pointed out, directly (Arbejdsgruppen for

Arbejdsmarkeds- og Erhvervsudvikling, 2007). Although Niels Thomsen's pro-posal was voted down in the Parliament, this does not necessary entail that the underlying logic of the proposal was rejected.

Mega-industrialization and climate change

What do mega-industries have to do with natural disasters like climate change? The political choice that Greenland is facing – that of diversifying and strength-ening the nation's economy by looking into mega-industries in a rapidly changing icescape, which is often described as posing the possibility of disaster for the world – can be viewed as a way of adapting to the natural changes and of seizing and actively creating opportunity. However, adaptation entails, in this case, a total transformation of society.

In Greenland, the adaptation to climate change cannot be regarded in isolation or separately from technology, political and economic ambitions, from the dele-gation of expertise or from the particular figurations of projects. The Greenlandic case presents a textbook illustration of the difficulties in demarcating adaptation from other societal processes, and to such an extent that one might even question whether the industrialization of Greenland can be termed 'adaptation to climate change' at all. Greenland is adapting to the melting ice sheet by turning it into a water resource that can furnish a new society, if mediated and socialized by a particular kind of technology.

I would like to emphasize here the attention on societal transformation as it is taking place in the Arctic where large-scale technology often plays a pivotal role. If we focus on processes of transformation instead of on adaptation, there are other normative and political questions that emerge. It is not a matter of finding the best possible (and preferably the cheapest and quickest) adaptation strategy or the best use of technology but rather a matter of asking, 'In what way would society like to transform itself, its values, and its relations to others, in order to avoid or overcome problems?' Furthermore, the focus on transformation compels us to ask another question: 'In what way will *this strategy* and *the chosen technology* transform society, our values, and relations to others?'

The discourse on climate change adaptation (and mitigation) manifests itself in financial allocations and political initiatives while the question of transforma-tion is seldom (or never) surrounded with funding or direct political attention. The upshot of this is that, all too often, the societal visions and the technological potentialities are not being addressed directly. It is by opening the 'black box' of technology that such issues may appear more accessible for analysis and public debate (Williams & Edge, 1996).

References

Andersen, Per. (2011, February 8). Find et erhverv, der kan betale sig, *Atuagagdliutit*, p. 10.
Arbejdsgruppen for Arbejdsmarkeds- og Erhvervsudvikling. (2007). *Arbejdsmarkeds- og erhvervsudviklingsmæssige betragtninger i forbindelse med etablering af tung energikrævende industri i Grønland*. Nuuk: Grønlands Hjemmestyre.

Avataq. (2010a). Pressemeddelelse November 15, 2010. Retrieved July 13, 2011, from www.avataq.gl/userfiles/NY_avataq_pressemedd_15_nov_2010.pdf

Avataq. (2010b). Pressemeddelelse October 17, 2010. Retrieved July 13, 2011, from www.avataq.gl/print.asp?lang=dk&num=2.

Bennetzen, Niels, & Lonka, Anders. (2008). *De byudviklingsmæssige konsekvenser ved etablering af en aluminiumssmelter i Grønland.* Nuuk: Greenland Development A/S.

Caine, Ken J., & Krogman, Naomi. (2010). Powerful or just plain power-full? A Power Analysis of Impact and Benefit Agreements in Canada's North. *Organization & Environment, 23*(1), 76–98.

Feenberg, Andrew. (1991). *Critical Theory of Technology.* New York, Oxford: Oxford University Press.

Ferguson, James. (1994). *The Anti-Politics Machine: Development, Depoliticization, and Bureaucratic Power in Lesotho.* Minneapolis: University of Minnesota Press.

Fidler, Courtney, & Hitch, Michael. (2007). Impact and Benefit Agreements: A Contentious Issue for Environmental and Aboriginal Justice. *Environments Journal, 35*(2), 49–69.

Greenough, Paul, & Tsing, Anna Lowenhaupt. (2003). Preface. In P. Greenough & A. L. Tsing (Eds.), *Nature in the Global South – Environmental Projects in South and Southeast Asia* (pp. vii–xii). Durham and London: Duke University Press.

Grønlands Selvstyres SMV arbejdsgruppe. (2010). *Regionaludvikling og migration – Strategisk miljøvurdering.* Nuuk: Grønlands Selvstyre.

Gyekye, Kwame. (1995). Technology and Culture in a Developing Country. In R. Fellows (Ed.), *Philosophy and Technology* (pp. 121–142). Cambridge: Cambridge University Press.

Hansen, Anne Merrild. (2010). *SEA Effectiveness and Power in Decision-Making: A Casestudy of Aluminium Production in Greenland.* Aalborg: University of Aalborg (Ph.D. handed in at The Danish Centre for Environmental Assessment).

Hansen, Klaus Georg, Sørensen, Frela Lund, & Jeppson, Steen R. (2009). Decision processes, communication and democracy; The aluminium smelter project in Greenland. In J. H. e. al. (Ed.), *Knowledge-Based Tools for Sustainable Governance of Energy and Climate Adaptation in the Nordic Periphery* (pp. 55–84). Stockholm: Nordregio.

Hjemmestyre, Grønlands. (2008). *Tilpasning af arbejdsstyrken til nye væksterhverv, bind 1 hovedrapport.* Nuuk: Grønlands Hjemmestyre (Projektgruppen vedr. tilpasning af arbejdsstyrke til nye væksterhverv).

Hughes, Thomas P. (2009). Technological momentum. In D. G. Johnson & J. M. Wetmore (Eds.), *Technology and Society. Building Our Sociotechnical Future* (pp. 141–150). Cambridge, Massachusetts: The MIT Press.

Kennedy, Meaev. (2010, October 10). Hungary braces for second wave of toxic sludge. *The Guardian.* Retrieved July 13, 2011, from www.guardian.co.uk/world/2010/oct/10/hungary-sludge-toxic-red-waste-spill?intcmp=239.

Latour, Bruno. (1999). *Pandora's Hope: Essays on the Reality of Science Studies.* Cambridge, Massachusetts: Harvard University Press.

Leth, Henrik. (2008, February 8). Alcoa-projektet kræver politisk omtanke og rettidig omhu, *Sermitsiaq (Inuussutit)*, p. 8.

Lyberth, Karl. (2011, February 23). Grønlændere som minoritet i vort eget land, *Atuagagdliutit*, p. 16.

Lyberth, Mette Larsen. (2011, March 11). De sælger vores land, samhørigheden udryddes, *Sermitsiaq.*

Marcuse, Herbert. (1964). *One-Dimensional Man.* London: Routledge & Kegan Paul.

Mumford, Lewis. (1966). Technics and the Nature of Man. *Technology and Culture, 7*(3), 303–317.

NIRAS. (2010). *Aluminiumsprojektets økonomiske betydning.* Nuuk: NIRAS.

Nordregio. (2010). *Mobilitet i Grønland - sammenfattende analyse.* Stockholm: Nordregio.

Naalakkersuisut. (2010). *White Paper on the Aluminium Project Based on Recent Completed Studies, Including the Strategic Environmental Assessment (SEA)*. Nuuk: Greenland Self-Government.

Naalakkersuisut. (2011). *Redegørelse om regional udviklingsstrategi*. Nuuk: Grønlands selvstyre.

Pacey, Arnold. (1983). *The Culture of Technology*. Cambridge, Massachusetts.

Padel, Felix, & Das, Samarendra. (2010). *Out of This Earth: East India Adivasis and the Aluminium Cartel*. New Delhi: Orient BlackSwan.

Pidd, Helen. (2010, October 7). Hungarians battle to hold back toxic sludge spill from Danube. Retrieved July 13, 2011, from www.guardian.co.uk/world/2010/oct/07/hungary-toxic-sludge-spill-danube.

Scott, James C. (1998). *Seeing Like a State: How Certain Schemes to Improve the Human Condition have Failed*. New Haven, Connecticut: Yale University Press.

Sejersen, Frank. (2003). *Grønlands naturforvaltning. Ressourcer og fangstrettigheder*. København: Akademisk Forlag.

Sejersen, Frank. (2004). Horizon of sustainability in Greenland: Inuit landscapes of memory and vision. *Arctic Anthropology, 41*(1), 71–89.

Simpson, Lorenzo C. (1995). *Technology, Time and the Conversations of Modernity*. New York: Routledge.

Tran, Mark. (2010, October 5). Hungary toxic sludge spill an 'ecological catastrophe' says government. Retrieved July 13, 2011, from www.guardian.co.uk/world/2010/oct/05/hungary-toxic-sludge-spill?INTCMP=SRCH.

Tsing, Anna Lowenhaupt. (2003). Agrarian allegory and global futures. In P. Greenough & A. L. Tsing (Eds.), *Nature in the Global South – Environmental Projects in South and Southeast Asia* (pp. 124–169). Durham and London: Duke University Press.

Williams, Robin, & Edge, David. (1996). The social shaping of technology. *Research Policy, 25*, 865–899.

Winner, Langdon. (1977). *Autonomous Technology*. Cambridge MA: MIT Press.

Winner, Langdon. (2009). Do artifacts have politics? In D. G. Johnson & J. M. Wetmore (Eds.), *Technology and Society: Building Our Sociotechnical Future* (pp. 209–226). Cambridge, Massachusetts: The MIT Press.

5   Place consciousness and the renewal of Maniitsoq

A great many people in Maniitsoq are excited about the prospects of having an aluminium smelter located in their back yard. Elsewhere in the world, strong opposition is very often aired when there is a plan in connection with large-scale development projects to establish facilities close to residential communities. Often, the position taken up by the opposition to such projects is termed 'NIMBY', the abbreviation for 'Not in My Back Yard'. In Maniitsoq, however, the local people's concerns and criticism have been met with expertise. The local excitement about a large-scale work place and other job opportunities, which could potentially boost the town's economy and its dynamics, has been reinforced by several trips to Iceland, made by community members, where they had a chance to visit similar smelters. The support for the project and the expectations have reached a point where the ideological position of the community's representatives that is currently dominating the discourse can be termed PIMBY – short for 'Please in My Back Yard'. Many in Maniitsoq point to the possibilities offered to the town by such a factory and feel that the project could potentially cause the town to regain a more central economic and political position in Greenland and will potentially make the town a place to live the good life once again.

The project has pushed for and initiated a process where people are re-evaluating the town as a place. This, in turn, has fostered a new and complex place consciousness, which gives rise to the emergence of special subject positions and possibilities for agency. In the following, I will present four cases of place constructions which have been dominant in the local and national debate:

1 Whales and urban place competition
2 Landscape redefinition and new commitments to the place
3 Creating a greener global environment from Maniitsoq
4 Creating a place for the good life in an expanding town

The cases indicate that the development of a new place consciousness is extensive and that it involves the construction of a variety of time-space relations. On a broader scale, the cases indicate that the introduction of new technology, new strategies for relating to (climate) change, new uses of water and the construction of new horizons of possibility may not only have ramifications for the way places are understood and approached, but also ramifications for how people creatively construct new positions for agency through a re-understanding of place. In the case of Maniitsoq (and in the case of Greenland in general), the re-construction of place consciousness is extensive, because there is a programmatic attempt under-way to change the social, cultural and economic focus from a fishing and block-grant economy to a more large-scale industrial and self-reliant economy. This is a transformation that will change the country and have irreversible ramifications. The discourse is primarily one of opportunity, empowerment and necessity rather than one of loss and retainment. As has been pointed out in Chapter 1, the Arctic peoples already have a history of industrial experience (J. K. Nielsen, 2005) and expectations hold that this experience is going to be advanced and elevated by conditions made possible by, among other things, climate change. In some cases, industrial activity has taken place in close collaboration with indigenous communities and the people living in such communities have used the activities to strengthen their local economies and their possibilities for self-determination (North Slope Barrow in northern Alaska is but one example). Due to the increase in the collective rights of indigenous peoples in the Arctic, a number of different political and economic possibilities and obligations for indigenous peoples have emerged and have served to empower them with a larger influence on industrial development and caused them to benefit more directly from industrial projects (Nuttall, 2010). In this perspective, the process in Maniitsoq can serve to illumi-nate some of the processes that might be at play when a community appropriates and interacts with a given industrial complex.

The new place consciousness emerging in Maniitsoq and the processes of re-territorialization can be better appreciated if the history of the town *as a place* is understood. In Maniitsoq, many of the people whom I met during my fieldwork made explicit references, at one point or another in our conversations, to the historical developments of the town and to its historical fluctuations of boom and bust economies. Their emphasis on this can be interpreted as a way of accentu-ating not only their concrete experiences of change and their love of the place, notwithstanding its ups and downs, but also – and perhaps moreover – as a way of pointing out to me that change itself is an inherent part of their lives and that change is not something that is unfamiliar – for them – to deal with. Furthermore, the potential construction of a smelter was integrated, through the vehicle of the constructed narrative, as an integral part and extension of the town's historical dynamics.

Maniitsoq as a place in history

In 1782, Maniitsoq was established as a small community by the Danish colonial trade on the southern part of the island of Maniitsoq (E. Lyberth, 1982). At that time, the town was also called Sukkertoppen (Bendixen, 1921, p. 151). This name is believed to refer to the hilly and mountainous characteristics of the island and is also believed to refer to the observation that freshly fallen snow on these hills looked much like a special Dutch cake (Zuykerbrood) that is topped with sugar. In fact, the name stems originally from the spectacular hills that are close to Kangaamiut, located 70 km north of Maniitsoq, the colonial trade centre that was also called 'Sukkertoppen' at the time. After a decision made by the Danes, allegedly for purposes of benefitting the Danish colonial trade's interest in whaling, the district's colonial trade centre was relocated from Kangaamiut (established in 1755) to its present day location. The colonial name, Sukkertoppen, moved in synch with the relocation of the trade centre. The island itself is roughly 150 km^2 in area and is only separated from the mainland by the small sound, Tuno (Hamborgsundet).

From Maniitsoq, one can easily get far inland on the mainland to hunt muskoxen and caribou and to fish for trout, either by entering through the mainland's many fiords along the coast or by taking the long trip down along the fiord of Kangerlussuaq (Søndre Strømfjord), which is 190 km long. The widespread use of the area by different Inuit groups in order to benefit from both its terrestrial and marine resources is apparent in the presence of archaeological (Bendixen, 1921, p. 120; N. Nielsen, Skautrup, & Vibe, 1970, pp. 483–484; R. Petersen, 1982) and contemporary camp sites. Today, small hunting cabins are scattered in the landscape and used as bases for hunting and fishing, both for commercial and private use. Furthermore, these cabins are used as places for relaxation and considered sites of leisure (Sejersen, 2010b). Many Maniitsormiut (the Greenlandic name for the people who are in living in Maniitsoq – Maniitsormioq being the singular form) point out that the places and areas in the landscape that can be reached within a few hours of sailing are integrated parts of the community's dynamics and orientation. This, they claim, makes the town very attractive. The capital of Nuuk, which is located 320 km south of Maniitsoq, can be reached by plane (30 minutes) or by boat (3 ½ hours), for an affordable price, which also makes living here especially desirable to many people, when taking into account Nuuk's opportunities as well as the many friends and family members that have moved there.

Whaling and fishing – a community of change

Despite great expectations, the whaling activities going on at Sukkertoppen never amounted to a success and this centre for whaling was shut down back in 1795 (E. Lyberth, 1982), at which time the equipment was moved north – to Holsteinsborg (which is called Sisimiut today). The colonial administration expected people to move north, as well, but the population of Sukkertoppen continued to grow, from 249 (in 1789) to 317 (in 1799), due – very likely – to the advantageous conditions presented by the place for good hunting and fishing (E. Lyberth, 1982, p. 44). These opportunities are also singled out by Louis Bobé, in his historical account of the district, where he mentions that Sukkertoppen was, in 1832, considered the best colonial production site in Greenland, with its abundance of resources and its large population of 485 Greenlanders (Bobé, 1921, p. 172). Of commercial interest were, in particular, the hides and skins (from seals, beluga whales, caribous, foxes and eider ducks) and the oil/blubber (from seals and whales) (Egede, 1982). At the beginning of the 1900s, as part of the so-called 'Tjalfe expedition', which was headed up by Adolf Jensen in 1908–09, the Danes explored the possibilities and potentials for commercial fishing in Greenland (apart from shark fishing, which was already being done very intensively, due to these creatures' enormous and oil-rich livers). The Danes were experimenting with new techniques and were trying to awaken an interest among the Greenlanders in increasing their fishing of cod, salmon, Greenland halibut and halibut (Egede, 1982). The primary processing activities that were being carried out before export-ing the goods were salting and drying the fish. During the 1910s and 1920s, higher temperatures in the sea waters (Kiilerich, 1970, p. 63; Mattox, 1973) caused the cod to swim from Iceland to Greenland. By 1922, people were already starting to catch sight of cod in the waters around Maniitsoq (Horsted, 1970, p. 168). This signalled the start of the pre-industrial phase of fishing, which was characterized by in-shore activities taking place on and near smaller boats and with simple tech-nology (such as lines and jigging), where the cods were salted in the summers and dried during the winter months (Smidt, 1989, p. 119). In terms of importance in the trading economy, from the 1930s (Mattox, 1973), fishing came to supplant seal hunting, and as fishing increasingly became the focus of the trade rather than seal hunting, Greenlanders started to obtain small wooden vessels that were also used for transportation – and over the years these gradually replaced the skin boats (umiaq/konebåd). This change is reflected in the following statistics: In 1880, 24 umiat and 31 wooden boats were registered; in 1935, the numbers were 2 umiat and 126 wooden boats; in 1927, a motorized boat was purchased by a private entrepre-neur and the number of these kinds of boats increased to 11 in 1939 (Egede, 1982, p. 79), and then to 16 in 1949 (Rask, 1993).

During the dramatic boom in cod fishing in the 1930s, the town became Greenland's most dynamic fishing centre. It can rightly be said that the modern Greenlandic cod fisheries were developed right here (Lauritzen, 1994, p. 183). After World War II, intensive cod fishing, for export, was started up in Greenland by two different companies from Denmark that operated close to Maniitsoq. And especially during the period from 1950 to 1975, the cod fisheries were abso-lutely extraordinary and many foreign vessels were engaged in these activities (Rasmussen & Hamilton, 2001, p. 36). In 1951, a factory for filleting the fish was established in Maniitsoq, although it was difficult to do this because of the hilly terrain, which had to be levelled out through the use of explosives. But this location offered good possibilities when it came to accessibility and production, and the population of the town was considered to be skilled and hard-working (Egede, 1982, p. 97). In the census that was taken in 1951, Maniitsoq, with its 983 inhabitants, ranked second after Nuuk by only 400 persons. The town indeed functioned as a magnet for people who wanted to become engaged in the fishing industry, which was, during the 1950s, entering a more intensive phase of indus-trialization, where land-based technology like freezers and factories as well as more effective fishing techniques, with bottom traps for cod and bottom trawls for shrimps, started to dominate the sector. From the beginning of the 1970s, the fisheries moved into a third phase (Smidt, 1989, p. 119), where the industry introduced electronic equipment, large-scale on-deck production facilities on the trawlers, off-shore fisheries, more efficient fishing gear and processing facilities (Poole, 1995), all of which served to make Maniitsoq a most dynamic place for the fishing industry. During the heydays of fishing in the 1970s and 1980s, the factory could boast of employing 500–600 people on a daily basis, according to the account of the man who was the production leader at the time. Then, the fishing sector overheated, as a consequence of overcapacity that was triggered by massive investments; since the end of the 1980s, it has been undergoing a process of structural rationalization, which has resulted in the reduction of jobs and vessels as well as in new ways of regulating the fisheries (Danielsen, Andersen, Knudsen, & Nielsen, 1998, pp. 37–65).

Up until the 1950s, Maniitsoq was one of the most populous communities in Greenland and it was used as an example of how the 'rational use' of fishing, as the Danes called it, could change the society, centralize it and improve the conditions of the population (Christiansen, 1959; Hamilton, Lyster, & Otterstad, 2000, p. 200).

In the 1950s and 1960s, urbanization and modernization strategies were implemented. As part of this process, large housing blocks were constructed in Maniitsoq in order to facilitate the concentration of the population. The town grew steadily, to 3,197 inhabitants in 1991, when the population peaked. The intensive activities of fishing and processing gave rise to a call for women to enter the job market. They organized themselves in the local Housewives' Association (Husmoderforeningen), which was later to become the Women's Association (Kvindeforeningen). Here, they worked hard to establish a political platform from where they could air their concerns about how the children were to be cared for while the women were working at the fish-processing plants. This movement was central in the establishment of daytime nursery schools (Biilmann & Heilmann, 1982) in Greenland.

It was during the 1980s that fishing for shrimp became the main activity; this compensated for the dramatic decrease in the catches of cod, which was the direct result of falling sea temperatures which were witnessed in 1970. The factory's statistics indicate this change quite clearly: in 1960, the factory received 6,240 tons of cod and no shrimps at all (N. Nielsen et al., 1970, p. 474); in 1970, there were 4,231 tons of cod and 27 tons of shrimp; in 1980, the numbers were, respectively, 2,447 tons and 1,761 tons (Egede, 1982, p. 97). And more recently, in 2010, according to statistics compiled by a local consultant, the relatively small fish- and meat-processing plant, Arctic Green Food A/S in Maniitsoq, managed only to take in 803 tons of cod. Today, the economy has stagnated and the town has been de-populating, both in absolute and relative terms; it is now the fifth largest town in Greenland, with a population of 2,747 in 2011 (Greenland Development A/S, 2011). The massive changes in the lucrative cod fishing industry that took place in the 1980s are described in the following way by Hamilton et al. (2000, p. 210):

> Two unusual severe 'ice winters' in 1982–1984 froze vessels into their harbors. Fishing effort soon recovered, but the fish themselves did not.

Cold water slowed cod growth and reduced their replacement through migration and reproduction; biomass fell 70% … Over the next few years, warmer water and lower catches allowed biomass to rebuild, which encouraged fisheries expansion. Reflecting this expansion, cod catches peaked again over 1988–1990. But temperatures had been cooling again since 1986, and biomass decreasing since 1987. The intensified fishing effort thus fell upon a declining fish population. Cod biomass plummeted more than 99% between 1988 and 1991, and has since shown no signs of recovery despite warming waters. Plants, communities and people that had adapted to cod fishing were left behind by this large-scale change.

The boom and bust of Maniitsoq

Over the years, the town's population has fallen. Many Maniitsormiut are concerned that this decrease and brain drain have brought the town to a critical point where it becomes difficult to maintain the town's dynamics. Even though the number of people of an age where they are expected to be active in the labour force (age 20–62) is increasing in comparison to the number of people in need of public support (in 2000, 71 out of every 100 persons between the ages of 20 and 62 were receiving support; in 2011, the analogous figures were 63 for every 100), there are some demographic changes that may be causes for concern. From 2000 to 2011, the number of people between the ages of 30 and 39 was drastically reduced by 50 per cent, and it is also expected that 15 to 25 years from now, the number of people in need of public support is going to increase as the relatively large generation of people born in the '60s begins to retire (Greenland Development A/S, 2011, p. 11). Another concern that has been aired by many Maniitsormiut is the decreasing population coupled with the number of people who are out of work: the latter has increased from 129 in 2009 to 151 in 2010. People point to the closing of the fish factory and the relocation of several administrative offices to other towns as a venisection of a kind (see e.g. Qeqqata Kommunia, 2011, p. 12), which has caused much of the life-dynamics to drain away from Maniitsoq. This has put the town in a position that makes it difficult to attract people, funding and investments – a fact that will potentially lead to a further downfall, people fear. When Royal Greenland closed down the fish factory in 2001, as part of a company-rationalization process, a group of local entrepreneurs bought the facility. However, the factory has been running at a reduced pace. Today, the company, Arctic Green Food A/S (Arctic Green Food A/S & Greenland Venture A/S, 2009), whose business is situated inside the old factory, buys fish and meat products for approximately DKK 13 million per annum from fishermen who are based in Maniitsoq. Hunters and fishermen also sell products at the local meat market for about DKK 2 million every year. This possibility of income for the hunters and the fishermen does not match, in any way, the heydays of the factory and the extensive impact it made on the dynamics of the town. The average age of hunters and fishermen in Maniitsoq is 57, which is also indicative of a general trend that the hunting and fishing occupation is undergoing a recruitment problem (Rasmussen, 2005). These figures stem from calculations made by the local hunting consultant who oversees and helps the approximately 70 professional hunters and fishermen in Maniitsoq.

The fishing bonanza periods that people in Maniitsoq have experienced despite the highly fluctuating cycles of catches and the introduction of new species of fish is often recalled with great excitement during conversations. What was continuously stressed was how all the family members (including the children, especially during holidays) worked in the fisheries and the factory during the peak seasons. Repeatedly, people pointed out to me that the country around Maniitsoq was rich in resources, and that the people were hard-working and skilled; in this way, the entrepreneurial history and potentials of the town were emphasized. However, this was also a way of expressing astonishment and frustration about the way the town had been abandoned as an upshot of priorities being formulated *elsewhere* (by the government and by the companies) and also a way of expressing that the problems should not be ascribed to inherent problems of the town. The prospected aluminium smelter is considered by many Maniitsormiut as the *new* chance (and some even expressed it as the *last* chance) to avoid the town's downfall. Therefore it might very well have been taken as an affront when concerns and critique of the project were raised by individuals and by the environmental organization, Avataq, which is based in the capital of Nuuk: 'Nuuk bulldozes Maniitsoq in the Alcoa debate. [...] Interest organizations and individuals in the country's capital, Nuuk, are telling us, speaking way over our heads, how bad the production of aluminium is for us' (Langhoff, 2010 translated by the author). According to this optics, the factory becomes a local project that need to be protected from outside criticism which is, per definition, considered illegitimate, because it does ('as usual', as seen from the local point of view) reflect other agendas and is regarded as a symptom of 'remote control' and interference.

Maniitsormiut feel strongly about Maniitsoq and about the prominent role it has played in the history of Greenland. The town is constructed as a significant and rich place, both with respect to the natural and the human resources. The cycles of resources and the concomitant boom and bust economy of the town have, up until now, been considered a natural part of town dynamics, where severe negative impacts have been avoided by shifting to new resources and production strategies. However, the political decisions that resulted in the closing of the fish factory and the removal of administrative offices from the town have cemented a local awareness of how the town's dynamics lie in the hands of decision-makers from elsewhere. The town narrative that is told by its people is one that spans the gamut from powerful to powerless and this, in turn, is related not only to changes in the presence of resources or to the diverse ways of resource use, but related just as closely to the shifting political and economic decisions that are being made by the Home Rule government and by the companies (which often are owned by the Home Rule itself).

The erosion of creative flexibility in the hunting and fishing sector

Hunters and fishermen, in general, seem to have a keen understanding of the changes in – and the cycles of – resources that they use. They are generally ready and willing to experiment with new resources or new ways of processing and selling their catch (Sejersen, 1998, 2003). In the 1980s, when the cod disappeared from Maniitsoq (it came back for a short period around 1990 [Rasmussen & Hamilton, 2001, p. 36]) the fisheries were also relying on Atlantic salmon until that species of fish also decreased sometime later in the 1980s (Rasmussen & Hamilton, 2001, pp. 38–39). One person who was talking about this period termed Maniitsoq 'a fishing Mecca' and referred to the salmon fisheries in the 1970s to 1980s as an adventure where even shrimp trawlers switched equipment for a period of one month in order to take part in the lucrative fishing activity. In the 1980s, the factory tried for a short period to process scallops in order to com-pensate for the decrease in the cod and salmon catch but concentrated its efforts nonetheless on shrimp on a more permanent basis. The changing ice, weather and sea conditions, the changing presence of resources as well as the fluctuating prices have always been crucial factors in the hunting and fishing sector. From time to time, these dynamics have given rise to much distress, and have required major investments, entrepreneurial skills, supplementary training and experimentation.

Being a hunter and fisherman thus requires the acceptance of a certain landscape of risk in which one has to be attuned continuously in order to take action at just the right moment and to maintain an intimate understanding of the aforementioned changes. Their creativity and readiness to change can be profiled as the most important strategy for hunters and fisherman when it comes to their ability to eke out a living that is based on the use of natural resources. In order to maintain their fishing and hunting livelihoods, many hunters and fishermen also rely on subsidies, on income from other household members and on income from alternative jobs that they might happen to take on during certain seasons. It is within this complex and ever-changing structure and network of activities that hunters and fishermen can maintain their ability to ascribe potentiality to an environment that is difficult to predict and control. Very often, hunters and fishermen face dire straits: even small events can make a great impact upon their activities. A broken motor, one broken finger or a broken appointment by a hunt-ing partner can hinder the person from pursuing a certain activity during a criti-cal period. In my conversations with hunters and fishermen in Sisimiut, during my previous field work visits, many of these individuals told me that they had experienced such problems during the peak season of beluga whaling, the season for lump sucker roe or the caribou hunting season, for example. These activities are critical and constitute an important source of income for the family if it is going to subsist through the leaner seasons and to make investments in new hunt-ing gear, among other things. Many hunters and fishermen are struggling to make ends meet; the landscape of risk is in constant movement and is highly unpre-dictable. From one year to the next, no season is the same, even though anthro-pologists (including myself [Sejersen, 1998]) have a habit of setting up elaborate charts indicating the yearly rhythms of hunters and fishermen. This point is also advanced by Hugh Brody (1982, p. 89) in his description of northern hunters:

> The seasonal round occupies grooves of cultural history, and draws upon archives of experience and knowledge. Hunting itself, however, must defy habit as well as follow it: no two seasons are identical, animal migrations are never wholly predictable. Hunters, following well-worn trails, must seize new opportunities, adjust the pace and direction of their movements to follow, intercept, or find the animals upon which life depends. At each point along the seasonal round, individuals must assess and process a mass of information. The habit and pattern of mobility set the scene; action within the scene keeps changing.

Harvey Feit (1994, p. 435) also notes the importance of understanding hunting as a forward-moving process: 'the essence of hunting ... is the experience of linking present anticipation and future events' (for a discussion of this, see Sejersen, 2004). Hunters and fishermen increasingly face restrictions in their possibilities and in their flexible strategies, restrictions that are imposed by the implementation of governmental regulations (quotas, seasons, equipment, license requirements, etc.), and effectuated in sector reforms (efficiency improvements with respect to technology, investment, subsidies, etc.) and in market possibilities (prices and places where the products can be sold). Mark Nuttall's (2009, p. 307) anthropological work in Greenland also points in this direction:

> Rather than Inuit hunters being prevented by climate change from catching seals, the reasons, I suggest, are rather more complicated. Long-term policies of shifting demographics, investment in a few major centers, a reluctance to introduce development policies for small villages and settlements, a redefinition of resources and rights of access to them, and a political desire to encourage the depopulation of some communities all perhaps have greater significance for changing hunting and fishing practices than climate change does.

A hunter who was speaking with the Danish Ph.D. student Lill Rastad Bjørst, during her fieldwork in Ilulissat in 2010, also put this quite clearly: 'I used to follow the animals – now I follow the rules of the Home Rule' (personal communication with Bjørst). Hamilton et al. (2000, pp. 206–207) even finds that the 'location' of resources nowadays depends partly on human artefacts like transportation, markets, and political decisions about where to support fish processing plants. Knowledge of and the skills to discover flexibility within these institutional dimensions of the hunting and fishing activities are becoming more and more important for the hunters and fishermen, and can be understood as significant aspects of what is often phrased as the 'local knowledge' that is important to their success.

Environmental changes (e.g. brought about by climate change) can have a severe impact on the activities of hunters and fishermen and on their households and communities throughout the Arctic (ACIA, 2005) but the institutional sphere that is fashioned by governmental regulations and reforms may also, to a significant extent, be restricting hunters and fishermen. In Maniitsoq, the decision handed down by the Home Rule-owned fishing company, Royal Greenland, to close down the factory struck the town's life-nerve. The closing of one of the town's major working places and, to boot, one that was based on the use of renewable resources, cut off economic possibilities for many individuals and households. In a sense, the factory was also a symbol of the town's position as an important historical place for the skillful use of resources, and was emblematic of the town's link to the important fishing industry, which has now come to concentrate its activities on fewer and more efficient units of production (ships and factories) in order to be competitive globally. As a result of similar shutdowns of local workplaces, which have been relocated to other places in Greenland (and *pari passu* with this, skilled labour has also been moved), Maniitsoq has become a place that some Maniitsormiut describe as an 'old and tired lady'. It is within this change of place consciousness (from productive, flexible and important, to unproductive, stiff and marginalized) that the prospects of the aluminium smelter have to be viewed.

The socialized conception of place

Maniitsormiut do indeed emphasize Maniitsoq as a place that is deeply engaged in a particular resource economy related to the marine environment. However, this particular place consciousness does not rule out that the town's economy is also linked to a multitude of other sectors – including public administration and services as well as mining and tourism. Furthermore, it does not necessarily reflect in detail the fishing and hunting sector's economic viability, as such. Place consciousness can be conceived as a legacy of history and geography, which is the discourse that is often employed by Maniitsormiut. In this discourse, Maniitsoq is understood as a place where what they perceive as the good life can be pursued and as an important town for Greenland due to its geographical location (and the resources that are available in this particular place) and the entrepreneurial and skillful investment of time, technology, energy and money by the town's population. Maniitsormiut often consider their town a nesting box and an arena for Greenland's influential personalities, intellectuals and politicians (see for example Biilmann, Heilmann, Lyberth, Møller, & Petersen, 1982) and thus inscribe the place (Maniitsoq) into a larger social, economic, cultural and political network of Greenland.

'Place consciousness' is understood by Doreen Massey (1994, p. 5) to be a socialized conception of place, which implies that

> the particular mix of social relations which are thus part of what defines the uniqueness of any place is by no means all included within that place itself. Importantly it includes relations, which stretch out beyond the global as part

of what constitutes the local, the outside as part of the inside. Such a view of place challenges any possibility of claims to internal histories or to timeless identities. The identities of places are always unfixed, contested and multiple. […] Places viewed in this way are open and porous.

Massey thus stresses place consciousness as not being dependent on boundedness or on the exclusion of extra-local relations. For Arif Dirlik (1999), this is an important contribution but it poses a problem because it disassociates place from location and because it potentially makes the concept of place meaningless when it can be stretched out on the basis of social relations (pp. 154–155). How is this place consciousness linked to globalism, which has emerged to a greater and greater degree as the radical antipole of place (the local)? Dirlik suggests that it is better to conceive of place and place consciousness as 'a project that is devoted to the creation and construction of new contexts for thinking about politics and the production of knowledge' (Dirlik, 1999, pp. 151–152). Place as metaphor, he proposes, indicates groundedness from below, and a flexible and porous boundary around it – without closing out the extra-local: 'What is important about the metaphor is that it calls for a definition of what is to be included in the place from within the place – [for] some control over the conduct and organization of everyday life, in other words – rather than from above, from those placeless abstractions such as capital, the nation-state, and their discursive expressions in the realm of theory' (Dirlik, 1999, p. 155). His argument about grounding place is neither tantamount to ascribing immutable fixity to place nor tantamount to repudiating flexible and porous boundaries. He wants to focus, instead, on how place is constructed and produced in order to avoid an understanding of place as a preordained location where things happen and social relations are stretched out. His suggestion to look at place from below and as a project also involves the production of figurations comprised of particular social relations, scales and boundaries. Place consciousness and place imagination (including the understanding of how far the social relations are stretched out) are in constant flow and being refigured from below and they may have something to offer in relation to people's ideas of development, social life and politics. Globalization and the global are understood and imagined *as part of* the process of constructing local identities and projects, as Bubandt (1999) also suggests.

This analytical take on globalization encourages us to see how people envision, create and deal with the world not from a place but moreover from a project's point of view, where the imagination and construction of place are crucial to the understanding of the world (see also Chapter 6). Geertz reminds us that creative forces are immanent in people's will to mobilize and pursue projects: 'Human beings, gifted with language and living in history, are, for better or worse, possessed of intentions, visions, memories, hopes, and moods, as well as of passions and judgements, and these have a more than a little to do with what they do and why they do it. An attempt to understand their social and cultural life in terms of forces, mechanisms, and drivers alone, objectivised variables set in systems of closed causalities, seems unlikely of success' (Geertz, 1995, p. 127). From this perspective, places are projects of place-makers.

The production of places or localities, according to Appadurai (1995), is not only context-driven, but is also context-generative. Thus, he proposes that as 'local subjects carry on the continuing task of re-producing their neighbourhood, the contingencies of history, environment and imagination contain the potential for new contexts (material, social and imaginative) to be produced' (Appadurai, 1995, p. 210). In essence, people continuously produce and scale contexts and wider sets of contexts for themselves and each other in order to set up frames or settings in which various kinds of human action can be initiated and conducted meaningfully. Localities and places thus become a multiplex interpretive site. Neither the global nor the local are demarcated a priori but are rather part of the continuous evoking and enacting of projects pursued by people, projects that these people find to be feasible, necessary and desirable. Such a view does not rule out asymmetries of power and does not rule out the limitations and forces of context and structure but is actually a recognition of the 'primacy of place, and its autonomy, and, on that irreducible basis, [supposed] to produce translocal or, better still, transplace alliances and cooperative formations' (Dirlik, 1999, p. 180). It is by applying this analytical focus on reflexive place consciousness as a project (related to development, culture and social categories), where people project themselves into much larger settings and networks, that we may approach some of the place dynamics appearing in Maniitsoq. Based on four short cases, I intend to show how people re-place, re-scale and rethink Maniitsoq as part of a process of society reorganization that is set in motion by the potentiality of having an aluminium smelter set up in the town's vicinity.

[1] Whales and urban place competition

In Greenland, nearly everywhere, the sea is a dominant part of life, and not only with respect to resources, transportation, and its influence on weather conditions. The sea is also a significant point of identity orientation and is significant with respect to commercial and leisure activities. The sea's social, economic, cultural and symbolic significance is deeply embedded in most stories because it plays a decisive role in people's narratives of movement and places. Aesthetically, the sea and the coastline are indeed valued to a considerable degree: when visiting people in their homes, the home's view of the sea is often brought up as part of the conversation (see also 70° N arkitektur, 2010, p. 27). In fact, the view from one's home is considered so important that one of the citizens' groups recommended that all buildings should be connected to the natural environment and that a view ought to be guaranteed (Borgerinitiativet i Maniitsoq, 2009, p. 4). In Maniitsoq, it is very common, during the right season, to observe humpback whales very close to the shoreline. This is indeed a phenomenon that Maniitsormiut still consider spectacular and unique. Even if one does not have a 'room with a view' of one's own, it is quite easy to find satisfying observation posts on some of the cliffs next to the roads. In some cases, the whales swim so close to the shore that you can almost touch them with your hand, a woman told me with great enthusiasm.

Easily accessible whale-watching can thus be considered an urban privilege of Maniitsormiut and an activity that many people value, whether they just happen to spot a whale on their way home from the grocery store or whether they actively go to watch the whales.

In February 2009, when the municipality organized citizens' groups to discuss how to reorganize town life to make it more attractive to visit and to settle in, the whale-watching opportunities were quickly mentioned. This was defined as an *asset* and one of the things that makes Maniitsoq special, when compared to other Greenlandic towns. The organization of citizens' groups was encouraged by the municipality as part of a process closely linked to the potential establishment of the aluminium smelter. A number of institutions and firms from *outside* Maniitsoq had already gotten involved in the development of different scenarios for the town. As a reaction to this, the municipality extended, via flyers distributed in the community, the following invitation (Maniitsoq kommune, 2009, translated by the author):

> It is important that we, the citizens of Maniitsoq, also take an active part in order to co-determine our own future. Therefore, the municipality encourages you to initiate projects that you might consider important for the development and the growth of the town, in order to develop cooperation, to provide more information, to secure welfare within the families, to think in new ways, and to be part of the creation of more and exciting work places – in new or existing businesses. This [invitation] is aimed at you and at your children's future.

At the meeting, citizens were informed about the aluminium smelter project and four different citizens groups were set up as part of a strategy to 'take responsibility for the development' (Maniitsoq kommune, 2009). People refer to this meeting as a very successful and informative one, and the four citizen groups worked hard during the spring of 2009 to produce a report and an idea catalogue to be handed over to the municipality. In its introduction, the final 20-page report, which was handed over in June 2009, stressed, among other things, that the people wanted to develop a society with the qualifications to deal with the challenges of the future: 'We want to create a town where we can develop our human resources and protect our environment, and a town that can express our history and simultaneously cherish our cultural values. We want to contribute to the creation of a sustainable development in Maniitsoq with an economic growth that will bring forth working places as well as advantageous social conditions that give rise to healthy and well-functioning families' (Borgerinitiativet i Maniitsoq, 2009, p. 1, translated by the author). In this same report, the group welcomed the aluminium project as an occasion to start rethinking the town's future, but later on, it was pointed out to me by several of the participants that the proposals which were put forward in the report were necessary for the town and its development, irrespective of the construction of the smelter.

As part of this process, the idea of making whale-watching more accessible and visible emerged. An idea was presented by the group that focused on 'culture and tourism', which yearned to have Maniitsoq 'positioned on the map' (Borgerinitiativet i Maniitsoq, 2009, p. 18) by creating a 'park-like' setting, from where the whales could be observed and people could relax on benches while enjoying the scenery. The proposal was based on two basic ideas: first, the town needed to develop a *brand* in order to appear attractive to citizens, visitors and newcomers (Borgerinitiativet i Maniitsoq, 2009, p. 18); and second, the surrounding environment close to town needed to be *opened up* for the citizens (Borgerinitiativet i Maniitsoq, 2009, p. 19). These ideas merged in the initiative to create a whale-watching observation post in town. The proposal was handed over to the technical section of the municipality, which took upon itself the notion that this was certainly one of the first tasks it had to realize.

Today, a large wooden platform with benches overlooks the sea and the spectacular shoreline. The platform is made easily accessible by a wooden walkway leading over the rocks, and many people visit the site just to take a break and to appreciate the landscape. People were indeed very satisfied with the project result – and not only with the construction itself, but also because the project symbolized a new social contract between citizens and the municipality. Despite its smallness, the project was regarded by many of the town's inhabitants as a milestone: it was singled out as an important milestone in the promotion of Maniitsoq and as symbolizing that the initiatives of citizens who aimed to improve the town's life were being supported and realized. One of the people who was involved in the promotion of the platform explained, in the following way (translation by the author):

> The guiding thought behind setting up the observation point was to signal that it is possible, at this special site in the landscape, to obtain an experience that is special for us and you can also share this experience together with others. In a way, you – somehow – make a dot on the map, marking out a spot where you can go to and have an experience. Of course, you can get such an experience many other places, but then it's something more accidental. I think that it has been a way of – somehow – making an environmental experience visible and accessible in a way that does not require a special effort. Yes, I think I have, moreover, emphasized a project that might make somebody proud about the town. How can one – sort of – find the feeling that we really have something we would like to show others, something we can talk about among ourselves and something that we can orientate ourselves toward … if you ask anybody, they think it's fabulous with the whales … and that it is so exciting. However, there are not so many things in the public space that make you feel that this is a town where you can share an experience together, something that you head for, together with people whom you don't know. Of course, you can bring your family, in a car, to the airport and enjoy the view from there and you can do this over and over … Of course, people do just that … enjoying the view together. But in any event, I think that, for me,

personally, this places an emphasis on how one can render it visible – also for people in the town – that something is happening here and that we are able to gather around it. That we can be happy about it. Actually, I was surprised about how well it was received. Really, it is being used a lot. One may ask why this is so, when you can simply stand on the rocks. It has become a gate to the sea for people on foot. It has become a destination for a walk.

In order to underline Maniitsoq as a special place, an artist was commissioned to create a statue in stone, of a whale's tail, a sculpture that would be placed right next to the platform. The wooden platform and the statue in stone co-produce Maniitsoq as a unique place, with its own symbol or brand which – in the words of one of the citizen groups – is 'positive' and appears attractive for the citizens, the future citizens and the guests (Borgergruppe for kultur og turisme, 2009, p. 4).

The wooden platform is a creation of a place where the consumer and leisure culture is positioned in the centre in order to make Maniitsoq appear attractive, in a particular way, within the competition between towns in Greenland. The need to attract and to hold on to skilled labour are some of the reasons for the urban initiatives that have also been taken in Nuuk, where, among other projects, a golf course has been established. The citizens' group very explicitly formulated the need for the leisure activities in the following way: 'To make the town attractive for newcomers, good leisure facilities are a prerequisite' (Borgerinitiativet i Maniitsoq, 2009, p. 16). The platform encourages and gives people the possibility of appropriating the whales, the sea and landscape in a new and more controlled way (signs with information telling about what you can see are also being developed) and in providing such an opportunity, the specificity of the place also becomes one of differentiation (from Nuuk, for example).

Maniitsoq has created a place that emphasizes and promotes its own uniqueness by actively turning the surroundings and the environmental dynamics of the town into 'a view'. The people are transforming the surroundings by applying demarcation and encouraging a certain kind of orientation and a certain kind of environmental appreciation. There are some people, of course, who contested the construction of the platform, because they found it to be unnecessary, considering that the sea, the landscape and the whales could be enjoyed from basically every point in town. However, the platform can be regarded as a particular kind of entrepreneurial place-making, where the ordinary is actively turned into something unique which can then be linked to a new vision of the town. In this way, the place helped to organize a new town narrative. It is functioning to figure the town and its resources in a new way, closely linked to a vision of a new and highly competitive economy, an influx of new capital and new people into the town, and a novel way of using the landscape (see also Granås & Nyseth, 2007). As a place, the platform actively mediates an encounter with whales and with a potential future. Thus, it is inevitably linked to negotiations of openness and closed-ness of places, not only of places in Maniitsoq but also of places in Greenland as a whole. Places are, indeed, never finished but are always becoming (Simonsen, 2008, p. 15).

Maniitsoq is facing the potentials of a huge factory and nearly a doubling of the number of inhabitants. It is a town that is expecting to – and that is wanting to – change. On first glance, the intention associated with choosing to start out by constructing a wooden platform for whale-watching might seem a bit obscure, when we consider all of the challenges that lie ahead. Nevertheless, what this indicates is that the potential new socio-economic context emerging from the construction of a factory has an impact on how people use, perceive and promote places. As one Maniitsormioq expressed it, the cliff had 'been turned into a des-tination'. One could add that it had been designed as 'an event', as well. Place-making, place creativity and the carving out of places are active drivers in staging and branding the town and in articulating new cultural and economic policies, which will re-make the town and move it away from the margins of develop-ment. This is a process that can be described as an enactment of places and new socio-scapes running across distinctions like the periphery-centre (Bærenholt & Granås, 2008, p. 1). Therefore, the wooden platform can be seen as a community enactment of potentiality, as a commitment to change, and as an enactment of networks on spatial and temporal scales that indeed surpass the platform's imme-diate purpose as an observation post.

[2] Landscape redefinition and new commitments to the place

Aluminium smelters need energy – in large, cheap and reliable quantities. To be able to power the factory in Maniitsoq, the plan is to dam two lakes in West Greenland. The Tasersiaq Lake, one of the two lakes, has been in focus as a source for hydroelectric power since the mid-1970s, when Greenland's Technological Organization investigated new energy potentials as a consequence of the oil crisis (Buch, 1981, p. 31; Lodberg, 2007) and also in connection with initiating alu-minium production (Ølgaard, 1981, pp. 59–61). The water supply stems from the melting ice cap and glaciers as well as from rainwater, and the amount of water is of such a magnitude that engineer Julius Galster proposed, in 1956, to use the water to power industries (Galster, 1956). In a short article, Galster even referred to discussions from the 1920s about how best to approach the hydroelectric power potentials presented in Greenland.

The area of Tasersiaq Lake itself is located on the mainland and is not being used today. This was made apparent upon a visit to the office of the municipal-ity's hunting officer (*jagtbetjent* in Danish), where a large map of the municipality that was pinned to the wall could be seen. This map demarcated the area that the officer was responsible for overseeing, but it did not include the lake – it was literally a white spot on the map! It is in an area that is difficult to access and is situated quite remotely from the town, in terms of the estimated time of transport to get there. For many Greenlanders, the area of Tasersiaq Lake is a place rich in historical and mythical connotations. In particular, they have a sense of the place through the stories and the watercolour paintings that were created by Aron of Kangeq (Aron fra Kangeq & Thisted, 1999) from 1858 until 1869, at which time the artist died of tuberculosis. Here, the famous story of Aariassuaq is told. Aariassuaq was an excellent hunter and song duellist but he died in his summer camp at Tasersiaq due to a disease, to the delight of many people in the area who were jealous of his success and who always lost to him in the song competitions. His cousin, who relied on Aariassuaq's skills, managed to resuscitate the deceased hunter and singer and bring him back to life. When the other hunting parties saw Aariassuaq standing in the grave, singing, they were all startled by the horrific sight and they all died of fear. Another of the stories told by Aron of Kangeq is one about a family that was hunting at Tasersiaq. Unfortunately, the son died and was buried together with his wife, who was placed alongside her deceased husband while she was still alive. Subsequently, her father-in-law tried to kill her by lancing her through the grave. Archaeologists have found the latter grave but the whereabouts of Aariassuaq's grave is still a mystery that puzzles people. The drawings of these two incidents by Aron of Kangeq are indeed frightening and they remain living stories.

Moreover, in 1863, Jens Kreutzmann made an elaborate map with place names that pertained to the area (Thisted, 1997, pp. 228–229). The place thus has a double meaning, which stresses both legend and historical use, and it is part of the mythical world of Greenlanders. The place can be said to be a non-destination (no one really travels there) but due to the importance it had for former generations up until 1950 (Knudsen & Andreasen, 2009, p. 5) and due to its mythical significance, it is still a place that people relate to. It is within this double nature of a destination and a non-destination that it obtains its position as a sort of hibernating monument. It is hibernating in the sense that it is neither used nor visited, as such, while at the same time, the lake, through naming, through drawing and through narrative, has been captured in social discourse and functions as a mnemonic device for the historical actions of individuals and groups, both real and mythical ones (Tilley, 1994, p. 18). One person whom I spoke to was particularly stricken by the rapid change in the discourse about Tasersiaq, which, according to her, had become transformed into a more utilitarian and standardized understanding. 'I acknowledge that it [the landscape] has to be standardized because we are going to be receiving a lot of different offers about industrial development projects – and not only about small-scale projects, but also about large projects with the dimensions of the aluminium smelter'. The understanding of the landscape as a useful and rational space for economic development has indeed started to dominate the landscape discussions and more and more land is being set aside and demarcated for industrial purposes. In the Self-Government's instructions on the regulation of the 'open land' (Grønlands Selvstyre, 2011), the government works with several land categories, each one having its own particular focus (for example, recreational, industrial/technical infrastructure and wilderness). Here, Tasersiaq is categorized as an 'N3 area', which has been demarcated for large-scale technical installations. This change in the land's categorization – notwithstanding the fact that nothing industrial has yet been constructed there – has, according to the person with whom I spoke, already changed the way people are talking about the area. In Maniitsoq, Tasersiaq was considered an appropriate place for a hydroelectric power plant, because it would not inflict encumbrances on their contemporary hunting and fishing activities. However, this redefinition of land-scape and place ran into problems, which nearly put a halt on the project.

As part of nearly any industrial project under development in Greenland, the entrepreneur has the obligation to initiate archaeological investigations in order to survey and look into questions related to cultural heritage issues. The alu-minium company, Alcoa, entered into cooperation with the Greenland National Museum and Archives, which then pursued intensive archaeological surveys in the Tasersiaq area during 2007 and 2008 (Knudsen & Andreasen, 2009).

Parts of Tasersiaq had previously been surveyed, but the archaeological com-munity was not fully aware of the extent of historical activity in the area. The results from the 2007 and 2008 were, in the words of the archaeologists, astound-ing (Knudsen & Andreasen, 2009, p. 3):

> The importance of the caribou hunts in the interior and the use of the big lakes for that activity is now obviously cemented by the amount of mapped cultural remains, as regards the Inuit. Samples collected from Saqqaq Culture settlements by Tasersiaq produced 14C dates telling that the very first peo-ple of West Greenland from an early period exploited the resources of the interior. Special attention is to be regarded to the complexes of unique and largely undisturbed contiguous cultural landscapes of the interior where tra-ditional knowledge and legends of cultural significance for the Greenlandic population are associated.

The large number of different stone structures like house walls, tent rings, shooting blinds, hunters' beds, cairn systems, fox traps, graves, meat caches and rock shelters indicate a large and highly concentrated effort focusing on caribou hunting by paleo-Eskimo hunters (the Saqqaq culture) as well as by Thule Eskimo hunters. The findings signify that Tasersiaq must have been an important hunting area for a sizeable part of the Inuit population of West Greenland and even a potentially important one for people from the East Coast of Greenland, as well. Therefore, the place provides more substantial material to the archaeologists' aggregate understanding of the coastal-inland duality of the Eskimos' annual cycle, of the importance of the interior for the Inuit groups, and of the complex patterns of mobility and exchange in Greenland. Furthermore, the system of different stone structures and middens indicates a highly complex and extensive settlement pat-tern. It is especially around the constrictions of the 80-km long Tasersiaq Lake that these structures are concentrated and very profound. For example, the set-tlement of what is termed Qoornoq Kangilleq, which encompasses more than 40 structures, is important because it is probably the largest caribou hunting camp in Greenland that was also in use 4,000 years ago (Knudsen & Andreasen, 2009, p. 16). Even though the individual finds are interesting in themselves and are indicative of paleo-Eskimo activity this far inland, it is primarily the *interplay* and overall *relationship* of the complex of structures and the landscape itself that come to form a substantial contribution to the understanding and interpretation of the livelihoods of Eskimo groups. Of special interest to archaeologists are the contours of a highly complex *cultural landscape*, which emerges out of the spatial distribution of finds. Because the hunting conditions in the area are analogous to those used by prehistoric hunters of the European Ice Age, the site is of great value in connection with the study of prehistoric hunting activity, in particular, and the study of the interplay between human being and nature, in general. Thus, the area may help archaeologists to better understand hunting techniques, social organization and adaptive strategies during an important period of human prehistory, when caribou hunting was important to people living in the Northern hemisphere. As a consequence of these findings, the Greenland National Museum and Archives, in November 2008, recommended that the cultural landscape here was to be preserved. Furthermore, the institution suggested that the government of Greenland include Tasersiaq as part of the neighbouring area of Aussivissuit-Arnangarnup Qoorua (Sarfartoq), which was already on the Tentative List as a UNESCO World Heritage Site (Knudsen & Andreasen, 2009, p. 17). The archaeologists understood the area, as a whole, as a cultural landscape having the importance of a cultural and historic monument. Furthermore, its importance was underlined by the historical records, folk tales, maps and stories collected by Aron and Jens Kreutzmann.

That recommendation was a 'deal-breaker', in the jargon of the people who were working for the establishment of a hydroelectric power plant, since the industrial project calls for a large water reservoir that will inevitably raise the waterline by 20 meters and consequently flood the archaeological sites. This posed a predicament, indeed, and many people in favour of establishing a smelter respected the recommendations of the Greenland National Museum and Archives and turned their attention to coming up with different approaches to solve the problem. One of the suggested strategies for dealing with the problem was to pursue a fragmentation of sites in what the archaeologists were arguing was essentially an *integrated* cultural landscape. This strategy of fragmentation was carried out in two ways: by creating rationalities of artefact *relocation* and of artefact *resemblance*. First, it was proposed that the cultural relics could simply be re-positioned, so that they would be situated above the water level of the flooded lake. Or the relics could be situated in museums. This idea of artefact relocation existed alongside the second suggestion, which was based on the idea that the cultural relics (which are basically very simple and not particularly distinctive or notable stone structures) could find their resemblance in already existing historical relics located elsewhere along the coast. Because of this resemblance, it would not be necessary to take any steps to preserve or protect any of the cultural relics in the Tasersiaq area; the cultural heritage was, so to speak, being preserved and taken care of *elsewhere*.

Through the means of the creative acts of fragmentation, deconstruction and dis-assemblage, these two processes transmute cultural heritage into moveable parts that are to be *re*placed in order to respect and protect the cultural heritage.

Both arguments carry some truth in the sense that (a) the structures (graves, cairns, etc.) could certainly be removed and re-positioned above water level and (b) that similar structures can easily be found elsewhere in Greenland. However, the point raised by the archaeologists, a point that lies at the heart of the matter, is that the *intimate interplay* between site structure and landscape makes the place archaeologically significant. It is the cultural landscape as a whole that the archaeologists are recommending be protected: the system of cairns and shooting blinds set up at particular places in the landscape; the location of camps and settlements in relation to each other, and the localities of the systems of hunting grounds and settlement areas constitute an integrated cultural heritage site.

This idea of the monumentalization of an entire *region* was certainly pitted in opposition to the two suggested processes of fragmentation (relocation and resemblance). Both strategies (fragmentation and integration) of respecting the cultural heritage were challenged by a third strategy springing from a very different sense of commitment, belonging and movement in the landscape. The respect for cultural heritage was turned away from the materiality of difference (how they used the landscape in a different way, in olden days) to one that emphasized praxis and the engagement of similarity ('we still use and we still need the land for our survival, today'). The latter-named strategy for overcoming the predicament of a total protection was put forward by Maniitsormiut as well as by some politicians. It is formulated very precisely by Maniitsormioq Karl Lyberth (2010, p. 1, translated by the author), MP for the political party, Siumut, in a written statement during a hearing in the Parliament concerning the white paper on the aluminium project (Naalakkersuisut, 2010) that was put forward in the autumn of 2010:

> Concerning the white paper on the aluminium project and the strategic environmental assessment, Siumut clearly wants to express, as we also did under the parliamentary gathering in the autumn 2009, that it is pointless to protect Tasersiaq but would be better if Tasersiaq was used to benefit from the hydroelectric power. Of course, it is necessary to take initiatives to protect the most important parts of our cultural heritage – Siumut needs to underline this. In relation to this, the following was stated by several citizens from Maniitsoq during a citizens' meeting, and I will take this opportunity to pass it on because it reflects a great truth: 'Our honourable forefathers, who pursued caribou hunting at Tasersiaq, would under no circumstances want to stand in the way of the development of our country, on the basis of their use of the area – on the contrary, it could be expected that they would have wanted a [productive] use of Tasersiaq on the basis of the needs that are present today'.

Persons arguing against an integrated landscape protection, as was suggested by the archaeologists, maintained a sense of strong commitment, relation and bond to the prehistoric hunters by applying three different rationalities: relocation, resemblance and similarity. The temporality of the landscape that is inscribed by the archaeologists (where it becomes a particular historical cultural landscape – a regional monument) is redefined by means of creating new meaningful continuities between fragments, in order to create a renewed space for movement and to approach places in new ways. Tasersiaq understood as an archaeological cultural landscape inhibits contemporary passage.

Today, people want to move in the landscape again (to construct dams, power plants etc.). Similarity between ancestors' and contemporary Greenlanders' interest in the landscape (albeit for different resources and for different purposes) and a continuation in social legitimacy are being evoked, by making the past speak to the present, as Karl Lyberth did in Parliament. The argument of similarity (as our ancestors were using the land around Tasersiaq to survive in prehistoric times, and so are we using the same land to survive, today) may destroy the materiality that clearly and unequivocally indicates and substantiates the presence of prehistoric hunters but it is not perceived as being an act of disrespect. When asked, in an interview, about how she perceived the prospects of the project, one woman in her fifties replied: 'There is always someone saying, "TAKE CARE of your own culture". But […] our ancestors would say, "Carry on, carry on, carry on!"'. The use of Tasersiaq for hydroelectric power is – from this point of view – a way of continuing to use and continuing to put value on the land. The respect for cultural heritage is not upheld merely by giving it a material form but furthermore by inscribing it in the contemporary movement in the landscape. The cultural heritage is performed, so to speak, by continuing to use the land and by maintaining a relation of dependence. A similar understanding of the land is expressed – by the Iñupiaq president of the NANA Regional Corporation, Marie Kasaŋnaaluk Greene (2008), from Alaska – in her message to the readers of the journal, The Hunter, under the headline, 'Our land is our future':

> Our land has always sustained us. From our ancient ancestors who crossed the sea thousands of years ago to our great, great grandchildren who will inherit the NANA Region, the land of northwest Alaska has provided food, shelter, and a home for our people. It was because of our land that we were able to form NANA with funds from the Alaska Native Claims Settlement Act (ANCSA). And today, our land provides us with jobs from business enterprises such as Red Dog Mine and with sustenance from hunting, fishing, and berries. Our land is not simply important to the Iñupiat people. Our land is vital … we also work very hard to ensure that resources within our land are available for our use and for our benefit.

Here, the Iñupiat ancestors and the contemporary population of Iñupiat are conjoined on the basis of their similar interest and dependence on the land, albeit for different purposes and with their different ways of livelihood; Greene is, in fact, arguing for the development of more mining prospects on the land.

The issue related to Tasersiaq is not only one of how to perceive and how to relate to what is demarcated as cultural heritage. It is, moreover, an issue about a reinvention of place in a situation where new paths of development and the contours of future horizons of possibilities are re-assembled. Through this process, Tasersiaq changed from being a mythical and historical place (a prehistoric destination), and a white spot on the map (a non-destination, today) to a cultural heritage site (as defined by archaeologists) and an area for use and development (both supported through area demarcation by the Self-Government and by the wishes of the ancestors). The development-related desires and socio-economic changes in Greenland and in Maniitsoq work as catalysts for a reinvention of place. The prospects of development whirl up a number of landscape and place approaches, where time-space relations are creatively modelled in new ways to match the requirements and expectations of a new social project.

[3] Creating a greener global environment from Maniitsoq

During a lunch break, I was sitting with a family discussing how Maniitsoq would benefit from the factory. All the family members were eagerly supporting the implementation of the plan. The daughter in the family was pointing out to me that she had stayed right here in Maniitsoq with her two children and her husband, even if Nuuk might have provided better job and welfare opportunities: 'I don't want to move. I really want to work for the cause – to get Maniitsoq back. […] It is exciting with the smelter. It may be a totally new town – if we succeed'. Apart from reflecting her strong sense of loyalty to place and her identity as Maniitsormiut, this focus on the town's potentials was a recurrent theme during the conversation. However, her father directed my attention to other benefits of the factory: 'The opponents have not understood the positive influence that the factory in Greenland will have on the reduction of pollution in the world. I have heard that if a smelter is built in Greenland, Alcoa will potentially close down 13 smelters elsewhere. This means that the global pollution will be reduced and in that case, [transboundary] pollution that is normally transported to the Arctic is going to be reduced as well'.

The factory is thus not solely understood as being good for Maniitsoq, but as being good for the world at large. At a meeting with the local pro-smelter organization, Aatsitsivik Soqutigaarput, one of the members pointed out that 'we have to think in a new way – to think of the whole globe as being sustainable rather than merely focusing on local rapid development. […] If we [the people in Maniitsoq] don't do it [build a smelter], then they [Alcoa] will find another place to build a factory. In that case, it will probably not be powered by hydroelectric power – it will be powered by coal'. Again, a specific kind of globality is being evoked and rendered meaningful and relevant to people's understanding of place relations.

Maniitsoq will be able, with its overwhelming water potentials, to provide CO_2-friendly hydroelectric power to an industry that is widely known as being energy-heavy and CO_2-polluting to a vast degree when the energy comes from sources like coal, petroleum and natural gas. A scientific life-cycle assessment report (Schmidt & Thrane, 2009) commissioned by the Home Rule administration, as part of the Strategic Environmental Assessment, deals with the total

CO_2 balance of aluminium production. The production of 1 kg of aluminium in Greenland is expected to create 5.92 kg of CO_2 while 1kg of aluminium produced elsewhere would result in 20.7 ± 9 kg of CO_2 due to the energy resources used (primarily, coal). This report (Schmidt & Thrane, 2009, p. 13) concludes with the following statement:

> In other words, the Greenland smelter will imply that we avoid GHG emissions of about 5 ± 3 million tons of CO_2 annually, in a global perspective. Since Greenland's annual CO_2 emissions are approximately 700,000 tons, the planned smelter has the potential for reducing global GHG emissions by 3 to 12 times Greenland's current GHG emissions, despite a nearly doubling of the domestic GHG emissions occurring in Greenland. In this respect, it should be stressed that the consequences of GHG emissions are independent of the location where they occur.

This doubling of Greenland's CO_2 emissions, however, potentially puts Greenland in a position where the Greenlanders could be accused of being 'climate extremists' in a world that is currently busy making gallant efforts to reduce emissions (Sejersen, 2010a). This political predicament was confronted by the premier, Kuupik Kleist, who argued constantly during the COP negotiations for a 'common but differentiated responsibility' on the part of the countries engaged in reducing emissions (Bjørst, 2008).

An aluminium smelter in Maniitsoq can thus be understood as a significant contributor to the world's effort to reduce emissions. In this way, Greenlanders create a meaningful place of their own in the world and relate actively to global issues. They stretch out the socio-spatial site of the smelter and produce a globality in which they can imagine themselves and can make a difference. One could speak of situated globalities, in which the global and globalization are understood and imagined as parts of the process of constructing local identities and projects, as Bubandt suggests (1999). 'The global' is not something that is detached from livelihood strategies but something that is evoked and rendered meaningful in particular ways by and for people. For opponents of the smelter, the same processes of creating situated globalities are at work, but in their optics, the smelter is socialized in a way that stretches out the global in other world-spanning structures that are perceived as destructive. Analytically speaking, the 'local' is not exposed to the 'global' – it is rather that case that the 'global' is invoked by giving it social-relational qualities (Blok, 2010, p. 188). 'The global' is, from this perspective, not an abstraction connoting the ultimate large-scale space, which is at once 'everywhere' and 'nowhere', wherein one has to pursue a mediation between 'the local' and 'the global' through, for example, finding links among what are understood as local conditions and global forces (this issue will be discussed in Chapter 6). The multiplicities of situated globalities and world-spanning processes cannot be understood by invoking a deep dichotomy between the local and the global (Blok, 2010).

In Maniitsoq, they re-interpret place and through the vehicle of active scale-making, they are inscribing the town in a globality of a certain scale and character that is meaningful and purposeful to them. It is not a question of linking 'the local' to 'the global' but rather a matter of using scale-making in order to reinvent place and create a subject position. With a strong reference to the work of Bruno Latour, John Law and Anna Tsing, the sociologist Anders Blok (2010, p. 197) proposes that '[t]he global is what the actors may, or may not, be projecting, building or otherwise achieving, and thus represents one amongst other situated standpoints'. Maniitsoq is, by means of politically loaded circulating entities (CO_2-molecules), actively being turned into a place of global importance *by proxy* by supporters of the smelter. With 'by proxy' I mean to imply that in spite of the large-scale production of emissions from the Greenlandic smelter, it is perceived as *replacing* or as *standing in* the place of another as of yet unbuilt and unplanned albeit potentially more polluting smelter, which would quite conceivably be located elsewhere. It is by invoking the *absent presence* of a polluting smelter, which would presumably be powered by coal, someplace in, for example, China, and by invoking the *present absence* of effective policies reducing CO_2 emissions that many Maniitsormiut engage in creative scale-making in order to reinvent a place for them to set up new place potentialities.

[4] Creating a place for the good life in an expanding town

The proposed smelter will need a labour force of approximately 600. Additionally, it is expected that another 350–450 jobs in sectors servicing the smelter and the labour force will be created in Maniitsoq. Overall, then, around 1,050 new jobs will appear in Maniitsoq because of the smelter. It is estimated that there are about 100 persons in Maniitsoq who can fill out some of these jobs. This entails that there will be a need to recruit around 950 persons from outside of town for the project. Taking the accompanying spouses and children into account, then, some 2,000 persons are expected to be moving to Maniitsoq (Grønlands Selvstyres SMV arbejdsgruppe, 2010, p. 8). The aforementioned demographic projections are also boosted by an anticipated increase in job opportunities in other sectors. In the first years (during the start phase), a large number of workers will be coming to Maniitsoq from other countries like Poland and China. Thus, Maniitsormiut await unprecedented urban dynamics, where infrastructural challenges and multicultural issues will be in the forefront.

The requirements and potentialities of the smelter have incited the town to rethink and re-imagine itself. First, the town expects to initiate major infrastructural projects in order to meet the demands with a substantial increase in housing possibilities, with improved school and health services, and with enhanced leisure time activities, etc. Second, the town intends to amplify Maniitsoq as a unique place in order for newcomers to appreciate the town's history and to explore and enjoy it. In order to trigger this process, the citizens' groups discussed and drew up suggestions for the organization of the future Maniitsoq. Several workshop members met on a weekly basis to discuss issues ranging from sewer systems and energy-efficient housing to artificial grass and street names. The work was organized in four groups: Education and labour market; Infrastructure and housing; Culture and tourism; and Family and spare time. The groups played the role of think tanks so that they could feed the municipality with ideas and stir up new energy 'from below'.

According to the written overall purpose of the groups (Qeqqata Kommunia, 2009), the initiative was aimed at motivating and engaging the citizens in the development of town and at stimulating them to take ownership over the projects. Specifically, the goal was to secure – through the accomplished projects – that the town and its citizens were prepared and had developed competences for being engaged in the expansion of the town, should an aluminium smelter be constructed. In a report submitted to the municipality, the coordinator of the work wrote the following: 'By establishing groups (and a network around these), it makes it possible to realize initiatives and projects which, in both the short- and long-term, can contribute to giving citizens a sense of co-influence on their future' (Engelsen, 2009, p. 1; translated by the author). The working groups were, so to speak, supposed to prompt thinking about life in Maniitsoq and supposed to formulate urban visions and concrete development projects. Even though many of the things discussed were concrete projects like pedestrian streets, flowerbeds, possibilities for traineeship, English language classes, a family advisory centre, poetry evenings, a cinema, transport and harbour facilities, and so forth, the discussions had a strong resonance in the people's ideas about what constitutes a viable and healthy community life. The group on Infrastructure and housing, for example, formulated their vision in the following way: 'one has to work on making a town that protects the environment and the Greenlandic values. With the international focus on climate and a changing Greenland, it is important to aim at creating a "green" town. [...] The new part of town must not develop into a new independent town, but instead has to be connected to the existing town so that the existing and the new will merge into one common Maniitsoq. It is therefore important that people from all social classes and cultures move to the new part of town' (cited in Engelsen, 2009, p. 2, translated by the author).

In fact, the groups were caught in a situation where they had to envision the fate of Maniitsoq both with and without a smelter; in both cases, they had to stretch their social imagination. Maniitsormiut often presented the case in terms of two parallel lines of potential development: either the town would dwindle and turn into a sleepy town, or it would expand into a dynamic centre that would function as an engine for the whole of Greenland. In any event, Maniitsoq, as a place, would never be the same again. To trigger the imagination, the municipality assigned to a group of Norwegian architects the task of producing a publication with sketches for potential solutions to the challenges that were faced by an expanding town (70° N arkitektur, 2010). The architects worked closely with the citizens – setting up lectures, meetings, workshops, focus groups, city walks, and interviews (70° N arkitektur, 2010, p. 19) and they focused a great deal of their efforts on trying to appropriate the town's special social, cultural and environmental conditions. This publication, with which everyone in Maniitsoq is familiar, often functioned as a point of reference and as a tool for communicating ideas. During meetings and conversations, the publication would typically be brought forth and opened up in order to explicate what 'a good view' or what 'a large building' might look like. The underlying and guiding notion of the report – expansion *within* the existing town structure – was, however, not in line with the idea that had been circulating about the development of a completely new part of town.

One of the workshops organized by the Norwegian architects brainstormed on the issues that lay ahead. People spoke up with free associations and blurted out keywords like: melting ice, energy, food, trees, light, Alcoa, laughter, infrastructure, self-government, a nice view, exercise, CO_2-emission 90 per cent higher, dependence on Denmark, bigger windows, 'the last wilderness', without Alcoa, empty villages, mountain top, benches, and industrial country, just to mention a few of the 'free associations' that were voiced (70° N arkitektur, 2010, p. 6). Issues, scales and causalities are laid out in a floating and levelled-out structure. In the report prepared by the 70° N arkitektur group (2010, p. 6), the keywords make their appearance – not in the form of an ordered list but rather as spread out all over the page, with no apparent system among the words. This serves to prompt the activities of making more free associations, of exploring new aspects in the complex field of issues and of assembling the keywords in new and meaningful ways. The words appear to be sprinkled all over the page and the page is difficult to read and appropriate because you are always uncertain about whether you have read all the words and whether you have made the right connections and thus whether you have gotten around all the issues. This may carry an important point, however. During interviews and conversations, people in Maniitsoq had some of these same experiences: many combinations of scales, issues and causalities served to fuel the imaginative reinvention of Maniitsoq as a place. Even though the vision and direction of the work had a clear focus, the imagination of how to create new ways of living and working together and of designing future social and economic sustainability amounted to an act of free and unfocused assemblage. People created story lines in order to set the local place-evaluation in motion. Abstract plans, theories and calculations – as are so often presented in the reports prepared by Greenland Development A/S (see Chapter 3) – were, so to speak, reassembled here, in order to animate (the) place, making it liveable and tangible – but at the same time making it fluid and negotiable.

Whereas many of the reports written or commissioned by Greenland Development A/S took the plans in a direction where close causalities were upheld and uncertainties were controlled for different purposes (see Chapter 3), the process locally was of a different nature. Here, expectations, dreams, stories, and myth were spun together in endless webs of narratives linking people and place, intimately. It is through these narratives that people help each other explore how ideas of 'the good life' can be made meaningful in a living town. Greenland Development A/S is working with a discourse of positive but radical national transformation, which can be understood as a shift in paradigm. In contrast to this, Maniitsormiut seem to be working with the possibilities of change in an analogue sense. They understand, embrace and work for change locally, but this is being done very largely on the basis of a projection of existing values and problems. It is not a paradigmatic shift in the life of town. It is rather an opportunity to get more of what one already appreciates and dreams of: more jobs, more dynamics, more leisure possibilities, more visitors, and more prestige and status in Greenland. In essence, Maniitsormiut are projecting a future town that *they* find to be concrete and inhabitable. Their ideas of a future Maniitsoq where the town dynamics will be organized around the smelter and the population nearly doubled are imagined by means of an analogue between the existing, real, and physical and the expected/envisioned. Their images thus have strong qualities of continuity and extension.

At one of the citizens' group meetings, several suggestions bearing on improving the appearance of the town were in their final stages of discussion. One person, who was in charge of keeping track of all the ideas and the texts and illustrations associated with each project, was struggling to keep up with the discussions while maps, photos, sketches, and text bits were being passed around among different hands over the meeting table. Project after project was presented and commented on, by the six participants. A4-sized photos of specific locations of projects were circulating and routes as well as markings on maps were being drawn. As do many other citizens' groups, this one had been meeting once every week throughout the winter and the group was now getting ready to make its final presentation before the open meeting of the town's citizens. The diversity of projects was evident. This citizens' group wanted, among other things, to have flowers planted close to the hospital, to have a huge sign created by a local artist – saying 'Maniitsoq Tikilluarit' (Welcome to Maniitsoq) – set up at the harbour, to have a water fountain, to have a new small entrance into the harbour that would make it easier for incoming small boats in rough weather, to have a warning sign for trucks unloading goods behind one of the supermarkets, to have a large board posted in the centre of town with a map of the town, and to have plates set up on each sign pole that would explain the historical background of the street names. One active member had been out and around, taking detailed photos of some of the locations in question and a friend of his had 'Photo-shopped' some of the pictures in order to make the suggestions more cogent, visually. In one picture, one could accordingly see what the result would look like with the flowers planted and in another, the warning sign for the trucks was manipulated right into the photo.

Maniitsoq, as a town, was the centre of a conversion that could be heard during a small break at one of the meetings, while three persons gathered around an old map of town that was pinned to the wall. Here, what could easily be appreciated – by means of simple cartography – were the rapid changes that had taken place since the 1950s, when the town was restructured and modernized by the Danes; a change that some of the members can still recall. In a jubilee publication celebrating the town's bicentennial in 1982, these rapid changes are described in the following way (see description by H. C. Petersen, 1982):

> The noise from machines and bulldozers, the banging sounds from the blasting of rocks, the sound of blows from hammers, and busyness characterized the town scene for the next 30 years [starting around 1950]. The generation

of people who grew up during this period have experienced the new buildings taking over the look of the town as the heritage sites have been disappearing, little by little. Up to 1950, everyone in Maniitsoq knew one another. Since then, many newcomers have come to town. This has necessitated the acquisition of skills for adaptation, not only to technical influences but also to human impact.

Between 1947 and 1982, nearly one million tons of rock were blasted and used to reorganize the layout of the town. The old map on the wall was a clear reminder of the turbulent changes of the townscape and changes in social life. The town has been undergoing a constant state of becoming. The suggestions put forward by the group can be perceived as rather limited when compared to the magnitude of challenges ahead and their historical experiences. However, the reinvention of Maniitsoq as a place, as reflected by the project proposals, is based on the significant approach to 'opening up' the town as a place to live and as a place that, in turn, opens up for new flows of people (and for this reason, maps and warning signs become even more necessary). By explaining why the streets have the names they have, the group opens up the townscape by explicating the historical significance of relations between the place and its people. In a former report by the group working specifically with culture and tourism, the street name idea is described as an attempt to aim to bring about 'continuity between a potential new part of town and the town we know today. It is a simple way to bring together the past, the present and the future and to use these in everyday life. New incomers will gain knowledge of the town's history' (Borgergruppe for kultur og turisme, 2009, p. 5, translated by the author). This particular project can be understood as a straightforward way of helping newcomers to appreciate the history of the town and a simple way of reflecting the townscape as a memory-scape (Nuttall, 1992; Sejersen, 2004). There was an expectation on the part of one former citizens' group that this initiative would eventually be combined with organized city-walks that would strengthen 'storytelling', as stated in their report (Borgergruppe for kultur og turisme, 2009, p. 5). These stories, buttressed and clarified through signs and city-walks, would contribute to the way that incomers make sense of and inhabit the town; or to put this more precisely, it would give Maniitsormiut a sense of ownership over the narrative of the town, as a *place*, while opening up for new flows of people, cultures and expectations.

Locally, abstract plans for future (and uncertain) development and change are met by grounding life historically, physically and practically – in projects that not only service and welcome incomers but also point at solutions to existing problems and serve to articulate a place that the present inhabitants find to be suitable for 'the good life'. Through the aestheticization of everyday life (Featherstone, 2007) and by creating a historical order, the town is envisioned as a new place for personal fulfilment. It is a process that may mirror what Lash and Urry (1994) term 'reflexive modernity', which is accompanied by a reflexive re-subjectivization of space. Maniitsoq becomes not only a place that is opening up for flows but also a place with particular and clearly singled-out aesthetic qualities to be consumed. The groups project Maniitsoq as an open space to be explored, used and consumed by newcomers but also as a place which, by means of signs, images and narratives, is not empty and without order. Maniitsoq is thus set up as a particular place with a particular history, a place that is not only to be consumed (and enjoyed) but also a place that is to be respected and appreciated for its historical achievements, its affinities and its morality.

Place-making in the making

No matter what happens, Maniitsoq as a place will never be the same. The water's energy potentialities and the political ambitions merge into a powerful driver and transformer of society. The uncertainty about the future of the town faced with closing industries and services has made Greenland and Maniitsoq welcome the potential establishment of an aluminium smelter. Such a smelter not only generates job opportunities but also sets in motion a complex process of re-interpreting place (see also Benediktsson & Suopajärvi, 2007). It is not solely a question of disentangling a fishing industry in order to instate an aluminium industry powered by hydroelectricity. Moreover, it is a question of place reinvention, which plays itself out creatively along several lines of thinking and which seems to ascribe multiplicity to place. People are actively constructing new senses of place that will be meaningful and purposeful in connection with the desired changes and the opportunities to come. The reinvention of place involves spatial and temporal scaling processes and various ways of accentuating change and continuity. Locally, people are not adapting to or adjusting to a context and a future to come. They are actively – through processes of place reinvention – constructing frameworks and subject positions that will empower them with a strong sense of control and ownership over and investment in the future paths made possible by the introduction of a new industry. The organization of water in new ways to facilitate mega-industries thus has far-reaching implications for the way townscapes and landscapes are linked to consumption and production, and furthermore to how places and networks are to be understood and constructed in relation to each other (whether real or imagined). Place is put in the foreground and given a considerable role in tasks of social engineering and social imagination.

The changes that lie ahead, which are due to the potential involvement in the aluminium business, can be understood as an expression of broader structural changes, where global capitalist logics and market systems have a concrete impact on marginal and local communities, and where global firms can claim to be local everywhere. However, the four cases dealt with in this chapter indicate that the process is everything but simple and that Greenland and Maniitsormiut are implicated centrally in the process. They are, so to speak, co-constituting the structural changes – among other things, by innovatively renegotiating and reinventing place. This is not only being pursued by state institutions but also by networks of citizen groups and political and administrative institutions.

I have presented four cases of place-making processes, each of which is related directly to the potential establishment of a large-scale industrial complex.

The efforts that were made to have a platform for whale-watching constructed indicates place-making in a new competitive economy, where towns have to brand themselves in relation to each other in order to stand out and promote uniqueness, but also to appear as attractive to people who are not only looking for jobs but who also want to consume a landscape in a particular way. By creating 'a view', 'a destination' and 'an event', the platform opens up the landscape and reinvents it as a place for cultural consumption in a novel way. Nature has been actively reinvented, so to speak, and promoted as a landscape of pleasure and enjoyment (Granås & Nyseth, 2007, p. 24). In this case, place-making of this kind goes hand-in-hand with perceptions of the landscape as a site of industrial production.

The large-scale use of water in a highly controlled way is fundamental for the implementation of the mega-industrial project. Although the actual water is neither being taken away from contemporary users nor would influence contemporary activities (two scenarios that are so often the case, elsewhere) the act of water control, in and of itself, triggered a process of place reinvention. The area at Tasersiaq lake that would be dammed turned out to constitute a cultural landscape which proved to be worthy of being listed as a potential UNESCO site, according to archaeologists. The historical and mythical significance of the place was taken seriously by people, although turning the site into a protected area would be a 'deal-breaker'. Tasersiaq, as a historical place deserving special respect, was reinvented by deconstructing it into a site of removable or replaceable historical objects and constructions. Furthermore, this *ex situ* protective strategy was promoted alongside an understanding of the location as a place that has, for many centuries, been used by Greenlanders for purposes of survival. It was argued that the act of protecting the area would close the place and cut off the historical relationship between people and land. The histories of places are thus revisited and actively laid out in new constellations in order to reinvent meaningful relations between people, land and projects. The histories of places and its meanings are thus never given a priori but are continuously being negotiated and continuously being related to contemporary projects. This remapping of memory is not a unique insight, but it adds further dynamics to the temporal and spatial dimensions of place innovations. In this instance, an act of place-destruction (in the view of archaeologists) is simultaneously perceived (in the view of industrial supporters) to be an act of cultural respect and historical affiliation to the place.

According to estimates, the smelter will put Greenland in the club of severe world polluters when tallied up on a *per inhabitant* basis (Price Waterhouse Coopers, 2009). It will nearly double the CO_2 emissions of Greenland, which is a politically precarious message to be sending out to a world that is trying to reduce emissions. In Greenland and in Maniitsoq, however, the aluminium smelter, set up at *this* particular place in the world, was understood as actually making a significant contribution to the world's efforts to reduce emissions, since it was thought to be taking the place of an even more polluting smelter that would potentially be built elsewhere. In this way, Greenlanders creatively construct a meaningful global place of their own and thus a sense of being-in-the-world. The global is not something detached from livelihood strategies and places but something that is evoked and made meaningful in different ways *by* and *for* people.

By constructing bottom-up initiatives, the citizens of Maniitsoq revisited their town as a good place to live and mobilized new ideas to open up the town for the large number of incomers. This kind of place-making requires social imagination and social engineering about how to perceive the good life. Faced with potential, rapid, multicultural and demographic changes, Maniitsormiut tried to maintain their commitment to a certain kind of social and cultural order by opening up the history of town and by creating an aestheticized townscape as a common platform for contemporary inhabitants and newcomers. Everyday problems and aspirations were in focus and formed the basis for most of the suggested projects related to town renewal. Locally, people accordingly paid close attention to contemporary problems in their dealings with an uncertain future. In order to get a sense of feeling for the contours of a future horizon of expectations, people mobilized a dynamic set of causality-relations and fluid scale-making processes. By doing so, they created a landscape of risk and potentialities, but not by means of mounting a controlled setting – with pre-determined causalities and contained uncertainties. Rather, their anticipation of the future was approached by creative thinking and an ever-shifting assemblage of issues that people found relevant, interesting and emergent. The highly hegemonic structure of knowledge production set up by the Greenlandic authorities who were busy demarcating a more and more controlled landscape of risk accordingly did not determine people's innovative associations, which were used to mobilize local initiatives for controlling the direction of change.

Nothing has happened as of yet in Maniitsoq with respect to the construction of the smelter and the hydroelectric power plant. However, apart from waiting, the people there are trying to prepare for future potentialities. One inherent aspect of preparation is, of course, the establishing of a new horizon of expectation, based on a re-structuring of place. It could be said that the potential factory is accompanied by a place-sensitivity, a place-awareness and a place-creativity. In fact, a reinterpretation of place has given people the possibility of setting up a multi-dimensional temporal and spatial setting, in which they can mobilize and negotiate ideas of community viability in the face of anticipated rapid change. Understanding 'the local point of view' is thus not necessarily an exercise in representing one's understanding of place (e.g. a dominating local discourse on place use or place protection) or one's understanding of a diversity of views (some local people may argue for and some may argue against a certain kind of place use) but more precisely, a question of appreciating how place-awareness can be multi-dimensional and can be entangled in dynamic spatial and temporal scale-making while, at the same time, being deeply embedded in everyday life and prevailing problems. In the reproduction and transformation of society, places are continuously revisited, recreated, and inflected in unexpected ways and interwoven in and among ever-changing ideas of the good life. As David Harvey (1996, p. 53, emphasis in original) reminds us:

> Space and time are neither absolute nor external to processes but are contingent and contained within them. There are multiple spaces and times (and space-times) implicated in different physical, biological, and social processes. [...] Processes do not operate *in* but *actively construct* space and time and in so doing define distinctive scales for their development.

If we apply such a view, people are not only carried along by specific time-space contexts (to which they must adapt) but are actively forming and transforming them in creative acts of reflexive place-making.

References

70° N arkitektur. (2010). *Takorluukkanut nalunaarusiaq // Visjonsrapport // Maniitsoq*. Tromsoe: 70° N arkitektur as.

ACIA. (2005). *Arctic Climate Impact Assessment*. Cambridge: Cambridge University Press.

Appadurai, Arjun. (1995). The production of locality. In R. Fardon (Ed.), *Counterworks. Managing the Diversity of Knowledge* (pp. 204–225). London: Routledge.

Arctic Green Food A/S, & Greenland Venture A/S. (2009). *Arctic Green Food A/S. Grønlandske råvarer, grønlandske arbejdspladser, grønlandske fødevarer*. Maniitsoq: Greenland Venture A/S.

Aron fra Kangeq, & Thisted, Kirsten. (1999). *Således skriver jeg, Aron. vol I–II*. Nuuk: Atuakkiorfik.

Bendixen, Ole. (1921). Sukkertoppen distrikt. In G. C. Amdrup, L. Bobé, A. S. Jensen & H. P. Steenby (Eds.), *Grønland i tohundredaaret for Hans Egedes landing* (Vol. Bind XLI i Meddeleser om Grønland, pp. 95–170). København: C.A. Reitzel.

Benediktsson, Karl, & Suopajärvi, Leena. (2007). Industrious northern cultures? The uneasy relationship between an industrial order and a 'Second Modernity'. In T. Nyseth & B. Granås (Eds.), *Place Reinvention in the North: Dynamics and Governance Perspectives* (pp. 27–38). Stockholm: Nordregio.

Biilmann, MagdâraK, & Heilmann, Marie. (1982). Kvinderne aktiveredes. In H. C. Petersen (Ed.), *ManîtsoK' Sukkertoppen. 1782–1982* (pp. 171–172). Maniitsoq: Manîtsup Kommûnia.

Biilmann, MagdâraK, Heilmann, Marie, Lyberth, Jens K'ujage, Møller, Karl, & Petersen, H.C. (1982). Biografier. In H. C. Petersen (Ed.), *ManîtsoK' Sukkertoppen. 1782–1982* (pp. 171–184). Maniitsoq: Manîtsup Kommûnia.

Bjørst, Lill Rastad. (2008). Grønland og den dobbelte klimastrategi. *Økonomi og Politik, 81*(4), 26–37.

Blok, Anders. (2010). *Divided Socio-Natures: Essays on the Co-Construction of Science, Society, and the Global Environment*. Copenhagen: University of Copenhagen (Ph.D. handed in at Department of Sociology).

Bobé, Louis. (1921). Distriktets historie. In G. C. Amdrup, L. Bobé, A. S. Jensen & H. P. Steenby (Eds.), *Grønland i tohundredaaret for Hans Egedes landing* (Bind XLI i Meddeleser om Grønland) (pp. 170–175). København: C.A. Reitzel.

Borgergruppe for kultur og turisme. (2009). *Vision og strategi for kultur og turisme i Maniitsoq*. Maniitsoq: Borgergruppe for kultur og turisme.

Borgerinitiativet i Maniitsoq. (2009). *Maniitsoqs fremtidige udvikling*. Maniitsoq: Borgerinitiativet i Maniitsoq.

Brody, Hugh. (1982). *Maps and Dreams: Indians and the British Columbia Frontier*. London: Norman and Hobhouse.

Bubandt, Nils. (1999). Imagined globalities. Fetishism of the global and the end of the world in Indonesia. *Folk, 40*, 99–122.

Buch, Dan. (1981). Forundersøgelser for vandkraftanlæg i Grønland. In G. Larsen (Ed.), *Vandkraft i Grønland* (pp. 31–52). København: Akademiet for de tekniske videnskaber.

Bærenholt, Jørgen Ole, & Granås, Brynhild. (2008). Places and mobilities beyond the periphery. In J. O. Bærenholt & B. Granås (Eds.), *Mobility and Place: Enacting Northern European Peripheries* (pp. 1–12). Aldershot: Ashgate Publisher.

Christiansen, Hans C. (1959). Erhvervsudvikling i Grønland. *Tidsskriftet Grønland*, 375–388.

Danielsen, Mogens, Andersen, Thomas, Knudsen, Thorkild, & Nielsen, Olafur. (1998). *Mål og strategier i den grønlandske erhvervsudvikling*. Nuuk: Sulisa A/S.

Dirlik, Arif. (1999). Place-based imagination: Globalism and the politics of place. *Review: A Journal of the Fernand Braudel Center for the Study of Economies, Historical Systems, and Civilizations, 22*(2), 151–187.

Egede, Peter. (1982). Erhvervslivet. In H. C. Petersen (Ed.), *ManîtsoK' Sukkertoppen. 1782-1982* (pp. 73–97). Maniitsoq: Manîtsup Kommûnia.

Engelsen, Birte. (2009). *Borgergrupper: Maniitsoqs byudvikling*. Maniitsoq: Qeqqata Kommunia.

Featherstone, Mike. (2007). *Consumer Culture and Postmodernism*. London: SAGE Publications.

Feit, Harvey. (1994). The enduring pursuit: Land, time, and social relationships in anthropological models of hunters and gatherers and in subarctic hunters' images. In E. Burch & L. J. Ellana (Eds.), *Key Issues in Hunter-Gatherer Research* (pp. 421–440). Oxford: Berg.

Galster, Julius. (1956). Kan de grønlandske vandfald udnyttes industrielt? *Tidsskriftet Grønland*, 20–26.

Geertz, Clifford. (1995). *After the Fact*. Cambridge, Massachusetts: Harvard University Press.

Granås, Brynhild, & Nyseth, Torill. (2007). Dimensions of place reinvention. In T. Nyseth & B. Granås (Eds.), *Place Reinvention in the North. Dynamics and Governance Perspectives* (pp. 9–25). Stockholm: Nordregio.

Greene, Marie Kasaŋnaaluk. (2008). Our land is our future. *The Hunter, 20*(3), 1.

Greenland Development A/S. (2011). *Fakta om Maniitsoq 2011*. Nuuk: Greenland Development A/S.

Grønlands Selvstyre. (2011). *Landsplandirektiv for det åbne land*. Nuuk: Grønlands Selvstyre.

Grønlands Selvstyres SMV arbejdsgruppe. (2010). *Regionaludvikling og migration - Strategisk miljøvurdering*. Nuuk: Grønlands Selvstyre.

Hamilton, Lawrence C., Lyster, Per, & Otterstad, Oddmund. (2000). Social change, ecology and climate in 20th-century Greenland. *Climate Change* (47), 193–211.

Harvey, David. (1996). *Justice, Nature and the Geography of Difference*. Cambridge: Blackwell publishing.

Horsted, Svend Aage. (1970). Fisk og fiskerierhverv. In N. Nielsen, P. Skautrup & C. Vibe (Eds.), *J.P. Trap Danmark, bind XIV Grønland* (pp. 166–190). København: G.E.C. Gads Forlag.

Kiilerich, Alf. (1970). Havene omkring Grønland. In N. Nielsen, P. Skautrup & C. Vibe (Eds.), *J.P. Trap Danmark, bind XIV Grønland* (pp. 57–63). København: G.E.C. Gads Forlag.

Knudsen, Pauline K., & Andreasen, Claus. (2009). *Culture Historical Significance on Areas Tasersiaq and Tarsartuup Tasersua in West Greenland & Suggestions for Salvage Archaeology and Documentation in Case of Damming Lakes*. Nuuk: Nunatta Katersugaasivia Allagaateqarfialu (Greenland National Museum and Archives).

Langhoff, Rune. (2010, November 22). Protest mod Alcoa-modstand. Retrieved August 4, 2011, from http://knr.gl/da/news/protest-mod-alcoa-modstand.

Lash, Scott, & Urry, John. (1994). *Economies of Signs and Space*. London: SAGE Publications.

Lauritzen, Philip. (1994). *Grønlandsguide*. Nuuk: Atuagkat.

Lodberg, Torben. (2007, March 9). Aluminium og vandkraft - før og nu, *Sermitsiaq*, p. 52.

Lyberth, Erik. (1982). Tiden omkring anlæggelse af 'Kolonien ManîtsoK'. In H. C. Petersen (Ed.), *ManîtsoK' Sukkertoppen. 1782–1982* (pp. 41–72). Maniitsoq: Manîtsup Kommûnia.

Lyberth, Karl (2010). *Siumut's landstingsgruppes kommentar til Redegørelse om aluminium-projektet med udgangspunkt i de nu gennemførte undersøgelser, herunder den strategiske miljøvurdering (SMV)*, Nuuk: Inatsisartut.

Maniitsoq kommune. (2009). *Aluminiumsmelteværk i Maniitsoq*: Maniitsoq kommune.

Massey, Doreen. (1994). *Space, Place and Gender*. Minneapolis: University of Minnesota Press.

Mattox, William G. (1973). Fishing in West Greenland. The development of a new native industry. *Meddelelser om Grønland, 197*, 1–469.

Nielsen, Jens Kaalhauge. (2005). Industrial development. In M. Nuttall (Ed.), *Encyclopedia of the Arctic* (Vol. 2, pp. 966–969). New York & London: Routledge.

Nielsen, Niels, Skautrup, Peter, & Vibe, Christian. (1970). Sukkertoppen kommune. In N. Nielsen, P. Skautrup & C. Vibe (Eds.), *J.P. Trap Danmark, bind XIV Grønland* (pp. 471–485). København: G.E.C. Gads Forlag.

Nuttall, Mark. (1992). *Arctic Homeland: Kinship, Community and Development in Northwest Greenland*. Toronto: University of Toronto Press.

Nuttall, Mark. (2009). Living in a world of movement: Human resilience to environmental instability in Greenland. In S. A. Crate & M. Nuttall (Eds.), *Anthropology & Climate Change. From Encounters to Actions* (pp. 292–310). Walnut Creek: Left Coast Press.

Nuttall, Mark. (2010). *Pipeline Dreams: People, Environment, and the Arctic Energy Frontier*. Copenhagen: IWGIA.

Naalakkersuisut. (2010). *White Paper on the Aluminium Project Based on Recent Completed Studies, Including the Strategic Environmental Assessment (SEA)*. Nuuk: Greenland Self-Government.

Petersen, H.C. (1982). ManîtsoK by. In H. C. Petersen (Ed.), *ManîtsoK' Sukkertoppen. 1782–1982* (pp. 120–125). Maniitsoq: Manîtsup Kommûnia.

Petersen, Robert. (1982). ManîtsoKs historie. In H. C. Petersen (Ed.), *ManîtsoK' Sukkertoppen. 1782–1982* (pp. 27–40). Maniitsoq: Manîtsup Kommûnia.

Poole, Graham. (1995). *The Development of Greenland's Shrimp Fishing and Processing Industry Since 1979: A Study in Applied Economics* (Ph.D. handed in at Scott Polar Research Institute). Cambridge: University of Cambridge.

PriceWaterhouseCoopers. (2009). *Grønland og CO$_2$ kvoter*. København: PwC.

Qeqqata Kommunia. (2009). *Formål og plan for temagruppernes arbejde*. Maniitsoq: Qeqqata Kommunia.

Qeqqata Kommunia. (2011). *Qeqqata Kommunias erhvervsplan 2011 med overslagsårene 2012–2014*. Sisimiut: Qeqqata Kommunia.

Rask, Sven. (1993). De første erhvervsmotorbåde. Om fangstens betydning for udviklingen af industrifiskeriet. *Tidsskriftet Grønland, 41*(3), 100–118.

Rasmussen, Rasmus Ole. (2005). *Analyse af fangererhvervet i Grønland*. Nuuk: Grønlands Hjemmestyre.

Rasmussen, Rasmus Ole, & Hamilton, Lawrence C. (2001). *The Development of Fisheries in Greenland*. Roskilde: NORS, Roskilde University.

Schmidt, Jannick H, & Thrane, Mikkel. (2009). *Life Cycle Assessment of Aluminium Production in New Alcoa Smelter in Greenland*. Nuuk: Government of Greenland.

Sejersen, Frank. (1998). *Strategies for Sustainability and Management of People: An Analysis of Hunting and Environmental Perceptions in Greenland with a Special Focus on Sisimiut*. Copenhagen: University of Copenhagen (Ph.D. handed in to the Faculty of Humanities).

Sejersen, Frank. (2003). *Grønlands naturforvaltning. Ressourcer og fangstrettigheder.* København: Akademisk Forlag.

Sejersen, Frank. (2004). Horizon of sustainability in Greenland: Inuit landscapes of memory and vision. *Arctic Anthropology, 41*(1), 71–89.

Sejersen, Frank. (2010a). De potentielle klimaekstremister: Grønlands nye udfordring i CO_2-samfundet. *Tværkultur, 1,* 61–67.

Sejersen, Frank. (2010b). Urbanization, landscape appropriation and climate change in Greenland. *Acta Borealia, 27*(2), 167–188.

Simonsen, Kirsten. (2008). Place as encounters: Practice, embodiment and narrativity In J. O. Bærenholt & B. Granås (Eds.), *Mobility and Place: Enacting Northern European Peripheries* (pp. 13–26). Aldershot: Ashgate Publisher.

Smidt, Erik L. Balslev. (1989). *Min tid i Grønland – Grønland i min tid. Fiskeri, biologi, samfund 1948–1985.* København: Nyt Nordisk Forlag Arnold Busck.

Thisted, Kirsten (Ed.). (1997). *Jens Kreutzmann. Fortællinger og akvareller.* Nuuk: Atuakkiorfik.

Tilley, Christopher. (1994). *A Phenomenology of Landscape: Places, Paths and Monuments.* Oxford: Berg.

Ølgaard, Hans. (1981). Mulighederne for anvendelse af den grønlandske vandkraft. In G. Larsen (Ed.), *Vandkraft i Grønland* (pp. 53–66). København: Akademiet for de tekniske videnskaber.

6 The social life of globalization and scale-makers

In the contemporary international discourse on climate change, two aspects appear to be dominant: first, climate change is supposed to be understood as a global phenomenon; and second, climate change will have a global impact. The twin emphasis on the increase in the global mean temperature and on the rise of sea levels are examples of this *globalization* of climate change. Climate change understood as global is all-embracing and inclusive. No human and no species will thus be able to position itself outside or avoid the consequences of this global change. The global extent of the issue is also accentuated by discussions about global tipping points and a 2 degrees Celsius maximum limit for the rise in global temperature. Increasingly, the dynamics in the climate models are becoming more and more complex and are working with system interrelations that cross-cut geographical regions, focus areas (melting ice, bleaching corals and hurricanes, for example) and spheres (hemisphere, stratosphere, cryosphere). Representations aimed at getting us to comprehend global climate change are indeed multiple and sometimes take on the shape of graphs (the famous 'hockey stick') or animals (polar bears), to mention but two examples of representations that operate as mediators and mobilizers of understanding and imagination.

Consequently, the present issues related to climate change are often understood as something radically different from climate issues that were formerly dealt with. Before the climate became global, so to speak, it was used to describe certain tendencies in large regions (or climate zones) where both stability and viability were inherent characteristics of any understanding of climate. The Arctic, for example, belonged to the polar climate zone, which had its salient characteristics and its inherent temperature fluctuations (see for example Vibe, 1967). The historical record of cooling and warming periods in Greenland is comprehensive. Basing his supposition on interviews with local hunters and fishermen as well as on various historical documents, the Greenlandic researcher, H.C. Petersen, has put forward a hypothesis concerning different temperature cycles in Greenland. His hypothesis conjectures highly viable *but* predictable changes between warming and cooling periods that impact on the environment and animal life, to a significant extent (Petersen, 2007, 2010). In Greenland, people very often express a sense of familiarity with or an understanding of changes in the climate (Bjørst, 2011; Nuttall, 2009) and do not necessarily apply a global perspective or blame mankind for the changes that are taking place. This point of view, which is not limited to Greenland alone, thus applies another scale of reference and relations of causalities when interpreting change than the one that is used by global climate change researchers and advocates.

In this chapter, the focus will be trained on the practices of scaling that are so immanent in the discussions of climate change, but are also crucial to the way that adaptation strategies and local people are approached and appreciated. Scaling is approached as a social praxis and as part of every cultural and political project (Li, 2007). The practices of scaling by scale-makers who belong to particular epistemic communities also move the discussion over into the scientific community, where scaling is, by nature, an inherent aspect of our analytical approaches. The chapter's discussions of different kinds of scaling practices do not reflect an intention, on the part of the author, to repudiate the scales applied by different research communities. The point is rather to draw attention to how scale-making is productive, not neutral, and how some scale-makings come to take on a hegemonic position.

Exposed people under stress

In the work of the Intergovernmental Panel on Climate Change (IPCC), the view on climate change as global and the global impact it makes are coupled with an elaborate understanding of the diversity of impacts it will have on countries, regions, sectors, socio-economic groups and gender. In connection with the Arctic region, for example, IPCC puts forth the following valuation: 'Climate change is probably going to drive changes in communities by challenging individuals' and communities' relationship with their local environment, which has been the basis of Arctic peoples' identity, culture, social and physical well-being' (Intergovernmental Panel on Climate Change, 2007, p. 672). Similar concerns have been put forward in the Arctic Climate Impact Assessment (ACIA, 2005).

The drivers for change and the potential impacts on people and environment have, among other things, triggered a strong and increasing research focus on assessments of vulnerability and adaptability capacity (Keskitalo, 2008; Orlove, 2009) which now dominates much of the discourse on climate change that is pursued by a large group of social scientists in the Arctic. The impacts on the particular object under study (e.g. a community, ethnic group or sector) are understood as being amplified by other processes that might concurrently be taking place or by the existing circumstances (Huntington et al., 2007). Poor and uneducated people may thus potentially be more vulnerable to the effects of climate change than rich and educated people in the same region, because poor people are understood as having a lesser capacity to adapt, due to lack of resources. In the framework used by James Ford to study Inuit communities, for example, vulnerability is conceptualized as a function of exposure to climatic stresses and also of the adaptive capacity to cope with such stresses (Ford & Smit, 2004). These stressors are produced along a number of lines: climate, loss of biodiversity, overpopulation, urbanization, neo-liberal market reforms and political institutions. Robin M. Leichenko and Karen O'Brien (2008), for example, speak about a 'double exposure', where people are living under pressure from both global environmental change and global economic change at one and the same time. Their theoretical framework includes an elaborate understanding of causalities, effects and feedback systems that provide food for thought inasmuch as they frame the discussions not only in relation to climate impacts but also because they cast light on how global processes can intensify one another. Looking at Sahel in Africa, Anette Reenberg (2009) adds population pressure to the list of significant stressors and suggests speaking about the 'triple exposure' of local livelihood strategies in an agricultural frontline that is under extreme pressure. People have multiple exposures, so to speak, in different combinations and intensities and this divergence has a tendency to create 'winners' and 'losers' (Leichenko & O'Brien, 2008).

Among the general public, Inuit are commonly perceived to be first-hand *witnesses* to these changes because they are, quite literally, seeing their world melt around them. Therefore, they are often singled out as the ultimate *victims* (or losers) of climate change (see Chapter 1). This particular position and role ascribed to the indigenous peoples in the Arctic is also seen in the media, where the Arctic is singled out as 'a sentinel' in climate research, the 'canary in the mine', the 'mercury in the thermometer', a 'Distant Early Warming System', a 'bellwether' and even as the 'linchpin' for global climate change. According to Inuit Circumpolar Council – one of the permanent participants in the Arctic Council - the Arctic is 'a barometer of the globe's environmental health. Inuit would add that they are the mercury in the barometer' (Watt-Cloutier, Fenge, & Crowley, 2006, p. 57). In the view of *National Geographic*, Greenland is the 'Ground zero for global warming', as was heralded on the front page of the magazine's June 2010 issue. Global processes are indeed making local impacts; with respect to the impacts on Inuit and the Arctic, these effects have been the focus of a great many studies and have captured the attention of a concerned public.

The study of exposures, adaptive capacities and vulnerabilities may help us to identify areas, sectors, peoples and communities in special need of assistance and we can also encircle the circumstances (or barriers) that stimulate or hinder adaptation (e.g. finances, education, political setting and technology). One dominant thought within adaptation research is the idea of 'resilience' (Pelling, 2011), which is a measure of the capacity of a unit in question to absorb shocks while maintaining functionality. This capacity fuels renewal and reorganization and may provide the potential for innovation, development and novelty and accordingly helps the unit in question to persevere through periods of pressure, shock and change. A social unit with little or no resilience is considered vulnerable: even minor impacts on such a unit may have devastating effects. Several analytical frameworks using the concepts of drivers, stressors, vulnerability, impact, adaptation and resilience are circulating in the research community. In particular, journals like *Global Environmental Change*, *Climate Change* and *Ecology & Society* reflect some of these different schools of thought and different scientific genealogies (Berrang-Ford, Ford, & Paterson, 2011; Janssen, Schoon, Ke, & Börner, 2006; Keskitalo, 2008; Manyena, 2006; Pelling, 2011; Smit, Burton, Klein, & Wandel, 2000; Smit & Wandel, 2006).

The use of these frameworks is very helpful seeing as they have been set up for purposes of examining a complex world under constant change as well as for purposes of providing us with a picture of challenges presented by – as well as the chances to understand – the coupled human-environmental system and feedback mechanisms which can enhance strategies for the protection of the environment and the protection of human well-being and security. However, many of these approaches apply the idea of 'exposure', in general, and grapple with the idea of being exposed to globalization, in particular. This is a complex of ideas that I choose to term a *scale-exposure perspective*, and the intention of this chapter is to discuss the implications of such a perspective and the scales that are implied. I will usher in this discussion on the basis of the interesting framework of 'double exposure' that has been set up by Leichenko and O'Brien (2008).

Double exposure

In the book by Leichenko and O'Brien (2008), an argument is put forth that the world is increasingly experiencing globalization and that, as a result of this, the human world is being compressed, shrunken, interlinked, connected and subjected to similar systems (primarily, to the neo-liberal market economy that staunchly advocates free-market regulation) and values (primarily, Western ones). Furthermore, we increasingly share the risks and threats of environmental destruction and change (whether it is biodiversity or climate change that is involved). The world is also experiencing a population expected to grow to around 9 billion by 2050 and projections hold that an increasing portion of this population will be migrating to and eventually living in urban areas. These processes are taking place at an accelerating pace. Furthermore, it is evident that these global processes are altering the biophysical, social and ecological systems. But how exactly do economic globalization and global environmental change affect society? In the 'double exposure' model developed by Leichenko and O'Brien (2008), the authors point toward some very interesting systems of causality and feedback. Leichenko and O'Brien argue that humans are exposed to *both* economic globalization *and* global environmental change (ergo, a 'double exposure') and that the outcomes of the interaction generate new contexts as well as 'winners and losers'. On this account, global change is deeply entangled in questions of equity. For Leichenko and O'Brien (2008, p. 5), a key concern is that these interacting processes are surpassing the capacity of both humans and ecosystems to adapt and are thereby undermining livelihood opportunities and long-term sustainability. When scrutinizing the double exposures, the authors observe that people who are experiencing negative effects of one of the global processes often also feel the negative effects of the other, and vice versa.

The aim of the 'double exposure' model is to couple the processes of economic globalization and global environmental change together and thus challenge the ordinary view where these two transformative changes are treated as being separate. Furthermore, Leichenko and O'Brien's model emphasizes multiple interactions between these two processes and they are, thereafter, analyzed systematically on the basis of different pathways of double exposure: (1) outcome double exposure, (2) context double exposure, and (3) feedback double exposure. This idea of pathways furnishes Leichenko and O'Brien with the very elaborate possibility of articulating and exploring a variety of specific interactions between the two global processes and with the chance to consider the implications on equity, resilience, and sustainability. *Outcome* double exposure reveals how overlapping exposures can aggravate regional and social inequalities; *context* double exposure points at how the processes can increase the vulnerabilities of individuals and groups to shocks and stresses; and *feedback* double exposure emphasizes how the processes can produce responses that may amplify the processes themselves and lead to new cycles of double exposure. The model is used to analyze a number of important process linkages, ranging from cases that look at climate change, trade liberalization and rural livelihoods in India through urban disaster in New Orleans in the wake of Hurricane Katrina to sea-ice change, shipping and oil extraction in the Arctic. The model indeed proves very useful when it comes to calling attention to certain very emergent and intertwined issues that are highly relevant to human welfare and security.

With respect to their analysis of the Arctic case, Leichenko and O'Brien are able to point out how economic globalization (industrialization and market mechanisms) has severely affected the Arctic environment, not only as a result of transboundary pollution generated by industries but also due to increasing temperatures that are directly related to global climate change. Consequently, the Arctic ecosystem is undergoing rapid change and the extent of the sea ice is diminishing with great speed. This environmental change not only has its own positive feedback mechanisms, which are accelerating the problem; it also opens up the Arctic for industrial development and commercial shipping activities that will not only power globalization processes but will, according to the authors, also lead to further environmental change. These intertwined processes may reinforce the processes of global climate change and industrialization. They conclude that '[w]hile the 'winners' from a warmer Arctic may be generally located outside the region, the immediate losers are likely to include many of the long-term residents of the region' (Leichenko & O'Brien, 2008, p. 101). Using a longer-term temporal perspective, they link changes in the Arctic to global sea rise and concomitantly add billions of people to the list of 'losers'. This Arctic case, which illustrates the *feedback* double exposure, not only draws attention to issues of sustainability and equity but also – according to the authors – suggests 'a fundamental rethinking, not only of energy and material consumption practices but also of what we value and why' (Leichenko & O'Brien, 2008, p. 103).

The three aforementioned suggested 'pathways of double exposure' whirl up a number of entangled issues while nonetheless maintaining a clear sense of analytical focus. Still, what does it imply to be *exposed* to *processes of globalization*? Leichenko and O'Brien (2008, pp. 34–35) define global exposure as the 'condition of being subjected to some effect or influence resulting from a process of global change' (2008, p. 34). Additionally, exposure is understood as describing how gradual transformations or discrete events occurring within a specific researcher-defined *exposure frame* that is relative to the study (e.g. a particular country or a particular household), impact directly upon particular units of analysis, or upon *exposure units* (e.g. particular communities or particular individuals).

'For each exposure unit, exposure is a function of the magnitude and intensity of the stress or shock, as well as of the contextual conditions present within the exposure frame that make each unit of analysis more prone or sensitive to a particular change' (Leichenko & O'Brien, 2008, p. 35). Global change – to which one is exposed – has *facets* (e.g. climate change or land use change), each of which has specific *manifestations* (e.g. higher temperatures or increased soil reduction). These manifestations are sometimes defined as *stressors* because 'they create conditions (stresses) that represent significant deviations from the status quo and require adjustments or responses' (Leichenko & O'Brien, 2008, p. 34). The book by Leichenko and O'Brien, taken as a whole, points our attention to existing, emergent and anticipated problems and transformations at all levels caused by the forces of globalization. Apart from furnishing a model to analyze the dynamics of these forces, the book also raises concern about the contemporary developments and contemporary values. Their model, their arguments and their analyses are very inspiring, but in the following discussion of exposure and globalization, I want to concentrate on a single sentence in the book, which I find to be particularly productive: '[a]lthough processes of global change entail large-scale transformations, they ultimately emanate from and are shaped by local activities, actions and decisions' (Leichenko & O'Brien, 2008, p. 34). This perspective is not pursued in their book.

In the framework set up by Leichenko and O'Brien, the transformations and processes taking place on a global scale operate to stress units on another (and more limited) scale (i.e. local). A similar perspective on the relationship between the global and the local is a commonly used vantage point. For example, the unprecedented increase in global food and grain prices in 2006–2007 translated directly into higher food prices on many local markets in the Sahel. This drastically diminished the food security for a number of people who were already poor, a fact described and discussed by Jonas Nielsen and Henrik Vigh (2012). The global food crisis brought about by multiple factors – including drought in grain-producing countries, rising prices of oil and fertilizer, and an increased use of land areas for the production of biofuels, to mention but a few potential causes – thus had a direct impact on local people. Locally, in the village of Biidi 2, in Burkina Faso – which was studied by Nielsen and Vigh – the inhabitants had to take adaptive actions in order to maintain human security and to reduce the impacts of the higher prices. The global food crisis placed additional stress on Sahel communities located on marginal terrain, where the inhabitants were already struggling with the unpredictability of precipitation, the movement of sand, soil degradation, the disappearance of plants, trees, wild fauna and watering holes, and growing problems with pests, all consequences of the changing climate.

The material and analysis presented by Nielsen and Vigh indeed amount to an example of double exposure, in relation to which people must navigate. The authors suggest that local people in the area in Burkina Faso that was studied actually adapted to this double exposure by means of pro-active political manoeuvring and initiatives. However, their analytical take on the matter serves to propel the adaptation discussion in an interesting direction. By introducing the concept of *social navigation*, they elucidate the way local actors simultaneously navigate many different uncertainties and possibilities across time and space when adapting to climate change (Nielsen & Vigh, 2012). Thereby, they emphasize that the concept of social navigation draws attention 'to the way human beings attempt to plan and actualize their life trajectories through a constant evaluation of the movement of the social environment, one's own possibilities for moving through it, and its effects on one's planned and actual movement' (Nielsen & Vigh, 2012, p. 661).

The concept of social navigation maintains an explicit focus on change in an *entire* social terrain. Adaptation to climate change, food prices or any other circumstances that have analytically been singled out as stressors to which people are exposed cannot be reduced, according to Nielsen and Vigh, to simple causalities because people adapt to a multiplicity of immediate, mediate and future perforations, aspirations and barriers, biophysical as well as social (Nielsen & Vigh, 2012, p. 661). People manage to do this by taking their bearings from many forces (biophysical, social, economic, political, etc.), attuning plot and practice to the many possible configurations of these (Vigh, 2006). When people take decisions – an activity that researchers often demarcate analytically as 'adapting to climate change' – they do *not* do so by isolating factors (e.g. climate change) but more correctly by navigating in a social terrain that is influenced by many conditions – and often by conditions that are more important than climate. Social navigation can thus be understood as an ongoing process of emplotment, which is constantly attuned to multiple movements and outcomes. Nielsen and Vigh explain how local people living in the area in Sahel that was studied were constantly surveying (or 'plotting' in the theory of social navigation) their socio-political environment in order to spot opportunities for warding off the high prices of food and for neutralising their lack of other strategies to withstand dire straits. By means of political negotiation, village branding, and skillful networking, and by activating international connections, the small village of Biidi 2 managed to obtain free and cheap sacks of millet. According to Nielsen and Vigh, '[t]he need for cheap food is intimately connected to the lack of rain and navigating the GFC [Global Food Crisis] is hence *also* a matter of adapting to the impact of climate change experienced in Biidi 2' (Nielsen & Vigh, 2012, p. 667). The decisions that were made in the village and the practices and strategies that were pursued can be understood, in the view of the authors, as adaptation to climate change albeit in ways that are not linked directly to climate. The process is analytically unfolded in an interesting manner by the use of *social navigation* as the analytical lens and Nielsen and Vigh conclude their article by stressing the need to explore more deeply the manner in which researchers go about understanding *how* and *what* local people are adapting to.

The introduction of *social navigation* opens up the social terrain and provides an analytical take on the situation that, with its emphasis on multiplicity and creativity, challenges some of the adaptation literature working within direct cause-and-effect relationships between what are termed 'stressors' (e.g. climate change) and human action (e.g. adaptive responses). The concept of social navigation may not only embrace the idea of seeing the world in constant motion, in which persons attentively navigate and position themselves in a setting of multiplicity, but also the idea of seeing a world that people constantly try to apprehend and make up. An inherent aspect of navigation, I would argue, is to relate to scale as a concept, both as size and extent, but also as perspective and ideology. In this chapter, the question of scale is approached not as something that is fixed but as a result of productive social and cultural creativity on the part of persons and communities. The creation of scales is not related exclusively to scientists who are busy attempting to grasp the complexities of the world but is also an activity of ordinary life. When I talk about scale-making, then, it is as an activity that can and does give direction to – and furnishes a framing around – social navigation and imagination: scale-making creates the horizon of potential action and certain ways of appreciating forces. It is important to address scale-making because it fundamentally frames the questions that are being asked, the models that are being constructed and the solutions that are being proposed. The choice of scale is, indeed, also a matter of strategic choice, with political and analytical implications (Nilsson, 2007, 2009).

Scale-making

Scaling – as a creative enactment of the world – is informed by human perspectives, agendas and circumstances. The 'locals' may thus, by means of scaling and social navigation, create and move in a space that is multi-scalable in order for them to create movement and opportunities, and in order for them to understand forces and changes. Scaling is a tool for creating subject positions and is essential for social navigation in the sense that acts of scaling draw attention to how people perceive and actualize their life trajectories. People may, by the use of scaling, pursue practices, position themselves and understand changes, opportunities and circumstances. In the words of Jones (1998, p. 26), scale can thus 'be understood as situated relationally within a community of producers and readers who give the practice of scale meaning. […] Scale is therefore both historically specific and subject to change.' In her view, scale does not exist as a fundamental structure of the world but is rather a way of apprehending the world – an apprehension that is dynamic as well as contested. When scale is understood as a representational practice, we must – according to Jones – accept that, for example, 'participants in political disputes deploy arguments about scale discursively, alternately representing their position as global or local to enhance their standing' (Jones, 1998, p. 27). Seeing that scale becomes a way to simplify, classify, frame and activate political-spatiality that may have material effects, it can no longer be regarded as neutral – rather, it is an act of productive creativity that produces subject positions, potentiality for navigation and particular forms of knowing. Smith argues (cited in Marston, 2000, p. 231) that '[a]t the very least, different kinds of society produce different kinds of geographical scale for containing and enabling particular forms of social interaction'. Producing and linking scales is thus a way to enact or cast the world and to demarcate what may be true or knowable about a subject matter within the proposed frame of scale. The need to turn scale from an ontological category into an epistemology is also suggested by Latour when he points out that the 'problem is that social scientists use scale as one of the many variables they need to set out *before* doing the study, whereas scale is what actors achieve by *scaling, spacing, and contextualizing* each other' (Latour, 2007, pp. 183–184). Similar critiques of the pre-configurations of scales are put forward by Yarrow (2008) and by Marston et al. (2005).

The setting of scales in prefixed geographical areas, positions or levels (e.g. the global level and the local level, the community level and the state level) is a (pre-)configuration that often emerges as a relationship between an 'inside' and an 'outside'. Despite the fact that most researchers subscribe to an approach where the 'local' and the 'global' are understood as embedded in each other and thus entangled, their methodologies and analyses, at times, reflect a demarcation of domains. For example, that processes taking place in the village of Biidi 2 (the lived 'inside') are *perforated* (Nielsen & Vigh, 2012) by processes taking place on the global financial market (the abstract 'outside'). 'Looking at the Arctic', Chapin III et al. (2004, p. 346, italics by the author) even interpret the processes as a '*penetration* of western culture into indigenous communities'. Chapin III et al. consider the changes taking place in Arctic indigenous communities as originating from pressures stemming from outside the Arctic. According to the authors, this configuration makes it difficult to reduce such trends. Instead, they claim, 'northern residents must be prepared to learn, cope, and adapt' (2004, p. 346). This understanding echoes the thoughts of sociologist Michael Burawoy, who also turns global forces into something privileged that lie above and behind everything and everyone – influencing local people on the ground, so to speak: 'The global force makes itself felt through mediators that transmit it as their interest or as the subjective internalization of values or beliefs. The locality in turn can fight back, adapt, or simply be destroyed' (cited in Blok, 2010, p. 192). The concept of exposure denotes a similar relation – a sense of externality – something 'the inside' is not fully a part of but indeed can be exposed to, penetrated by and impacted by – see a critique of this way of thinking in Gibson-Graham (2002) or Nielsen and Sejersen (2012). Thus, when claiming that someone is exposed to processes of globalization, both the unit in question (the someone) and the stressor (the processes of globalization) are potentially turned into ontological categories. Furthermore, the unit in question may become locked in a relation to one or several stressors – thus the unit can be under double, triple or multiple exposures, which dominate social and economic life. The power of scale in the scale-exposure perspective is, namely, its 'taken-for-granted' quality, which it imparts to their users (for example, the term 'local' is seldom questioned), and this power (of scale) privileges a particular sight that can indeed divide and order space as well as move the world.

The work of researchers employing the scale-exposure perspective is important, interesting and eye-opening, and can challenge or stabilize the ways we understand and imagine the shifting world around us. However, if scale-making (including the hypothesis about relations between scales) is looked upon as a creative act of a particular community (for example, a scientific community), we can open up for *additional* ways of understanding how ideas of climate change and other exposures are evoked, represented, played out, contested and given material consequences. An emphasis on scale-making as a creative social act may re-focus our understanding of change. Change does *not* take place *within* a scale (e.g. in a local community) or *between* scales (e.g. macro-scale influencing micro-scale). Change is immanent in the scale-making process itself, which is a relational performance constantly in the making, and scale-makers work with and shift between multiple scales at one and the same time (Orlove, 2009). By doing so, they are evoking, scaling and framing what is understood as change itself. Scale-makers and their epistemic communities conceptualize scales and relations, and in the process of doing so, they shape, constitute and transform social practices in particular places and across space. Scale-making is thus a central determinant of what transpires in places (e.g. localities, cities, regions), of how places coalesce – or do not coalesce – as entities, of how social relations in places are constructed and of how the politics of place matter (Amin, 2001, p. 389). Scale-making actively configures the spatiality of social practices and relations and is a central aspect of contemporary global interactions and transactions.

Anna Tsing (2005, p. 4) approaches these interactions and transactions as based on 'friction', because they are often fragmented, awkward, unequal, unstable, and have creative qualities of interconnection across differences. That scale-making is a process which is always deeply heterogeneous, conflictual and contested is also argued by Erik Swyngedouw (1997). Tsing is – among other things – apprehensive about the simple local-global relation that is so often applied, by fiat, when trying to understand the world (Tsing, 2005, p. 58). Her concern is that such an approach supports and produces a simple imaginary notion of the global as a homogeneous space opposed to the heterogeneity of locality. Looking at global connections as characterized by messiness and friction, she is reluctant to see the global as predictable and homogeneous. In her work, she analyzes how globalist financial conjuring links itself with other connections and scale-making projects. It is accordingly not merely a question of seeing global force and local response, which constitute the essence of the scale-exposure perspective, but rather a matter of analyzing how people 'form and reform themselves in shifting alliances, mobilized for reasons of power or passion or discipline or dis-ease, and mounting campaigns for particular configurations of unit and scale' (Tsing, 2000, p. 327). Tsing proposes an analytical approach, which urges us to trace globally interconnected, messy and fractious networks without reducing them to external forces, to one program, or to one commitment, which is so often done when looking at globalisms. In this sense, her ideas share similarities with the theory of social navigation (Vigh, 2006). By tracing global connections and encounters, she renders the question of globalization very concrete and ethnographic while maintaining the perspective of larger structures. A global framework allows us, according to Tsing (2000, p. 330), to 'consider the making and remaking of geographical and historical agents and the forms of their agency in relation to movement, interaction, and shifting, competing claims about community, culture, and scale'. Globalization is not taken for granted but is instead turned into powerful claims that can be made and unmade, pursued and given up, and which have consequences. Tsing insists that there is a lot going on and that we may miss this multiplicity if we insist on stressing interconnected circulation and flows rather than on focusing on the shifting and contested makings of connections, and on the creation of tracks and grounds and scales and units of agency.

The social life of globalization in Greenland

When examining the aluminium project in Greenland, it would be easy to apply a more traditional analytical framework that stresses the distinction between 'global' forces and 'local' responses. Such an analysis would focus on how Maniitsoq and Greenland are exposed to – and are dealing with – global capitalism and market forces. The analysis would presumably emphasize the perceptions of capitalism about localities, extractive resources, fluctuating market prizes and the aluminium needs of global consumers. In this way, the 'local' can be seen as exposed to, impacted and penetrated by or included in globalization. The Greenlanders will have to adjust or adapt to these processes – and this is going to be a 'take-it-or-leave-it' chance. By adapting to aluminium production, the Greenlanders are simultaneously whirled into the economy that is simultaneously dependent upon and fuelling globalization. The study could be about how they, more or less, successfully adapted locally by improving their language skills, by requiring certain culturally sensitive project adjustments, by integrating the project into their risk environment, by reorganizing the town so as to facilitate the factory, and by organizing differently and mobilising power and knowledge, etc. In a similar way, we could also analyze how local places in Greenland are exposed to global climate change and how they adapt to it, more or less successfully, in order to avoid disaster. However, following Tsing, this will produce the 'local' and the 'global' as scales that are taken for granted. In answering my initial question, 'What is implied by being *exposed* to *processes of globalization*', it may then be prudent to analyze how communities of scale-makers and scale-readers construct, contest and work the global scales and connections, perceive the processes and make them meaningful. There are no monocausal relations between 'local' and 'global' that can be taken for granted. Two examples from Greenland indicate that the global scale and global processes can be constructed in quite different ways, by means of different tropes: (1) the global as a competitive marketplace; and (2) the global as interlinked and dependent. These tropes are only two out of many constructions of the global, but they might serve to point our attention to some of the ways that claims of, for example, agency, community, movement, interrelationships, culture and scales are being made and being played out and to how they enable particular relationships of power and space, which benefit certain groups while operating to the detriment of others.

The global as a competitive marketplace

Entrepreneurs and workers living in Greenland cannot, by themselves, construct the massive industrial complex consisting of a 1.5-km-long smelter and two large-scale hydroelectric projects that are needed for the aluminium project to become a reality. Now, Greenland actually needs to 'import' skilled workers in order to meet the demands of the present construction projects. Therefore, it has been quite clear and has been appreciated from the very beginning that the 2,500–3,000 workmen needed to construct the hydroelectric plants as well as the 1,500–2,000 workmen needed to construct the smelter will have to come from outside Greenland (Grønlands Hjemmestyre Erhvervsdirektoratet, 2007, p. 25). These figures have changed during the preparations: in 2010, the number was reduced to 2,600 workmen in total (Departementet for Boliger Infrastruktur og Trafik, 2010, p. 4). Increasingly, it has become clear that the workers were to come from China, and people in Greenland have not to any great extent voiced objections to having foreigners construct the industrial facilities. It has also been a clear perception that when these thousands of foreign workers come to Greenland for a period of approximately 5 years, they are going to be working under the existing rules and agreements applicable to the Greenlandic labour market – a fact that the Home Rule stated explicitly in 2007 (Grønlands Hjemmestyre Erhvervsdirektoratet, 2007, p. 26).

This perception of the global as a space from which it is possible to import needed labour, which is then to be controlled by state regulations, is not unique. Often, around the world, foreign workers fill out the lowest paid jobs or receive the lowest wages. However, in Greenland, the colonial legacy is that the foreigners often were Danes and that it was they who manned the best jobs. Between 1964 and 1991, a Greenlander and a Dane who were filling out the exact same job function could thus be paid two different salaries; the reasons for this were primarily based on ethnic criteria, specifically on *where* the particular worker happened to be born (*fødestedskriteriet* in Danish) (Janussen, 1995). The elimination of this system was considered a great step forward by the Greenlanders in severing the colonial relations that they found themselves stuck in. This also came to play an important role in the Greenlandic nation-building process, where a labour market free of ethnic differentiation was considered to be a milestone. However, at a meeting in Ottawa in February 2011, Alcoa made it clear to the Greenlandic delegation that the projected construction had to be *internationally competitive*; otherwise, it would not be worthwhile for the aluminium manufacturer to pursue the project in Greenland. By situating the project in a globally competitive situation, Alcoa provided a frame in order to accentuate that the expenses had to be reduced substantially. This means that the idea of a 'globally competitive marketplace' is interposed into the discussions and evoked as 'part of the game', which is supposed to drive decisions and priorities, not only with respect to *how* the construction and the running are going to be carried out but also with respect to the question of *whether* the factory should be constructed at all. Thus, Greenlanders found themselves entangled in a situation where the global is evoked as a competitive marketplace, where both *labour* and *place* are competitively interlinked parameters. Alcoa suggested that in order to make the project internationally competitive, the construction would have to be done by Chinese contractors using Chinese workers who were to be paid international wages that are below the minimum wage in Greenland. Furthermore, the use of technology and labour should be pursued under the same regulations that are effective in other countries with similar large-scale industrial projects (Naalakkersuisut, 2010, p. 7). This would reduce the costs by 1.7 billion Danish kroner (Benson & Sørensen, 2011) but would also require that the parties of both the labour market and the Parliament contribute to the 'creation of the required legislative framework', as it was put in the white paper put forward by the Greenland government in 2010 (Naalakkersuisut, 2010, p. 7). As a comment on the need to have Chinese workers who were being compensated with 'international-level' wages, the Minister for Industry and Mineral Resources, Ove Karl Berthelsen, stated clearly that Greenland had to be realistic, 'even though we are based in the land of Santa Claus' (Berthelsen, 2011).

By establishing a framework of a 'global competitive marketplace', Greenland not only has to manoeuvre within a space of international capital flows and world market possibilities but also to *actively* relate to framework conditions that are present elsewhere in the world. Rules for international capital investments that could be expected to enable foreign investments in Greenland thus go hand in hand with changes and requirements on the labour market as well as with other rules and regulations that ensure the accumulation and circulation of capital in a fully integrated economy. Greenland has to establish a new situation of societal coherence that is fit for the new actors. According to Neil Smith, as reviewed by Marston (2000, p. 229), '[t]his equalization is accomplished through the universalization of the wage-labor relation through both formal and real spatial integration into a global system'. The international division of labour is accompanied by a converse process, where poor workers are moved to developed countries. Workers are, with reference to the mechanisms of *global competition*, expected to work under 'special' rules and 'special' regulations, and for 'special' wages. It is accepted that they are working in a 'state of exception' from the rules and regulations that might be in place in the countries in question – or to put this more precisely: the rules and regulations in a particular place are changed and bent in order to open up for this kind of labour mobility and thus make the 'state of exception' more or less permanent.

In Greenland, this was one of the concerns that was aired after Alcoa announced their new requirements, which were fuelled by arguments based on global competition: How could this 'state of exception' be contained in order to make sure that similar requirements were not going to be used in connection with other parts of the project and in other large-scale projects? The president of the Greenland Labour Union, Jess G. Berthelsen, came forth with the following statement: 'I am warning the government against opening up for low-paid Chinese. Foreign workers are to have proper salaries. No firm should try to bypass the existing agreements in Greenland. This is a pre-set ticking bomb. If we to say 'yes' to Alcoa, then other companies will line up and demand the same meagre agreements when the oil production and mining are set in motion' (Benson & Sørensen, 2011, translated by the author). Also, the president of the Employers' Association of Greenland was sceptical, primarily because such special arrangements would benefit only a single company and thus create competitive distortion in Greenland (Leth, 2011).

When the global scale is evoked as a 'global competitive marketplace', in which low-paid workers can be moved around in a constant 'state of exception', this gives rise to certain subject positions, potentials and limitations for stakeholders, governments and companies. The Greenlandic parliament has to actively set up new rules, regulations and frameworks, has to creatively rethink the country's future labour market situation and has to differentiate between businesses, in order to meet their aspirations for basing a future economy on a mega-industrialization of the country. The Greenlandic authorities 'faced' these unexpected political challenges in concrete negotiations with Alcoa and later produced specific and new legislation (a set of regulations that were later termed *storskalaloven*, i.e. legislation governing large-scale industrial projects). The process can be understood as a commercial pressure being put on Greenland to allow its labour market to operate in a manner that is unfettered by national regulations and agreements – in order to create a gateway for the mobility and circulation of a transnational low-paid labour force.

Pressure on governments from transnational companies are, according to the post-Marxists Michael Hardt and Antonio Negri (2000), characterizing the transition from the modern to the postmodern world, in which the power of the nation-state is being challenged by an 'Empire' of ruling powers that are held firmly in the grasp of transnational institutions and companies. Colin Crouch (2004) also puts forward a similar argument in his book, *Post Democracy*. The decisions potentially to be taken by the Parliament to open up for this mobility can be interpreted as a way of adapting to globalization or as an example of how Greenland is exposed to globalization. This opening-up can, however, also be seen as a way that Greenland itself is actively co-producing, evoking, enacting and mobilizing the global scale and the logics of partnership, integration and mobility which have been identified and which are expected to transpire. The 'global' and 'global processes' cannot simply be located as 'outside' Greenland. It is rather the case that 'global' and 'global processes' delineate a scale that is enacted along a trope of the 'global as a competitive marketplace', which Greenland actively imagines, relates to and alters in order to maintain what is considered the 'proper' roles and relations of governments, unions, workers and companies in a new geometry of power. In the event that the Greenland government opposes the employment of low-paid workers, the company can move elsewhere in the global space and engage in other places, with less friction and opposition (Bauman, 1998); this was also a point that was made explicit by industrial leaders at a public meeting in Greenland (Nyvold, 2011). Greenland's parliament and Denmark (which would have to approve the work permits) thus actively need to formulate the framework for a new contract between the public and private sectors, which are being mobilized and reconfigured in relation to a scale that is being defined and understood as 'global'.

The global as interlinked and dependent

The trope of the global as interlinked and dependent is widespread. It is utilized to apprehend the global as a scale where action that is taken in one place has consequences elsewhere, despite the geographical distances involved. This notion of interconnectedness and dependence creates a kind of imagined intimacy across time and space, where everything (for example, goods, information and people) is circulating with even greater speed and power (Robertson, 1992). David Harvey's description of this phenomenon as 'space-time compression' (1990) has become one of the most common ways of understanding what globalization is all about. The objective of evoking imagination and responsibility on this scale has been one of the main drivers of the environmental movement since the 1970s. With respect to the political discourse of climate change, this scale of understanding indeed also lays the very basis for both concern and action. In practice, people have to imagine that their desires and actions have consequences for people elsewhere in the world. We are made to understand that even simple routines and consumption patterns (e.g. driving a car to work or using a mobile phone) may potentially have severe impacts on (other) people and environments in places that we have never even heard about. These connections are difficult to appreciate and they are not easily observable. In order for us to transcend our immediate experience in the world, the relations have to be mediated. The many images of Pacific Islands supposedly experiencing sea level rise, and Inuit (and polar bears) moving around in a melting (and thus vanishing) world are among the means of mobilising this scale of understanding. However, this scale has to be mobilized and evoked, in much the manner of any other scale. In Greenland, the act of using this scale as an integral part of a political argument became an issue during a discussion of the impacts of the aluminium smelter. The central point of what I want to communicate in what follows from here is to show how the global can be used and contested as a relevant scale. I have already elaborated on the issue in the chapter on place consciousness (Chapter 5) and will therefore refrain here from delving more deeply into the details.

In November 2010, the Greenlandic environmental organization, Avataq, accused the Greenlandic government of keeping the public in the dark about the human and environmental impacts of having an aluminium smelter. Their claim was raised in a press release (Avataq, 2010a) and was heard on the radio's news program just when the government was about to present its white paper on the smelter (Naalakkersuisut, 2010). Avataq criticized the white paper for being manipulative and inadequate, and for containing misinforming propaganda that was spread primarily by Greenland Development A/S. Their critique was focused primarily on the *scale* on which the sustainability and the impact assessments of the aluminium production were being apprehended and conveyed. Avataq complained that the impact assessments focused too narrowly on the situation being envisioned in Greenland. By way of posing a contrast, the organization argued that aluminium production was 'a production that in its totality can be characterized as one of this planet's most socially and environmentally destructive industrial processes' (Avataq, 2010a, translated by the author). The minister in charge of the process, Ove Karl Berthelsen, quickly commented on the critique and aired his concern over Avataq's choice of words because they 'complicate an exciting and substantive debate about such an important issue as a potential aluminium production in Greenland' (Sermitsiaq, 2010, translated by the author). Furthermore, Berthelsen raised two other points to which he objected: that Avataq did not put forward any documentation to substantiate their claims; and that Avataq 'takes the matters out of context' (Sermitsiaq, 2010, translated by the author). Two days later, Avataq distributed a new press release (Avataq, 2010b) that included a list of references (Internet links) in order to give substance to their accusations about the destructive nature of the aluminium industry. They pointed to environmental issues in the Amazon, to human rights violations in Guinea and to community health problems in Australia as direct consequences of the industry's activities. One basic argument in the environmental organization's press release was that '*the reality* does not match the information that has been made available until now' (Avataq, 2010b, italics and translation by the author). Avataq was trying to mobilize 'a reality' that was based on the trope of the global as 'interlinked and dependent' – a trope that inscribes local projects into larger networks of dependencies and, accordingly, consequences. If one evokes 'a reality' on a global scale, potential new subject positions and relations emerge. In the wake of this, new responsibilities emerge, as well. This is a scale where even the best Strategic Environmental Assessment or Life Cycle Assessment may be forced to give up.

It may seem like a battle between scales: the government tried to scale the project in order to maintain a focus on Maniitsoq and Greenland, primarily in order to make sure that the project would not have negative impacts on the Greenlandic economy, society, environment and population. Avataq, on the other hand, wanted to link the Greenlandic factory into a connected and globally dependent production line, which may have severe consequences for people and environments elsewhere. In doing so, the environmental organization was evoking a very different landscape of risk and responsibility than the one propagated by the government. Even though the minister in charge of the process elaborated on some of Avataq's accusations, he pointed out that 'without in any way defending or taking a stand on Alcoa's doings out in the great wide world, it is widely known that Alcoa is recognized for its efforts in the extraction of bauxite and the refining of bauxite into aluminium oxide in a manner that is, in relation to the environment and the surroundings, as responsible as possible' (Minister Ove Karl Berthelsen cited in Sermitsiaq, 2010, translated by the author). The minister appealed to Avataq that they base their contributions to the debate on documented facts. I would propose, however, that the encounter between the minister and Avataq has nothing to do with facts: both parties may actually prove to be suffering under a shortage of facts. What we have here is rather a matter of competing scale-makers who – by demarcating and following different impacts – are evoking different 'realities' and thus diverging 'facts' that have to be produced, discussed and evaluated. What are considered relevant 'facts' and 'costs' within the trope of the global as 'interdependent and interlinked' may turn out to be quite irrelevant and outside the scale of interest, concern and priority of a government that is focusing on local and national scales or that may want to focus on other global dependencies like market fluctuations related to aluminium. In the political and very aluminium-critical book, *Out of this Earth*, Padel and Das (2010) address this question by asking: 'Our modern lifestyle depends on extracting and processing huge quantities of minerals and oil. But what is the real cost we are making our earth pay?' (Padel & Das, 2010, p. xv). Their account of the aluminium industry focuses on how the industry affects the environment, people and Third World countries. Like Avataq, Padel and Das propose looking at the 'real' cost-benefit analysis of aluminium production – an analysis that includes all links in the production. The demarcation of 'real' is, again, scale-dependent and highly contestable and stakeholders spend a great deal of energy maintaining their particular level of scale and orientation in order to give relevance to the production of a particular genre of facts. Avataq's engagement and the inspiration that it gathers from a global network of environmental organizations fashion a background for the claims that they put forward. For Greenland Development A/S, the notion of the global as being interlinked is primarily maintained by following the market fluctuations of aluminium – these are contours that are vital in the evaluation of the smelter's eventual profitability. Whereas Avataq trains a strong focus on the global *pre*-factory interdependencies, Greenland Development A/S focuses on the *post*-factory interdependencies. Both stakeholders thus work with a global scale as interlinked and dependent. However, they focus on different aspects along the chain of dependencies: Avataq produces a pre-factory gaze, which positions the factory as a *consumer* of resources, while Greenland Development A/S pursues a post-factory gaze, where the factory is a *producer* of resources.

In both cases, the global is utilized as a trope – or a framing device – in order to demarcate different terrains in which potential navigation is meaningful, and as a way of organising and mobilising imagination, knowledge production, social responsibility and politics in certain constellations. It is difficult if not impossible to summarize the discussions in Greenland and the choices being made and boil them down to being a consequence of exposure to globalization. Rather, stakeholders are involved in living off and adding to the circulation of capital, workers, material, knowledge and ideas that can be framed and scaled as global. Greenlanders are creating their place in the world, and they are also placing their world in the creation – and these acts of *worlding* are highly political, contested and have consequences. The examples do not imply that the global is the appropriate scale for the discussions, but it is nonetheless being evoked, in a certain way, and is being rendered powerful. As has been astutely pointed out by Anna Tsing (2005, p. 111), making the globe our frame of reference is indeed *hard work*.

The scaling of climate change adaptation

If scale is considered as being analytically evoked and as privileging certain subject positions and particular relations of causalities and dependences, it may be important to discuss how the climate change adaptation discourse is handling this scaling issue and to discuss, also, what consequences this might have. The point is not to question the quality or the importance of climate change adaptation research but rather to investigate the question of what direction it may lead our gaze. As James Ford et al. (2008, p. 47) point out (see Chapter 2), their particular down-scaled community-based methodology is important and central in linking research to policy action, which is becoming more and more important. The exposure framework that they analytically demarcate for their vulnerability studies is closely related to down-scaled projections that provide detailed regional and site scenarios of climate change (Ford & Smit, 2004). In fact, these researchers are representative of an Arctic research trend, as has been pointed out by Emilie Cameron (2012), and thus a discussion of Ford and his team's work – and a discussion of the very academically productive James Ford in particular – may cast some light on the perspectives that have been applied by many other researchers.

The scale they use puts people in the very foreground and sees exposures, vulnerabilities and coping strategies from the users' point of view; in this case, from that of the Inuit hunters. This allows Ford and his collaborators to make detailed analyses on multiple limits and potentials in the local setting, which may, by turns, hinder or improve the adaptation required to protect the livelihoods in a changing climate. Their study not only integrates local knowledge, hunting techniques, flexible resource use and sharing practices but also hunting quotas, governmental subsidies, wage employment, communication technology and school requirements, just to mention a few of the many elements that are considered in their studies. By stressing that the need to integrate economic and institutional support is just as important as understanding Inuit's ability to manage harvesting-related exposures, the researchers were most certainly operating with a highly complex understanding of system dynamics. Their conclusion is that climate change will alter the environmental setting and accessibilities, which will then require a response from the Inuit communities. The capacities of the people, who are part of these communities, to respond and adapt will vary, indeed, among different communities and different (age-) groups, but Ford and his fellow researchers conclude that 'the changing climatic conditions, superimposed on changes in harvesting behaviour, have altered, and have tended to increase, exposure to climatic risks' (Ford et al., 2008, p. 59). This concern is mirrored in many of James Ford's studies and several suggestions for improving the communities' capacity to adapt have been put forward. It is, for example, suggested that the communities need enhanced training in GPS usage and in traditional skills (Ford, 2008, 2009; Ford, Pearce, Duerden, Furgal, & Smit, 2010). The applied framework of adaptation is dependent on a conscious choice to demarcate and rank exposures and drivers and thus to evoke a certain scale that can be considered relevant.

In Ford's work, vulnerability to climate change is the primary research focus. This analytical grasp conjures up some very insightful understandings of the dynamics that are linked to environmental change. His work is policy-oriented and thus helps in identifying significant policy entry points and, by doing so, occasions the examination of policy initiatives for adaptation that will reduce Inuit vulnerability and will increase their adaptive capacity (Ford et al., 2010) when it comes to climate change. In his work, climate change adaptation is set into a larger socio-historical-political framework within which Inuit will experience and respond to climate change. In Ford et al. (2010, p. 179), there is a chart, for example, which illustrates the major societal changes that have transpired after modernization policies were implemented in the North in the 1950s and directs our attention to the drastic and traumatic upheavals that made such an enormous impact on individuals and on communities. Ford points out that the changes and the contemporary conditions have had effects on Inuit's adaptive capacity: 'These determinants of vulnerability are influenced by social, economic, cultural, and political conditions and processes operating at multiple scales over time and space, and change in these non-climatic conditions play[s] an *important* role in determining vulnerability to climate change. Importantly, the emphasis on multiple stresses broadens the scope for adaption to include initiatives to reduce sensitivity and exposure while increasing adaptive capacity' (Ford et al., 2010, p. 181, italics by the author). This is indeed a significant point when we consider that the problems in the North are tremendous, as is also underlined by Jack Hicks (1999, p. 43) in his study of Nunavut governmental structures and challenges:

> [The new Nunavut government] [...] will face enormous challenges: a young work force with high levels of unemployment, low (but rising) educational levels, low average incomes with heavy and mounting dependence on social assistance, high costs for goods and public services, seriously inadequate public housing, high levels of substance abuse and other social problems (including suicide), and escalating rates of violence and incarceration.

Inuit's exposure to – and capacity to adapt to – climate change are thus entangled in larger issues which may actually be designated as being quite decisive. Poverty, for example, as a factor, may amplify or attenuate vulnerability (Ford et al., 2010, p. 181) and communities may be rather limited in their possibilities to adapt due to barriers related to their capabilities to act collectively and to mobilize social capital (Adger, 2003). Still, the vulnerability framework that was used in the study (Ford & Smit, 2004) focuses only on adaptation to risks associated with resource harvesting, travel, food systems, and community infrastructure (Ford et al., 2010, p. 183). I argue that this focus is a particular analytical act in which societal dynamics are not only delimited by activities within only one sector (hunting) and one narrow group of agents (hunters), but are also downscaled to such an extent that societal action, problems and needs become silenced.

The studies of Ford integrate political institutions at different levels as well as more than 25 per cent of the communities in the Canadian North, which is in itself an impressive accomplishment, furnishing a magnificent ground for comparative studies. By doing this, a number of new stakeholders emerge (e.g. international and national institutions influencing hunting regulations and trade), although the scale of analysis is maintained as local and as focusing solely on hunting. According to Ford et al. (2010, p. 183), it is important to uphold this scale because it will make policy intervention easier and help it obtain relevance, credibility, and legitimacy. The analytical focus, however, leaves us rather uninformed about the livelihoods, the problems, strategies, choices and potentials in the households, communities and their networks. Such an analytical opening would stimulate the analysis to take into consideration that local actors simultaneously navigate many different uncertainties and possibilities across time and space when operating in a social environment that is related not only to climate change adaptation. This emphasis on social navigation maintains an explicit focus on change in an *entire* social terrain rather than solely in a human-environment nexus, where social, economic, political and cultural issues and actions become reduced to stressors or constrainers.

The framework used by Ford provides us with interesting food for thought and with 'easy' policy entry points, but it focuses only on a single activity/sector (hunting) within the community and on a single and all-pervasive frame of exposure (climate change). The critique being voiced here is not to be interpreted as a way of underestimating the great impacts that climate change will have in the Arctic, changes that are expected to be accelerating here faster than they are anywhere else, nor to be interpreted as a comment that climate change is not the root of genuine concern, locally (Ayles, Bell, & Fast, 2002; McDonald, Arragutainaq, & Novalinga, 1997). To put this more explicitly, the critique is that many down-scaled vulnerability studies, for example, those that are represented by the work of Ford, reduce the dynamics of lnuit communities and point political interventions in narrow directions that might potentially fail to address urgent and critical issues, fail to improve the livelihoods of Northern Inuit communities or fail to reduce vulnerability in the long run.

The subject positions and subject relations that are activated and mobilized within the scale evoked in Ford's analyses are understood in a rather different way by polar researcher George Wenzel (2009). In an article, he focuses on the social reality of the food system as the core of the matter when it comes to understanding vulnerability and adaptation. Basically, by expanding scale and analytical focus, he unfolds what is kept as background, context or stressor in Ford's analyses and turns this into an integrated part of the social landscape in which subjects navigate. In a novel way, Wenzel analyzes the elaborate meat distribution systems and complex economic systems in order to 'dispel the false notion that Inuit subsistence is the sum of seals or caribou caught. Rather, Inuit subsistence in the past and today is not only about the production of food, but is equally about all the Inuit behaviours [...] that provide individuals with the security of a well-functioning economy' (Wenzel, 2009, p. 93). On the basis of archaeological, historical and contemporary data, he contends against the idea that a warming Arctic presents an insurmountable threat to the subsistence system. The real challenges to adaptation, he suggests, are to be found elsewhere: in the politics of global warming. In an act of temporal and spatial upscaling, he creates other subjects, locally and internationally. This scaling manoeuvre is necessary because 'the Arctic is no longer an environment in which the Inuit are the sole actors' (Wenzel, 2009, p. 94). These actors are kept in the shadows, as being merely contextual, in Ford's analyses. By adopting a more encompassing understanding of the sociality and politics of subsistence economy, Wenzel includes a number of new actors that influence the livelihoods of northern peoples 'at least as much

as any shifts in the ranges or even the disappearance of important food species'
(Wenzel, 2009, p. 94). In particular, he claims that the Western perceptions and
concern for charismatic Arctic animals like polar bears and seals may undermine
any adaptive and scientifically regulated use of the resources. The adaptive
choices and capacities of Inuit may thus be hampered by global, environmental, political regimes that are influenced by the environmental movement, whose
organizations are 'ignorant of their [i.e. the regimes'] cultural impact' (Wenzel,
2009, p. 97). By introducing the management regimes as part of the very environment in which Inuit have to navigate, he concludes that *political negotiation* may
constitute an important part of their adaptive tool kit. Wenzel thus coaxes the
adaptation and vulnerability discussion in a more political direction by working
with a different scale than Ford, even though he maintains a strong focus on the
local. Wenzel's upscaling is not a matter of leaving the local behind for the sake
of moving onto an extra-local level, but is more a matter of scaling the local in a
different way, and by doing so, Western environmental political activists become
part of the socio-political terrain in which northern communities have to navigate and influence. Scaling is thus more than a question of size and extent but just
as much a matter of perspective and room for social agency.

In order to understand a number of local and sector-specific adaptability problems related to climate change in Scandinavia, E. Carina Keskitalo (2008) finds
it productive to regard adaptation and adaptive capacity, and thus also vulnerability, as being determined within frameworks of governance. In all her studies,
she analyzes how political regulatory systems limit resource use and distribute
privileges and support to different actors and how, by doing so, these systems
play a major role in mediating and determining vulnerability to climate change.
Her scale-making is opening up for understanding the national and international
markets and institutions as operative in the social, economic and political field
of hunters, herders and loggers: 'On the whole, this study illustrates that general adaptive capacity should be analyzed in terms of the principal impacts of
ongoing and anticipated economic, political and social changes on stakeholders'
livelihoods. There are also clear inter-linkages between economic and political
systems, particularly regarding employment, within broad, multi-actor and multi-
level systems of governance for the sectors and areas' (Keskitalo, 2008, p. 184).
Her conclusions are quite different from Ford's when it comes to the assessments
of climate change vulnerabilities and when it comes to adaptive strategies of local
stakeholders. According to Keskitalo (2008), people act in response to situations
as a whole and do not necessarily sort out distinguishable areas or factors. Instead,
people adapt continuously, 'with a focus on what they need to do to maintain
or improve their current livelihood and socioeconomic situation' (Keskitalo,
2008, p. 192). She draws attention to how people yearn to influence regulatory
bodies as part of their adaptive strategy and how they communicate in a complex social, economic and political network. Although Keskitalo explicitly positions herself close to vulnerability approaches that have been advanced by, for
example, Leichenko and O'Brien (2008), Smit and Wandel (2006), and Eakin
and Lamos (2006), she is more attentive to scale-making practices, and to the

subject-positions that are evoked in these processes. When she posits governance as one of the crucial factors in how adaptive capacity is distributed, she is pointing not only at how international processes may influence the capacities of local actors (taking up the scale-exposure perspective) but moreover at how 'local' actors are entangled and actively engaged in norm-making and at how stakeholders' interests and powers influence the definition of the problem at hand. Actors are understood as framing themselves in terms of narratives, so as to link themselves onto other levels of authority (Keskitalo, 2008, p. 24) and so as to generate and construct their own scales and spaces of engagement and exposures; these scales are produced as part of particular projects (e.g., political negotiations and the promotion of special interests). In order to make these scales apparent, Keskitalo analyzes actions and institutions that are considered important in 'the eyes of the stakeholders' (Keskitalo, 2008, p. 41). In her study of the fishing sector's vulnerability, for example, small-scale fishermen call attention to how their projects (catching fish) are deeply entangled in the actions and projects of others who are considered 'non-local' (e.g. politicians, industrial fishermen and financial investors), and to how the fishermen suggest new scales of involvement and agency (e.g. more regionally regulated quota distribution schemes) in order to improve the field of action and projects. Scale does not only become something that should be crossed, but something that is evoked as a means toward understanding and as a vehicle for producing potentiality.

We can see, when moving from the work of Ford through Wenzel's approach and over to Keskitalo's approach, an analytical widening of the social terrain of action. Concomitantly, the understanding of processes of change is gradually being expanded. Each of the three researchers mentioned above is pursuing different scale-making projects and accordingly presenting different analytical understandings of subject positions, subject potentialities and subject relations. The ideology of scale thus has consequences for how people, sectors, groups, localities, institutions, regions, states and peoples are conjured and rendered imaginable. When exploring the works of vulnerability researchers, one must (as would be the case in any other kind of research project) remain aware about what scale-making projects are being promoted and keep an eye on how 'the local' and 'the global' come into being. Even Keskitalo, who devotes certain sections of her research to how the global impacts local vulnerability, asks whether globalization is a key determinant of change (Keskitalo, 2008, p. 186ff). In one shorter section, she unfolds how difficult it really is to differentiate between the 'internal' and the 'external' because people's concerns and strategies are entangled in complex systems of interactions and networks of political, environmental and social agents – a network which they themselves have spun, are suspended in and act in. This brings me back to the question, 'What is implied by being exposed to processes of globalization?' To answer this question, one has to accept the scale-making project that is inherent in the question itself and appreciate the vitality the question brings to any discussion. In relation to climate change, which has been demarcated as one aspect of globalization, the question has indeed given vitality and focus to political, academic and public discussions while leaving other concerns, changes, actions and relations in the shadows or has even left them forgotten and forsaken. It is tempting to complement the question that was just raised with the following rejoinder: 'and what kind of answers and narratives does this question produce?'

In the Arctic, people are struggling to deal with a multitude of problems and potentials. Having the dynamics of this complex social terrain narrowed down to a question of exposure to globalization (and primarily, to climate change) can distort the work that people are doing to create and maintain livelihoods. For example, the focus on climate change and the hunting sector in the work of Ford can be seen as being based on three implicit 'exposure assumptions' or 'exposure narratives': that the vulnerability of hunters is a proxy of the vulnerability of northern communities; that climate change is the most immediate problem which hunters and communities have to relate to; and finally, that climate change will make its most deeply felt effect on the hunting sector. Maintaining a focus on climate change, on hunters as the vulnerable group, and on their hunting activities as an indicator of community well-being can indeed be said to produce a strained understanding of the quality and dynamics of Northern livelihoods and social well-being, as was discussed in the Arctic Council's Report on Arctic Social Indicators (Larsen, Schweitzer, & Fondahl, 2010), which is a result of and a follow-up study of the Arctic Human Development Report (2004). Here, what is explicated is that even though climate change may be seen as an obvious and widely acknowledged influence on the future of circumpolar societies, other factors play a more immediate role in the lives of Arctic residents, in many areas (Larsen et al., 2010, p. 11). Even with respect to hunters, climate change may only pose a relatively minor problem, as has been noted by Mark Nuttall (2009, p. 307):

> Rather than Inuit hunters being prevented by climate change from catching seals, the reasons, I suggest, are rather more complicated. Long-term policies of shifting demographics, investment in a few major centers, a reluctance to introduce development policies for small villages and settlements, a redefinition of resources and rights of access to them, and a political desire to encourage the depopulation of some communities all perhaps have greater significance for changing hunting and fishing practices than climate change does.

It is within this complex world that hunters listen and make choices, remember and anticipate, work and network, settle and move, vote and lobby, sell and buy, as well as scale and imagine. From this point of view, the discourse of climate change and adaptation can indeed seem bounded and limited (Bravo, 2009; Marino & Schweitzer, 2009; Orlove, 2009), even when scaled to include what researchers demarcate as 'global exposures'. The 'local–global' binary is a fantastic framing device for setting up some general reflections on potential interrelationships and causalities between the concrete (local) and the structural (global), but it may paradoxically overlook many of the often muddy, surprising, sticky, and evolving actions, choices and encounters of people, actions, choices and encounters that are neither simple nor causal (Krauss, 2009). Anna Tsing's metaphor of 'friction' (Tsing, 2005), which she uses to describe the diverse and conflicting social interaction, is indeed welcome as it moves away from the idea of globalization as a unified force, whether in the shape of climate change or liberalization of markets. We might actually learn more about the vulnerabilities and capacities of people if we stop talking about globalization and stop framing our research questions after that fashion (see also Marino & Schweitzer, 2009). Foregrounding and privileging processes of globalization amount to pre-ordaining their significance and primacy and doing so hinders us from appreciating both minor and mega trends in the Arctic and in pursuing what Anders Blok (2010, p. 197) terms 'ethnographies of scale-making'. The rethinking of scale-making as something that assembles and connects causes the forces that are usually referred to as 'outside' and 'global' to emerge as an inherent part of social life, where problem-framing and agency are demarcated. Scale-making indeed fuels the imagination, thus allowing distinctive voices and forms of agency to emerge while others can be left in the analytical shadows.

References

ACIA. (2005). *Arctic Climate Impact Assessment*. Cambridge: Cambridge University Press.

Adger, W. Neil. (2003). Social capital, collective action, and adaptation to climate change. *Economic Geography*, 79(4), 387–404.

Amin, Ash. (2001). Spatialities of globalisation. *Environment and Planning A*, 34, 385–399

Arctic Human Development Report. (2004). Akureyri: Stefansson Arctic Institute.

Avataq. (2010a). Pressemeddelelse November 8, 2010. Retrieved September 12, 2011, from www.avataq.gl/userfiles/avataq_pressemeddelelse_8nov2010.pdf.

Avataq. (2010b). Pressemeddelelse November 15, 2010. Retrieved July 13, 2011, from www.avataq.gl/userfiles/NY_avataq_pressemedd_15_nov_2010.pdf.

Ayles, G.B., Bell, R., & Fast, H. (2002). The Beaufort Sea Conference 2000 on the Renewable Marine Resources of the Canadian Beaufort Sea. *Arctic*, 55(Supp. 1), iii–v.

Bauman, Zygmunt. (1998). *Globalization: The Human Consequences*. New York: Columbia University Press.

Benson, Peter Suppli, & Sørensen, Bent Højgaard. (2011, March 11). Alugigant kræver billige kinesere i Grønland. *Business.dk*. Retrieved September 7, 2011, from www.business.dk/industri/alugigant-kraever-billige-kinesere-i-groenland.

Berrang-Ford, Lea, Ford, James, & Paterson, Jaclyn. (2011). Are we adapting to climate change? *Global Environmental Change*, 21(2011), 25–33.

Berthelsen, Ove Karl. (2011). Grønland satser på væksterhverv. Retrieved September 7, 2011, from http://dagenssynspunkt.blogs.business.dk/2011/03/31/gr%C3%B8nland-satser-pa-v%C3%A6kst-erhverv/.

Bjørst, Lill Rastad. (2011). *Arktiske diskurser og klimaforandringer i Grønland. Fire (post) humanistiske klimastudier*. København: Institut for Tværkulturelle og Regionale Studier (Ph.D. indleveret til det Humanistiske fakultetet).

Blok, Anders. (2010). *Divided Socio-Natures: Essays on the Co-Construction of Science, Society, and the Global Environment*. Copenhagen: University of Copenhagen (Ph.D. handed in at Department of Sociology).

Bravo, Michael. (2009). Voices from the sea ice: The reception of climate impact narratives. *Journal of Historical Geography*, 35(2), 256–278.

Cameron, Emilie S. (2012). Securing indigenous politics: A critique of the vulnerability and adaptation approach to the human dimensions of climate change in the Canadian Arctic. *Global Environmental Change, 22*(2012), 103–114.

Chapin III, F. Stuart, Peterson, Garry, Berkes, Fikret, Callaghan, Terry, Angelstam, Per, Apps, M., Beier, Colin, Bergeron, Yves, Crépin, Anne-Sophie, Danell, Kjell, Elmqvist, Thomas, Folke, Carl, Forbes, Bruce, Fresco, Nancy, Juday, Glenn, Niemelä, Jari, Shvidenko, Anatoly & Whiteman, Gail. (2004). Resilience and vulnerability of Northern regions to social and environmental change. *Ambio, 33*(6), 344–349.

Crouch, Colin. (2004). *Post Democracy.* Cambridge: Polity Press.

Departementet for Boliger Infrastruktur og Trafik. (2010). *Regional social og samfundsmæssig konsekvensanalyse ved mulig etablering af aluminiumsmelter i Grønland.* Nuuk: Grønlands Selvstyre.

Eakin, H., & Lamos, M.C. (2006). Adaption and the state: Latin America and the challenge of capacity-building under globalization. *Global Environmental Change, 16,* 7–18.

Ford, James. (2008). Climate, society, and natural hazards: Changing hazard exposure in two Nunavut communities. *Northern Review, 28,* 51–71.

Ford, James. (2009). Sea ice change in Arctic Canada: Are there limits to Inuit adaptation? In W. N. Adger, I. Lorenzoni & K. L. O'Brien (Eds.), *Adapting to Climate Change: Thresholds, Values, Governance* (pp. 114–127). Cambridge: Cambridge University Press.

Ford, James, & Smit, Barry. (2004). A Framework for Assessing the Vulnerability of Communities in the Canadian Arctic to Risks Associated with Climate Change. *Arctic, 57*(4), 389–400.

Ford, James, Smit, Barry, Wandel, Johanna, Allurut, Mishak, Shappa, Kik, Ittusarjuats, Harry, & Qrunnut, Kevin. (2008). Climate change in the Arctic: Current and future vulnerability in two Inuit communities in Canada. *The Geographical Journal, 174*(1), 45–62.

Ford, James, Pearce, Tristan, Duerden, Frank, Furgal, Chris, & Smit, Barry. (2010). Climate change policy responses for Canada's Inuit population: The importance of and opportunities for adaptation. *Global Environmental Change, 20,* 177–191.

Gibson-Graham, J.K. (2002). Beyond global vs. local: Economic politics outside the binary frame. In M. W. Wright & A. Herod (Eds.), *Geographies of Power: Placing Scale* (pp. 25–60). Oxford: Blackwell.

Grønlands Hjemmestyre Erhvervsdirektoratet. (2007). Redegørelse om energiintensiv industri i Grønland. Nuuk: Grønlands Hjemmestyre.

Hardt, Michael, & Negri, Antonio. (2000). *Empire.* Cambridge, Massachutts: Harvard University Press.

Harvey, David. (1990). *The Condition of Postmodernity.* Cambridge, Massachusetts: Blackwell.

Hicks, Jack. (1999). The Nunavut land claim and Nunavut government: Political structures of self-government in Canada's eastern Arctic. In H. Petersen & B. Poppel (Eds.), *Dependency, Autonomy, Sustainbility in the Arctic* (pp. 21–54). Aldershot: Ashgate.

Huntington, Henry P., Hamilton, Lawrence C., Nicolson, Craig, Brunner, Ronald, Lynch, Amanda, Ogilvie, Astrid E. J., & Voinov, Alexey. (2007). Toward understanding the human dimensions of the rapidly changing arctic system: Insights and approaches from five HARC projects. *Regional Environmental Change, 7*(4), 173–186.

Intergovernmental Panel on Climate Change (IPCC). (2007). Polar Regions (Arctic and Antarctic). In M. Parry, O. Canziani, J. Palutikof, P. v. d. Linden, & C. Hanson (Eds.), *Climate Change 2007: Impacts, Adaptation and Vulnerability. Contribution of Working Group II to the Fourth Assessment Report of the Intergovernmental Panel on Climate Change* (Vol. 15, pp. 654–685). Cambridge and New York: Cambridge University Press.

Janssen, M.A., Schoon, M. L., Ke, W., & Börner, K. (2006). Scholarly networks on resilience, vulnerability and adaptation within the human dimensions of global environmental change. *Global Environmental Change*, 16(3), 240–252.

Janussen, Jakob. (1995). Fødestedskriteriet – og hjemmestyrets ansættelsespolitik. *Tidsskriftet Grønland* (2), 73–80.

Jones, Katherine T. (1998). Scale as epistemology. *Political Geography*, 17(1), 25–28.

Keskitalo, E. Carina H. (2008). *Climate Change and Globalization in the Arctic: An Integrated Approach to Vulnerability Assessment*. London and Sterling: Earthscan.

Krauss, Werner. (2009). Localizing climate change: A multi-sited approach. In M.A. Falzon (Ed.), *Multi-Sited Ethnography: Theory, Praxis and Locality in Contemporary Research* (pp. 149–164). Surrey: Ashgate.

Larsen, Joan Nymand, Schweitzer, Peter, & Fondahl, Gail (Eds.). (2010). *Arctic Social Indicators: A Follow-up to the Arctic Human Development Report*. Copenhagen: Nordic Council of Ministers.

Latour, Bruno. (2007). *Reassembling the Social. An Introduction to Actor-Network-Theory*. Oxford: Oxford University Press.

Leichenko, Robin M., & O'Brien, Karen. (2008). *Environmental Change and Globalization: Double Exposure*. Oxford: Oxford University Press.

Leth, Henrik. (2011). Det er ikke særordninger men handlekraft, der er brug. Retrieved September 7, 2011, from www.ga.gl/Nyheder/Nyhedsarkiv/Nyhedsarkiv2011/Marts2011/Deterikkes%C3%A6rordningermenhandlekraftdererb/tabid/1572/language/da-DK/Default.aspx.

Li, Tania Murray. (2007). *The Will to Improve: Governmentalilty, Development, and the Practice of Politics*. Durham: Duke University Press.

Manyena, Siambabala Bernard. (2006). The concept of resilience revisited. *Disasters*, 30(4), 434–450.

Marino, Elizabeth, & Schweitzer, Peter. (2009). Talking and not talking about climate change in Northwestern Alaska. In S. A. Crate & M. Nuttall (Eds.), *Anthropology & Climate Change: From Encounters to Actions* (pp. 209–217). Walnut Creek: Left Coast Press.

Marston, Sallie A. (2000). The social construction of scale. *Progress in Human Geography*, 24(2), 219–242.

Marston, Sallie A., Jones, John Paul, & Woodward, Keith. (2005). Human geography without scale. *Transactions of the Institute of British Geographers*, 30(4), 416–432.

McDonald, M., Arragutainaq, L., & Novalinga, Z. (1997). *Voices From the Bay: Traditional Ecological Knowledge of Inuit and Cree in the Hudson Bay Bioregion*. Ottawa: Canadian Arctic Resources Committee and Municipality of Sanikiluaq.

Nielsen, Jonas Østergaard, & Sejersen, Frank. (2012). Earth System Science, the IPCC and the problem of downward causation in human geographies of Global Climate Change. *Danish Journal of Geography*, 112(2), 194–202.

Nielsen, Jonas Østergaard, & Vigh, Henrik. (2012). Adaptive lives. Navigating the global food crisis in a changing climate. *Global Environmental Change*, 22(3), 659–669.

Nilsson, Annika E. (2007). *A Changing Arctic Climate: Science and Policy in the Arctic Climate Impact Assessment*. Linköbing: Linköping University, Department of Water and Environmental Studies.

Nilsson, Annika E. (2009). A changing Arctic climate: Science and policy in the Arctic Climate Impact Assessment. In T. Koivurova, E. C. H. Keskitalo & N. Bankes (Eds.), *Climate Governance in the Arctic*. New York: Springer, Environment & Policy 50.

Nuttall, Mark. (2009). Living in a world of movement: Human resilience to environmental instability in Greenland. In S. A. Crate & M. Nuttall (Eds.), *Anthropology & Climate Change: From Encounters to Actions* (pp. 292–310). Walnut Creek: Left Coast Press.

Nyvold, Mads. (2011, October 21). Socialistisk regering med alt for få hotelværelser, *Sermitsiaq*, p. 18.

Naalakkersuisut. (2010). *White Paper on the Aluminium Project Based on Recent Completed Studies, Including the Strategic Environmental Assessment (SEA)*. Nuuk: Greenland Self-Government.

Orlove, Ben. (2009). The past, the present and some possible futures of adaptation. In W. N. Adger, I. Lorenzoni & K. L. O'Brien (Eds.), *Adapting to Climate Change. Thresholds, Values, Governance* (pp. 131–163). Cambridge: Cambridge University Press.

Padel, Felix, & Das, Samarendra. (2010). *Out of This Earth. East India Adivasis and the Aluminium Cartel.* Hyderabad: Orient Blackswan.

Pelling, Mark. (2011). *Adaptation to Climate Change. From Resilience to Transformation.* New York: Routledge.

Petersen, Hans Christian. (2007). Iagttagelser over klimaets svingninger. *Tidsskriftet Grønland, 55*(2–3), 94–104.

Petersen, Hans Christian. (2010). *Kalaallit Ilisimasaat. Pisuussutit Uumassusillit Nunatsinnilu Pinngortitap Pisuusutai. Local Knowledge. Living Resources and Natural Assets in Greenland.* Montreal: IPI International Polar Institute Press.

Reenberg, Anette. (2009). Embedded flexibility in coupled human-environmental systems in the Sahel: Talking about resilience. In K. Hastrup (Ed.), *The Question of Resilience. Social Responses to Climate Change* (pp. 132–158). Copenhagen: The Royal Danish Academy of Sciences and Letters.

Robertson, Roland. (1992). *Globalization*. London: SAGE.

Sermitsiaq. (2010). Landsstyremedlem forsvarer Alcoa. Retrieved September 12, 2011, from http://sermitsiaq.ag/node/76748.

Smit, Barry, & Wandel, Johanna. (2006). Adaptation, adaptive capacity and vulnerability. *Global Environmental Change, 16*(3), 282–292.

Smit, Barry, Burton, Ian, Klein, Richard J.T., & Wandel, J. (2000). An anatomy of adaptation to climate change and variability. *Climatic Change* (45), 223–251.

Swyngedouw, Erik. (1997). Neither global nor local: 'Glocalisation' and the politics of scale. In K. Cox (Ed.), *Spaces of Globalization* (pp. 137–166). New York: Guilford.

Tsing, Anna Lowenhaupt. (2000). The global situation. *Cultural Anthropology, 15*(3), 327–360.

Tsing, Anna Lowenhaupt. (2005). *Friction. An Ethnography of Global Connection.* Princeton and Oxford: Princeton University Press.

Vibe, Christian. (1967). Arctic animals in relation to climatic fluctuations. *Meddelelser om Grønland, 170*(5), 1–227.

Vigh, Henrik E. (2006). *Navigating Terrains of War: Youth and Soldiering in Guinea-Bissau.* Oxford: Berghan Books.

Watt-Cloutier, Shiela, Fenge, Terry, & Crowley, Paul. (2006). Responding to global climate change: The perspective of the Inuit Circumpolar Conference on the Arctic Climate Impact Assessment. In L. Rosentrater (Ed.), *2° is Too Much! Evidence and Implications of Dangerous Climate Change in the Arctic* (pp. 57–68). Oslo: WWF.

Wenzel, George. (2009). Canadian Inuit subsistence and ecological instability – if the climate changes, must the Inuit? *Polar Research, 28*, 89–99.

Yarrow, Thomas. (2008). Paired opposites: Dualism in development and anthropology. *Critique of Anthropology, 28*(4), 426–445.

7 Indigenous knowledge and indigenous future-makers

'Indigenous knowledge' as a demarcated category of knowledge, understood as separate and distinct from other knowledge categories – from scientific knowledge, for example – has gained an upswing in interest and attention among anthropologists, development workers and indigenous human rights activists. In the Arctic research community, the increased interest is apparent in the large number of articles and policy documents that compile, look into, document, describe, promote, analyze and accentuate indigenous peoples' knowledge under headings like 'local knowledge', 'traditional ecological knowledge' (TEK), 'traditional knowledge', 'Inuit knowledge', 'indigenous knowledge' or 'Inuit Qaujimajatuqangit' (IQ). The overwhelming interest came as a surprise to an Inuk from Canada who, in the early 1990s, stated: 'As indigenous peoples, we are amazed at the excitement the existence of indigenous knowledge seems to have created. We have always known we have it' (cited in Brooke, 1993, p. 32). The excitement, however, can be understood, because the knowledge discussion opens up new perspectives, solutions and epistemic communities to take into consideration when discussing climate change issues; the essential question is whether the role and position given to Inuit that are based on focus on knowledge fully captures and appreciates their diverse experiences, aspirations, anticipations and acts of shaping futures.

In this chapter, I will explore how Inuit have become integrated in the climate change literature, primarily on the basis of their 'knowledge' and on the basis of how their 'knowledge' is related to a theoretical field of cultural ecology, which has been stretched out between concepts like adaptation, vulnerability and resilience. A basic argument running throughout the chapter is that the perceived empowerment of indigenous peoples through the vehicle of 'knowledge' may be disempowering and, at worst, may even be undermining circumpolar peoples' possibilities to engage in, add to, address the direction of and benefit from the development taking place in the Arctic during this era of climate change. In the course of argument, I will point to a new way of appreciating circumpolar peoples' historical and contemporary experiences in the North as epitomized in their accentuation of being 'indigenous'. Rather than having a grip on the 'indigenous' aspect as being related to a cultural complex (which is often referred to as 'traditional') or an ecological one (focusing on their close relationship to the environment) I choose to use the term 'indigenous' in a political-historical manner, in which it stresses a structural position in an asymmetrical colonial power relation. 'Indigenous' as a historical identity is produced in what Quijano (2008) calls a global structure of control of people and labour. Thus, 'indigenous' is a particular position from which to enunciate an interpretation and critique of power structures and cultural paradigms (Dahl, 2013). It is in the flux of constantly changing power relations, bearing the colonial legacy in mind, that Inuit have had to navigate, live under, appropriate, contest, develop, mimic and set up new livelihoods, according to what can be understood by employing the term, 'indigenous knowledge'. The concept of 'indigenous knowledge' thus turns our attention to knowledge of events, practices, experiences and experimentations that are related to a particular position within an asymmetrical relation.

The chapter's argument is that the concept of indigenous knowledge, understood in this way, may prove more fruitful to understanding how Inuit can be perceived, moreover, as *future-makers* rather than merely as environmentally knowledgeable adaptors to climate change. *Future-making* can be understood as social praxis which implies, among other things, narrating, social imagining and social creativity, knowledge production, institutionalization and political mobilization, in order to anticipate and establish viable horizons of expectations and potentialities. The concept of future-maker is invoked in order to redirect the focus away from the dominant climate change adaptation discourse over towards the question of how humans, groups and communities navigate in and create life-worlds of socially informed choices and possibilities. One of the interesting political experiments that has been fostered in the Arctic was the strategy of including the indigenous peoples as permanent participants in the Arctic Council, thus giving them a strong voice at the negotiation table. This can be interpreted as an act of including other voices, experiences and knowledge systems but it can be regarded, moreover, as a new category of *rights-holders* that has historically been politically squeezed in between states and stakeholders. As the years have passed, the role of indigenous peoples has changed from being 'local experts' and 'knowledge providers' in the Arctic Environmental Protection Strategy, where they were integrated *because* it was 'recognized that this strategy [AEPS], and its implementation, must incorporate the knowledge and culture of indigenous peoples' (Arctic Environmental Protection Strategy, 1991, p. 6), to standing a more cooperative relationship in the Arctic Council, where their status as subjects in communication and policy recommendations has certainly been upgraded.

This chapter takes a critical look at how indigenous communities in the Arctic – despite the increased recognition of them as political and creative rights-holders – have been down-scaled, contextualized and figured, with the environment as the primary organising device. On this account, I would propose that Inuit knowledge is caught in a number of constraints that spring primarily from the emphasis that researchers so often put on the close, local and intimate relationship between Inuit and the environment and on the role of Inuit's knowledge in maintaining adaptive capacity. The majority of climate change studies in the Arctic are based on this line of thinking and are deeply rooted in cultural-ecological approaches. Emphasizing their role as future-makers when addressing the issue of indigenous knowledge does not imply that other approaches and perspectives on Inuit knowledge production are not valid (Huntington [2005], too, argues for a diversity of approaches and perspectives), but doing so underscores that the approach taken here is not studying Inuit knowledge by looking at some inherent qualities that their knowledge possesses. Rather, it is an analytical take, which points our attention – and attempts – to recognize certain aspects of people's being in and knowing the world, where people both shape and find themselves in combinations of natural, cultural and political events that influence their horizon of expectations. A historical-political focus on knowledge production may not only produce other subjects but may also draw attention to the experiences, practices and competences of Inuit during a rapidly changing North, with changes that are the upshot of colonization processes. This perspective points at human resources, and this is a perspective that seems to vanish in much of the academic and non-academic writing about Inuit and climate change. It is also a perspective that may potentially modify the discussions about prediction, anticipation and forecasting as well as the widespread preoccupation with traditional ecological knowledge.

Creating more promising futures

The historical-political (colonial) dimensions of contemporary anticipation and future-making became apparent to me during a conversation I had with a Greenlandic woman in Maniitsoq. She was attending several social and official arrangements but it was extraordinarily difficult to make an appointment with her. One afternoon, after work, she was able to find a gap in her busy schedule and we found a quiet classroom overlooking the town. She was very active in the citizen's groups, and while I was interviewing her about her engagement, her ideas about the town's future and her experiences of the town's development since the time of her childhood, she created a narrative that indicated to me that she knew the world from a particular colonial point of view. To emphasize this, she foregrounded the politically asymmetrical relationship to the colonial Denmark, as she had experienced it. She was very pleased about the contemporary initiatives that had been set in motion by her municipality and about the ideas that had been formulated by the citizens in order to boost development in Maniitsoq: 'I think it is a very good idea compared to what was previously going on, where everything […] came from above'. She continued speaking with a firm voice as if she were imitating a dominating Dane: 'This is how it's going to be! This way!' Using her normal voice, again, she explained: 'The difference lies with how we are getting involved in how things are going to be organized'. I asked her to elaborate on what she meant by 'previously'. She said, 'it is difficult to put an exact year on this. But all I know is that during the period of development, we did not have a say in how things were going to be'. Later on in our conversation, she returned to the issue of how the town of Maniitsoq developed during the 1950s and 1960s: 'I mean, there was a lot of construction work. We [Greenlanders] were just spectators, at that time. People [i.e. workmen] were just coming from outside [i.e. Denmark]. Once in a while, it occurred that [she pauses] a man met a woman and they got children. And then it came to be known that those men often had wives and children at home [i.e. in Denmark]. Then they just left, and things ran aground. Unhappy families are created that way. And all those men were living in barracks. It was not so far away from here [she points out the window]: just behind Brugsen [one of the local supermarkets], where the little path winds up the hill. There were four or five barracks and a canteen, and there were more barracks further away, as well. They did their job, and that can be regarded as good [she pauses, for a few seconds] [...] As opposed to that, I think we should be part of it. We should not just be spectators. It should be us [she emphasizes *us*] who want it [i.e. development]. If there are consequences, then we are the ones who have wanted it. If we do not try it, then we will just keep standing still. The development will just stand still if we do not try something'.

She attuned my awareness to how the past's colonial history and the rather traumatic experience of being marginalized as a spectator to your own development, which was defined by the Danes, were still important movers of future-making, even after more than 30 years of Greenlandic self-governance (Home Rule and Self-Government). Of extreme importance to her was the sheer act of taking action into your own hands, creating your own horizon of expectations and engineering your own pathways of development.

This woman, like most Maniitsormiut, was preoccupied with the potentialities in the construction of the aluminium smelter, but she was painfully attentive to the problems it may bring into being, precisely because of her historical experiences. The concept of future-maker puts the focus on a relationship between historical experiences and expectations about the future where people are thinking about and laying the ground for potentiality. She related to the potentials of a future factory, but in fact expressed a much larger vision of empowerment, agency, development and social welfare, in which the factory only plays a role. One could say that she is neither concerned about adapting to climate change (the factory is going to be powered by hydroelectricity from the melting ice), nor about adapting to a factory; she is trying, rather, to adapt the factory to her societal vision. It is her coherent societal vision that is the moving force and the focus of her enthusiasm. Her ideas for a certain kind of society and a new subject position in development practices are central and difficult to distil away, if one should want to understand her appreciation of the factory.

Mechanical, tactical, and practical solutions to problems of the factory and climate-related issues are often the focus of many discussions, and it is important to demarcate these issues in order to 'get things going and done' or to produce operational knowledge. However, choices and concerns in a changing Arctic can also be approached by paying more attention to processes and enactments of anticipation and vision, in which the (colonial) past plays a significant role.

People are future-makers at different scales, and in the Arctic, the colonial legacy indeed plays a role. Questions of factory construction, climate change adaptation and food security are, for this reason, to be understood as being deeply entangled in the anticipatory engagement that lies far beyond the concrete challenge. In this perspective, the concept of 'indigenous' takes on a double connotation. It stresses a past (and present) relation dominated by a colonial power, and it stresses a strong vision of obtaining a collective involvement in the politics of societal change.

One important point that emerges from this woman's narrative is the significance placed on the capacity to engage actively in future-making as a creative subject and the ability to be responsible for your own visions of the good life. For peoples with a history that has been dominated, in part, by a colonial power, the desire to experience empowerment is present in most discourses and constitutes an intrinsic aspect of indigenousness. In order to appreciate the crux of the concept of indigenous peoples as future-makers and the value of their knowledge in this relation, this chapter will, first, critically explore the position of indigenous peoples and indigenous knowledge in the climate change discourse, with a special focus on the analytical emphasis that adaptation research puts on the human-environment relation. Later in the chapter, I will present a perspective that inflects research in a new direction, where indigenous peoples' visions and positions as future-makers appear in the foreground.

Knowledge and the local gaze

Bringing to light, in a powerful and cogent way, the close and positive feedback link between global climate change and melting ice in the Arctic has served to station Inuit in the forefront of climate discussions. They are portrayed as the ultimate witnesses to climate change because they are literally seeing their world melting around them. This is a disposition that finds resonance in the conception of the North and Inuit as marginal (see Chapter 1). The role that has been assigned to them as witnesses and victims of climate change has certainly affected the academic studies of Inuit and their livelihoods. Many researchers have prioritized a focus on Inuit as 'ground truthers' of climate change and as 'vulnerable' people who need to have their adaptive capacities improved in order to handle the pressing situation. The work of these researchers is elaborate; it unfolds, in very detailed ways, both the contemporary and the historical use by Inuit of – and observations of Inuit in relation to – the changing environment, on which their way of life depends. Historically, Inuit have been upheld as epitomising the most precarious human adaptation on earth (see Wenzel, 2002). While the emphasis, in this connection, is placed on environmental use, other aspects of northern life that hinder, limit, or act as barriers for adaptation are brought into the analysis. Many of these studies are pursued in partnerships with Inuit organizations, communities and experts (primarily hunters and elders) (Pearce et al., 2009), and in some cases, Inuit are referred to as consultants (Marino & Schweitzer, 2009) while in other projects, Inuit are engaged in explorative research (Krupnik, Aporta, Gearhead, Laidler, & Holm, 2010) or in reciprocal dialogue (Leduc, 2007). The production of knowledge in these research endeavours takes place within a particular understanding of the temporal and spatial scale, where it is the local scale that is stationed at the forefront.

In Canada, extensive studies of sea-ice use and knowledge have been pursued by James Ford. He relates these studies, in analogous ways, to discussions of Inuit vulnerability to climate change (Ford, 2008, 2009a; Ford, Pearce, Duerden, Furgal, & Smit, 2010; Ford & Smit, 2004; Ford et al., 2008). The issues of vulnerability, Inuit's ability to adapt, and their inherent resilience in applying a flexible resource use are also put in the forefront by the Intergovernmental Panel on Climate Change (IPCC). In one of its reports, for example, it is stated that '[t]he vulnerable nature of Arctic communities, and particularly coastal indigenous communities, to climate change arises from their close relationship with the land, geographical location, [and] reliance on the local environment for aspects of everyday life such as diet and economy' (Anisimov et al., 2007, p. 661). Traditional knowledge of the ice and the environment is foregrounded as an essential and significant component of the resilience of these communities. According to the IPCC (Anisimov et al., 2007, p. 674), such knowledge, however, is under stress; this is due to acculturation:

> Although Arctic peoples show great resilience and adaptability, some traditional responses to environmental change have already been compromised by recent socio-political changes. [...] The generation and application of traditional knowledge requires active engagement with the environment, close social networks in communities, and respect for and recognition of the value of this form of knowledge and understanding. Current special, economic and cultural trends, in some communities and predominantly among younger generations, towards a more western lifestyle have the potential to erode the cycle of traditional knowledge generation and transfer, and hence its contribution to adaptive capacity.

Researching Inuit knowledge of ice and environment is thus understood not only as serving to promulgate a Western understanding of changes in Arctic systems (to the benefit of scientific communities) but may concomitantly serve to furnish Inuit with valuable narratives, observations, data, terminology and interpretations which could potentially help them to adapt to the changing icescape and to navigate a new landscape of risk. Therefore, there is, according to Ford et al. (2007), a need to teach young hunters about the ice in order to strengthen the adaptive capacity of communities. In a similar way, Anisimov et al. (2007, p. 674) air concerns about what they see as an erosion of the cycle of traditional knowledge generation and transfer, and hence an erosion of what they term 'Inuit adaptive capacity', due to an orientation towards a more Western lifestyle among the younger generations. Accordingly, Inuit knowledge of the environment is in the forefront of these studies and is understood as being pivotal for securing life in a climate changing Arctic.

Inuit's extremely complex understanding of ice is approached in two ways (or in combinations of the two). One approach elaborates on Inuit's detailed observations, categorizations and interpretations of changing ice and its influence on mobility, animal presence and behaviour as well as on its interrelationship with factors like the wind and the ocean currents (Aporta, 2002, 2004; Fienup-Riordan & Rearden, 2010; George et al., 2004; Krupnik & Jolly, 2002; Krupnik & Weyapuk, 2010; McDonald, Arragutainaq, & Novalinga, 1997). This is an approach that appreciates that ice is a world in a constant process of becoming, where nothing is ever fixed or certain (Fienup-Riordan & Rearden, 2010). It is indeed a world of transformation and movement and ice can be understood as volume, i.e. as matter, and also as motion, where continuities and discontinuities are, in themselves, significant tendencies that require attention. Another approach focuses quite specifically on change that is understood to be brought about by climate change. This latter category of research often concentrates on changes and is thus framed by *comparative* terms: *more* rain and *less* snow, *less* ice, *thinner* ice, *rougher* storms, *looser* snow, *earlier* break-up, *later* freeze-up and *more* open water that lies *closer* to communities (for example, Berkes, 2008; Jolly, Berkes, Castleden, Nichols, & the community of Sachs Harbour, 2002; Nichols, Berkes, Jolly, Snow, & the community of Sachs Harbour, 2004; Riedlinger & Berkes, 2001; Thorpe, Eyegetok, Hakongak, & Elders, 2002). Both of these approaches are based on a deep respect for Inuit understandings of ice and for their abilities to pursue livelihoods in the North. Berkes (2008, p. 179), for example, notes that Northern peoples are experts when it comes to adapting to conditions that outsiders would consider difficult. This is a focus which is also reflected in both Franz Boas' work, carried out among the Inuit on Baffin Island in 1883–1884 (Boas, 1964 [1888]) and Richard K. Nelson's work, carried out among the Iñupiat in Alaska in the 1960s (Nelson, 1969). The contemporary adaptation and knowledge studies are a continuation of the classic focus on man-environment relations within Arctic anthropology. Knowledge also plays an important role in the assessments of environmental changes by northern communities. According to Riedlinger and Berkes (2001, p. 315, italics by the author), Inuit's assessments are based on 'cumulative knowledge of *local* trends, patterns, and processes, derived from *generations* of *reliance* on the land'. In their perspective, Inuit knowledge has evolved by '*adaptive* processes and [has been] handed down through generations by cultural transmission'. The sustained emphasis on local adaptation as the driving force of community processes and peoples' strategies is indeed striking.

In their book, *The Earth is Faster Now* (Krupnik & Jolly, 2002), the authors point to the alienation that people experience in a changing landscape. The extreme changes that we see in the Arctic actually put people in a situation where they find themselves in a totally *new* and *transformed* environment, even if they might not have moved at all. One could say – as Susan Crate (2009, p. 148) has – that the environment is moving. An environment can move in different ways. The rapid change from ice-covered sea to open sea is one example. One hunter, who normally travels over the ice, explained to a team of researchers that he now has to sail: 'it just felt odd' (Huntington, Gearheard, & Holm, 2010, p. 264). The researchers ascribed this feeling to a sense of dislocation that was due to the change in a familiar environment. For hunters, the environment has turned into something alien, out of balance, disintegrating and unpredictable. The Inuit of Baffin Island in Canada use the term *uggianaqtuq* to describe the changing weather. The term describes a situation where a friend might be acting strangely or acting in an unpredictable manner (Fox, 2004). When anthropologist Sherry Fox interviewed Iyerak, an Inuit from Igloolik in Nunavut, *uggianaqtuq* was explained to her in the following way: 'For example, I am very close to my sister. Let's say I wasn't feeling myself one day and I went to go visit her. As soon as I walk into the room, or say something, she would know right away that something is wrong. She would ask me, 'Is there something wrong with you?' She would say *uggianaqtuq*: I was not myself, acting unexpectedly or in an unfamiliar way' (Fox, 2002, pp. 43–44). In the Greenlandic language, a person who has gone crazy (lost his or her mind/intelligence) or is out of his/her mind is referred to as *silaqaraluarneq*; this term, interestingly enough, also carries the meaning, 'the weather is out of its mind' (Nuttall, 2009, p. 299).

Both of the foregoing approaches to Inuit's understandings of the environment are of paramount importance to a general understanding of the changes taking place in the Arctic. Hence, Inuit observations of changes have played a significant role in the elaboration of the Arctic Climate Impact Assessment (ACIA, 2005). However, it is noteworthy that Inuit's contributions and perspectives are only valued because they are rooted in a *generational adaptive reliance* on the *local*. Consequently, Inuit knowledge is ascribed value only when it works within a very specific temporal (primarily, the past) and spatial (primarily, the local) scale.

Today, many researchers and environmental stakeholders are preoccupied with finding ways to bridge traditional knowledge and scientific knowledge, in order to expand the 'picture', so to speak (see for example, Riewe & Oakes, 2006; Weatherhead, Gearhearh, & Barry, 2010). First, there is an acknowledgement that Inuit knowledge can enhance the understanding of climate change in the Arctic seeing that 'climate models cannot provide the full story' (Laidler, 2006, p. 436), and it is also acknowledged that Inuit input is important when it comes to providing climate history, 'important clues on climate change' (Berkes, 2008, p. 170), and 'firsthand' (Riedlinger & Berkes, 2001) baseline data, especially when we reflect that there is considerable uncertainty about how climate change will impact northern ecosystems (Riedlinger & Berkes, 2001). Second, science can provide synoptic insights into large-scale climate processes, about which it is important for communities and local decision-makers to be informed (Laidler, 2006, p. 435). Combining the knowledge of Inuit and scientists is believed to be down-scaling global processes of climate change and to be making potential climate impacts at the local level more perceptible. However, cooperation on these issues is still in its infancy, although past experiences hold out a lot of promise, according to Eicken (2010). The publication, *SIKU: Knowing Our Ice* (Krupnik et al., 2010) contains a number of examples of how the exchange and development of ice knowledge can be approached methodologically. It also shows how rewarding this process of complementation can be.

The research on the environmental knowledge of Inuit (encompassing the weather, the ice etc.) often maintains that its value stems from its embeddedness in the *local*. For example, Duerden and Kuhn (1998, p. 34) maintain that

> [a]lthough northern indigenous [people] inhabit vast 'traditional territories', their knowledge of the land constitutes intense, highly functional local geographies. They integrate a wide and eclectic range of land-use information and depict discrete features of large areas in tremendous detail. [...] It is at this local level, from which the information is drawn, that [traditional ecological knowledge, TEK] has the greatest utility from the standpoint of both describing the varied geographies of the north and providing locally useful information.

Duerden and Kuhn also claim that 'TEK in its purest sense' (Duerden & Kuhn, 1998, p. 35) has a low degree of abstraction, which is a consequence of its local scale. A consequence of this is, therefore, that the validity and integrity of TEK are closely linked to the maintenance of a particular *local* scale and context. It is easy to appreciate the authors' legitimate concern about how Inuit knowledge can potentially be deconstructed by other epistemic communities and can, in that process, be torn asunder, into fragments that are detached from Inuit frameworks of interpretation and understanding – a crucial problem also pointed out several times by other authors (for example, Cruikshank, 1998, 2004; Nadasdy, 2003). The very same authors, however, are also running the risk of confining Inuit agency, knowledge production and view on the world to a certain scale (local), while simultaneously demarcating it in relation to a specific context (the environment). As a consequence, the study of climate change issues in the Circumpolar North is often focused on sector (e.g. hunting) and community problems related to changes in sea ice, weather and animal presence.

Inuit knowledge is caught in a number of constraints which spring primarily from an emphasis that researchers put on the close, local and intimate relationship between Inuit and the environment, and on the role of knowledge in maintaining adaptive capacity. The majority of climate change studies in the Arctic are based on this line of thinking and are thus deeply rooted in cultural ecological approaches. Faced with the huge changes in society due to climate change and Inuit's involvement in extractive industries and hyper-industrialization, this perspective does not in a sufficient way support analytical approaches which help us to understand the challenges and potentials that lie ahead.

New cultural ecology

By approaching the situation and changes in Northern communities and considering these to be driven primarily by struggles to adapt to the local ice and ecosystem, adaptation emerges as the prime functional imperative. Such an analytical approach is based in the paradigm of cultural ecology, which focuses primarily on how society and its institutions further a given culture's survival by adapting to an ecosystem. The classic works of Roy Rappaport and his monograph, *Pigs for the Ancestors: Ritual in the Ecology of a New Guinea People* (Rappaport, 1968), are particularly renowned for taking this ecosystemic approach, which is underpinned by the notion that cultural processes ought to be understood as adaptive devices. Today, Inuit's 'direct' relationship to resources is, however, understood to be blurred and mediated by the state and its management institutions; this has incited researchers who subscribe to the cultural ecology approach to add a strong management-related component to their research, often accompanied by suggestions for improvements (such as co-management or integration of local knowledge) in order for Northern communities to be given better possibilities for adaptation. It is within this politically sensitive, novel, and cultural-ecological approach that Inuit knowledge is understood, ascribed importance, and closely linked to what is perceived to be their adaptation to the Northern environment. In a recent study, for example, the importance of locally based knowledge on adaptation is formulated in the following way: 'Traditional and local ecological knowledge and the institutions in which this knowledge is embedded are critical reservoirs of understanding about interactions between people and their environment and therefore a key source of resilience in northern systems' (Chapin et al., 2004, p. 346). In particular, the elders are singled out, because the stories they tell are 'the "libraries" of traditional knowledge to ensure the integrity of indigenous cultures' (Chapin et al., 2004, p. 347) and their survival (Chapin et al., 2004, p. 344).

The continued focus of many Arctic anthropologists on game distribution, resource-hunter seasonality, extractive technology and on knowledge and skills is centred on an analytical approach that is closely linked to the cultural ecology paradigm that was originally developed by Julian Steward (1955). He pointed people's attention to those features that empirical analysis shows to be most closely involved in the utilization of the environment in culturally prescribed ways. As such, Steward's paradigm signalled a departure from the thinking of Leslie White (1949), who argued that technology determined the social and technological aspects of life. This was largely because Steward – although inspired by White's materialist ideas – was more interested in adaptation as the organizing principle of societies. He searched, among other things, for institutions and values that aided and furthered a culture's survival in a set environment. Cultures could evolve in multi-linear ways, depending upon the given environment and on the cultures' adaptation strategies. He understood each culture as having a *cultural core*, which is tightly connected to salient characteristics of the culture (like settlement patterns, institutions, kinship, ownership, leadership, and values) that are closely related to important subsistence practices. If his view is applied narrowly, the elaborate meat-sharing practices of Inuit can be understood as having a decisive adaptive imperative that is characteristic of the cultural core.

For many of the resilience and vulnerability researchers in the Arctic, the following characteristics of Inuit culture are promulgated as important interrelated clusters with respect to successful adaptation: traditional knowledge and land-based skills; resource use diversity and flexibility; group mobility; and strong social networks (see for example, Berkes & Jolly, 2001; Ford, Smit, Wandel, & MacDonald, 2006). The focus applied by these researchers on community vulnerability, in the face of climate change, has much in common with Steward's analytical and theoretical emphasis on the cultural core and its importance in adapting to a given environment. Any changes in the cultural core (such as shifts in shared values or differences in settlement patterns) are looked upon as constituting a potential threat to adaptation and to the integrity of the cultural core and thereby considered potential threatening to the culture's survival. Adaptation as an organizing principle for Arctic societies is referred to in so much of the literature. Most writings on Inuit and climate change subscribe to cultural ecology and maintain a strong focus on Inuit's vulnerability because their basic adaptive relationship to the environment is perceived to be under stress due to either climate change or social change. Hence, Ford et al. (2006) point out that the most important characteristics of successful Inuit adaptation, apart from environmental knowledge and skills, are resource use diversity, group mobility and strong social networks – aspects that Steward, long ago, pointed out as being seated inherently in the cultural core and as being important for adaptation. The social practices of community sharing are, in this view, understood as facilitating adaptive capacity, and changes in sharing practices (e.g. due to what is termed 'Westernization') are thus considered to be undermining Inuit's adaptive capacity and also to be increasing their vulnerability. When social institutions like the elaborate sharing systems that are present in Inuit communities are simplistically perceived as strategies for risk reduction for the group during periods of scarcity or environmental stress (see e.g. Ford, Smit, Wandel et al., 2006, p. 134), a particular image of the Inuit emerges: this is the environmentally dependent Inuit who has adapted through a number of interdependent techniques (culture, social structure, technology, skills, knowledge, etc.). Although this intimate relation between man and environment has changed historically, the authors maintain that the relation may be put under considerable stress and strain if the environment changes (e.g. as a result of climate change), if the communities change (e.g. effectuated by Westernization and globalization), or if the relation is constrained (e.g. by management regulations). It is probably as a direct consequence of this view that the Arctic is considered the best place to study human adaptations to climate change, as has been argued by Berkes and Jolly (2001).

For researchers applying the cultural ecological approach, much effort has been put into distilling characteristics that tend to facilitate adaptation to the environment from those that are perceived to erode, hinder or restrict adaptation.

The environment becomes demarcated as a significant point of reference from which many processes have to be related and evaluated. In such a perspective, 'the local scale' becomes the centre of focus and the research emerges in the form of place-specific analyses because it is here, at the local stage, that the adaptive response is central and needs to function. The approach does not look exclusively at the environment or at the social aspects, but also at an *interlinked* social-ecological system, where the question of resilience is at the forefront (Adger, 2000). These studies of the impacts of climate change in the Arctic and the resilience, vulnerability, and adaptability of Inuit have also become conspicuously dominant in the IPCC's dealings with Arctic communities, as can be observed in Anisimov et al. (2007). The approach of cultural ecology certainly dominates the understanding of climate change issues in the Arctic and also serves to frame the Inuit in a particular way, where this particular indigenous group's knowledge has to be distilled in a certain way in order to be serviceable. My argument is that such an approach turns our analytical attention in directions that do neither reflect the resources and challenges of indigenous communities.

Adaptive responses of Inuit

An instructive example of the logic of this cultural ecology approach can be found in the work of Fikret Berkes and Dyanna Jolly (2001). They have, as part of their project, 'Inuit Observations of Climate Change', analyzed the strategies for coping and for the adaptation of the small community of Sachs Harbour located on Banks Island in the western part of Canada. This community is the smallest of the six Inuvialuit communities and consists of 13 households. The environmental changes experienced there are multiple and have had impacts on subsistence activities. With the help of local experts in Sachs Harbour, Berkes and Jolly have described seasonal variations and the yearly cycle of activities. Moreover, they have delved into changes in access, safety, predictability and species availability that are due to climate change. The interlinked social-ecological system is articulated by the authors in the following way: 'Problems and opportunities related to climate change need to be considered against a background of a highly variable Arctic ecosystem and an equally variable social-ecological system of harvesting activities' (Berkes & Jolly, 2001). The shifting seasons and the shifting presence of animals make the hunters exceedingly reliant upon their own abilities to forecast environmental phenomena, such as ice conditions, weather, and animal migration. As is the case elsewhere in the Arctic, the hunters from Sachs Harbour feel deprived of their ability to predict because things have changed too much, recently. One hunter expressed it in the following way: 'Years ago, we knew when the weather was going to change – mild weather meant a storm was going to come, and so we would get ready for it. But today it changes so much' (Berkes & Jolly, 2001). According to Berkes and Jolly, the changes are affecting the activities, but many of the impacts have been 'absorbed[,] thanks to the flexibility of the seasonal cycle and the Inuvialuit way of life' (Berkes & Jolly, 2001). The Inuvialuit hunters' coping strategies are thus considered successful and they are able to minimize risk and uncertainty by pursuing a multi-species hunting strategy. Such a perspective finds resonance in Krupnik's point that 'dynamic and flexible use of the environment constitutes the chief adaptive strategy of Arctic communities' (Krupnik, 1993, p. 210). Waiting is one out of many cultural practices that Berkes and Jolly (2001) consider to be adaptive responses to the Arctic environment. The list also includes mobility and flexible group size, flexible resource use and seasonal cycles, detailed local knowledge and skills, sharing mechanisms and social networks to provide mutual support and minimize risks, and, finally, intercommunity trade. Hence, in the adaptation perspective deployed by Berkes and Jolly, the Arctic environment exerts a profound influence on social organization and social practices (e.g. sharing), and even to such an extent that 'the adaptive strategy of sharing requires the development and reinforcement of cultural values that favor generosity, reciprocity, and communitarianism and discourage hoarding and individualism' (Berkes & Jolly, 2001).

The emphasis on the environment as the primary frame of reference for the understanding of social and cultural dynamics has certainly been a dominant theme in Arctic anthropology, which has increasingly been dealing, also, with environmental management issues. Berkes and Jolly include, as well, a political dimension in their study. In Sachs Harbour, the hunters are engaged in a number of political networks and institutions that have been undergoing development since the 1980s – political networks and institutions that allow them to participate in management decisions. These so-called 'co-management regimes' are furnishing hunters with the possibility of responding to hunting policies immediately and these new institutional linkages can serve, according to Berkes and Jolly, to 'increase the resilience of the social-ecological system by providing for cross-scale communication that did not exist before the 1980s, and by increasing the capability for self-organization and the capacity for learning' (Berkes & Jolly, 2001). In this perspective, then, political mobilization and engagement also become part of an adaptive strategy. These adaptive strategies are put under threat by climate change, seeing as it threatens to undermine the delicate balance of the socio-ecological system. When every social and cultural act becomes a question of adaptation (even the sheer act of waiting) in the face of change, the environment becomes a framework for every analysis. Furthermore, human agency, anticipation and the social and cultural life of people become reduced to responses, subject to being analyzed and reviewed – as successful or unsuccessful.

Policies of adaptation

In order to judge and evaluate the resilience of communities and the susceptibility of people to climate risks, the cultural ecology approach applies certain analytical parameters and scales. Notwithstanding its rather narrow analytical focus on human-environmental relations and despite its emphasis on interpreting social and cultural practices as a function of adaptation to the environment, the cultural ecology approach has a rather potent political and applied ambition. In the words of Ford et al., who are also pursuing this line of research, the goal is to 'identify what policy measures are required to moderate or reduce the negative effects of climate change, as well as how best to develop, apply and fund such policies' (Ford et al., 2007, pp. 151–152). Thus, there can be a strong policy and an applied component in these studies. Knowledge takes up a decisive position in the study of coping, adaptation and resilience and many projects, indeed, are focusing on what Arun Agrawal (2002, p. 288) critically terms the 'harvesting' of 'specific elements of indigenous knowledge'. Agrawal adopts a critical stance not only because the knowledge harvesting is politically saturated but also because it has political consequences. The cultural ecological approach to comprehending the climate change challenges faced by northern communities puts an emphasis on people's proximity to nature: in order to maintain this analytical focus, other aspects of community life, well-being and livelihoods are overlooked or set aside altogether. Furthermore, these kind of studies tend to place people in a position demarcated by certain constraints and possibilities for the future – by invoking their proximity to nature as the essential relation to focus on, by depicting the survival of northern communities as contingent upon preserving their relationship to the environment, and by focusing on practices that demonstrate insight into the environment. This act of delineation of community orientation, practices and knowledge production is valuable but it generates its own problems because it fails to reflect any further on what it leaves unaddressed and thus fails to reflect on the way in which it partakes in a political process, through which particular ideas of communities are produced and maintained.

One of the important stated goals of resilience and vulnerability studies is to guide policy makers on all scales by putting 'the problem in place' and, in doing so, to identify target areas and potential futures. However, what this demands, I would argue, is something more than preparing elaborate local studies of weather and ice observations, examining changing resource use strategies, and working up local risk assessments related to hunting practices. In these cultural ecology studies, the complexity and diversity of community resources, processes, challenges, concerns and anticipations are instrumentalized. What we have here is an analytical take that has the potential to make the enterprise itself (investigating local environmental knowledge and local risk assessments) stand out as positive, necessary and obvious. Hence, we see a tremendous number of vulnerability studies in, for example, Canada, studies that follow the same line of thinking without little, if any, reflection on either the applied concept of culture or on the political implications of the studies. In her elaborate post-colonial critique of these Canadian adaptation and vulnerability studies, Emilie Cameron (2012) argues that the researchers are politically blind and are even extending the colonial relations in the region: 'Colonialism fails to appear as a word or concept in these studies, in spite of the fact that the projects are carried out in communities profoundly shaped by colonialization and movements towards decolonialization and Inuit self-determination' (Cameron, 2012, p. 104).

Adaptation and practices of sharing

The adaptation perspective embeds people in their environmental surroundings. However, by doing so, it also runs the risk of removing them from the livelihood context in which they live and navigate. In fact, the adaptation perspective may lead to a distortion of their livelihoods. By focusing on flexibility and change, the perspective may result in lifting Inuit out of the timelessness and placelessness of the idealized hunter-gatherer, which have been criticized, but it may also position Inuit in a situation that is perhaps overburdened with the time and place of a particular (local) scale. The adaptation perspective may distort the realities of the Inuit because the researchers might be ignoring structures, changes and values that they actually set out to study. For example, very few of the resilience researchers who claim that sharing is a way of adapting to uncertain resources have studied the complex sharing practices in depth and very few have studied how they actually strengthen resilience.

David Damas, however, is one researcher who has pursued some of the most outstanding studies on sharing practices among Inuit in Canada. He has applied, to a certain extent, a cultural-ecological approach (although he was actually more interested in social structure), and in an elaborate article on his comparative study of Netsilik, Igloolik and Copper Eskimos (as they were called at that time), an article that was re-printed in the anthology, 'Cultural Ecology. Readings on the Canadian Indians and Eskimos', he points out that a number of social practices can be logically defended as adaptive and related to facts of exploitation, 'but the relationship was far from complete. Both features of settlement pattern and community pattern were found to relate internally to other social features but not always convincingly to external adaptation' (Damas, 1973, p. 298). Although he (Damas, 1972, p. 236) finds that the sharing practices served to help insure survival during bad times and also helped to even out unequal possession of food during more fortunate times, he is always cautious about interpreting the diversity of sharing practices in terms of adaptive responses to the Arctic environment, as has been proposed by Berkes and Jolly (2001). Sharing systems in Inuit communities are extensive, diverse and complex, and have taken up a central focus in Arctic anthropology. However, these studies also carry different implicit understandings of Inuit life and their position as subjects, as will be made apparent in the following presentation of different studies of a particular important food-sharing practice known as *ningiq*.

Ningiq, which is considered a strategy for ensuring the widest possible intra-community distribution of food (*niqi* in Inuktitut), was studied by David Damas (1972) and has more recently been examined by George Wenzel (2000) in the High Arctic community of Clyde River, on Baffin Island. Wenzel uses the term *ningiqtuq* and conceptualizes the strategy as a set of socio-economic operations that also encompass labour and non-traditional resources. Clyde River Inuit critically rely on the marine and terrestrial resources of the region, but their subsistence activities are as limited by and as dependent on access to money as they are on weather and prey conditions. Thus, Wenzel underlines that 'in the Baffin Inuit economy [...] cash has become as fully a part of the resource environment as food or other natural raw materials' (Wenzel 1986 cited in Wenzel, 2000, p. 67). The elaborate system of *ningiqtuq* reproduces social and material relations that sustain the Inuit subsistence system. Today, *ningiqtuq*, which contains several interactive sets, rules, responsibilities and obligations, has been altered so as to include the sharing of technology as well as the sharing of money because it may optimize their resource access, according to Wenzel.

One of these sub-systems of *ningiqtuq* – the so-called *tugagaujuq-tigutuinnaq* subsystem – ensures equal access to food within the extended family, even though Wenzel is careful to note that it also has the potential to engender differences among the participants, with the potential to establish unbalance and to sometimes put young women, especially, in a disadvantaged position. This can be the case when younger kinfolk are obliged to respond to the demands of a genealogically older person. A relationship of this kind is termed *naalaqtuk* and is a critical structural element that underpins *ningiqtuq* relations. Thus, through the avenue of 'demand sharing', a superior can now ask for expensive equipment, which puts a great deal of pressure on the younger generation's financial situation. In some cases, it was the female consanguineal kin of hunters, typically unmarried daughters holding wage-paid positions, who were focal with respect to the demand sharing of money. The *naalaqtuk* obligation is very binding and it compels persons to help and assist superior members of the family. In one case, which is mentioned by Wenzel, a male who was generously complying with the sharing requests from other kin members decided to relocate his own household to another community, possibly because of the considerable economic disadvantage that the obligation to share put him in. In another publication, Wenzel renders the community conflict even more apparent by stating that 'the current economic situation in Clyde River is approximately one in which the 'haves' resent the demands of the 'have nots', while the latter consider the 'haves' ungenerous' (Wenzel, 1995, p. 54). Wenzel concludes that *ningiqtuq* is very flexible and it forms a crucial component of Inuit ecological adaptation, but the central *naalaqtuk* obligation potentially gives rise to tensions and conflict, and Wenzel finds that *ningiqtuq* is 'considerably less operationally flexible with regard to incorporating new material resources' (Wenzel, 2000, p. 71).

Wenzel's observations and analyses are important when we consider that Berkes and Jolly (2001) also notice changes in food-sharing practices in Sachs Harbour as the number of hunters providing 'country food' to the rest of the community is decreasing. They consider this to be an unsustainable situation. However, new forms of reciprocities, which have brought money and equipment into the sharing relationship, have, according to Berkes and Jolly, addressed the imbalance. Although, Wenzel and Berkes and Jolly all seem to agree that *ningiqtuq* is a cultural practice with adaptive consequences, there is an interesting disparity between their respective interpretations of the success in incorporating and importing the essential requirement for cash and new technology into the *ningiqtuq* system. Whereas Berkes and Jolly find this to be unproblematic and consider it to be an example of flexibility and adaptability, in order to maintain mutual support and to minimize risk (and by stating this, they are reiterating

Asen Balikci's comment on *ningiqtuq* made at the 'Man the Hunter' conference in 1968: 'Clearly, such a system is adaptive' (Balikci, 1968, p. 81), Wenzel calls attention to potential unbalances and dissatisfactions that *ningiqtuq* may foster within extended families (the same does Ford, Smit, Wandel et al., 2006). These researchers seem to be subscribing to two different variations of cultural ecology: while Berkes and Jolly consider the social structure and cultural values as *adaptive responses* to the environment (the material), Wenzel (1995, pp. 56–57) sees them as constituting *relations* that serve to sustain Inuit social life in a broader perspective:

> Ningiqtuq cannot simply be described as a system for the generalized allocation of food, goods, or labor. [...] In a very real sense, therefore, ningiqtuq relations socially ratify the production and consumption aspects of Inuit subsistence. As such, ningiqtuq relations should be seen as the critical means by which harvesting [...] is joined to the social process of local economy.

And in Wenzel's optics, access to cash is a paramount part of these relations and as deserving of study as weather and animals (Wenzel, 1991). The latter point is interesting because it turns our attention to how significant discussions of the cash, wage and transfer economy could prove to be when looking into what is ordinarily referred to as adaptation to climate change. In fact, one could argue, based on Wenzel's work that, in the first place, the continued access to money is essential for the continuation of hunting and, second, that cash and hunting have to be regarded as co-related within the same system. There is nothing novel in this (see e.g. Lonner, 1986), but in many of the vulnerability and resilience studies that have more recently been pursued in the Arctic, money becomes a means or an instrument for an adaptive system that is viewed as being detached from social dynamics in general.

Many of the cultural ecology research approaches struggle with the predicament of change. On the one hand, change and involvement in a formal economy and the use of new technology constitute an inherent part of Inuit lives and the sustainment of Arctic communities. On the other hand, it seems difficult for the researchers to include this change as a strategy and as a way for Inuit to create new futures of their own. Paradoxically, the authors often portray communities as having adaptive capacity that is due, on the one hand, to certain characteristics that underpin flexibility and openness to social change (dynamic traditional knowledge and land-based skills, resource use diversity and flexibility, group mobility, and strong social networks). The very same adaptive capacity and flexibility are considered, on the other hand, to be undermined due to societal change (Ford, Smit, Wandel et al., 2006, pp. 131–132). Even though a *declining* number of people are engaged in hunting (Ford, Smit, Wandel et al., 2006, pp. 134–135), and even though considerable changes have taken place within food-sharing networks, researchers persist in seeing Inuit communities as hunting communities and in typically regarding such a community with an economy based on hunting rather than regarding it as an Arctic community with a hunting sector among other important sectors that constitute complex social, economic and cultural dynamics. Their analysis maintains that the vulnerability of this hunting system (and thus, of the community as such, in their optics) is linked to environmental changes that are being accelerated by climate change. Climate change related vulnerability research is thus 'parked' in the environmental domain and the strong discursive position of this domain splinters the lifeworld of people and undermines a broader, and perhaps more inclusive, understanding of the threats and challenges that particular communities are struggling with. Only seldom does the research unfold or examine the question of money and wages, or the question of jobs and transfer payments, even though the viability of both hunting activities and the community as such are exceedingly reliant on the cash-economy. In fact, one could argue that people in the Arctic could maintain their livelihoods, even in an era of climate change, if they had the financial means to experiment along a diversity of lines, to acquire the appropriate technology, and to maintain food security. Securing the full-time and part-time jobs could strengthen the community without necessarily undermining hunting activities. The juxtaposition of the cultural ecology model and the acculturative paradigm which emphasizes that involvement in the wage-economy weakens Inuit socio-cultural life seems to create a 'blind angle', where the economy and the societal dynamics are deformed and reduced to hunting-related concerns of a very narrow kind. The hunter may, in fact, be more at risk if his wife happens to lose her job than if the slower freeze-up, due to climate change, forces the hunter to postpone his hunting activities on the skidoo as a consequence of dangerous ice conditions.

According to Krupnik (1993, p. 211), the historical record shows that a warming Arctic may improve the availability of resources for coastal communities. The ability to pursue these opportunities is – apart from knowledge, skill and political will (Wenzel, 2009) – dependent on the financial capital that is available for investments. The formal and informal economy of the communities are thus significant factors to be taken into account when trying to understand how future climate change may affect Arctic communities, how communities will respond and what processes will reduce or heighten vulnerabilities. Economy is also a matter of concern for hunters and their families and they spend a great deal of their time considering socially viable strategies (Sejersen, 1998).

The limits of Inuit cultural ecology

When Inuit knowledge is framed in the paradigm of cultural ecology, it may have political consequences (Sejersen, 2004). In an analysis of how TEK has been approached and understood as '"facts" about animals and other elements of the natural world', George Wenzel (2004, p. 239) points at, among other things, his dissatisfaction with the inadequacy of the concept when it comes to including Inuit attitudes, perspectives and practices: the concept of TEK seems to be more and more devoid of people. In Canada, the Inuit themselves have promoted the concept of Inuit Qaujimajatuqangit (IQ), which they consider a more inclusive concept, since it encompasses all aspects of traditional culture including values, worldview, language, social organization, knowledge, life skills, perceptions and expectations (Wenzel, 2004, p. 240). An important contribution of IQ to the knowledge discussions is that it underlines that Inuit does not understand and relate to animals, ice and the environment as merely material relations. Rather, the relationship is rooted in worldviews where agency, causality, anticipation, time and place are appreciated in ways that may indeed pose a challenge to scientists subscribing to a modern worldview (Nadasdy, 2011). It is from this perspective that ice can emerge as more than frozen water, sharing can emerge as more than adaptation, and storytelling can emerge as more than knowledge being transferred to the younger generations. Because sea ice is entangled in a system of values and social relations and because sea ice, in itself, can be seen as having agency (drift ice can crush boats or an ice floe can carry hunters out to the open sea), Michael Bravo (2010) argues that we should look at sea ice as a social object: 'In that sense, sea ice has a profound social ontology, an existence as a social object by virtue of the deep-seated meanings and relations that connect it to Inuit life' (p. 446). Understanding ice as a social object may break with the rather positivistic approaches pursued by Arctic adaptation researchers. However, by doing so, certain new community dynamics and new futures may emerge, where the post-colonial complexities of Arctic dynamics are not distilled and reduced to questions of climate change impact and adaptation, but are put up front in the analysis. Furthermore, the formal and informal economies, the new sharing practices, and community concerns of a broader kind can be integrated in the analysis as more than mere context but rather as inherent aspects of anticipation and future-making.

Problems of research reductionism and the production of contexts

In those instances when Inuit are presented primarily as subjects with intimate and detailed knowledge of ice as the dominant discourse – a discourse that is also accentuated by the Western perception of Inuit as having a large vocabulary pertaining to snow and ice (Krupnik & Müller-Wille, 2010; Pullum, 1989) – they are, as part and parcel of the very same process, undergoing a qualitative transformation of subjectivity, in which their concerns and problems are related primarily to their environmental dependence. The approach of cultural ecology distils the complexity of societal change and climate change into a simple vocabulary of impacts and adaptation, which implicates climate change as being solely responsible for the problems and the potentialities of northern communities, families or sectors. The extreme focus on the presumed environmental dependence propels the research in particular directions. This has prompted Claudio Aporta (2010, p. 164), who has pursued extensive studies of Inuit ice knowledge, to put forward the following critical comment: the 'very definition of research topic […] involves severing one particular aspect of Inuit knowledge (in this case, the sea ice) from the rest of a multidimensional approach to life and the world, where concepts as apparently diverse as social and environmental health are not completely understood without the other'. His concern over a fragmentation of the Inuit world as a consequence of the research questions that are being pursued is indeed valid, when we consider that climate-related research in the North predominantly focuses on knowledge of weather, ice and animals, and by doing so, upholds and maintains an environmental and even an instrumentalist and tactical approach. This is neither to say that the environment does not matter nor that ice knowledge is unimportant. However, this research focus produces certain subjects and subsequent ideas of social dynamics. In the 1990s, a similar concern was raised by James Fairhead (1993, p. 199) that touched on a shift among development experts. He critically discussed how these experts initially perceived farmers as ignorant but later started to see farmers as persons in possession of valuable technical knowledge:

> What has not changed in the switch from ignorance to knowledge seems to be the 'social distance' between the farmer and the agricultural development researcher. The focus on 'technical knowledge' helps isolate agriculture from the social context, or put another way, the farmer from the person. Researchers who are permitted to examine agriculture in terms of agricultural knowledge can maintain themselves in ignorance of the multitude of non-agricultural influences which inform farming practices.

This is an essential point: any aprioristic assumption of Inuit's environmental dependence could actually obscure more than it reveals, and could serve to disassociate Inuit from their daily lives. The continued focus on the environmental knowledge of Inuit directs our attention towards certain 'resources', 'problems' and 'solutions', and away from other aspects of Northern livelihoods. It is striking, for example, how little the more encompassing perspectives of the Arctic Human Development Report (AHDR) (2004) and of subsequent publications have been used by northern climate adaptation researchers. The report is groundbreaking because it is issue-inclusive in its understanding of circumpolar processes. Land rights and economic structures are dealt with, in parallel with gender issues and environmental use. The entangled issues that, according to AHDR, play a significant – if not a decisive – role in the decisions, anticipations and livelihoods of Arctic peoples seem to be downplayed in much of the adaptation writing, where the focus is solely on environmental knowledge and use. By isolating climate change concerns and separating them from other societal issues, and also by localizing knowledge production (in the form of 'local knowledge'), the climate researchers fail to recognize the multitude of issues that move, inform and influence choices and knowledge production – issues that may be understood to be scaled beyond 'the local'. This reductionism may, in fact, downplay local agency, potentiality and heterogeneity, as has also been suggested by Agrawal (1995) and Nadasdy (2003).

There seems to be a contradiction here. On the one hand, vulnerability and adaptation researchers are trying to localize and contextualize the rather abstract conceptions of climate change. This amounts to a practice of crossing scales. On the other hand, I argue, this scale-crossing exercise is alienated with respect to community life and northern livelihoods. In order to understand this contradiction, it is prudent to examine how climate-related cross-scaling practices have been played through. Mike Hulme (2008) points our attention to specific cross-scaling practices of climate change knowledge production, and some of the problems may lie here. In particular, I want to focus on how these practices give rise to *context*. Hulme notices that when pursuing climate change research, local measurements and observations are standardized and circulated in centralized bureaucracies. Such a practice makes it possible to quantify (local) weather and subsequently to construct statistically aggregated climates, thus enabling the scientific community to construct an abstracted 'global climate'. This is a practice of purification and domestication of local observations, which detaches local observation from its original human and cultural setting. Local weather phenomena that are significant to local people are thus transformed into standardized numbers that are propagated by the 'globalised and universalising machinery of meteorological and scientific institutions and assessments where [the weather] loses its identity' (Hulme, 2008, p. 7). This act of *up-scaling* gives numbers a new identity and creates a new context. However, Hulme points out that today, much research on climate change is devoted to finding 'ways of restoring these lost values and meanings [...] to reconnect purified climate indicators with local practices and to re-situate and re-contextualize putative future climates in unique geographical settings' (Hulme, 2008, p. 8). This act of *down-scaling* is central in much of the recent research that is devoted to climate change adaptation, as well as being central in many vulnerability, coping and resilience studies. This is important work and it has been widely supported by local people because this research and these studies have enabled them to understand and relate to the predicted changes. However, this circulation of knowledge back and forth does create a pitfall. Whereas the global climate change researchers actively *de*-contextualize local weather phenomena in order to create an abstract 'global climate', the climate adaptation researchers do not *re*-contextualize future climates or *re*-situate climate change within a relational context that includes the places people live, their histories, daily lives, cultures or values, as claimed by Slocum (cited in Hulme, 2008, p. 8), as if it were truly an act of bringing the data back home. Rather, they produce new – and seductive – contexts that are analytically demarcated by the dominant discourse of climate change and the approach of cultural ecology.

By maintaining an analytical focus on climate change impacts and adaptation strategies, value and significance are being ascribed to certain aspects of local life while others are toned down. What is understood as *de-* and *re*-contextualization of climate related issues and phenomena are actually acts of *context* production. That contexts are analytically evoked rather than given is, of course, intrinsic to all research activity (Dilley, 1999). On this account, it may be important to discuss the possibilities and constraints of a selected context construction. In climate vulnerability studies, the analyses of social, cultural, economic and political life become primarily focused on *how* these factors influence environmental relations, because climate-related issues are understood to be located here. Elaborate and in-depth understandings of environmental knowledge, perceptions, practices and dependences are situated in the foreground of the research and considered analytically interesting while other aspects of community life are portrayed as background elements. Vulnerability researchers have a keen eye trained on this background and have an elaborate insight into how issues of gender, politics and historical changes impact human-environment relations. However, because they have defined the environmental relations as *the* most relevant focus when evaluating climate change vulnerability, other aspects of people's histories, experiences, lives and anticipations are omitted or – at best – are described as 'the setting'. What becomes important in 'the setting' crystallizes around the environmental relation. In the case of Inuit, their knowledge of ice and mobility, environmental regulations (quotas and trade restrictions, etc.) and their meat-sharing practices are, for example, pointed out as being important to take into consideration for the purpose of identifying community vulnerabilities. Indeed, these aspects *are* important for resource use, but people's problems, practices, strategies, choices and aspirations are seldom linked solely to the environment. To put this differently, when people are faced with the challenges of climate change, questions of human vulnerabilities, resource use and points of orientation, from the perspective of cultural ecology, are determined *a priori* to be understood in relation to the environment; this results in the construction of a particular understanding of what constitutes *the context*. In Ford et al. (2006), to cite but one example, the focus is on the introduction of – and the dependence on – new technology like snowmobiles and VHF radios, etc., on technology's influence on hunting practices and on the implications for the ecological relations of harvesting. The authors (Ford, Smit, Wandel et al., 2006, p. 130, italic by the author) conclude that the

> adoption of these modern technologies has occurred in the *context* of the decreasing time availability for hunting due to participation of hunters in the formal economic sector, a reduction in land based skills especially among younger generations and the requirements of hunting with snowmachines and motorized boats, and the perceived safety that many of these devices provide.

Such a perspective not only turns important societal changes into a 'context' but relies, moreover, on an acculturative perspective, where adaptive capacity, by fiat, becomes threatened by change. The authors demarcate the acculturative dimensions of the context as one where '"Westernization" has changed many social relationships and has resulted in rising inequality, individualized behaviour, and withdrawal from the subsistence economy' (Ford, Smit, Wandel et al., 2006, p. 134). All in all, these changes prompt the authors to conclude that new vulnerabilities have been created, old vulnerabilities attenuated and others exacerbated. Because of this, the Inuit are perceived to have become even more vulnerable and more exposed to climate change.

A living, dynamic and resourceful community may, for example, be considered deformed according to these optics, because what the people living in such a community locally perceive as their world is judged by its properties as a function of adaptation to the environment. A community where teenagers are pursuing an education, where adults have community-based jobs, where people are engaging in a social dynamic sphere, pursuing complex sharing practices and continuously trying to establish viable futures can, according to the adaptation optics, be described in the following way, which was formulated by Ford et al. (2007, pp. 156–157):

> While subsistence activities remain important to younger–generation Inuit, fewer are displaying the same degree of commitment or interest in harvesting. This decline has been attributed to southern requirements, which result in decreased time to participate in hunting; increased dependence on wage employment; a general shift in social norms; and segregation of the young and older generations.

The functionalistic and environmentally focused approach may thus describe a community in cultural decay, and 'cultural preservation' becomes one of the logical and suggested solutions by the authors: 'Policies that promote and preserve Inuit knowledge, culture, and values have the potential to increase safe hunting practices among vulnerable groups' (Ford et al., 2007, p. 158). In the IPCC reports, similar ideas are presented, and in its review of climate change problems bearing on Arctic indigenous peoples, Anisimov et al. (2007) state the following: 'Current social, economic and cultural trends, in some communities and predominantly among younger generations, towards a more western lifestyle, have the potential to erode the cycle of traditional knowledge generation and transfer, and hence its [traditional knowledge] contribution to adaptive capacity' (2007, p. 674). Such an acculturalistic and environmental functionalistic approach destabilizes our perception of the communities in question and the total social, political, cultural and economic terrain that community members navigate in and co-produce. Having the environment as the organizing device for climate analysis thus produces a particular context and a foreground as well as giving rise to a number of blind angles.

The localization of climate change impacts – problems and perspectives

Maybe the challenges of climate change will not emerge as we think they will – even in the Arctic, where many consider the causalities to be straightforward (less ice creates more problems; less Inuit culture makes them more vulnerable). However, one could ask whether climate change adaptation and vulnerability problems are related to the hunting sector and whether hunters are the most vulnerable? If the analytical gaze focuses on hunting, the answer to these suppositions might appear, by fiat, as being in the affirmative. However, climate change related challenges and vulnerabilities may emerge elsewhere. Actually, the use of hunters and hunting as proxy for Inuit climate change related vulnerability may potentially circumvent and squander the opportunity to see a living community as a whole and may consequently miss the chance to appreciate capacities and vulnerabilities in depth. In Greenland, this problem emerges quite clearly. Some hunters and fishermen are concerned about the changes they observe, both with respect to changing animal presence and accessibility. If one adds the unfamiliar weather patterns, their horizon of anticipation and their ability to navigate the environment indeed becomes challenged. However, as I have argued, communities, households, sectors and individuals in Greenland can face the climate change issues from another angle. The very introduction of mega-industries in Greenland for purposes of breaking away from the economic dependence on Denmark is intensified and underpinned by the climate-induced environmental changes. The development of and engagement in these industries call for major transformations of the society, the labour market, the educational system, and economic priorities, and the country crosses over into a new political and environmental landscape of risk. For a Greenlandic hunting household or a small Greenlandic community, climate change related problems may thus emerge from an unexpected angle, where the economic priorities afforded the hunting sector can change due to new political priorities, or where the community loses resourceful and skilled persons due to labour migration, only to mention two among the many potential consequences of hyper-industrialization in Greenland. In fact, hunters and fishermen may have better possibilities for dealing successfully with climate related environmental conditions than navigating in a Greenlandic society that is transforming so as to benefit as much as possible from climate change. One thing is to focus narrowly, when judging vulnerability, on immediate environmental changes and problems; another is to regard climate change as a driver for other albeit less apparent processes, which may have an impact as well. This requires the evocation of another context of understanding. However, it is often very difficult to approach these issues analytically, because the context emerging from climate adaptation research appears so obvious.

Food security and context production

An instructive example of how contexts are produced is the research that has been pursued in the Inuit community of Igloolik in the Canadian High Arctic, with a population of 1,540. Here, James Ford and Lea Berrang-Ford (2009) have very elaborately described and analyzed the community's food insecurity and thus its vulnerability to climate change. They point at conditions that both facilitate and constrain food security and argue that the study may be appropriate in identifying key food security trends in Nunavut as a whole. This indeed infuses additional perspectives to the study. In Igloolik, as elsewhere in the North, people rely on store-bought food (referred to 'southern foods') as well as on food that is obtained from hunting and fishing (often referred to as 'country food'). A dual food system of this kind is reliant on a mixed economy, where wage-earning activities are as important as subsistence activities. It is also important to understand, as has been pointed out by the authors, that subsistence activities are dependent upon income-generating activities so that hunters can invest in equipment (see for example Langdon, 1986; Sejersen, 1998). Their survey bears out that all of the respondents reported eating traditional foods/country foods, with 21 per cent obtaining more than half of their food from traditional sources. Furthermore, 79 per cent of respondents obtained half or more of their food from the store (this is also noted by Furgal & Prowse, 2008, p. 103). Reduced access to natural resources (e.g. due to late freeze-up, increasing prices of equipment, or decreasing access to cash) and reduced access to food from the store (e.g. due to shortages, increasing prices, or decreasing access to cash) have a severe influence on people's food insecurity. The survey concludes that food insecurity is a problem, with 64 per cent of the respondents reporting that they have experienced some degree of food insecurity and 24 per cent being categorized as having a very low food security status (Ford & Berrang-Ford, 2009, p. 230). This is far above the average of 9.2 per cent of the Canadians, in general, experiencing some degree of food insecurity, and the survey thus reveals the precarious nature in which many Northern community members find themselves. The survey also stresses the significant role of 'country foods' in providing food security. Participants who hunt for a living were, for example, more likely to be food secure than those who are engaged in the wage-paid employment sector. Furthermore, people who had country foods as more than half of their total consumption were significantly more likely to be food secure. In this perspective, climate change could stand out as a major threat to food security if its impacts result in reducing access to natural resources and thus curtail the production of country foods (Ford, Smit, & Wandell, 2006). The report, 'Canada in a Changing Climate 2007' (Lemmen, Warren, Lacroix, & Bush, 2008), contains a chapter on the northern part of the country, where it is clearly stated that the discussion of the impact of climate change on the livelihoods of indigenous peoples 'is about sustaining relationships between humans and their food resources, as well as being aware that this impact poses the threat of irreversible social change' (Furgal & Prowse, 2008, p. 103).

The relationship to the resources is indeed important; this is corroborated by the study prepared by Ford and Berrang-Ford (2009). Furthermore, the report by Lemmen et al. specifies that the 'ability to adapt [to climate change] is influenced by factors such as access to economic resources, technology, information and skills, institutional arrangements, equity among members of a group, risk perception and health status' (Furgal & Prowse, 2008, p. 108). Adaptation to climate change, in this report, is thus understood to be about maintaining a healthy and productive interaction with the environment and 'clearing away' factors that work as hindrances to the production of country foods. This means to say that adaptation can be improved by working with the list of factors stipulated above – factors that may not necessarily be directly linked to climate change. Ford and Berrang-Ford (2009) also point out access to income and income sharing networks as major factors that determine the availability and access to country foods, because they affect the ability to engage in hunting and fishing. The *context* that emerges from this analytical approach is still based on the environment as the organizing device, which figures in certain factors and relations as being important for adaptation to the environment. What we see is an increase in the complexity of analytical aspects and, simultaneously, a sustainment of what is perceived as context. A different context may emerge, however, if we approach Igloolik from another perspective. In the socio-economic base-line study of Igloolik by Sheena Kennedy and Frances Abele (2011), the authors took into account many aspects of the economy – including wage-paid work, unpaid and volunteer work, harvesting, businesses and artistic production. Most areas of community life are thus considered relevant to the economy. Their report covers a wide variety of topics, ranging from language use, education and employment, to harvesting and questions of health and wellness, as well as individuals' involvement in community affairs. The socio-economic project was designed as a baseline study so that the hamlet could, in three to five years, repeat the study in order to measure changes in the community over time that were evidently brought about by internal and external influences like environmental changes, political institutions, resource development projects and shifts in demographics.

If we are to understand the vulnerability of Igloolik with respect to climate change, such a baseline study – with all its inherent limitations – may help us see the complex socio-economic landscape in which Igloolik residents have to navigate, because the organizing principle is less focused on the environment. Suddenly, issues like mining and shipping routes, the impacts of the Nunavut government on community services, employment, and income support programs appear to be central to community life and emerge as choices rather than as mere factors for adaptation. Such a study can serve to remind us about the fact that climate change may be only one factor out of many that residents in Igloolik have to relate to when understanding and driving the social dynamics. For example, the study directs our attention to the question of resource development in the region as an issue of concern and attention, especially when it comes to the construction of the Mary River Iron Mine, which may provide 400–500 jobs, as well as millions of dollars to the Nunavut government, and may come to necessitate large-scale shipping through the area. Interviews with Igloolik residents concerning this enormous project have been posted on-line, namely, on the homepage of Isuma Productions (Isuma Productions, n.d.): some of the residents are concerned about the consequences on the environment and on the hunting of walrus while others are focusing on the positive and negative impacts on family life and on the community dynamics generated by the new job opportunities. Overall, community change, potentialities and vulnerabilities emerge more fully when the analytical organizing device is not solely limited to climate change or the environment. An analytical approach that is more open to dynamic scaling may also have an impact on our understanding of food security. In fact, when Ford and Berrang-Ford (2009, p. 232) argue that the 'most commonly identified reasons for difficulty in obtaining traditional and store food included lack of income, the high price of store food and fuel, lack of hunting equipment, the increasing costs of hunting, and social problems including addiction', this can be considered an invitation to develop a multi-scale analysis integrating biophysical, institutional, economic, social and political processes in order to obtain a more solid understanding of food security. But presumably, and by way of response to the dominant discourse of climate change, one of the authors (Ford, 2009b), in another project, approaches food security with a focus on the direct and indirect stresses on the food system stemming from climate change. Here, climate-related conditions are rendered particularly important in affecting Inuit food security, and it is argued that the impacts of current climate change and the prognosis of accelerating change have increased the need to understand links between climate and food security (Ford, 2009b, p. 87). The article develops a conceptual model for examining the vulnerability of Inuit food systems to food insecurity as a consequence of climate change. According to Ford, this model 'illustrates that food system vulnerability is *determined* by the exposure and sensitivity of the food system to climate-related risks and its adaptive capacity to deal with those risks' (Ford, 2009b, p. 83, italics by the author). The need to understand the food system is not only necessary when it comes to improving food security in the North but also, as the author points out, it is 'essential for identifying entry points for policy to strengthen food systems in the context of a changing climate' (Ford, 2009b, p. 87). Once again, climate change is employed in order to organize the analysis and doing this turns societal processes, aspirations and problems into background, setting and context. In this case, they are referred to simply as a 'context of underlying vulnerabilities in the community as a consequence of long-term changes in Inuit livelihoods and community dynamics' (Ford, 2009b, p. 96). The research of Ford (2009b) calls attention to the direct and indirect problems that climate change is expected to inflict on the food system, and the concerns that are put forward are developed in close collaboration with local residents. The author explicitly points out the importance of this kind of research in policymaking and financial programs and it can be expected that future adaptation policies focusing on climate change issues will find inspiration in the model, in the concerns, and in the points that have been put forward.

The critique that can be lodged is that when we pursue the analysis with climate change as our organizing device, our understanding of food security cannot be adequate, because so much of what is important in people's lives and so many of the factors that drive decisions, mobilize resources and action are then parked in the background, as context. 'Context' does indeed matter in people's lives, as more than simply 'context', and the Mary River iron mine project generates a telling illustration of this. It is expected that large-scale shipments of ore will take place in the sea close to Igloolik; this has incited the mayor of Igloolik, P. Quassa, to express concern about the effects that a year-round shipping route might have on marine mammals and sea ice (CBC News North, 2008). For Igloolik resident J. Palluq, the matter is so important that he will, according to his own declaration, oppose the company's current plans to the bitter end. He points out, furthermore, that residents in Arctic Bay and Clyde River also share his concern about the project's impact on their walrus hunting (Muse, 2008). Aside from environmental concerns, other residents have expressed worries about the impact on family life and hunting activities (see their testimonies at the Isuma productions website). Viewed from a food security perspective, this project may give rise to both positive and negative impacts. On the one hand, it may potentially improve people's income opportunities (which Ford and Berrang-Ford [2009] have pointed out as being *decisive* for food security) while on the other hand, it might reduce the time available for hunting and could potentially alter the environment and resource accessibility.

Livelihood decisions, which need to be taken in Igloolik by the community, by families and households, by groups of hunters, and by individuals, are composed of a multitude of parameters, scales, and frames of orientation and it is in their capacity as *future-makers* that their livelihoods are given direction and potentiality. If we approach human beings as future-makers, their horizon of orientation becomes broader and more inclusive than if their actions, capacities, resources, concerns, conflicts, and problems are to be framed more specifically and narrowly in the light of adaptation to climate change or if their lives are simply seen as a 'context'. If we take a look at food security, just one centrally important issue, then the problems with addiction and the lack of income-generating opportunities become just as important as climate change problems; or to put this more precisely, those issues deserve analytical attention as well. In fact, when we analytically allow people's worlds to be opened up without making an a priori assumption about figure and ground that is dominated from the outset by considerations about the environment (i.e. ascribing, by fiat, paramount importance to climate change), we can approach the issues of climate change and adaptation from a new angle. This will be the focus of the next section.

Climate as figure and the concept of future-makers

The 'climate' can be approached from a number of strategic perspectives that influence how we understand adaptation to climate. 'Climate adaption' can be seen as a strategic perspective which draws our attention to certain elements, relations and phenomena while drawing our attention away from others. Discussions about climate change and climate adaptation are fundamentally a negotiation between figure and ground, a relation that is analytically evoked. By figuring the elements of a world, it becomes navigable: this activity serves to move our understandings and mobilize action because figuring points our attention to relevance, the extension of a perceived problem and the contours of solutions. However, at one point, it may be useful to revisit the analytical and strategic perspective in order to see whether the figure-ground relation can be infused with new potential and new dynamics by means of reconsidering what is appreciated as ground and what is appreciated as figure. I would argue that when using 'climate' to configure the world and vulnerabilities in the Arctic, doing so brings important local perspectives and vulnerabilities 'to the fore', so to speak. However, using climate to figure the world and the vulnerabilities in the Arctic is also an *analytical* take that relegates other parts of social life to the background, as 'context', as 'setting', as 'influencing factors', or merely as 'conditions'. Presently, the relation between background and figure in the climate change discussions draws our analytical attention to man-environmental relations. As has been pointed out earlier on in this chapter, this disposition ascribes a great deal of significance to environmental knowledge. A large number of research projects have unfolded indigenous peoples' extensive and detailed observations and have expounded their interpretations of the environment. This line of studies has focused on changing ice, snow, weather, animal behaviour and distribution, to mention but a few examples. This perspective configures climate change as an environmental matter, albeit with human consequences. However, if we change our analytical perspective and approach climate change as a societal matter, we consequently not only change the relation between background and figure – we set up a totally new figuration of what is important and what is relevant.

If we use 'climate' to figure the world in such a way that our analytical focus pays more attention to political and societal matters than it does on environmental matters, this could serve to figure human agency in new ways without devaluing the understanding that man and environment exist in an entangled and reciprocally coupled human-environment system. Such a figuring could inspire us to approach studies related to climate change and climate adaptation as studies of social stability, dynamics, change and transformations, and such a way of figuring might allow us to focus more attention on societal, economic and political issues, not as an important background, but as the *centre* of our analysis of how people relate to climate change. If we understand climate change issues as emerging from social, political and environmental processes and entanglements, we might be able to pay more attention to people's everyday practices, concerns and anticipations.

Navigating a climate changed world

In peoples' lives, climate change related issues have a tendency to adhere to other aspects of their livelihood and are often difficult to separate and isolate as an easily demarcated field. In some research projects, climate issues are isolated from social life. This sometimes provokes social scientists to call for the 'integration of the human dimension' as if 'the human' were some kind of add-on. In order to gain a better understanding of Arctic societal transformations in a climate change era, it is useful to change the focus from environmental change as the centre of attention (although the changes are enormous) and move it over to an examination of how people navigate a complex space of social interaction, in which the natural environment is an active part. The emphasis on *navigation* (Vigh, 2006) (see also, Chapter 5) points our attention to how people attend to immediate concerns and opportunities and simultaneously draw trajectories into the future, and thus to how they not only orientate themselves towards a horizon of potentialities but also actively make choices, imagine and envision trajectories and create futures. This is more than adaptation or coping: it is navigation as 'motion within motion, that is, as action in a terrain that is not a stable field or surface but changeable as well as opaque' (Vigh, 2006, p. 128). From the perspective of anthropologist Henrik Vigh (2006), the term 'navigation' gains strength from having the capacity to encompass some of the more dense, yet analytically elusive, dimensions of social action by addressing the praxis of *moving through* a social environment in motion.

In his discussion of Arctic hunting and climate change, Mark Nuttall (2010) also directs our attention to the navigational praxis of anticipation as an inherent part of being a hunter. He criticizes the concept of adaptation for being too mechanistic and for being a reactive response to climate change. Instead, he wants to draw our attention to the importance of anticipation when discussing local preparedness and responses to climate change. For him, anticipation is about intentionality, action, agency, imagination, possibility, and choice – aspects that I consider intrinsic to future-making. When navigation is used to cover a duality of action that is related to both present and future orientation, this has consequences to bear on our analysis. According to Vigh (2006), we have to position our informants' actions within their experience of their 'being' – as part of a historical process, within their experience of their individual lives as process, and within their experience of their lives as immediacy; that is, as both position and movement. When navigating, manoeuvring, and moving within a space where one only can expect the unexpected, it is crucial to pay attention to the practices of anticipation and the envisioning of social horizons. Using such an analytical lens, drug addiction and money-sharing networks are not only important factors in the context that might exert some influence on food security but are also, to be sure, integral parts of the terrain that agents necessarily have to engage in, navigate, stabilize, change, transform or move. The concept of navigation also turns our attention to shifting interpretations of 'social order', imagined futures and possible movements through time. One particularly interesting aspect of Vigh's navigation concept is his inclusion of social imaginaries as more than a set of immediate practical understandings. The social imaginaries involve a form of understanding that offers a wider grasp of our history and social existence (Goankar cited in Vigh, 2006, p. 173). Movement *in* and *of* worlds stands in relation to ideas about where we come from, what we have become and where we are headed, accordingly constituting a special way of appreciating how social life is made up and how social life offers *horizons* of possibilities.

This focus on navigation, movement and anticipation gives rise to a new proposition about the figure-ground relation, where climate change issues cannot solely be reduced to an environmental matter, with positive or negative consequences for human societies, but need also to be configured as an inherent part of the social. Nuttall (2010) points our attention to the concept of anticipation as being a prerequisite for thinking about adaptation to climate change, and goes on to argue that researchers need to study its social, cultural and cognitive aspects within local settings. His focus on anticipation as a means of orientation, exploration and as a way of imagining, framing and viewing the world draws climate change issues deeply into social capabilities, knowledge-making, experiences and skills. Basing his thinking on the work of Derrida and Pannenberg, Nuttall (2010, p. 25) argues that thinking about possibilities (which are so important when looking on adaptation) entails anticipation 'not just of the future but also of the past, a past that is "reconstituted by the originary present and by the anticipated future"'. For Nuttall, it is important to underline that the Inuit have not merely adapted to the environment, but moreover, that they have 'anticipated the possibilities and conditions for successful engagement with it' (Nuttall, 2010, p. 25). Anticipation becomes part of the pursuit of the desirable. As such, engagement and movement in the landscape are embedded in ideas of what is socially desirable, possible and needed. When movements of social life are understood as being entangled in environmental movements that are unified in a world of constant becoming, the enactment of anticipation is decisive in the local choices of environmental engagement – choices that are often understood merely as strategies of adaptation to the environment, but which are, more correctly, enactments of the desirable.

This approach has consequences for how we get climate change to configure our understanding of processes in the Arctic. First, climate change issues emerge as inherent parts of people's everyday lives and cannot easily be demarcated from the social, economic, political and cultural aspects. Second, people's continuous practices of anticipation and navigation have a wider grasp of history and social existence. The focus we obtain from concepts like anticipation and navigation veers our climate change related research away from studying climate change impacts, vulnerability, and adaptation, and so forth, and redirects our research towards a more integrative approach, where climate change can never be considered alone or understood as being detached from human aspiration, desire and anticipation. In Greenland, climate change issues cannot be viewed as being detached from the desire to gain more economic self-reliance in a new self-governed Greenland, nor can a local fisherman's concerns about melting ice be understood as being isolated from quota systems and prices on the market. The point here is not that this could lead us into studying everything or that it might lead us into studying nothing, simply because it is so difficult to demarcate climate change issues. The argument is rather that we have to be attentive to how climate change is perceived and how it is to be considered an interwoven part of social life and dynamics. When, for example, researching food security and climate change, it may be important to integrate the social world that people move in and move. This entails the inclusion of thorough studies of addiction problems and cash-generating possibilities, which the research studies and the local people actually single out as being important factors in people's social navigation. It must not be parked in the background, as is the case right now. I am not arguing for the *elaboration* of context, but rather for a figuration of climate change that cannot be understood as isolated from the social or from people's horizons of expectations.

Indigenous peoples as future-makers

From this perspective, research inquiries into local people's knowledge-making that is related to climate change, which have so elaborately been pursued in the Arctic, should not only revolve around environmental issues and environmental use, but should also include social issues that are not necessarily related directly to the environment. In Maniitsoq, for example, it could prove instructive to relate the ways of understanding welfare-developments, technology socialisation and town-futures directly to climate change issues because these ways of understanding the situations play a significant role in the way people establish a horizon of possibilities. It is not just a context but also an active part of people's navigating, capacity building and the resources on which they are to move their world as active future-makers. Local (non-environmental) knowledge can be important in understanding local ways of navigating social complexity and moving life and can also serve to cast light on desires, anticipations, and concerns that are important in people's lives. The colonial experience of indigenous peoples and their aspiration to self-determination are indeed strong elements in anticipated futures and the value they put on different knowledge regimes.

If climate change challenges are approached from this perspective, it is not enough to study environmental knowledge and the use of the land and sea. These activities must be related directly to people's other concerns. Concepts like navigation and anticipation render other aspects of social life matter and render them relevant and they also draw our attention to historical experiences and contemporary vision. As future-makers, people move societies towards a horizon of expectations and potentialities; this involves misgivings, doubts, and uncertainties as well as hope, imagination and encouragement. As Mark Nuttall states: 'hunting and fishing involve not merely procurement, but also anticipating, waiting, hoping, pondering, and imagining the movements of seals, narwhals, fish, and other animals to be caught, as well as anticipating and apprehension of the return home' (Nuttall, 2010, p. 25). 'The return home' in his article is, among other things, about anticipating a safe travel home, but it may also be interpreted in a broader sense. I propose that 'the return home' can be understood as being about caring and creating a future by providing: this is what hunters do.

The Greenlandic word for hunter is *piniartoq*, which can be translated into 'one who wants'. Nuttall elaborates on the several uses of the word-root *piniarpoq*, and he reveals how a *piniartoq* is, by the term itself, inscribed in social life rather than simply indicating a given occupational category: '*Piniartoq*, the Greenlandic word for hunter, translates literally as "one who wants". It derives from *piniarpoq*, "to make an effort to get or to do something," "to want," and "to acquire." *Piniarpaa* means "to strive after something," while *piniarluarpoq* indicates that the hunter has been "striving in the right way" and is diligent and successful. To hunt, therefore, is to strive for something one wants and needs. A second meaning of *piniartoq* is "provider"' (Nuttall, 2010, p. 30). 'The return home' is thus more than safe travelling. It is about giving the social (i.e. home) a navigational value for one's activities and choices. Hunting can, as Nuttall states, be understood as more than securing food. Hunting has to be regarded as being entangled in social life and as an evocation of a future. This has implications on the way we approach 'adaptation to climate change'. Here, Inuit hunters are understood to be in dire straits and the research is predominantly focusing on how hunters have been, are, and may continue to be pursuing coping and adaptation strategies. However, 'the return home' accentuates that we have to pay more attention to what is going on 'at home', and that hunters are constantly navigating in a *total* social terrain when they are out hunting.

While doing fieldwork in the 1990s in Sisimiut, I participated in a meeting of hunters who were meeting in the cafeteria of the local seamen's home. The Home Rule Government had granted the town's small-scale hunters a quota of one minke whale and the hunters had convened to choose the right date for pursuing the collective hunt. Being successful in this kind of hunt requires an extreme knowledge of whales' behaviour and presence as well as skills in cooperating. Being very interested, at that time, in local environmental knowledge, I was much attuned to these issues and I judged the setting to be extremely promising for my studies in these hunters' perception of animals and the environment, and in a larger perspective, in these hunters' ideas of sustainability. However, I was (partly) wrong. It only took them a few minutes to exchange sightings of whales that had the proper size, to make sure that they had the right equipment and to agree that a hunt would be a feasible operation. Over the course of the next hour, they discussed *when* to pursue the hunt, in order to make the most out of it – socially. It was not so much about understanding and hunting the whale, but was more a matter of *socializing* the whale. The hunters were discussing 'the return home', so to speak. One hunter needed the meat and *mattak* (whale skin) by a certain date, for his daughter's eighteenth birthday dinner. Another one wanted to time the hunt with a surgery appointment, while a third hunter was asking whether the expedition could be put off, for the time being, and could wait until a spare part for his boat's motor had arrived from Denmark. The demand at the market as well as the purchasing power of the consumers were, in fact, the most discussed issues and part of the reason for this was to forecast anticipations of other whale hunts along the coast, seeing as these other hunting expeditions could result in saturating the local market with meat. Organizing what was, socially speaking, the most appropriate 'return home' was the decisive aspect of the hunters' preparation and anticipation.

The episode bears out how ideas of the 'future social' were important to the group of hunters and also shows how they navigate a total social terrain, where decisions cannot be reduced to pure economic or environmental matters that are isolated from social life. In order to fully grasp the world in which the hunters navigate, we can pay more attention to how people's activities and ideas are entangled in memory and vision (Sejersen, 2002, 2004) and to how their involvement in, concerns and excitements about activities are deeply embedded in anticipations and ideas about future social life. It is difficult to reduce this to functionalistic approaches, as is so often done in adaptation research, where environmental matters are typically situated in the foreground.

Taking the social world as the analytical starting point, different social, political, cultural and economic groups emerge. In the North, indigenous peoples stand out, *both* as a political category and as an identity that is linked to certain experiences and interpretations. For indigenous peoples, the social history and the colonial relation become important matters and have to inform our studies of observations and interpretations of – as well as use of – the ice and the environment. From this perspective, concepts like local knowledge and traditional ecological knowledge may not be sufficiently useful. Rather, other ways of knowing and other experiences of the world come into view as being important. Historical and contemporary experiences, observations, interpretations and institutionalizations, as well as anticipations of social and political life, all come to be significant, and one item – among others – of relevant knowledge is, of course, the colonial experience.

The colonial experience is an important frame of reference when mobilizing agency, when legitimizing actions, and when anticipating and creating futures. 'Indigenous', from this perspective, is seen as underlining peoples' historical status and political experience lived out under a colonial regime, regulation and direction, a status and a storehouse of experiences that have altered their use of and relation to the environment. Furthermore, social, cultural, technical and political practices that were pursued by the colonial state have influenced and altered these peoples' social organization and their resource use. In the Baffin Island region, for example, the dogs that were used by Inuit to travel over the ice to hunting grounds were shot and killed by the Royal Canadian Mounted Police, thus reducing Inuit's mobility in a landscape of ice and de facto containing them in settlements, concomitantly making them all the more dependent on the state. An experience of such a traumatic nature, where a certain sense of human agency is undermined, causing a more sedentary settlement pattern and consequently giving rise to new resource use practices and new dependencies (on the colonial state), is not to be disregarded and demoted to the status of being a historical context but rather, as I am arguing, needs to be treated as a decisive experience of Inuit in a transformed world. At the time of increased sedentarism, Inuit were supposed to reestablish a new meaningful world and potential futures from this point of departure.

Indigenous peoples have experienced relocation, sedentarization, urbanization, isolation, and changes in their economic, occupational, technological, political, religious, educational, health, social and cultural systems as part and parcel of their position within a colonial system. The experiences of indigenous peoples over the course of many generations make the colonial world more than simply a setting or a mere context; it is rather the case that these experiences emerge as a dominant aspect of life, making certain pathways and certain horizons of potentialities possible and desirable to pursue. It is within a total social terrain that indigenous peoples have established livelihoods in which they navigate and create their worlds. Environmental changes and resource use do not protrude as being demarcated from other challenges and conflicts (as underlined by political ecology). Nor do society and resource use function independently of the environment itself. There is a conflation of the social and the environmental, and it is difficult, indeed, to distinguish between them: where does the environmental end and where does the social begin? With respect to Inuit, as with many other indigenous peoples, there seems, however, to be a tendency to approach their vulnerability to climate change and their adaptation strategies as being very closely linked to their interaction with the environment. This is certainly the case in Greenland, where many Greenlanders themselves point at the northern hunters as being the most vulnerable or as being those who are most knowledgeable about climate change (Bjørst, 2011). When climate change is understood as, primarily, an environmental issue, certain groups are positioned at the forefront, by fiat, and certain aspects of their lives get singled out. The predominant configuring of climate knowledge and Inuit adaptation leads to certain understandings about their agency. However,

Inuit never simply react to climate change as an isolated issue, but engage, instead, in complex social, political and moral practices of re-orientation and envisioning.

It cannot be boiled down to a question of avoiding context-making, but rather becomes a matter of placing a question mark beside the 'taken-for-granted' context in climate change research. An analysis always demarcates a context that might appear relevant to the subject matter. The context makes certain subjects and relations emerge as obvious and important but the context also underpins certain understandings of agency. If we approach climate change issues from the perspective of *indigenous peoples*, as defined here, the colonial (whether we are speaking about the historical or the contemporary colonial) aspect becomes important. And knowledge, solutions, aspirations, problems and world-making have to be weighed in this light. Such an approach draws our attention away from the environment as the primary point of interest and directs it over to the social, political and economic world, where climate change not only affects but is also an integral part of a total social terrain. This approach redirects our attention towards the role that Arctic peoples can play in envisioning decolonized futures and the role that this very aspiration possesses, as a driving force. I propose to turn the discussion upside down, so to speak. Researchers should not be preoccupied with the study of how people adapt to climate change but rather with the study of how people adapt climate change to their lives and future imaginaries. Such an approach allows the social to be central in the analysis. By doing so, the subject position of people becomes one of future-makers. With respect to indigenous peoples, it is neither a question of invoking the past as a guiding mechanism nor a matter of taking recourse in pre-colonial ways of living, but more fundamentally a question of acknowledging that Arctic peoples' colonial history and position cannot be reduced to context but are permanent aspects of the way that these indigenous peoples anticipate and make futures. This applies to both an Inuit hunter in Nunavut and a Greenlandic supporter of hyper-industrialization in Maniitsoq.

References

ACIA. (2005). *Arctic Climate Impact Assessment*. Cambridge: Cambridge University Press.

Adger, W. Neil. (2000). Social and ecological resilience: Are they related? *Progress in Human Geography, 24*(3), 347–364.

Arctic Environmental Protection Strategy (AEPS). (1991). *Rovaniemi Declaration*. Rovaniemi.

Agrawal, Arun. (1995). Dismantling the divide between indigenous and scientific knowledge. *Development and Change, 26*(3), 413–439.

Agrawal, Arun. (2002). Indigenous knowledge and the politics of classification. *International Social Science Journal, 54*(173), 287–297.

Anisimov, Oleg, Vaughan, David, Callaghan, Terry, Furgal, Christopher, Marchant, Harvey, Prowse, Terry, Vilhjálmsson, Hjalmar & Walsh, John. (2007). Polar regions (Arctic and Antarctic). In M. L. Parry, O. F. Canziani, J. P. Palutikof, P. J. v. d. Linden & C. E. Hanson (Eds.), *Climate Change 2007: Impacts, Adaptation and Vulnerability. Contribution of Working Group II to the Fourth Assessment Report of the Intergovernmental Panel on Climate Change* (pp. 653–685). Cambridge: Cambridge University Press.

Aporta, Claudio. (2002). Life on the ice: Understanding the codes of a changing environment. *Polar Record*, 38(207), 341–354.

Aporta, Claudio. (2004). Routes, trails and tracks: Trail breaking among the Inuit of Igloolik. *Ètudes Inuit Studies*, 28(2), 9–38.

Aporta, Claudio. (2010). The sea, the land, the coast, and the winds: Understanding Inuit sea ice use in context. In I. Krupnik, C. Aporta, S. Gearhead, G. J. Laidler & L. K. Holm (Eds.), *SIKU: Knowing Our Ice. Documenting Inuit Sea-Ice Knowledge and Use*. (pp. 163–180). London: Springer.

Arctic Human Development Report. (2004). Akureyri: Stefansson Arctic Institute.

Balikci, Asen. (1968). The Netsilik Eskimos: Adaptive processes. In R. B. Lee & I. DeVore (Eds.), *Man the Hunter* (pp. 78–82). Chicago: Aldine Publishing.

Berkes, Fikret. (2008). *Sacred Ecology (second edition)*. New York: Routledge.

Berkes, Fikret, & Jolly, Dyanna. (2001). Adapting to climate change: Social-ecological resilience in a Canadian western Arctic community. *Conservation Ecology*, 5(2), article 18.

Bjørst, Lill Rastad. (2011). *Arktisk Diskurser og klimaforandringer i Grønland. Fire (post) humanistike klimastudier*. København: Ph.D. – afhandling forsvaret den 29. november ved Det Humanistiske Fakultet. Københavns Universitet.

Boas, Franz. (1964 [1888]). *The Central Eskimo*. Lincoln: University of Nebraska Press.

Bravo, Michael T. (2010). Epologue: The humanism of sea ice. In I. Krupnik, C. Aporta, S. Gearhead, G. J. Laidler & L. K. Holm (Eds.), *SIKU: Knowing Our Ice. Documenting Inuit Sea-Ice Knowledge and Use*. (pp. 445–452). London: Springer.

Brooke, L. F. (1993). *The Participation of Indigenous Peoples and the Application of their Environmental and Ecological Knowledge in the Arctic Environmental Protection Strategy*. Ottawa: Inuit Circumpolar Conference.

Cameron, Emilie S. (2012). Securing indigenous politics: A critique of the vulnerability and adaptation approach to the human dimensions of climate change in the Canadian Arctic. *Global Environmental Change*, 22(2012), 103–114.

CBC News North. (2008, April 7). Baffin Island residents resist proposed iron mine plans. *CBC News North*. Retrieved July 2, 2012, from www.cbc.ca/news/canada/north/story/2008/04/07/mine-walrus.html

Chapin III, F. Stuart, Peterson, Garry, Berkes, Fikret, Callaghan, Terry, Angelstam, Per, Apps, M., Beier, Colin, Bergeron, Yves, Crépin, Anne-Sophie, Danell, Kjell, Elmqvist, Thomas, Folke, Carl, Forbes, Bruce, Fresco, Nancy, Juday, Glenn, Niemelä, Jari, Shvidenko, Anatoly & Whiteman, Gail. (2004). Resilience and vulnerability of Northern regions to social and environmental change. *Ambio*, 33(6), 344–349.

Crate, Susan. (2009). Gone the bull of winter? Contemplating climate change's cultural implications in Northeastern Siberia, Russia. In S. Crate & M. Nuttall (Eds.), *Anthropology & Climate Change. From Encounters to Actions* (pp. 139–152). Walnut Creek: Left Coast Press.

Cruikshank, Julie. (1998). *The Social Life of Stories. Narrative and Knowledge in the Yukon Territory*. Vancouver: UBC Press.

Cruikshank, Julie. (2004). Uses and abuses of 'Traditional Knowledge': Perspectives from the Yukon Territory. In D. G. Anderson & M. Nuttall (Eds.), *Cultivating Arctic Landscapes: Knowing and Managing Animals in the Circumpolar North* (pp. 17–32). New York: Berghahn Books.

Dahl, Jens. (2013). *The Indigenous Space and Marginalized Peoples in the United Nations*. New York: Palgrave Macmillan.

Damas, David. (1972). Central Eskimo systems of food sharing. *Ethnology*, 11(3), 220–240.

Damas, David. (1973). Environment, history and Central Eskimo society. In B. Cox (Ed.), *Cultural Ecology. Readings on the Canadian Indians and Eskimos* (pp. 269–300). Toronto: McClelland and Stewart.

Dilley, Roy (Ed.). (1999). *The Problem of Context*. New York: Berghahn Books.

Duerden, Frank, & Kuhn, Richard G. (1998). Scale, context, and application of traditional knowledge of the Canadian north. *Polar Record*, 34(188), 31–38.

Eicken, Haja. (2010). Indigenous knowledge and sea ice science: What can we learn from indigenous ice users? In I. Krupnik, C. Aporta, S. Gearhead, G. J. Laidler & L. K. Holm (Eds.), *SIKU: Knowing Our Ice. Documenting Inuit Sea-Ice Knowledge and Use.* (pp. 357–376). London: Springer.

Fairhead, James. (1993). Representing knowledge. The 'new farmer' in research fashions. In J. Pottier (Ed.), *Practising Development: Social Science Perspectives* (pp. 187–204). London: Routledge.

Fienup-Riordan, Ann, & Rearden, Alice. (2010). The ice is always changing: Yup'ik understandings of sea ice, past and present. In I. Krupnik, C. Aporta, S. Gearhead, G. J. Laidler & L. K. Holm (Eds.), *SIKU: Knowing Our Ice. Documenting Inuit Sea-Ice Knowledge and Use.* (pp. 295–320). London: Springer.

Ford, James. (2008). Climate, society, and natural hazards: Changing hazard exposure in two Nunavut communities. *Northern Review, 28*, 51–71.

Ford, James. (2009a). Sea ice change in Arctic Canada: Are there limits to Inuit adaptation? In W. N. Adger, I. Lorenzoni & K. L. O'Brien (Eds.), *Adapting to Climate Change: Thresholds, Values, Governance* (pp. 114–127). Cambridge: Cambridge University Press.

Ford, James. (2009b). Vulnerability of Inuit Food Systems to Food Insecurity as a Consequence of Climate Change: A Case Study from Igloolik, Nunavut. *Regional Environmental Change, 9*(2), 83–100.

Ford, James, & Smit, Barry. (2004). A framework for assessing the vulnerability of communities in the Canadian Arctic to risks associated with climate change. *Arctic, 57*(4), 389–400.

Ford, James, & Berrang-Ford, Lea. (2009). Food security in Igloolik, Nunavut: An exploratory study. *Polar Record, 45*(234), 225–236.

Ford, James, Smit, Barry, & Wandell, Johanna. (2006). Vulnerability to climate change in the Arctic: A case study from Arctic Bay, Canada. *Global Environmental Change, 16*(2), 145–160.

Ford, James, Smit, Barry, Wandel, Johanna, & MacDonald, John. (2006). Vulnerability to climate change in Igloolik, Nunavut: What can we learn from the past and present. *Polar Record, 42*(221), 127–138.

Ford, James, Pearce, Tristian, Smit, Barry, Wandel, Johanna, Allurut, Mishak, Shappa, Kik, Ittusujurat, Harry & Qrunnut, Kevin. (2007). Reducing vulnerability to climate change in the Arctic: The case of Nunavut, Canada. *Arctic, 60*(2), 150–166.

Ford, James, Smit, Barry, Wandel, Johanna, Allurut, Mishak, Shappa, Kik, Ittusarjuats, Harry, & Qrunnut, Kevin. (2008). Climate change in the Arctic: Current and future vulnerability in two Inuit communities in Canada. *The Geographical Journal, 174*(1), 45–62.

Ford, James, Pearce, Tristan, Duerden, Frank, Furgal, Chris, & Smit, Barry. (2010). Climate change policy responses for Canada's Inuit population: The importance of and opportunities for adaptation. *Global Environmental Change, 20*, 177–191.

Fox, Shari. (2002). These are things that are really happening: Inuit perspectives on the evidence and impacts of climate change in Nunavut. In I. Krupnik & D. Jolly (Eds.), *The Earth is Faster Now* (pp. 12–53). Fairbanks: Arctic Research Consortium of the United States.

Fox, Shari. (2004). *When the Weather is Uggianaqtuq: Linking Inuit and Scientific Observations of Recent Environmental Change in Nunavut, Canada.* Boulder: University of Colorado (Ph.D. handed in to the Geography Department).

Furgal, Christopher, & Prowse, Terry. (2008). Northern Canada. In D. S. Lemmen, F. J. Warren, J. Lacroix & E. Bush (Eds.), *From Impacts to Adaptation: Canada in a Changing Climate 2007.* Ottawa: Government of Canada.

George, John C., Huntington, Henry P., Brewster, Karen, Eicken, Hajo, Norton, David W., & Glenn, Richard. (2004). Observations on shorefast ice dynamics in Arctic Alaska and the responses of the Iñupiat hunting community. *Arctic, 57*(4), 363–374.

Hulme, Mike. (2008). Geographical work at the boundaries of climate change. *Transactions / Institute of British Geographers* (33), 5–11.

Huntington, Henry P. (2005). 'We dance around in a ring and suppose': Academic engagement with traditional knowledge. *Arctic Anthropology*, 42(1), 29–32.

Huntington, Henry P., Gearheard, Shari, & Holm, Lene Kielsen. (2010). The power of multiple perspectives: Behind the scenes of the Siku-Inuit-Hila project. In I. Krupnik, C. Aporta, S. Gearhead, G. J. Laidler & L. K. Holm (Eds.), *SIKU: Knowing Our Ice* (pp. 257–274). London: Springer.

Isuma Productions. (n.d.). Homepage of Isuma Productions. Retrieved July 6, 2012, from www.isuma.tv/isuma-productions.

Jolly, Dyanna, Berkes, Fikret, Castleden, J., Nichols, T., & the community of Sachs Harbour. (2002). We can't predict the weather like we used to: Inuvialuit observations of climate change, Sachs Harbour, Western Canadian Arctic. In I. Krupnik & D. Jolly (Eds.), *The Earth is Faster Now: Indigenous Observations of Arctic Environmental Change* (pp. 92–125). Fairbanks: ARCUS.

Kennedy, Sheena, & Abele, Frances. (2011). *2009–2010 Igloolik Socio-Economic Baseline Study*. Ottawa: Carleton Centre for Community Innovation.

Krupnik, Igor. (1993). *Arctic Adaptations: Native Whalers and Reindeer Herders of Northern Eurasia*. Hanover: University Press of New England.

Krupnik, Igor, & Jolly, Dyanna (Eds.). (2002). *The Earth is Faster Now: Indigenous Observations of Arctic Environmental Change*. Fairbanks: ARCUS.

Krupnik, Igor, & Müller-Wille, Ludger. (2010). Franz Boas and Inuktitut terminology for ice and snow: From the emergence of the field to the 'Great Eskimo Vocabulary Hoax'. In I. Krupnik, C. Aporta, S. Gearhead, G. J. Laidler & L. K. Holm (Eds.), *SIKU: Knowing Our Ice. Documenting Inuit Sea-Ice Knowledge and Use* (pp. 377–400). London: Springer.

Krupnik, Igor, & Weyapuk, Winton (Utuktaaq). (2010). Qanuq Ilitaavut: 'How we learned what we know' (Wales Inupiaq Sea Ice Dictionary) In I. Krupnik, C. Aporta, S. Gearhead, G. J. Laidler & L. K. Holm (Eds.), *SIKU: Knowing our ice. Documenting Inuit sea-ice knowledge and use.* (pp. 321–356). London: Springer.

Krupnik, Igor, Aporta, Claudio, Gearhead, Shari, Laidler, Gita J., & Holm, Lene Kielsen (Eds.). (2010). *SIKU: Knowing Our Ice. Documenting Inuit Sea-Ice Knowledge and Use*. London: Springer.

Laidler, Gita J. (2006). Inuit and scientific perspectives on the relationship between sea ice and climate change: The ideal complement? *Climatic Change*, 78(2–4), 407–444.

Langdon, Steven J. (Ed.). (1986). *Contemporary Alaskan Native Economies*. Lanham: University Press of America.

Leduc, Timothy B. (2007). Sila dialogues on climate change: Inuit wisdom for a cross-cultural interdisciplinarity *Climate Change*, 85(3–4), 237–250.

Lemmen, D.S., Warren, F.J., Lacroix, J., & Bush, E. (Eds.). (2008). *From Impacts to Adaptation: Canada in a Changing Climate 2007*. Ottawa: Government of Canada.

Lonner, Thomas D. (1986). Subsistence as an economic system in Alaska: Theoretical observations and management implications. In S. J. Langdon (Ed.), *Contemporary Alaskan Native Economies* (pp. 15–27). Lanham: University Press of America.

Marino, Elizabeth, & Schweitzer, Peter. (2009). Talking and not talking about climate change in Northwestern Alaska. In S. A. Crate & M. Nuttall (Eds.), *Anthropology & Climate Change: From Encounters to Actions* (pp. 209–217). Walnut Creek: Left Coast Press.

McDonald, M., Arragutainaq, L., & Novalinga, Z. (1997). *Voices From the Bay: Traditional Ecological Knowledge of Inuit and Cree in the Hudson Bay Bioregion*. Ottawa: Canadian Arctic Resources Committee and Municipality of Sanikiluaq.

Muse, Ben. (2008, July 29). Baffin Island Iron. Retrieved July 2, 2012, from http://benmuse.typepad.com/arctic_economics/2008/07/baffinlands.html.

Nadasdy, Paul. (2003). *Hunters and Bureaucrats: Power, Knowledge, and Aboriginal-State Relations in the Southwest Yukon*. Vancouver: UBC Press.

Nadasdy, Paul. (2011). 'We don't harvest animals; we kill them': Agricultural metaphors and the politics of wildlife management in the Yukon. In M. J. Goldman, P. Nadasdy & M. D. Turner (Eds.), *Knowing Nature: Conversations at the Intersection of Political Ecology and Science Studies* (pp. 135–151). Chicago: The University of Chicago Press.

Nelson, Richard K. (1969). *Hunters of the Northern Ice*. Chicago: The University of Chicago Press.

Nichols, Theresa, Berkes, Fikret, Jolly, Dyanna, Snow, Norman B., & The community of Sachs Harbour. (2004). Climate change and sea ice: Local observations from the Canadian Western Arctic. *Arctic, 57*(1), 68–79.

Nuttall, Mark. (2009). Living in a world of movement: Human resilience to environmental instability in Greenland. In S. A. Crate & M. Nuttall (Eds.), *Anthropology & Climate Change: From Encounters to Actions* (pp. 292–310). Walnut Creek: Left Coast Press.

Nuttall, Mark. (2010). Anticipation, climate change, and movement in Greenland. *Études Inuit Studies, 34*(1), 21–37.

Pearce, Tristian, Ford, James, Laidler, Gita, Smit, Barry, Duerden, Frank, Allarut, Mishak, Andrachuk, Mark, Baryluk, Steven, Dialla, Andrew, Elee, Pootoogoo, Goose, Annie, Ikummaq, Theo, Joamie, Eric, Kataoyak, Fred, Loring, Eric, Meakin, Stephanie, Nickels, Scott, Shappa, Kip, Shirley, Jamal & Wandel, Johanna. (2009). Community collaboration and climate change research in the Canadian Arctic. *Polar Research, 28*(1), 10–27.

Pullum, Geoffrey K. (1989). The great eskimo vocabulary hoax. *Natural Language & Linguistic Theory, 7*(2), 275–281.

Quijano, Aníbal. (2008). Coloniality of power, eurocentrism, and social classification. In M. Moraña, E. Dussel & C. A. Jauregui (Eds.), *Coloniality at Large: Latin America and the Postcolonial Debate* (pp. 181–224). Durham: Duke University Press.

Rappaport, Roy A. (1968). *Pigs for the Ancestors: Ritual in the Ecology of a New Guinea People*. New Haven: Yale University Press.

Riedlinger, Dyanna, & Berkes, Fikret. (2001). Contributions of traditional knowledge to understanding climate change in the Canadian Arctic. *Polar Record, 37*(203), 315–328.

Riewe, Rick, & Oakes, Jill (Eds.). (2006). *Climate Change: Linking Traditional Knowledge and Scientific Knowledge*. Winnipeg: Aboriginal Issues Press, University of Manitoba.

Sejersen, Frank. (1998). *Strategies for Sustainability and Management of People: An Analysis of Hunting and Environmental Perceptions in Greenland with a Special Focus on Sisimiut*. Copenhagen: University of Copenhagen (Ph.D. handed in to the Faculty of Humanities).

Sejersen, Frank. (2002). *Local Knowledge, Sustainability and Visionscapes in Greenland*. Copenhagen: Department of Eskimology.

Sejersen, Frank. (2004). Horizon of sustainability in Greenland: Inuit landscapes of memory and vision. *Arctic Anthropology, 41*(1), 71–89.

Steward, Julian. (1955). *Theory of Culture Change: The Methodology of Multilinear Evolution*. Urnana: University of Illinois Press.

Thorpe, Natasha, Eyegetok, Sandra, Hakongak, Naikak, & Elders, Kitikmeot. (2002). Nowaday it is not the same: Inuit Qaujimajatuqangit, climate and caribou in the Kitikmeot region of Nunavut, Canada. In I. Krupnik & D. Jolly (Eds.), *The Earth is Faster Now: Indigenous Observations of Arctic Environmental Change* (pp. 201–239). Fairbanks: ARCUS.

Vigh, Henrik E. (2006). *Navigating Terrains of War: Youth and Soldiering in Guinea-Bissau*. Oxford: Berghan Books.

Weatherhead, E., Gearhearh, S., & Barry, R.G. (2010). Changes in weather persistence: Insight from Inuit knowledge. *Global Environmental Change, 20*(3), 523–528.

Wenzel, George. (1991). *Animal Rights, Human Rights: Ecology, Economy and Ideology in the Canadian Arctic*. Totonto: University of Toronto Press.

Wenzel, George. (1995). Ningiqtuq: Resource sharing and generalized reciprocity in Clyde River, Nunavut. *Arctic Anthropology*, 32(2), 43–60.

Wenzel, George. (2000). Sharing, money, and modern Inuit subsistence: obligation and reciprocity at Clyde River, Nunavut. In G. W. Wenzel, G. Hovelsrud-Broda & N. Kishigami (Eds.), *The Social Economy of Sharing: Resource Allocation and Modern Hunter-Gatherers* (pp. 61–85). Osaka: Senri Ethnological Series. National Museum of Ethnology.

Wenzel, George. (2002). *Hunter-Gatherer Subsistence: A Canadian Inuit Perspective*. Paper presented at the International Conference on Hunting and Gathering Societies, Edinburgh.

Wenzel, George. (2004). From TEK to IQ: Inuit Qaujimajatuqangit and Inuit cultural ecology. *Arctic Anthropology*, 41(2), 238–250.

Wenzel, George. (2009). Canadian Inuit subsistence and ecological instability – if the climate changes, must the Inuit? *Polar Research*, 28, 89–99.

White, Leslie. (1949). *The Science of Culture*. New York: Grove Press.

Index

For Product Safety Concerns and Information please contact our
EU representative GPSR@taylorandfrancis.com Taylor & Francis
Verlag GmbH, Kaufingerstraße 24, 80331 München, Germany